Comic Invective in Ancient Greek and Roman Oratory

Trends in Classics – Supplementary Volumes

Edited by
Franco Montanari and Antonios Rengakos

Associate Editors
Stavros Frangoulidis · Fausto Montana · Lara Pagani
Serena Perrone · Evina Sistakou · Christos Tsagalis

Scientific Committee
Alberto Bernabé · Margarethe Billerbeck
Claude Calame · Jonas Grethlein · Philip R. Hardie
Stephen J. Harrison · Stephen Hinds · Richard Hunter
Christina Kraus · Giuseppe Mastromarco
Gregory Nagy · Theodore D. Papanghelis
Giusto Picone · Alessandro Schiesaro
Tim Whitmarsh · Bernhard Zimmermann

Volume 121

Comic Invective
in Ancient Greek
and Roman Oratory

Edited by
Sophia Papaioannou and Andreas Serafim

DE GRUYTER

ISBN 978-3-11-127104-0
e-ISBN (PDF) 978-3-11-073553-6
e-ISBN (EPUB) 978-3-11-073566-6
ISSN 1868-4785

Library of Congress Control Number: 2021938923

Bibliographic information published by the Deutsche Nationalbibliothek
The Deutsche Nationalbibliothek lists this publication in the Deutsche Nationalbibliografie;
detailed bibliographic data are available on the Internet at http://dnb.dnb.de.

© 2023 Walter de Gruyter GmbH, Berlin/Boston
This volume is text- and page-identical with the hardback published in 2021.
Editorial Office: Alessia Ferreccio and Katerina Zianna
Logo: Christopher Schneider, Laufen
Printing and binding: CPI books GmbH, Leck

www.degruyter.com

Contents

Acknowledgements —— VII

Sophia Papaioannou and Andreas Serafim
Killing with a Smile: Comic Invective in Greek and Roman Oratory —— 1

Part I: Intertextual and Multi-genre Invective

Jasper Donelan
Comedy and Insults in the Athenian Law-courts —— 25

Kostas Apostolakis
Comic Invective and Public Speech in Fourth-Century Athens —— 43

Andreas Serafim
Comic Invective in Attic Forensic Oratory: Private Speeches —— 65

Emiliano J. Buis
Rhetorical Defence, Inter-poetic *Agōn* and the Reframing of Comic Invective in Plato's *Apology of Socrates* —— 81

George Kazantzidis
"You are Mad!" Allegations of Insanity in Greek Comedy and Rhetoric —— 107

Dennis Pausch
Comic Invective in Cicero's Speech *Pro M. Caelio* —— 125

Hanna Maria Degener
How to Start a Show: Comic Invectives in the Prologues of Terence and Decimus Laberius —— 147

Part II: The Cultural Workings of Invective

Thomas K. Hubbard
Comic Somatisation and the Body of Evidence in Aeschines' *Against Timarchus* —— 171

Nathan Kish
Comic Invective, Decorum and *Ars* in Cicero's *De Oratore* — 191

Jan Lukas Horneff
No Decorum in the Forum? Comic Invective in the Theatre of Justice — 211

Part III: Invective in Ancient Socio-political Contexts

Ioannis Konstantakos
Political Rhetoric and Comic Invective in Fifth-Century Athens: The Trial of the Dogs in Aristophanes' *Wasps* — 235

Wilfred E. Major
Democracy, Poverty, Comic Heroism and Oratorical Strategy in Lysias 24 — 257

Notes on Editors and Contributors — 273
General Index — 275
Index Locorum — 279

Acknowledgements

The editors would like to acknowledge a number of individuals and institutions whose help and support have been invaluable in the conception and completion of this volume. We would like to thank, first and foremost, the two editors of Trends in Classics at De Gruyter, Professors Antonios Rengakos (Aristotle University of Thessaloniki/Member of the Academy of Athens) and Franco Montanari (University of Genova), for having extended to us an honorary invitation to prepare the volume at hand.

The editors would also like to thank the contributors, who have been very patient and helpful throughout the process of putting together this volume, in the face of many rounds of revisions. As editors, we have been fortunate to work alongside the contributors right from our initial inquiries and theoretical meanderings, and we have been delighted to see how those exchanges of initial ideas and outlines have led to the formulation of chapters that will enhance our knowledge and understanding of the features, purposes and limits of comic invective in a wide range of Greek and Roman texts and contexts. We are sure the contributors will forgive us for having bombarded them with countless questions and requests which placed a huge demand on their time. The fruitful and fascinating result of our admirably smooth cooperation reimburses us all for our labours.

Andreas Serafim would like, finally, to thank the Research Centre for Greek and Latin Literature of the Academy of Athens for providing excellent research facilities that made the timely completion of this volume possible; and Millie Gall for reading and commenting on several drafts of the Introduction and of other chapters within the volume.

Abbreviations throughout this volume follow those in *L'Année philologique* or the *Oxford Classical Dictionary*. A certain level of formatting standardisation has been imposed to ensure consistency across the volume, but individual stylistic distinctiveness has been respected. The volume is intended for the specialist scholars and graduate students of rhetoric, comedy, theatre and invective both in Classics and beyond. All long quotations of Greek and Latin are accompanied by English translation. Only key passages are included in the *Index Locorum*, which does not aim to provide an exhaustive list of all textual references in this volume.

Sophia Papaioannou and Andreas Serafim
Athens, March 2021

Sophia Papaioannou and Andreas Serafim
Killing with a Smile: Comic Invective in Greek and Roman Oratory

1 Invective, Comicness and Laughter

Several scholarly studies discuss the use of comic invective in Greco-Roman literature. These studies aim, in most cases, to explore how invective can become comic and/or how this is used in (especially forensic) oratory as a means of triangulating relationships and thus fulfilling the persuasive ends of a speech. Subsequently, they set out to pin down the most recurrent, distinct and fundamental patterns of comic invective in oratory, and, in some cases, also to explain how specific thematic and institutional dichotomies (i.e. public vs private, prosecution vs defence and logographic vs non-logographic speeches) affect or determine the use of the technique.[1] This volume acknowledges the centrality of comic invective in a range of oratorical institutions (especially forensic and symbouleutic), and aspires to enhance the knowledge and understanding of how this technique is used in such contexts of both Greek and Roman oratory. This exploration addresses some understudied multi-genre and interdisciplinary topics: first, the ways in which comic invective in oratory draws on, or has implications for, comedy and other verse genres, or how these literary genres are influenced by oratorical theory and practice, and by contemporary socio-political circumstances, in articulating comic invective and targeting prominent individuals; second, how comic invective sustains relationships and promotes persuasion through unity and division; third, how it connects with sexuality, the human body and male/female physiology; fourth, what impact generic dichotomies, as, for example, public-private and defence-prosecution, may have upon using comic invective; and fifth, what the limitations in its use are, depending on the codes of honour and decency in ancient Greece and Rome.

Let us start with definitions. There is a term of fundamental importance for the purposes of this volume that should be discussed at this introductory stage: *invective*. This is roughly synonymous with "vituperation" and defined as "criti-

---

[1] One of the most recent works to pursue both goals is Serafim 2020, 23–42 where the use of comic invective in public forensic speeches of Attic oratory is explored. On the use of laughter in private speeches: Serafim in this volume.

cism that is very forceful, unkind, and often rude" (*Cambridge Dictionary*) or as "a form of rude expression or discourse intended to offend or hurt" or as "a denunciatory or abusive expression or discourse" (*The American Heritage Dictionary of the English Language*). For G. Kennedy, "invective is a statement expressive of inherent evils",[2] while S. Koster notes that invective is a structured, literary form (*eine strukturierte literarische Form*), the objective of which is to diminish (*herabsetzen*) openly a named person according to applicable values.[3] V. Arena defines invective as "a literary genre whose goal is to denigrate publicly a known individual against the background of ethical societal preconceptions, to the end of isolating him or her from the community".[4] For C.E. Schutz "invective, ridiculing or insulting of someone, becomes the substitute for violence. Political adversaries can express their anger, contempt, sense of difference without disrupting the fragile peace of political societies";[5] and E. Dussol describes invective as a means of demolishing the image of individuals, institutions and social groups, through an act of verbal violence.[6] Aggression and violence are, therefore, fundamental defining features of invective.[7]

Despite the polemical and aggressive character of invective, this has been considered, from antiquity to the present day, as having a comic dimension. We argue that this may be possible in two different ways: first, if invective has a humorous and/or a laughter-provoking character; second, if invective is associated with comedy as a genre, i.e. if it uses the generic markers of comedy in terms of diction and language register, imagery and story or character patterns. The seeming paradox that is created by the attribution of comic qualities to aggressive invective takes us back to the discussion about how *comicness* (τὸ γελοῖον) can be used as a means of attack. Several ancient sources (e.g. Aristotle, *Nicomachean Ethics* 1127a21–23; Plato, *Philebus* 48c-49c; Xenophon, *Memorabilia* 1.7.2–3) refer, for example, to bragging as provoking laughter, which is then used to lambast individuals, who, in lack of self-awareness, boast about qualities that they do not have.[8] This points to S. Halliwell's theory about the *consequential* character of laughter, which exemplifies the qualities of an attack and causes social division, in a sense that the members of an audience are invit-

---

[2] Kennedy 2003, 10.
[3] Koster 1980, 21.
[4] Arena 2007, 149.
[5] Schutz 1977, 67. On invective as a means of interpersonal violence, see also: Riess 2012.
[6] Dussol 2006, 164; in a similar vein: Powell 2007, 1–2; Novokhatko 2009, 12.
[7] Classen 2004; Garambois-Vasquez 2007; Applauso 2019.
[8] See further: Serafim 2020, 23–42.

ed to laugh *with* the speaker *at* the target of ridicule (cf. social identity theory which is discussed below).[9]

Humour and *laughter* are considered in scholarship two fundamental qualities of invective that effectively make it comic. According to Morreall, "the word humo[u]r was not used in its current sense of funniness until the 18th century";[10] thus in ancient literature discussion always refers to laughter or comedy. *Humour*, in general, can be considered a mental facility that is attached to invective and has the potential to disguise its violent and aggressive character, leading to *laughter*. The connection between humour and laughter is not inevitable or self-explicable: the stimuli that make an audience laugh are not necessarily humorous or amusing, and so the two terms cannot be used interchangeably.[11] A complete detachment of humour from laughter, however, may seem to be paradoxical: as N. Applauso rightly points out, humour without laughter seems to be "humourless".[12] Applauso, trying to draw a semantic line between the two notions, argues that humour is an expression, while laughter is a reaction.[13] This distinction is influenced by that of S. Attardo, who sees humour as a "mental phenomenon" and laughter as a "neurophysiological manifestation".[14]

For the purposes of this volume, we phrase this useful distinction between humour and laughter in terms that relate to comic theatre in ancient Greece and Rome: humour is the source of semantic or mental stimuli, which can be laughter-provoking, if performance before a lively audience allows it to be so. This distinction is analogous to that of the "text" and the "context": the text has provisions that may affect the audience of any sort (i.e. a lively audience or readers) and generate a reaction of any sort (i.e. cognitive/emotional or physical/sensory/somatised), but it is the context (e.g. innate or empirical factors, and others that have to do with external circumstances) that determines whether that reaction would happen. It is, therefore, the context – in Greco-Roman times, the lively, performative context – that determines whether laughter is provoked when a humorous story is told, as it is the context that gives a comic dimension to invective. The importance of context is rightly highlighted by R. Rosen, who, in his lecture "Roasting, Boasting and the Varieties of Greek Invec-

---

9 Halliwell 1991, esp. 280–287; 2008. On social identity theory: pp. 11–12 in this chapter.
10 Morreall 2012, online publication: https://plato.stanford.edu/entries/humor/. On the invention of the modern understanding of humour in the 18th century philosophy and social theory, see recently: Zuroski 2019.
11 Olbrechts-Tyteca 1974.
12 Applauso 2019, 5.
13 Applauso 2019, 6.
14 Attardo 1969, 10.

tive" at Université Catholique de Louvain in 2014, argues that there is *composed* and *spontaneous* invective (the same applies to humour): invective can take a textual form, but it can also be the lively hurling of insults in real time and place, and in front of a real audience. Invective, in the second case, equates to performance,[15] i.e. "the communication between a performer and an audience, which is informed by the etiquette of a specific occasion [what we call above "context"] and is based on the interactive communication, explicit or otherwise, between the transmitter of a message and its receiver".[16]

The main argument that this volume puts forward is that, in Greek and Roman oratory (or in oratorical passages that are incorporated in other literary texts or genres, e.g. the *Apology of Socrates* and the speeches in comic plays), an element of the comic permeates invective performance. "Invective, seen as performance, resembles a comic *agōn*: the competition between two contestants, in which one is conceived as the antagonist and the other as the ironist, who retaliates humorously. [...] Invective in court draws on, or has implications for, patterns that are related to comedy, such as the inversion of tragic patterns into comic ones and the use of stock comic characters".[17] It should be noted, at this point, that invective in fourth-century oratory mostly draws on, or has affinities with, Old Comedy of the fifth century because this works best in the confrontational and politically-charged environment of the cases the Attic orators were fighting. The so-called *onomasti kōmōidein*, i.e. "insult and ridicule directed at particular prominent individuals" when someone laughs or provokes laughter at his enemy wishing to see him suffering,[18] mostly features in Old Comedy, as exemplified by Aristophanes. As has been argued, "Old Comedy is generally recognised to be more politically engaged than Middle Comedy and it is therefore the techniques of Old Comedy that are appropriate to the cut and thrust of the court (although it should be noted that Middle Comedy is also relevant, such as in the use of stock characters like the braggart)".[19] This observation poses a

---

15 The performative dimension of invective, which is explored in the chapters this volume comprises, does not focus on Roman Satire, the genre which revolved around the employment of invective for corrective purposes, and during the later phrase of the genre, in the early imperial era, was fundamentally political. On the employment of invective as core rhetorical tool for laughter-generating mockery for political purposes in Persius and Juvenal: Roller 2012, acknowledging (p. 211) that invective in Latin literature has not been "deeply explored", and "in verse satire, still less so".
16 Serafim 2017, 16–17.
17 Serafim 2020, 25.
18 Griffith 2013, 7. Also: Halliwell 2008, 243–263; Sommerstein 2009, 107–115.
19 Serafim 2017, 92; also: Miner 2006, 21.

question about why comic invective features saliently in the speeches of the fourth century, when Old Comedy was by then attenuated to the extent of being replaced by Middle Comedy. This is because, we contend, rhetoric as *technē* (rhetoric as oratory, i.e. theory in action) was systematised in the fourth century: it was then that a great wealth of speeches were composed and delivered, and it is this corpus of speeches that has come down to us in a textual form.[20]

The link that exists between invective in Attic oratory and Old Comedy is also manifest in the ways in which invective is used in the contexts of public speaking. One of these is incongruity, i.e. the construction of a set of expectations which are then juxtaposed with an unexpected conclusion, or the gathering of antithetical or anomalous components into the same event or image. This is reminiscent of Aristophanes' comic style: P. Harding is right to argue that incongruity as a means of giving invective a comic character is used in ancient texts, as for example in Aristophanes, whose "action does depend on the unexpected, the incongruous, the fantastic, the grotesque and the inconsequential".[21] Cicero discusses comic invective based on incongruity in a detailed account in his treatise *On the Orator* 2.255, where it is mentioned that the most familiar kind of joke is "when we expect one thing and another is said; in which case our own disappointed expectation makes us laugh".[22]

The embrace of invective by comic theatre becomes an essential tool in the effectiveness of Greek and Roman oratorical performance. By the fifth century, invective in the courts evolved, "from an initial 'serious expression of hostility'

---

20 We are aware, of course, that the issue of systematisation of rhetoric is intricate enough to still generate debate in classical scholarship on the Greek orators, with scholars such as Usher 1999 claiming that this happened as early as in the fourth quarter of the fifth century. We tend to agree, however, with scholars who argue for the opposite, such as Cole 1991, Schiappa 1999 and Whitehead 2003. The art of public speaking had, in fifth-century Athens, only a modest form: that of preparing handbooks and model speeches, such as Gorgias' *Encomium of Helen* and Antiphon's *Tetralogies* (dated back in the mid-fifth century; Gagarin 1997, 8), i.e. paradigmatic models for composing homicide trials; see Whitehead 2003. On the *Tetralogies*: Carawan 1993, 235–270. On early rhetorical handbooks: Kennedy 1959, 169–178; Barwick 1963, 43–60.
21 Harding 1994, 197.
22 Two modern theorists, I. Kant and A. Schopenhauer also discuss the incongruity theory. For Kant, in his *Critique of Judgement*, "laughter is an affection arising from the sudden transformation of a strained expectation into nothing"; Kant ²1914, 223. Schopenhauer explains incongruity in terms of the difference between human perceptions and the reality around us, while Kierkegaard explains the "comical" in terms of the discrepancy between what is expected and what is experienced. Morreall 2009, 11 rightly argues that "the core meaning of incongruity in various versions of the Incongruity Theory, then, is that some thing or event we perceive or think about violates our standard mental patterns and normal expectations".

to a sophisticated composition of critique and stinging wit".[23] The works of Aristotle, Cicero and Quintilian on the nature, structure and effectiveness of vituperation establish a solid connection between blame and humour, confirming that invective is most effective when it aims at ridiculing one's opponent. Ancient thinkers are negative in their assessments of ridicule and the hostile. A philosophical commentary associates laughter with invective, considering it scornful, a means of enabling a speaker to devastatingly attack and undermine the opponents. Plato sums up this view when, in *Republic* 388e, he warns the guardians against the behaviour that includes laughter: in his words, "when one abandons himself to violent laughter, his condition provokes a violent reaction". In the same section, Plato expresses his aversion to Homer, who does not hesitate to describe the gods making Mount Olympus resound with their loud laughter, and opines that people should strongly oppose the tendency to represent men of power and merit as overpowered by laugher. In *Philebus* 48–50, Plato also expressly entwines ridicule with malice, putting Socrates define "the ridiculous" in terms of self-ignorance. In his discussion of "derisive laughter", Socrates is also presented as rejecting it because he thinks it provokes an unjust emotion, *phthonos* ("envy" or "malice").

Aristotle underlines the significance of wit in provoking laughter, but he overall agrees with Plato that laughter expresses scorn (*Rhetoric* 2.12). In *Nicomachean Ethics* 4.8, even though he admits that there are witty and educated people who tell jokes in a tasteful way, he seems to believe that these are few and far between, and that most people who strive to raise laughs at all costs are vulgar buffoons, indifferent to the pain they will thus cause to the object of their fun. The cause of pain determines the distinction between joking well and joking badly. Even so, the employment of invective typically aiming to insult the target is best realised when the invective is received by a third party/audience, and as such it is a form of performance and requires training.[24] The courts obviously are a setting uniquely suited to the study of invective accompanied by laughter. In Nathan Kish's words "laughter effected through humour, wit, and insult could be an effective means for orators to attain their ends, since by means of invective, an orator could attempt to reduce his opponent to an object of ridicule".[25]

---

23 Applauso 2019, 244, citing also Harding 1994, 201.
24 See Richlin 1992 on the entwinement of invective and laughter in Roman culture more broadly.
25 Kish 2018, 55.

Roman comedy, *fabula palliata*, the only extant form of Roman literary comic drama, unlike Old Attic Comedy, does not revel in shaming. As a matter of fact, personal invective on the *palliata* stage is strictly avoided at all levels: Roman comedy never refers or even alludes to contemporaries in Rome,[26] while profanities are never uttered onstage. Obscene words, which are rare and often difficult to identify, are always mild.[27] And yet, Roman comedy was popular with audiences of all social classes because it invested in ongoing and witty deployment of structures, characters, plot themes and motifs, as well as language and style, and dramatised various cases of interpersonal conflict, resolved through a combination of intrigue and good fortune. It was only natural for orators, another group of public performers, to look to the comic stage for inspiration in their own attempts to outwit their opponents and win over the judges and onlookers.

The *fabula palliata* features plots that are built upon set themes and are executed by standardised characters or types. Comic invective in Roman oratory, at least as we may surmise from Cicero's court speeches and the allusions therein to the speeches of his opponents (whose arguments the great orator dismantles, often by turning them on their heads), relied routinely on the manipulation of tropes and conventions of comic characterisation and stage conduct, not least because the denizens of the *palliata* world were people who bore traits and exhibited behaviours that conventionally fed accusation and invective in the Roman tradition: they were people from the lower classes, often slaves, foreigners, who practiced non-elite occupations and were prone to committing petty crimes, especially thievery; when they are free-born men, especially older ones, crack sexual jokes and exhibit unchecked sexual appetites; and the younger ones are coward and spendthrift, and all-consumed by improper love-affairs with prostitutes.[28] D. Pausch, in this volume, offers an insightful reading of the humorous outcome of invective in the *Pro Caelio*,[29] a most successful and mem-

---

[26] The only two likely references to real people are the jab at Pellio, Plautus' manager, in *Bacch.* 215, and for that reason its authenticity has been doubted: Lennartz 2014; and the allusion to Naevius and his incarceration by the Metelli in *Mil.* 210–212, which is hardly an abuse, and it recently has been seriously contested: Fontaine 2020.

[27] Fontaine 2010 chapter 5, "Double Entendre".

[28] According to Corbeill 2002, 200–201, these traits fueled some of the "most commonly identified topics of accusation" and invective in Roman oratory; see also pp. 8–9 below in the Introduction.

[29] The cornerstone study of comedy in Cicero is Geffcken's 1973 monograph, *Comedy in the Pro Caelio*. The comedic element in the *Pro Caelio* has attract considerable attention since, and some notable studies of the relationship between this speech and the stage include Arcellaschi

orable performance on the trial stage on Cicero's part because of the comparison of the case on trial to a *palliata* plot. Another celebrated example from one of Cicero's early court speeches concerns the disparagement of Q. Fannius Chaerea in *Pro Q. Roscio*. In this speech Cicero defends the actor Roscius against Fannius who had brought a lawsuit against Roscius, demanding the sum of 50,000 sesterces. Roscius, arguably the most famous actor of his day, had become particularly renowned for his performance on stage of the role of the pimp Ballio, the leading evil character in Plautus' *Pseudolus* and the most expressly portrayed pimp in surviving comic drama.[30] In *Pro Q. Roscio* 20 Cicero takes advantage of Fannius' unattractive physical appearance—the latter being another popular topic of invective, for apparently it denoted deceit and wickedness—which could evoke the *imago* (comic mask) of a pimp (Fannius was balding and had shaved eyebrows), and casts him as a really "bad" Ballio: his shaved head and eyebrows indicate *malitia* ("evilness") and *calliditas* ("shrewdness"); and his overall appearance, including his conduct during the trial, implies *fraus* ("cheating"), *fallacia* ("deceit") and *mendacia* ("mendacity").

What is more, it evokes the stage performance of that very character by Roscius. Cicero's invective against Fannius primarily intends to portray him as a person lacking credibility, but his comparison not just to the famous pimp Ballio, but the Ballio as impersonated and enacted on stage by Fannius' opponent, Roscius, also intends to enforce the strength of the invective by infusing it with humour: the audience is entertained as they are invited to envision a (badly executed) re-enactment of the Ballio part in Fannius and compare it with the (masterly) re-enactment of Roscius. Fannius in other words is a crook, a liar and a fraud, as his *imago* bespeaks. The performance of his real identity is worse than the stage performance of the same identity by Roscius; instead of seeking to intimidate Roscius by drawing inspiration for his actual behaviour from his close physical resemblance to the comic pimp, he should rather take lessons from Roscius on how to properly conduct himself.

Besides the ancients, influential modern thinkers, philosophers and scholars also discuss the nature of invective, and the features and functions that make it comic in specific circumstances and contexts. Disparagement or superiority theory explains that "humour originates from an act of aggression that stirs an ill-natured laughter at the wrongdoings of other individuals considered

---

1997; Leigh 2004; Tatum 2011. Recent studies on the influence of Roman comedy on Cicero beyond the *Pro Caelio* include Harries 2007; Harries 2011. A detailed study on the presence of Terence in Cicero is Manuwald 2014.

30 Harries 2007, 10–13; Harries 2011, 137–142.

morally inferior, and thus bestows a sense of superiority".[31] The most influential proponent of disparagement/superiority theory is T. Hobbes, who argues, in his work *Human Nature*, that "the passion of laughter is nothing else but sudden glory arising from some sudden conception of some eminency in ourselves, by comparison with the infirmity of others, or with our own formerly".[32] Whenever invective results in laughter at someone, in other words, this becomes a powerful means of belittling and devaluing the target's authority, character and existence. A similar approach to comic invective is also adopted by R. Descartes, who, in his treatise *Passions of the Soul*, argues that "derision or scorn is a sort of joy mingled with hatred, which proceeds from our perceiving some small evil in a person whom we consider to be deserving of it; we have hatred for this evil, we have joy in seeing it in him who is deserving of it; and when that comes upon us unexpectedly, the surprise of wonder is the cause of our bursting into laughter".[33]

Another manifestation of disparagement/superiority theory is the targeting of individuals with a physical handicap: "the target is attacked on the grounds of birth, upbringing and 'banausic' occupation (see artisans and craftsmen; labour), moral defects such as avarice or drunkenness, physical shortcomings (lameness, warts and the like), eccentricities of dress, ill fortune, and so on".[34] The theory of S. Freud, in his treatise *The Joke and Its Relation to the Unconscious*, about the qualities of "tendentious humour" to promote hostility (whether for the sake of aggressiveness, satire or defence) or obscenity, is also close to the disparagement/superiority theory of Hobbes and Descartes. Modern theories echo ancient thinking about invective and the comic: Plato, for example, emphasises the aggressive feelings that fuel hostile comic invective. In *Philebus* 47d-50e, he tries to expose the "mixture of pleasure and pain that lies in the malice of amusement". We also know that, in comedy, we take malicious pleasure from the ridiculous, mixing pleasure with a pain of the soul.[35] Demosthenes points out that invective produces pleasure for the listener and appeals to humankind because "by nature all people listen with pleasure to slander and invective" (18.3).[36]

---

[31] Applauso 2019, 11.
[32] Hobbes 1812, 65.
[33] Descartes 1989 [1649], 178–179.
[34] Watson 2015.
[35] For a comprehensive discussion of the ancient roots of superiority theory: Arena 2007, 149–50; Perks 2012, 119–132; Serafim 2020, 27.
[36] This claim of Demosthenes has a twofold purpose. It underlines the importance of invective for orators: on the one hand, if the law-court audience enjoys listening to it, then the orators

In a recently completed doctoral thesis, *The Ethics and Politics of Style in Latin Rhetorical Invective*, N. Kish, who also contributes a chapter to this volume, discusses four major features of invective in Roman rhetorical theory and oratorical practice: character, anger, humour and spin/smear.[37] Cicero mocks his opponents by using language that is conducive to provoke laughter (*De orat.* 216–290), noting specifically that referring to "something unseemly in no unseemly way produces the greatest degree of laughter" (*De orat.* 236).[38] Comic invective, in other words, entails picking on another's stigmatised attribute or action and thereby opens this third party to derision and ridicule. Quintilian mentions that humour is possible even by physical contact/touch (*Inst.* 6.3.7; cf. Cicero, *De orat.* 239 on the use of bodily faults as a means of constructing comic invective). In his words, "laughter will be derived either from the physical appearance of our opponent or from his character as revealed in his words and actions, or from external sources; for all forms of raillery come under one or other of these heads; if the raillery is serious, we style it as severe; if, on the other hand, it is of a lighter character, we regard it as humorous" (*Institutio Oratoria* 6.3.37). Cicero's and Quintilian's discussions of comic invective shed light on its purposes, when used in oratory; as Kish rightly notes, "exposing and ridiculing an adversary's faults could accomplish three things for an orator: make the adversary look bad, entertain the judges and audience, and win their goodwill by presenting the speaker as an entertaining individual with discerning and urbane taste".[39]

Disparagement/superiority theory underlines the potential of comic invective to triangulate relations and promote unity and division by means of communal superiority that contrasts with individual inferiority: the constant purpose of speakers is to align themselves with the audience ("You, the audience"

---

can benefit from using it; on the other hand, Demosthenes' claim can also be seen as the first step towards preparing his audience for his own use of invective against Aeschines in his *On the Crown* speech (18).

37 Kish 2018, 14.
38 The reference of Cicero to the discussion of "the unseemly in no unseemly way" harks back to the belief that a speaker who talks about a shameful act, even if not his own, runs the risk of incurring shame for merely discussing shameful things. A speaker could also incur shame if he were thought to be speaking slanderously (regardless of whether the accusations were true or false), since slander, along with abusive speech and foul language, was understood as a species of *aischrologia*. To avoid that risk, Attic orators regularly ask the audience to pardon them if they use bad expressions to describe the shameful deeds of their opponents; see, for example, Aeschines 1.37–38.
39 Kish 2018, 65.

and "I, the speaker") against their adversary ("that man/these men" or "him/they"). This leads to a "We-They" pattern of contrast: comic invective functions as a means for the speaker artfully to construct the audience's frame of mind, by binding himself with the judges/onlookers ("We"), while simultaneously estranging his opponents from the group ("They"). S. Critchley argues that "joking is a specific and meaningful practice that the audience and the joke-teller recognise as such. There is a tacit social contract at work here, namely some agreement about the social world in which we find ourselves, as the implicit background to the joke".[40] M. Beard, similarly, suggests that "aggressive communal laughter at the deviant, or rather at the man Cicero [and any other speaker] chose to present as such, was a means of simultaneously creating and enforcing the community's ethical values. Jokes become a means of ordering social realities".[41] S. Halliwell, whose theory about *consequential laughter* has been discussed at the beginning of this chapter, also talks about the potential of laughter to create social divisions.[42] The creation of division is the purpose of invective, as used in the transmitted speeches of ancient Greek and Roman oratory: it is an exercise of the power of A (the speaker and invective-producer) over B (the adversary and invective-receiver) before C (the audience) which is invited to side, cognitively, emotionally and by voting, with one of the two parties. Another way of articulating these same issues is H. Tajfel's and J. Turner's social identity theory, which explores how the activation of group attitudes and identities and inter-group relations – i.e. in-group solidarity and out-group hostility – has a huge impact upon behaviours and attitudes in target audiences.[43]

Modern psychological studies have shown that the use of the language of invective is an effective way of conveying that one feels very strongly about an individual or a situation, or of evoking negative feelings in someone else. This potential of invective to arouse emotions is even more pronounced when expletives and profane language are used. "Besides literal or denotative uses, the primary use of swearing is for emotional connotation, which occurs in the forms of epithets or as insults directed toward others. Epithets are offensive emotional

---

40 Critchley 2007, 20.
41 Beard 2014, 106. In the same vein, Corbeill 1996, 9 argues that "political humour, no less than serious political discussion, both creates and enforces a community's norms" so that what emerges is a system of values. Cf. Corbeill 2002, 197–218 on the potential of invective to generate faction or promote unity in the speeches of Cicero.
42 On Halliwell's *consequential laughter*: pp. 2–3 above in this introductory chapter.
43 Tajfel and Turner 1979, 33–37. Also: Miller et al. 1981, 494–511; Conover 1984, 760–785; Lau 1989, 220–231; Carey 1990, 44–51; Huddy 2003, 511–558; Hall 2006, 388; Arena 2007, 151.

outbursts of single words or phrases used to express the speaker's frustration, anger or surprise".[44] Invective invites people's negative emotional attitudes towards the target, or underscores the hostile emotions of the speaker by its very lack of restraint, thereby inviting the target audiences to share the same emotions. This invitation can be seen as an attempt to forge a rapport between the speaker and the audience, known as "emotional community".[45]

Before proceeding to the description of the current scholarship on comic invective and the content of the chapters this volume consists of, a caveat is necessary: in this chapter and elsewhere in the volume at hand, the main argument we put forward, that there are strong affinities between oratory and comedy, does not invalidate the suggestion that there are also notable differences between them, in terms of both frequency and use of comic invective. There is no doubt that comic invective is a powerful weapon in the arsenal of the speaker, but it is used with caution: as Serafim argues, it is used relatively sparingly in Attic forensic (public and private) oratory. "Th[is] restrained use may indicate that speakers are conscious of the risk of giving the impression that they are buffoons (βωμολόχοι). A buffoon suffers from lack of restraint and perception: '[he] is one who cannot resist a joke. He will not keep his tongue off himself or anyone else, if he can raise a laugh, and will say things which a man of refinement would never say, and some of which he would not even allow to be said to him' (Arist. *Eth. Nic.* 1128a34–1128b1; cf. *Eth. Nic.* 1108a24–25, Cicero, *De orat.* 2.337–347). Such behaviour would be annoying, if not offensive, in court where matters ought to be taken seriously".[46] Beyond frequency, the use of comic invective in the two genres, oratory and comedy, is also marked by differences. Orators, for example, are not free to use *aischrologia*, "profane language", in the ways in which Aristophanes and other comedians are. A speaker who talks about a shameful act, even if not his own, runs the risk of incurring shame for merely discussing shameful things (cf. Aeschines 1.37–38).[47]

---

44 Jay 2009, 155; also Pinker 2007; Fägersten 2012; Vingerhoets, Bylsma and Vlam 2013, 287–304.
45 On emotional community: Rosenwein 2002, 821–845; Rosenwein 2006; Plamper, Reddy, Rosenwein and Stearns 2010, 253.
46 Serafim 2020, 32. On the matter of frequency in the use of comic invective in oratory: Rabbie 2007, 211; Beard 2014, 107–108.
47 Aeschines asks the audience, in 1.37, to pardon him if he uses "some expression that is as bad as Timarchus' deeds", while in 1.38 he points out that "the blame should rather be his [meaning Timarchus], if it is a fact that his life has been so shameful that a man who is describing his behaviour is unable to say what he wishes without using expressions that are likewise shameful".

2 Comic Invective in Ancient Greek and Roman Oratory

The nature and the features of comic invective have already attracted adequate research interest among scholars. In the last few decades, several studies have offered in-depth examinations of comic invective, humorous attacks, satire and their likely result, laughter, in verse and prose genres. Since the groundbreaking study of K.A. Geffcken on *Comedy in the Pro Caelio*, there have been a lot of works on the topics this volume explores. A not at all exhaustive list of references should include seven books (A. Richlin's *The Garden of Priapus: Sexuality and Aggression in Roman Humor*; A. Corbeill's *Controlling Laughter: Political humour in the late Roman Republic*; N. Worman's *Abusive Mouths in Classical Athens*; R. Rosen's *Making Mockery: The Poetics of Ancient Satire*; S. Halliwell's *Greek Laughter*; M. Beard's *Laughter in Ancient Rome: On Joking, Tickling and Cracking Up*; and more recently, D. Dutsch's/A. Suterand's *Ancient Obscenities: Their Nature and Use in the Ancient Greek and Roman Worlds* and D. Kamen's *Insults in Classical Athens* – both on the laughter-producing dynamics of insults)[48] and three dissertations (J.J. Hughes' *Comedic Borrowings in Selected Orations of Cicero*; J. Miner's *Crowning Thersites: The Relevance of Invective in Athenian Forensic Oratory*; and N. Kish's *The Ethics and Politics of Style in Latin Rhetorical Invective*).[49] There are also discussions in shorter works, such as three articles, one by S. Halliwell, "The Uses of Laughter in Greek Culture", one by D. Spatharas on "Persuasive ΓΕΛΩΣ: Public Speaking and the Use of Laughter" and another by A. Serafim that discusses "Comic Invective in the Public Forensic Speeches of Attic Oratory"; and several chapters in volumes, such as P. Harding's "Comedy and Rhetoric", B. Harries on "Acting the Part: Techniques of Comic Stage in Cicero's Early Speeches", E. Rabbie's "Wit and humor in Roman rhetoric", W.J. Tatum on "Invective identities in *Pro Caelio*" and J. Miner on "Risk and Reward: Obscenity in the Law-Courts at Athens".[50]

---

48 Richlin 1992; Corbeill 2006; Rosen 2007; Halliwell 2008; Worman 2008; Beard 2014; Dutsch and Suterand 2018, Kamen 2020.
49 Hughes 1987; Miner 2006; Kish 2018.
50 Halliwell 1991, 279–296; Harding 1994, 196–221; Spatharas 2006, 374–387; Harries 2007, 129–147; Rabbie 2007, 207–217; Tatum 2010, 165–179; Miner 2015, 125–152; Serafim 2020, 23–42. There are also debates about whether invective should be approached as a genre or a mode of discourse, e.g. Powell 2007, 1–23, while there is an ever-growing bibliography on invective (not necessarily comic) in oratory, e.g. the studies of Rao 1988–1990, 261–267; Craig 2004, 187–213; Arena 2007, 149–160; Novokhatko 2009; Hammar 2013.

There are, however, two significant limitations: firstly, the majority of bibliographical works on comic invective are old, and therefore lacking updated references to interdisciplinary theories and topics, such as performance and theories about sex and/or gender. Secondly, the current scholarly work does not focus necessarily on ancient oratory (e.g. there are only occasional references to oratorical invective in Halliwell's book, with a specific focus on *aischrology*, "foul language"), and when it does, it only examines a small proportion of the transmitted speeches (e.g. Miner's dissertation explores only four public speeches, Demosthenes' *On the Crown*, *Against Androtion* and *Against Aristogeiton*; and Aeschines' *Against Timarchus*).[51] Many of the studies on comic invective in Roman oratory are mostly, if not exclusively, focused on late Republican oratory and, more specifically, on Cicero. Such a narrow approach does not allow scholars to draw overarching conclusions about the (semantic, intertextual, multidisciplinary and other) features of comic invective, nor about the limits and restrictions in its use that are imposed or affected by the codes of honour and decency in ancient Greece and Rome. There remains, therefore, scope for further and deeper research investigation regarding the features and purposes of comic invective, and the impact that cultural and moral contexts may have had upon its use.

What is more, despite the important work that has been done in discussing the patterns of using invective in Greek and Roman texts and contexts, there are still notable gaps in our knowledge of the issue. Scholars tend to recognise ten themes and topics that generate, or relate to, invective against opponents. Here follows the list that is cited by Corbeill, with a reference to W. Süss as being the first who compiled it: "servile heritage; barbarian (non-Roman) back-ground; having a non-elite occupation; thievery; non-standard sexual behaviour; estrangement from family and community; melancholy disposition; unusual appearance, clothing, or demeanour; cowardice; bankruptcy".[52] Human physiognomy (without any sexual innuendoes) is often presented in ways that underline the association of individuals with stock comic characters. This succinct catalogue of the themes and topics ignites further research in two directions with regard to comic invective in particular, thus leaving scope for further work in new publications, as this volume is. The first direction has to do with the use of comic invective: not all of these ten patterns of invective are discussed in scholarship as having an element of comicness. Scholarly works ex-

---

[51] The last chapter of Miner's dissertation examines four private forensic speeches of Demosthenes: 36, 37, 45 and 54; see Miner 2006.
[52] Corbeill 2002, 201; cf. Süss 1920, 247–254; Nisbet 1961, 192–197; Opelt 1965, 129.

plore, for example, how references to sexuality and cowardice are used by speakers to poke fun at opponents,[53] but less work focuses on the use of melancholy for comic invective – the chapter of G. Kazantzidis, in this volume, offers a refreshed approach to a similar, medically-flavoured issue, i.e. madness. But even in topics that have been discussed in scholarship, there is still room for more work. For example, T.K. Hubbard and W.E. Major, in this volume, shed new light on two much-discussed topics, i.e. sexuality and the socio-political dimension of the ways in which speakers attack their adversaries comically.

The second direction in research that new and forthcoming publications (should) follow is the discussion about the convergences and divergences in how Greek and Roman oratory use comic invective. There are several techniques that are used in common, as, for example, having a non-elite occupation (cf. Demosthenes 18.209, Lysias 30.28; Cicero, *In Pisonem* fr. 9 (Nisbet), where Piso is accused for being the son of a herald), non-standard sexual behaviour (cf. Aeschines 3.209; Aulus Gellius 6.12.5 = *ORF* 21.17, on P. Sulpicius Galus' quirky sexuality; Cicero, *In Clodium* 25; *Pro Milone* 17 on Clodius sexual appetites) and unusual clothing (cf. Aeschines 1.131, 181 on effeminate clothing; Aulus Gellius 6.12.5 = *ORF* 21.17; *In Verrem* 2.5.13.31; 2.5.33.86; *Phillipics* 2.18.44–45). There are also common techniques for comically exploiting these themes and topics of invective, e.g. the use of stock-comic characters (e.g. *kolax*, the flatterer: Demosthenes 19.113, Aeschines 3.76; *leno*, the pimp: Cicero, *Pro Roscio* 20; meretrix, the comic courtesan: Cicero, *Pro Caelio* 1.14; 32.12–15; 47–8–11). Some chapters in this volume (e.g. the ones by D. Pausch, H.M. Degener and J.L. Horneff) exploit the comparison between Greek and Roman sources, and help us better understand how socio-political, legal, moral and cultural differences between the two worlds affect the use of comic invective.

This volume consists of three parts and twelve chapters, which aim to advance research on comic invective. Part I, "Intertextual and Multi-genre Invective", comprises seven chapters that explore the features and the use of comic invective in texts and contexts in which oratory is fertilised by comedy and other genres. The first chapter, "Comedy and Insults in the Athenian Law-courts", by Jasper Donelan, examines similarities and differences between the insults found in Old Comedy and those spoken in the Athenian law-courts. The chapter also discusses how judges might have reacted to the insults exchanged by litigants and analyses how verbal abuse is talked about in the extant speeches. The chapter suggests that law-court speakers faced two diverging pressures: on the one hand, to deliver a pertinent and logical case against their adver-

---

[53] See, for example, Serafim 2015, 96–108; 2020, 23–42.

saries, but on the other, to satisfy their judges' desire for pleasurable though largely baseless *loidoria*.

The second chapter of Part I, "Comic Invective and Public Speech in Fourth-century Athens", by Kostas Apostolakis, explores patterns of comic invective (e.g. attacks on deception, bribery, social status and family tradition) in Attic forensic and deliberative oratory, particularly in Demosthenes' and Aeschines' speeches. The chapter suggests that invective recycles from comedy to oratory and vice versa, and that both genres share weapons from the same arsenal. A wide range of texts, including both Old Comedy and the surviving fragments of Middle Comedy, are examined, with the aim of shedding new light on the reciprocal interplays between the rostrum and the comic stage.

The third chapter of the first part of the volume has the title "Comic Invective in Attic Forensic Oratory: Private Speeches". In this chapter, which supplements the one by Apostolakis on comic invective in public forensic speeches, Andreas Serafim examines three "hows": how comic invective is used in private speeches, how differently it is used in comparison with public speeches, and how comic invective is used in defence and prosecution speeches. Three conclusions are drawn: the first is that the patterns of comic invective in private speeches are largely the same as those used in public speeches; these patterns have been identified and discussed in the context of salient passages that the chapter analyses. The second conclusion is that the dichotomy between public and private speeches affects the frequency of using patterns of comic invective: there are only a few limited instances of comicness in the attacks against the opponents in private speeches. The third conclusion is that the other generic dichotomy between private defence and prosecution speeches also affects the use of comic invective, but not in a coherent and consistent way in all private speeches of Attic oratory. Techniques differ from orator to orator: Demosthenes uses comic invective both in private defence and prosecution speeches; Lysias makes use of comicness (not, strictly speaking, invective) in his private defence speech 1; and Isaeus uses comic invective in one *diadikasia* speech only, speech 8 – so neither in defence nor in prosecution orations.

The fourth chapter by Emiliano Buis has the title "Rhetorical Defence, Inter-poetic *Agōn* and the Reframing of Comic Invective in Plato's *Apology of Socrates*". This chapter examines a comparison between Plato's *Apology of Socrates* and Aristophanes' *Acharnians*, which provides us with interesting insights on the use of comic invective in political/forensic rhetoric. It is argued that, by reframing some of the key elements which are present in Aristophanes' defence in the *Acharnians*, Plato uses comedy and plays with its literary features through the construction of an inter-poetic *agōn*. The *Apology* then manages to subvert the techniques of theatrical defence elaborated in Old Comedy in order to ensure a poetic victory by discrediting Socrates' accusers in a comically devastating way.

The fifth chapter by George Kazantzidis, which has the title "'You are Mad!' Allegations of Insanity in Greek Comedy and Rhetoric", examines the affinities between comedy and rhetoric in terms of staging characters who accuse their opponents of being mad. This chapter examines this common ground in two complementary ways: on the one hand, through a close reading of Aristophanes, *Eccl.* 250–251, it shows that some of the instances of comic slander revolving around an opponent's alleged insanity owe a lot, and are designed as sustained allusions, to the practices of contemporary oratory. On the other hand, it argues that when an orator resorts to this kind of language, labeling individuals or larger groups of people as "mad", he might be engaging in dialogue with comic tradition, not necessarily in the sense that he is aiming for a specifically "comic effect" but, more broadly, by virtue of the fact that the discourse of exaggeration attached to madness as well as the idea that madness can be a matter of perspective – something to be debated and be decided by people – are distinctively comic notions.

Two more chapters in Part I examine comic invective in Roman texts and contexts. The first, chapter six, "Comic Invective in Cicero's Speech *Pro M. Caelio*", by Dennis Pausch, examines Cicero's pleading for Marcus Caelius Rufus, delivered in 56 BC, as a prime example of the entertaining as well as aggressive use that can be made of a combination between rhetoric and comedy. Whereas the speech has been analysed mainly with regard to the strategic use of Cicero's presentation of the persons involved in the trial as if they were figures in a comedy, namely his client as *adulescens* and Clodia as *meretrix*, the complex invective dynamics between the two genres, but also between the speaker, his opponents and the audience can be described with more precision.

The seventh and final chapter of Part I, "How to Start a Show. Comic Invectives in the Prologues of Terence and Decimus Laberius", by Hanna Maria Degener, examines the rhetorical use of comic invective in the prologues of Roman playwrights as part of the *captatio benevolentiae* strategy in passages from Terence and Decimus Laberius. In Terence's prologues, one can trace the narratological construction of a conflict that extends over a longer period of time. While occasionally staging his dispute with a spiteful old poet as a court-scene, Terence's attacks on Lanuvinus remain focused on his accuser's actions, not his appearance, descent, education or sexuality. Decimus Laberius uses auto-invective to criticise Caesar's actions and cast him as an enemy of the Roman *populus*.

Part II, "The Cultural Workings of Invective", examines two of the many cultural dimensions of comic invective: sexuality and the limits of using invective in the public speaking forum in antiquity. The first chapter in this section belongs to T.K. Hubbard and has the title "Comic Somatisation and the Body of Evidence in Aeschines' *Against Timarchus*". This chapter examines Aeschines' rhetorical techniques for drawing attention to the physical body of his opponent Timarchus as a visible piece of evidence in the court. It argues that Aeschines, a former actor, draws on his knowledge of Old and Middle Comedy, exploiting comedy's obsessive focus on the body as a source of humour and the common stereotype of the hypersexual wastrel. His rhetorical bluster and techniques of comic characterisation not only make up for the weakness of Aeschines' actual evidence concerning youthful prostitution, but also the emptiness of his legal case that such behaviour, if it had occurred, statutorily barred Timarchus from speaking before the court.

The second chapter of Part II, "Comic Invective, Decorum and *Ars* in Cicero's *De Oratore*", by Nathan Kish, examines how the discussion of the limits of humour in Cicero's *De oratore* sheds light on the roles that *ars* and *natura* play in oratorical success. In the dialogue, Julius Caesar Strabo espouses a markedly aggressive type of humour and yet stresses that an orator should observe decorum and not strive to be funny in the manner of a mime or a buffoon. Although he attributes success in this regard to *natura* rather than *ars*, Caesar's emphasis obscures the fact that for him humour often entails warping how things would naturally appear through the use of artful language.

In the third chapter, "No Decorum in the Forum? Comic Invective in the Theatre of Justice", Jan Lukas Horneff examines Roman forensic invectivity and the role of the comic in it by relating the importance of performativity, character assassination and legal argumentation. Discussing the correspondence between Fronto and Marcus Aurelius, Horneff observes a great awareness of the imminent risks of heavy polemics in legal interactions that is contextualised by invectives in the theatre of justice from various sources. Further, Horneff argues that Fronto planned to stage contempt in a rather comedic manner and to describe his opponent as a *Graeculus*, a variant of the *cinaedus*, a popular (comic) stock figure for effeminacy.

The final part of Part III, which comprises two chapters, explores the sociopolitical dimensions of the comic invective – thus the title "Invective in Ancient Socio-political Contexts". The first of these chapters, entitled "Political Oratory and Comic Invective in Fifth-Century Athens: The Trial of the Dogs in Aristophanes' *Wasps*", is composed by Ioannis Konstantakos and examines the close interaction between fifth-century comic invective and Athenian political oratory through a particular case-study, the episode of the dogs' trial in Aristophanes' *Wasps*. In this episode the satirical depiction of the two opponents, the archdemagogue Cleon and general Laches, reflects rhetorical devices taken from their public discourses. Aristophanes' use of animal imagery and fable motifs is inspired by the animal metaphors and Aesopic stories which the two politicians or their supporters employed in their orations. The portraits of the two rivals reverberate with standard ideological tenets of the political struggle between radicals and moderates in contemporary Athens.

The second chapter, "Democracy, Poverty, Comic Heroism and Oratorical Strategy in Lysias 24", by Wilfred E. Major, examines the political and ideological positions that undergird the defence in Lysias 24, wherein a working class Athenian defends his right to a continued state stipend granted because of his physical disability. Whereas previous scholars find the defence comical, the analysis here argues that the speech attacks the prosecutor as an elite anti-democratic bully because the struggle of the democratic working class against oligarchic financial elites would have resonated with the members of the *Boulē*. As such, this is rare and valuable testimony to the tension between rich and poor in democratic Athens in the fourth century BC.

Bibliography

Applauso, N. (2019), *Dante's Comedy and the Ethics of Invective in Medieval Italy: Humor and Evil*, Lanham/Boulder/New York/London.
Arcellaschi, A. (1997), 'Le *Pro Caelio* et le théâtre', in: *Revue des Études Latines* 75, 78–91.
Arena, V. (2007), 'Roman Oratorical Invective', in: W. Dominik and J. Hall (eds.), *A Companion to Roman Rhetoric*, Malden, MA, 149–160.
Attardo, S. (1969), *Linguistic Theories of Humor*, Berlin/New York.
Barwick, K. (1963), 'Das Problem der Isokrateischen *Techne*', in: *Philologus* 107, 43–60.
Beard, M. (2014), *Laughter in Ancient Rome: On Joking, Tickling and Cracking Up*, Berkeley/Los Angeles/London.
Carawan, E.M. (1993), 'The Tetralogies and Athenian Homicide Trials', in: *American Journal of Philology* 114, 235–270.
Carey, C. (1990), 'Structure and Strategy in Lysias XXIV', in: *Greece & Rome* 37, 44–51.
Classen, C.J. (1991), 'The Speeches in the Courts of Law: A Three-cornered Dialogue', in: *Rhetorica* 9, 195–207.
Cole, T. (1991), *The Origins of Rhetoric in Ancient Greece*, Baltimore/London.
Conover, P.J. (1984), 'The Influence of Group Identifications on Political Perception and Evaluation', in: *The Journal of Politics* 46, 760–785.
Corbeill, A. (1996), *Controlling Laughter: Political Humor in the Late Roman Republic*, Princeton.

Corbeill, A. (2002), 'Ciceronian Invective', in: J.M. May (ed.), *Brill's Companion to Cicero: Oratory and Rhetoric*, Leiden, 197–218.
Craig, C.P. (2004), 'Audience Expectations, Invective and Proof', in: J. Powell (ed.), *Cicero the Advocate*, Oxford, 187–214.
Critchley, S. (2007), 'Humour as Practically Enacted Theory, or, Why Critics Should Tell More Jokes', in: R. Westwood and C. Rhodes (eds.), *Humour, Work and Organization*, London, 17–32.
Descartes, R. (1989) [1649], *The Passions of the Soul*. Transl. S. Voss, Uxbridge.
Dussol, E. (2006), 'Petite introduction à l'invective médiévale', in: D. Girard and J. Pollock (eds.), *Invectives, quand le corps reprend la parole*, Perpignan.
Dutsch, D. and Suterand, A. (eds.) (2018), *Ancient Obscenities: Their Nature and Use in the Ancient Greek and Roman Worlds*, Ann Arbor.
Fägersten, K.B. (2012), *Who's Swearing Now? The Social Aspects of Conversational Swearing*, Cambridge.
Fontaine, M. (2010), *Funny Words in Plautine Comedy*, Oxford.
Fontaine, M. (2020), 'Before Pussy Riot: Free Speech and Censorship in the Age of Plautus', in: S. Papaioannou and C. Demetriou (eds.), *Plautus' Erudite Comedy: New Insights into the Work of a doctus poeta*, Newcastle upon Tyne, 239–264.
Gagarin, M. (1997), *Antiphon: The Speeches*, Cambridge.
Garambois-Vasquez, F. (2007), *Les Invectives de Claudien: une poetique de la violence*, Brussels.
Geffcken, K.A. (1973), *Comedy in the Pro Caelio*, Leiden.
Griffith-Williams, B. (2013), *A Commentary on Selected Speeches of Isaios*, Leiden/Boston.
Hall, E. (2006), *The Theatrical Cast of Athens*, Oxford.
Halliwell, S. (1991), 'The Uses of Laughter in Greek Culture', in: *Classical Quarterly* 41, 279–296.
Halliwell, S. (2008), *Greek Laughter. A Study of Cultural Psychology from Homer to Early Christianity*, Cambridge.
Hammar, I. (2013), *Making Enemies: the Logic of Immorality in Ciceronian Oratory*, Ph.D. Dissertation, Lund University.
Harding, P. (2004), 'Comedy and Rhetoric', in: I. Worthington (ed.), *Persuasion: Greek Rhetoric in Action*, London, 196–221.
Harries, B. (2007), 'Acting the Part: Techniques of the Comic Stage in Cicero's Early Speeches', in: J. Booth (ed.), *Cicero on the Attack: Invective and Subversion in the Orations and Beyond*, Swansea, 129–147.
Hobbes, T. (1840), 'Human Nature', in: W. Molesworth (ed.), *The English Works of Thomas Hobbes of Malmesbury*, vol. IV, London, 1–76.
Huddy, L. (2003), 'Group Identity and Political Cohesion', in: D. Sears, L. Huddy and R. Jervis (eds.), *Oxford Handbook of Political Psychology*, Oxford, 511–558.
Hughes, J.J. (1987), *Comedic Borrowings in Selected Orations of Cicero*, Ph.D. Dissertation, University of Iowa.
Jay, T. (2009), 'The Utility and Ubiquity of Taboo Words', in: *Perspectives on Psychological Science* 4, 153–161.
Kamen, D. (2020), *Insults in Classical Athens*, Madison, WI.
Kennedy, G. (1959), 'The Earliest Rhetorical Handbooks', in: *American Journal of Philology* 80, 169–178.

Kennedy, G. (2003), *Progymnasmata: Greek Textbooks of Prose Composition and Rhetoric*, Leiden/Boston.
Kish, N. (2018), *The Ethics and Politics of Style in Latin Rhetorical Invective*, Ph.D. Dissertation, University of California at Los Angeles.
Koster, S. (1980), *Die Invektive in der griechischen und römischen Literatur*, Meisenheim am Glan.
Lau, R. (1989), 'Individual and Contextual Influences on Group Identification', in: *Social Psychology Quarterly* 52, 220–231.
Leigh, M. (2004), 'The *Pro Caelio* and Comedy', in: *Classical Philology* 99, 300–335.
Lennartz, K. (2014), 'True Plautus, False Plautus: *Pellio restitutus – uxor excisa*. Annotations to Plautus' *Bacchides*', in: J. Martínez (ed.), *Fakes and Forgers of Classical Literature. Ergo Decipiatur*, Leiden/Boston, 125–141.
Manuwald, G. (2014), 'Cicero, an Interpreter of Terence', in: S. Papaioannou (ed.), *Terence and Interpretation*, Newcastle upon Tyne, 179–200.
Miller, A.H., Gurin, P., Gurin, G. and Malanchuk, O. (1981), 'Group Consciousness and Political Participation', in: *American Journal of Political Science* 25, 494–511.
Miner, J. (2006), *Crowning Thersites: The Relevance of Invective in Athenian Forensic Oratory*, Ph.D. Dissertation, The University of Texas at Austin.
Miner, J. (2015), 'Risk and Reward: Obscenity in the Law-Courts at Athens', in: D. Dutsch and A. Suter (eds.), *Ancient Obscenities: Their Nature and Use in the Ancient Greek and Roman Worlds*, Ann Arbor, 125–152.
Morreall, J. (2009), *Comic Relief: A Comprehensive Philosophy of Humor*, Malden/Oxford/Sussex.
Morreall, J. (2012), "Philosophy of Humor", in: *Stanford Encyclopedia of Philosophy*, https://plato.stanford.edu/entries/humor/
Nisbet, R.G.M. (ed.) (1961), *M. Tulli Ciceronis in L. Calpurnium Pisonem Oratio*, Oxford.
Novokhatko, A. (2009), *The Invectives of Sallust and Cicero: Critical Edition with Introduction, Translation, and Commentary*, Berlin.
Olbrechts-Tyteca, L. (1974), *Le Comique du Discours*, Bruxelles.
Opelt, I. (1965), *Die lateinischen Schimpfwörter und verwandte sprachliche Erscheinungen: Eine Typologie*, Heidelberg.
Perks, L.G. (2012), 'The Ancient Roots of Humor Theory', in: *Humor* 25, 119–132.
Pinker, (2007), *The Stuff of Thought. Language as a Window into Human Nature*, New York.
Plamper, J., Reddy, W., Rosenwein, B. and Stearns, P. (2010), 'The History of Emotions: an Interview with William Reddy, Barbara Rosenwein and Peter Stearns', in: *History and Theory* 49, 237–263.
Powell, G.F. (2007), 'Invective and the Orator: Ciceronian Theory and Practice', in: J. Booth (ed.), *Cicero on the Attack: Invective and Subversion in the Orations and Beyond*, Swansea, 1–23.
Rabbie, E. (2007), 'Wit and Humor in Roman Rhetoric', in: W.J. Dominik and J. Hall (eds.), *A Companion to Roman Rhetoric*, Malden, MA.
Rao, E.I. (1988–1990), 'The Humanistic Invective as Literary Genre', in: G.C. Martín (eds.), *Selected Proceedings of the Pennsylvania Foreign Language Conference*, Pittsburgh, 261–267.
Richlin, A. (1992), *The Garden of Priapus: Sexuality and Aggression in Roman Humor*, Oxford.
Riess, W. (2012), *Performing Interpersonal Violence: Court, Curse, and Comedy in Fourth Century BCE Athens*, Berlin.

Roller, M. (2012), 'Politics and Invective in Persius and Juvenal', in: S. Braund and J. Osgood (eds.), *A Companion to Persius and Juvenal*, Malden, MA, 283–311.
Rosen, R. (2007), *Making Mockery: The Poetics of Ancient Satire*, Oxford.
Rosenwein, B. (2002), 'Worrying about Emotions in History', in: *American Historical Review* 107, 821–845.
Rosenwein, B. (2006), *Emotional Communities in the Early Middle Ages*, Ithaca, NY.
Schutz, C.E. (1977), 'It's a Funny Thing', in: A. Chapman and H. Foot (eds.), *Humour: Proceedings of the International Conference on Humour*, New York, 225–228.
Schiappa, E. (1999), *The Beginnings of Rhetorical Theory in Classical Greece*, New Haven/London.
Serafim, A. (2015), 'Making the Audience: *Ekphrasis* and Rhetorical Strategy in Demosthenes 18 and 19', in: *Classical Quarterly* 65, 96–108.
Serafim, A. (2017), *Attic Oratory and Performance*, New York/London.
Serafim, A. (2020), 'Comic Invective in the Public Forensic Speeches of Attic Oratory', in: *Hellenica* 68, 23–42.
Sommerstein, A. (2009), *Talking about Laughter*, Oxford.
Spatharas, D. (2006), 'Persuasive ΓΕΛΩΣ: Public Speaking and the Use of Laughter', in: *Mnemosyne* 59, 374–387.
Süss, W. (1920), *Ethos. Studien zur älteren griechischen Rhetorik*, Leipzig/Berlin.
Tajfel, H. and Turner, J.C. (1979), 'An Integrative Theory of Intergroup Conflict', in: W.G. Austin and S. Worchel (eds.), *The Social Psychology of Intergroup Relations*, Ann Arbor, 33–37.
Tatum, W.J. (2007), 'Invective Identities in *Pro Caelio*', in: R. Corvino and C. Smith (eds.), *Praise and Blame in Roman Republican Rhetoric*, Swansea, 165–180.
Usher, S. (1999), *Greek Oratory: Tradition and Originality*, Oxford.
Vingerhoets, A.J.J.M, Bylsma, L.M. and Vlam, C. (2013), 'Swearing: A Biopsychosocial Perspective', in: *Psychological Topics* 22, 287–304.
Watson, L.C. (³2003), 'Invective', in: S. Hornblower and A. Spawforth (eds.), *The Oxford Classical Dictionary*, Oxford, 762.
Whitehead, D. (2003), 'Tradition and Originality: Aspects of Athenian Forensic Oratory in the Late Fifth and Early Fourth Centuries B.C.', in: *Electronic Antiquity* 7, https://scholar.lib.vt.edu/ejournals/ElAnt/V7N1/whitehead.html
Worman, N. (2008), *Abusive Mouths in Classical Athens*, Cambridge.
Zuroski, E. (2019), 'British Laughter and Humor in the Long 18th Century', in: *Literature Compass* 16.3–4: e12521. https://doi.org/10.1111/lic3.12521

Part I: **Intertextual and Multi-genre Invective**

Jasper Donelan
Comedy and Insults in the Athenian Law-courts

Abstract: This paper first presents similarities between the insults spoken by characters in Old Comedy and those employed by litigants in the classical Athenian law-courts. The comparison demonstrates how Old Comedy and Athenian legal oratory relied (albeit with a few important exceptions) on shared topics of invective as well as an overlapping vocabulary of abuse. The discussion then progresses to the way that insulting language is talked about in the preserved law-court speeches. Litigants claim that certain insults could offend the judges' sensibilities. There is, moreover, evidence of formal restrictions on the use of invective in the public sphere. Nevertheless, it appears that judges did enjoy hearing opponents exchange insults and that they could – much like audiences of comedy – respond to this with delight and laughter. This paper concludes by arguing that litigants in Athens faced two competing pressures: on the one hand, to make a pertinent, respectful, and logical case against their adversary, but on the other, to satisfy the judges' desire for pleasurable and often baseless invective.

1 Introduction

The use of personal, let alone humorous invective might, to a modern observer, seem inappropriate during legal proceedings for crimes carrying penalties as weighty as political disenfranchisement or execution. In the corpus of Attic orators, however, which contains speeches composed for just such settings, there are multiple instances of litigants insulting their adversaries, and often with language similar to that of the verbal abuse found in Old Comedy. In this contribution, I wish to explore that phenomenon and advance arguments about

---

An earlier version of this paper was presented at the 2019 FIEC/CA conference in London. I would like to thank Sophia Papaioannou and Andreas Serafim for their invitation to contribute to this volume. Many thanks also to Francesco Mari for sharing his thoughts on a draft and to Jon Hesk, who not only read and critiqued the paper in its final stages, but also sent me a copy of his unpublished essay "Vicious humour and virtuous argument in the Attic orators". Unfortunately, Deborah Kamen's book *Insults in Classical Athens* appeared too late for me to take its arguments and analysis into account.

https://doi.org/10.1515/9783110735536-002

what the use of insults meant for Athenian orators as well as for the judges they hoped to persuade. I first consider the similarities between the insults of Greek oratory and those of the dramatic genre of Old Comedy, reinforcing but also adding nuance to the work of scholars who have established parallels between the invective in the two genres. The discussion then progresses to the anticipated effects of invective on the judges and the way that verbal abuse is talked about in the speeches. Demosthenes criticises the use of insults, yet this stands at odds with their prevalence in Greek oratory, not least in Demosthenes' own surviving work. This discrepancy is discussed in the conclusion, where I suggest that Athenian litigants could find themselves needing to navigate a path between, on the one hand, indulging their audiences' desire for enjoyable insults and, on the other, presenting themselves as moderate speakers capable of making cogent legal arguments.

2 Invective in Old Comedy and the Law-courts: Thematic and Verbal Similarities

The resemblances between comic and politico-judicial invective in classical Athens have not gone unperceived. Heath, for example, in his study of Aristophanes and the discourse of politics, uses Aristophanes' *Knights* to demonstrate continuity between the disparagement of rivals on the Old Comic stage and that of rivals in the political struggles that played out in Athens's law-courts.[1] Heath wants to show that Aristophanic drama is political because it mimics or echoes patterns of real-life political discourse. In support of this thesis, Heath notes how in *Knights*, the character Paphlagon is accused of deception, flattery, slander, sycophancy and corruption, is charged with exploiting fear for his own political ends, colluding with foreign powers, undermining the principles of democracy, being of foreign or servile origin, being sexually depraved, having no shame and, finally, of adopting a vulgar rhetorical style. Following this roll-call of the Aristophanic Paphlagon's crimes and character flaws, Heath goes on to identify, and again enumerate, plentiful instances in the speeches by both Demosthenes and Aeschines of precisely these same charges – sycophancy, deception, sexual depravity, collusion, servile origins, shamelessness, a deplorable speaking style and so forth – thus pointing to a distinct over-

---

[1] Heath 1997, 232–233. On the law-courts as an arena for settling political scores in Athens, see e.g. Cohen 1995; Lape 2016.

lap in the topics of Athenian comic and Athenian judicial invective.[2] Speakers in the two genres drew their derogatory accusations, Heath concludes, from the same pool of negative traits and behaviours. The shared motifs of verbal attacks, regardless of whether these provoked laughter, show that legal rhetoric and Old Comedy depended on a similar value system for the vilification of opponents.

The likenesses that Heath observes between the topics of invective in Old Comedy and those of judicial oratory are perhaps unsurprising. They occur not so much because comedy displays a keen interest in politics and the law (although that is a factor, as Konstantakos demonstrates in this volume), but rather because the two genres evolved and flourished under the same cultural conditions and invective typically reflects, in inverse fashion, the attributes or behaviours that a given community deems desirable. It is only insulting to say that someone employs a vulgar rhetorical style if one's cultural group, and especially the addressee as well as any immediate audience, finds a vulgar rhetorical style to be objectionable. Insults operate, as Koster recognises in his study of Greek and Roman invective, against the backdrop of cultural norms and attempt to locate targets beyond the boundaries of those.[3] Successful speakers will tap into the "social presumptions held by [an] audience" in order to depict their opponents as marginalised deviants.[4] Seen in this light, the types of comic and politico-legal invective catalogued by Heath emphasise a distinction not only between the speaker and the addressee (viz. you belong to a negative category that I, the insulter, do not), but also between the insultee and the wider group – here Athenian citizens – from which the target is distanced. In the democratic law-courts of classical Athens, this could have been an effective way to alienate opponents from the judges and establish oneself as a relatable and therefore trustworthy narrator of events.[5] Finally, as discussed in the Introduction to this

---

2 Sycophancy: e.g. Aeschin. 2.145; Dem. 19.2. Deception: e.g. Aeschin. 2.124, 3.99; Dem. 18.282, 22.4. Sexual depravity: e.g. Aeschin. 2.88, 3.162; Dem. 19.287, 309, 22.73. Collusion: e.g. Aeschin. 2.141–143; Dem. 18.149, 158–159, 284, 19.27–28, 175. Servile origins: e.g. Aeschin. 2.78, 180, 3.171–172; Dem. 18.129–131, 22.61; further Kamen 2009. Shamelessness: e.g. Aeschin. 2.150, 3.16; Dem. 19.16, 72, 206. Deplorable or unpleasant speaking style: e.g. Aeschin. 3.166–167, 218; Dem. 18.82, 122; further Worman 2008, 256–258, 269–270. Apostolakis and Serafim (in this volume) explore several of these tropes in more detail. See also Dover 1974, 30–33; Harding 1994; Serafim 2017, 92–99.
3 Koster 1980, 38–39.
4 Quote from Conley 2010, 40, discussing Ciceronian invective.
5 Cf. Arist. *Rhet.* 1356a4–6. Compare also Hyp. 2.9 Jensen for an alleged further advantage of using *loidoria* in court: the target must either respond, thus veering from the matter of the case, or let it slide, thus tacitly admitting that the insults are true.

volume, if the insults and invective also draw laughs from the judges, this can help ingratiate the speaker with the audience, while the target suffers a double disgrace, experiencing not just the affront of the verbal abuse, but also the humiliating laughter of their peers.[6]

Invective's distancing of the target from the wider social group is reified in Old Comedy when Paphlagon, at the end of *Knights*, is driven out beyond the city walls as a "scapegoat" (ὁ φαρμακός, *Eq.* 1405), when sycophants and other obnoxious characters are forcibly removed from comic utopias, or when the apex of comic celebrations involves expelling the politician Hyperbolos (*Pax* 1318–1319; cf. *Eq.* 1362–1363, with Olson 1998, 208). The Athenian orators too sought to depict their adversaries as people who, because they failed to abide by the dominant moral and ethical codes of the *polis*, were undeserving of its advantages and protection. Thus, for pseudo-Lysias, the impious Andocides is a *pharmakos* whose expulsion from Athens will "cleanse the *polis*" (τὴν πόλιν καθαίρειν, [Lys.] 6.53). The judges, as the speaker frames it, must choose between banishing the man and jettisoning the laws of the city (§8). For Dinarchus, Demosthenes is a despicable barbarian (τὸν δὲ κατάπτυστον τοῦτον καὶ Σκύθην, Din. 1.15) equated with "offscourings" (τοῦτο τὸ κάθαρμα, §16) who deserves to be executed and his body "thrown out of the city" (§77). And for Demosthenes, Aristogeiton is a "monster" or a "beast" (τὸ θηρίον, Dem. 25.31, 58), a venomous "snake" or "scorpion" or "spider" (§§52, 96) whose presence upsets the good order of the *polis* (§19) and impedes religious practices (§99). Demosthenes encourages the judges to excise this "cancer" (καρκίνον, §95) and "throw it out of the city". In these cases and others, the distancing effect of invective is accompanied, as it is in the aforementioned examples from Old Comedy, by real acts of purging intended to cleanse a community despoiled by the target's asocial conduct.[7]

Worman, in her study of insults and the metonymic mouth in classical Greece, concludes that the "abuses tossed back and forth between prominent [Athenian] speakers utilise comic vocabulary".[8] The accusations levelled by Demosthenes at the wealthy citizen Meidias verge on the "caricaturish", Worman writes, and call to mind the labels "used of lowbrow demagogues in Aristophanes".[9] In that particular case, replete with invective, Demosthenes calls Meidias a host of insulting names that include "revolting" (βδελυρός, Dem.

---

6 See also Halliwell 1991b, 283, 285–287; Spatharas 2006, 380.
7 See further Rosenbloom 2002, 329–337.
8 Worman 2008, 216.
9 Worman 2008, 223–225.

21.2, 98, 151), "brazen" (θρασύς, 21.2, 98, 201), "shameless" (ἀναιδής, 21.185) and, perhaps most offensively, "defiled" (μιαρός, 21.114, 117, 135). These words are all used also by Aristophanes' characters to disparage their adversaries. The most frequently employed is *miaros*. The chorus of Acharnians uses the word to insult Dicaeopolis (ὠπίτριπτε καὶ μιαρώτατε, *Ach.* 557), for example, as does Demos Paphlagon (ὦ μιαρέ, *Eq.* 1224), Strepsiades his unruly son (*Nub.* 1324, 1327, 1332), or the Proboulos Lysistrata (ὦ μιαρὰ σύ, *Lys.* 433). In oratory, the word is employed always in a hostile or negative fashion.[10] The customarily reserved Lysias, for example, uses *miaros* to describe Agoratus, who dared approach men whom he had earlier gotten expelled from Athens (πῶς ἂν γένοιτο ἄνθρωπος μιαρώτερος; 13.77). Aeschines twice uses the word to besmirch his rival Demosthenes (ὁ μιαρὸς ἄνθρωπος, 3.79; ὁ μιαρὸς καὶ ἀνόσιος ἄνθρωπος, 3.101). Dinarchus does the same (1.18, 21, 24), while Demosthenes himself uses *miaros* over forty times in his surviving speeches to malign and insult opponents, including his assaulter Meidias (ὦ μιαρὰ κεφαλή, 21.135 = Ar. *Ach.* 285), the mercenary sycophant Euctemon (21.103), the rapacious debt-collector Stephanos (45.70) or Aristogeiton who savagely bit off another man's nose (25.28 [ὦ μιαρώτατε πάντων τῶν ὄντων ἀνθρώπων], 32, 62, 81).

The insult *bdeluros* ("revolting", "obnoxious"), which Demosthenes uses three times against Meidias (21.2, 98, 151), is also common in both comedy and oratory. The most frequent target in the corpus of orators is Timarchus (ὁ πρωτεύων βδελυρίᾳ, Aeschin. 1.192) in Aeschines' speech against the spendthrift inheritor. There, the adjective and its cognates appear no fewer than thirteen times.[11] It is employed to describe Timarchus at the moment his drunken and neglected body caused onlookers to shield their eyes in shame (§§26, 31), in reference to the defendant's alleged enthusiasm for prostituting himself (§§41, 54), or to characterise his desire for depraved pleasures (§95). Demosthenes, for his part, directs the insult *bdeluros* at Androtion in connection with that man's anti-democratic and impious lifestyle (ὦ βδελυρέ, 22.66), at Conon who encouraged his son to engage in violently antisocial behaviour (πάντων βδελυρώτατος γεγένηται, 54.22), and at the defaulter Lacritus who, the orator adds, "surpasses all humankind when it comes to being bad" (35.46). Just as it is in oratory, the

---

10 Elsewhere, *miaros* is found spoken in a cheeky (Kinesias to the Spartan herald who has been concealing an erection [ὦ μιαρώτατε, Ar. *Lys.* 989]) or friendly tone (always in Plato's dialogues, such as when Socrates addresses Phaedrus [Pl. *Phdr.* 236e4; further Halliwell 1995, 113–115]).

11 Fisher 2001, 155; see also Spatharas 2017. On *bdeluros* in Demosthenes' *Against Meidias*, see Fisher 2017, 115–123.

insult *bdeluros* is connected in Aristophanes to behaviour that oversteps the acceptable.¹² The chorus of Acharnians, for instance, insults Dicaeopolis with the word when it learns the protagonist has negotiated a treaty with Sparta (ἀναίσχυντος εἶ καὶ βδελυρός, *Ach.* 287–288). The chorus in *Knights* establishes its hostility toward Paphlagon by insulting him, in the very first line that it speaks, with the word *bdeluros* (ὦ μιαρὲ καὶ βδελυρέ, *Eq.* 304–305). And the angry doorkeeper in *Frogs* berates Dionysus – believed to be the despised Heracles returned to Hades – with an emphatic string of insults that opens with *bdeluros* (ὦ βδελυρὲ κἀναίσχυντε καὶ τολμηρὲ σύ, *Ran.* 465). This short overview of the insults *miaros* and *bdeluros* should suffice to demonstrate that, in addition to common topics of invective, Old Comedy and Athenian legal oratory also exploited an overlapping vocabulary of abuse.¹³

3 Invective in Old Comedy and the Law-courts: Some Distinctions and Restrictions

We saw in the previous section that several of the same adjectives and labels were used to insult real-life adversaries in the Athenian courts as they were fictional antagonists in Old Comedy. While these insults and accusations can thus rightly be called comic – in the sense that they appear also in comedy – the vocabulary of comic insults does display some features that are not (or only rarely) echoed in the works of the orators. These differences have not fully been taken into account in discussions of the comic aspects of Greek legal invective. Take again the word most frequently used to insult another person in both Old Comedy and oratory: *miaros*. In about two-thirds of the instances from Aristophanes, the insult occurs in the superlative, yet in the orators, that form is found only in Demosthenes and there in just three out of the forty-two instances, two of which come from speeches whose authenticity and authorship are doubted (Dem. 25.28 [with Ps.-Long. *Subl.* 27.3], [35].52, [43].68). While one could attribute this difference to the trope of employing gratuitous superlatives

---

12 See Parker 1983, 4–5; Olson 2002, 154–155; Fisher 2017, 103–109. Compare also Theophr. *Char.* 11, where the *bdeluros* man engages in asocial acts (exposing his genitals to free women, belching in public [cf. Ar. *Vesp.* 914], etc.).
13 For the two other insults highlighted by Worman in her analysis of *Against Meidias*, namely "brazen" and "shameless", compare e.g. Ar. *Ach.* 289; *Eq.* 181; *Nub.* 915, 1380; *Pax* 362; *Thesm.* 611, 638, 744; *Ran.* 465.

purely for comic effect (a trope whose use in Aristophanes extends beyond insults; see Peppler 1918, 181–183), it might also suggest that the superlative *miarōtatos* was felt to be excessively forceful for the law-courts.[14] Another difference between the language of Greek comic and judicial abuse is the intensifying prefix *pan-*, twice combined with *miaros* in Aristophanes to create the insult *pammiaros* (*Pax* 183; *Ran.* 466). This prefixal construction, which Aristophanes also uses to coin the insults *pagkatapugon* (*Lys.* 137), *pagkataratos* (*Lys.* 588) and *pambdeluros* (*Lys.* 969; *Eccl.* 1043), is absent from classical oratory, again hinting that – for whatever reason – it was thought unsuited to the public politico-legal arena. And lastly, whereas Aristophanes' characters frequently employ *miaros* in vocative addresses (over twenty times), this occurs just once in surviving classical oratory (Dem. 25.28).[15] Could this vocative insult, common as it was in Aristophanic comedy, have been regarded as overly harsh or offensive even for the characteristic "rough-and-tumble" of the Athenian *dikastēria*?[16]

It is not only particular forms of insults that are avoided by the orators. Certain words too are eschewed. Noticeably absent from the speeches are *katapugōn*, *euruprōktos* and *laikastēs*. These words all refer, either directly or indirectly, to sexual acts, although their semantic range stretches beyond the literal meaning, suggesting traits such as licentiousness or effeminacy.[17] While accusations of those traits do occur in the law-court speeches, the insulting words themselves are attested in the classical period only as anonymous graffiti or in comedy.[18] For

---

14 Other insults in the superlative do occur, e.g. ὦ πρὸς μὲν τὰ μεγάλα καὶ σπουδαῖα τῶν ἔργων τῶν ἀνθρώπων ἁπάντων ἀχρηστότατε, "O man of all mankind most useless for great and serious deeds" (Aeschin. 3.152); τίνα τῶν ἐν τῇ πόλει φήσαιτ' ἂν βδελυρώτατον εἶναι καὶ πλείστης ἀναιδείας καὶ ὀλιγωρίας μεστόν; οὐδεὶς οὐδ' ἂν ἁμαρτὼν ὑμῶν ἄλλον εὖ οἶδ' ὅτι φήσειεν ἢ Φιλοκράτην, "Whom would you call the most detestable person in all Athens, and the most swollen with impudence and superciliousness? No one, I am sure, would name, even by a slip of the tongue, anyone but Philocrates" (Dem. 19.206); ὦ φαυλότατ' ἀνθρώπων, "most worthless of men" (Dem. 37.30); Στρατοκλεῖ τῷ πιθανωτάτῳ πάντων ἀνθρώπων καὶ πονηροτάτῳ, "Stratocles, the smoothest-tongued of men and the basest" (Dem. 37.48); ὁ γὰρ πονηρότατος τῶν ἐν τῇ πόλει, μᾶλλον δὲ καὶ τῶν ἄλλων ἀνθρώπων, Ἀριστογείτων, "The worst character in the city, I should say in the whole world, Aristogeiton" (Din. 2.1).
15 Although Dinarchus (1.50) does use the adjectival form in a vocative (ὦ μιαρὸν σὺ θηρίον "you abominable beast" = [Dem.] 58.49).
16 Carey 1999, 377.
17 On εὐρύπρωκτος, see Dover 2002, 94. On καταπύγων, see Davidson 1997, 167–182, who argues that the vulgar word was supplanted in the fourth century by the term *kinaidos* (not found in Aristophanes). On λαικαστής, see Jocelyn 1980; Bain 1991, 74–77; Olson 2002, 96.
18 For these words in graffiti, see Milne and von Bothmer 1953; Fraenkel 1955, 42–45; Lang 1976, 14–15; Brenne 2002, 132.

example, the tragic playwright Agathon is insulted in Aristophanes' *Thesmophoriazusae* as both a *euruprōktos* and a *katapugōn* (*Thesm.* 200), the Stronger Argument in *Clouds* insults the Weaker Argument as a "shameless *katapugōn*" (*Nub.* 909) and Athens's politicians are accused wholesale by Dicaeopolis of being both *laikastai* and *katapugones* (*Ach.* 79). These vulgar insults, found nowhere in the corpus of Greek orators, bear witness to comedy's propensity for exploiting language that exceeds what would elsewhere be tolerated. Audiences of Greek comedy, as a litigant from a Lysianic fragment puts it, were exposed "year in, year out" to things that other people found "shameful merely to mention" (ἃ τοῖς μὲν ἄλλοις αἰσχρόν ἐστι καὶ λέγειν, τῶν κωμῳδοδιδασκάλων ⟨δ'⟩ ἀκούετε καθ' ἕκαστον ἐνιαυτόν, Lys. fr. 195.10–12 Carey).

It is to be expected, in a society attentive to the potency of speech, that explicit and implicit limits were placed on what could be said in certain contexts. The manifestation of such limits in Athenian legal oratory has been explored by Carey, who rightly concludes that the matter is complex and dependant on several factors, not least the considerable "emphasis [in Greek oratory] on moral character" and its upshot, that "reservations and hesitations on the part of the speaker may reflect the image desired by the speaker as much as any objective constraints to which he is subject".[19] Impressions of a litigant might to a large extent be based on "his own and his opponent's ethical discussion; no matter what the facts of the case, he had to prove that he was the sort of person deserving of the jury's respect and that his opponent was not".[20] Moderating one's speech and lexical choices to match the *ēthos* one wished to portray was doubtless a common tactic (cf. Arist. *Rhet.* 1404b1–1405a2, 1408b11–16). With that in mind, speakers in the Athenian law-court sometimes apologise for using words that describe shameful acts (Aeschin. 1.37–38 with Fisher 2001 *ad loc.*) or claim that insults to which they have been subjected are so disgraceful they cannot be repeated in front of a jury. Thus Demosthenes, in describing the home invasion he suffered at the hands of Meidias and Thrasylochus, recounts how the two aggressors burst through the doors of his house and used "foul language" (ἐφθέγγοντ' αἰσχρά) and directed all sorts of bad words at Demosthenes' family (ῥητὰ καὶ ἄρρητα κάκ' ἐξεῖπον), words which the orator dare not repeat in front of the judges (οὐ γὰρ ἔγωγε προαχθείην ἂν εἰπεῖν πρὸς ὑμᾶς τῶν τότε ῥηθέντων οὐδέν, Dem. 21.79). Similarly, the speaker in *Against Conon* narrates how, after receiving a violent beating, he heard his aggressors insult him terribly (αὐτῶν

---

19 Carey 1999, 371.
20 Ober 1989, 147. Compare e.g. Lys. 14.23–40; Aeschin 1.153; Dem. 19.199–201, 52.1, 54.38; Isae. 4.27–29; Arist. *Rhet.* 1366a8–12.

ἤκουον πολλὰ καὶ δεινὰ λεγόντων). He hesitates, however, to reproduce this verbal abuse in court (καὶ τὰ μὲν ἄλλα καὶ βλασφημίαν ἔχει τινὰ καὶ ὀνομάζειν ὀκνήσαιμ' ἂν ἐν ὑμῖν ἔνια, Dem. 54.8–9; cf. 18.126). The litigants' unwillingness in these two cases to repeat insults supports the view that some words could offend the sensibilities of judges and may help to explain the absence of the vulgar terms discussed in the previous paragraph. That said, the professed reluctance is also an effective rhetorical strategy because it: a) draws a neat distinction between the modest victims and their unrefined aggressors, b) can be framed as an act of respect toward the judges, who are shielded by the speaker from hearing the offensive words and c) lets the judges imagine for themselves the most outrageous terms of abuse. Separating genuine concerns from rhetorical affectation is therefore difficult.

Beyond considerations of propriety and politeness, there is evidence of formal restrictions in Athens on the use of insulting or slanderous words. Lysias mentions, and Aeschines cites, a law that imposed fines on anyone who employed *loidoria* in public meetings, especially when the abuse was directed at magistrates. Such a measure is certainly plausible, although both the Lysianic speech in which the reference occurs (*On Behalf of the Soldier*) and the citation by Aeschines (1.35) have had their authenticity questioned.[21] The evidence for limits on invective among private citizens is more secure. An Athenian law against slander dates back at least to the 420s (Ar. *Vesp.* 1206–1207). Lysias' *Against Theomnestus I*, a prosecution speech in a slander case, provides us with basic information about the regulations.[22] There we learn that the fine for guilty parties was a hefty five hundred drachmas (Lys. 10.12; cf. Isocr. 20.3), roughly the annual salary of a skilled labourer in the fourth century, suggesting that the crime was considered to be serious.[23] The plaintiff in the case does admit that taking someone to court for using one of the forbidden, slanderous words is the hallmark of an "excessively litigious" (λίαν φιλόδικον, §3) or "petty" (ἀνελεύθερον) person but, despite his own use of insults (he repeatedly calls the defendant "stupid", at §§14, 15, 20), there is little suggestion of pettiness in this case. The accuser recalls his "legitimate anger" (ἄξιον ὀργισθῆναι, §28) at Theomnestus' "shameful allegation" (§26), the latter complaint expressing the power of slander to dishonour the target.

---

[21] See respectively Todd 2007, 581–585, 592–593 and Fisher 2001, 164. If the measure was real it cannot have been overly effective since there are several accounts of public speakers and magistrates being subjected to verbal abuse (e.g. Lys. 30.10; Dem. 19.210, 24.13).
[22] For all the evidence about the law, see Halliwell 1991a, 49–54; Wallace 1994.
[23] For fourth-century wage-labour costs, see Loomis 1998.

The anger felt by the speaker in Lysias 10 was deemed, by Aristotle, to be a natural reaction to insults.²⁴ Particularly painful, Aristotle says in the *Rhetoric*, is when others are perceived to be "deriding and ridiculing and mocking" us (καταγελῶσι καὶ χλευάζουσιν καὶ σκώπτουσιν, 1379a30–32). We grow angry, Aristotle continues, when others claim that we do not possess the qualities we aspire to possess (1379a38–40). We grow angry when those who previously respected us now cease to do so.²⁵ And finally, our anger is amplified when insults occur in the presence of our rivals or people whom we admire and respect (1379b23–27). It is this anger-inducing quality of verbal abuse that is cited, by one Athenian speaker, as the rationale behind the city's slander laws. The legal measure against slander, which Ariston in Demosthenes' *Against Conon* refers to by its official name (κακηγορίας δίκαι, 54.17–18), allows for verbal injustices to be resolved in a civilised manner and stops them, he says, from "being decided by the anger or will of just anybody" (τῇ τοῦ προστυχόντος ὀργῇ μηδὲ βουλήσει ταῦτα κρίνεσθαι, §§19–20). Ariston detects an intrinsic danger in insulting speech: it is not only hurtful in itself, but when left unresolved it can, because of the *orgē* that it engenders in the victim, trigger more serious forms of extra-legal retaliatory violence.²⁶ Or, as he puts it in an impressive anaphora, "insults can lead to blows, blows to grievous bodily harm, and grievous bodily harm to death" (ἐκ μὲν λοιδορίας εἰς πληγάς, ἐκ δὲ πληγῶν εἰς τραύματα, ἐκ δὲ τραυμάτων εἰς θάνατον, §19). While this chain of escalation might come across as hyperbolic, it in fact finds support in various Athenian narratives of insults turn-

---

24 Anger is one of the emotions that cause people to "differ in their judgements" (διαφέρουσι πρὸς τὰς κρίσεις, *Rhet.* 1378a20), Aristotle says, hence its importance for effective persuasion. On anger in the law-courts, see e.g. Allen 2004; Rubinstein 2004.
25 Arist. *Rhet.* 1379b4–7. Compare the speaker at Lysias 8.2, 17 who complains that the insults he received were doubly painful because they came from those he had thought to be his friends.
26 Compare Plato's comments in the *Laws*, which segue into a discussion on comic performances. Plato argues that invective is "incommensurate with a well-ordered *polis*" (οὐ πρέπον ἐν εὐνόμων πόλει, 934e1) and that disputes should be settled by reason, with each party taking turns to listen and then speak (934e4–6). Insults are dangerous because "when men take to... calling each other offensive names (αἰσχρῶν ὀνομάτων)", these words "soon lead to hatreds and disputes of the most serious kind" (934e7–935a3). In exchanging insults and thus indulging his passion (θυμός) and anger (ὀργή), an insulter "drives back into savagery (ἐξαγριῶν) a side of his character that had once been civilised by education, becoming wild" (θηριούμενος, 935a5–6). For Plato, insults cannot resolve an argument, because they are antithetical to logical turn-taking debate; they can only promote minor matters to cases of serious enmity. Insults thus endanger the stability of the community, Plato concludes, and have no rightful place in the public sphere (935b8–c8).

ing to blows (Lys. 3.43 [hypothetical]; Dem. 40.32, 47.36–38; Hyp. fr. 97 Jensen), insults turning to kidnapping and a severe beating (Lys. fr. 279 Carey), or insults turning to blows and indeed murder (Dem. 21.71; Pl. *Leg.* 866e4–8). The consequences of verbal abuse could be severe. Regulations governing slander and *loidoria* may have been designed to moderate this and help contain the risk.

4 Invective and the Athenian Audience

To recap the discussion so far, we have observed both thematic and linguistic similarities between the verbal abuse meted out by characters on the Old Comic stage and that directed at litigants in front of popular Athenian juries. From this perspective, the plentiful abuse in the courts can indeed be considered comic, although we have seen too that the verbal parallels are not universal. At the same time, formal limits on insulting speech and anecdotes about the damage that it can cause, as well the anger it provokes, suggest that invective could be a serious matter in Athens. Questions therefore arise as to why law-court speakers thought it profitable to employ invective and whether, given the crossovers with Old Comedy, this in fact provoked laughter.

Athenian litigants relied on a variety of emotive strategies to impress the judges and, ultimately, get them to vote in their favour. Philocleon's description of some of these strategies, in Aristophanes' *Wasps* (560–575), is supported by other sources and underscores the performative nature of the Attic law-courts.[27] Philocleon mentions speakers ingratiating themselves with judges through flattery (cf. Antiph. 5.8; Lys. 3.2), getting sympathy through lamentation (cf. Dem. 25.47, 37.48), distracting judges with amusing stories or passages from Aesop (cf. Lys. 3.7–8; Aeschin. 1.81–84; Arist. *Rhet.* 1393a28–31, 1394a2–5), bringing children into court to garner pity (cf. Lys. 20.34; Dem. 21.186; Isocr. 15.321) and using personal ridicule to obtain laughs (οἱ δὲ σκώπτουσ', ἵν' ἐγὼ γελάσω, *Vesp.* 567).[28] It is this last tactic that interests us here, as it would add a further, not insignificant parallel between the invective found in Old Comedy and that of legal oratory.

---

27 For law-court speeches as performances, see Hall 1995; Apostolakis 2017; Serafim 2017.
28 The verb that Philocleon uses to denote laughter-eliciting mockery, *skōptein*, is closely tied to Old Comedy and the aims of the comic poet. Aristophanes claims, for example, that the career of the playwright Magnes ended "because he lost his ability to *skōptein*" (*Eq.* 525), while in *Wealth*, *skōptein* and *kōmōidein* appear as virtual synonyms (*Plut.* 557). See further Edwards 1991, 168–178; Olson 2002, 285; Halliwell 2008, 18–19.

Comments in the surviving speeches corroborate Philocleon's claim that Athenian judges could laugh at invective and other law-court spectacles. The disabled pensioner in Lysias 24, analysed in this volume by Major, argues that the plaintiff wants to mock him by drawing attention to his physical handicap and poverty. The defendant frames the litigation as a kind of theatrical *mise-en-scène*, whereby the plaintiff is "composing something elegant" (τι καλὸν ποιῶν) for the judges and "indulging in comic ridicule" (κωμῳδεῖν, Lys. 24.18). In another speech by Lysias, the speaker tries to draw laughs by making a joke at an old woman's expense ("it was easier to count her teeth than it was to count her fingers", fr. 1.5 Carey), reminiscent of a quip from Aristophanes' *Wealth* (1057–1059). In the mid-fourth century, Hyperides accuses Philippides of acting the clown in court and escaping charges by "dancing comic dances and cracking jokes" (κορδακίζων καὶ γελωτοποιῶν, Hyp. fr. 4.7 Jensen). Demosthenes, for his part, links laughter with *loidoria* when he upbraids citizens for preferring speakers who turn serious debates into matters of "jokes and verbal abuse" (τὸ πρᾶγμ' εἰς γέλωτα καὶ λοιδορίαν ἐμβαλόντες, Dem. 10.75), the same tactic that Ariston, in Demosthenes 54, expects his assailants will adopt (ἀπὸ τῆς ὕβρεως καὶ τῶν πεπραγμένων τὸ πρᾶγμ' ἄγοντ' εἰς γέλωτα καὶ σκώμματ' ἐμβαλεῖν πειράσεσθαι, §13). The risk is that instead of pitying Ariston, the judges will find the story of his assault funny and, laughing together (γελάσαντες, §20) with Conon and his sons, dismiss the charge.[29] Finally, in *On the Crown*, Demosthenes reproaches Aeschines for relying on "jokes" (*skōmmata*) and "insults" (*loidoria*) rather than on proofs, arguing that funny vilification and verbal abuse are inadequate substitutes for a serious refutation of the charges (18.15).[30] That said,

---

29 See further Halliwell 2008, 33–38.
30 Further contrasts between *loidoria* and rational argument can be found at e.g. [Dem.] 57.34; Isae. 6.65. And in *Against Androtion*, Demosthenes opines that invective lacks substance and is "empty" (λοιδορίας κενάς, 22.21), before stating that *loidoria* is "wholly opposed to refutation" (πάμπολυ λοιδορία τε καὶ αἰτία κεχωρισμένον ἐστὶν ἐλέγχου, 22.22). Demosthenes and Dinarchus also argue that verbal abuse could be employed to mislead the people. Demosthenes observes how public speakers "insult and badmouth each other using unrepeatable words", but can later be seen celebrating together and partaking in joint sacrifices (58.40). These men pretend to be enemies yet "privately they work together and share the profits" (ἰδίᾳ δὲ ταὐτὰ πράττοντας καὶ μετέχοντας τῶν λημμάτων). Along similar lines, Dinarchus suggests that speakers "deliberately trade insults and abuse one another" (λοιδορῶνται καὶ προσκρούωσιν ἀλλήλοις ἐξεπίτηδες, 1.99), while in private they follow the same illicit pursuits. The exchange of verbal blows allows these men to "deceive" (ἐξαπατῶντες) Athens's citizens, Dinarchus claims, by creating an illusion of personal animosity that diverts attention from acts of bribe-taking (cf. Antiphanes fr. 194 K-A). Invective, according to those interpretations, was aimed

Demosthenes must admit the probable success of Aeschines' loidoric strategy. This is because it is, as the orator puts it, "in the nature of all people to enjoy listening to insults and slander" (φύσει πᾶσιν ἀνθρώποις ὑπάρχει τῶν μὲν λοιδοριῶν καὶ τῶν κατηγοριῶν ἀκούειν ἡδέως, §3). This universal "bad habit" causes law-court judges, Demosthenes remarks, to rank the "pleasure and gratification of *loidoria*" (τῆς ἐπὶ ταῖς λοιδορίαις ἡδονῆς καὶ χάριτος, §138) above what is advantageous for the city. Watching litigants trade insults is so captivating, in other words, that it distracts judges from adjudicating rationally and voting in the interests of the *polis* as they privilege spectacle over substance, led astray by their enjoyment of verbal abuse.[31]

Two further Demosthenic observations support the view that Athenian citizens enjoyed listening to invective in public settings and could react to it with laughter. Although not from a law-court speech, Demosthenes, in his *Third Philippic*, upbraids the Athenians for "laughing whenever speakers insult each other" (γελᾶτε ἄν τισι λοιδορηθῶσιν, 9.54) and for positively demanding that "hireling" orators speak so they can listen to those men's *skōmmata* and *loidoria*. Demosthenes characterises this behaviour as a "folly" (μωρίας) or "mania" (παρανοίας) of the people, highlighting the popularity of verbal abuse and implying that there was substantial pressure on speakers to indulge their audiences' desire for it. And lastly, in the Funeral Oration, Demosthenes notes that even those who "themselves would never speak ill of others, rejoice when hearing another do so" (οἱ μηδὲν ἂν εἰπόντες αὐτοὶ βλάσφημον ἄλλου γε λέγοντος χαίρουσιν ἀκούοντες, 60.26). While he is describing here how fear of reproach can spur men into excellent military behaviour, Demosthenes' comment does underscore the universal appeal of invective, even among the most reserved members of society. Taken at face value, this would suggest that speakers had little to lose when it came to using insults in the courts or other public settings.

The evidence presented above describes a citizenry that could take pleasure and laugh when others were insulted in public, supporting Philocleon's description of law-court tactics from Aristophanes' *Wasps*. It is, therefore, unsurprising that litigants adopted verbal abuse as a strategy for appealing to the judges. Demosthenes in particular seems to have been adept at generating vibrant insults and pejorative epithets, some of which we can assume gained him laugh-

---

less at amusing the judges or damaging an opponent's reputation than it was at purposely distracting Athenians with fabricated enmities.
31 Cf. Dem. 36.61.

ter. Not only was Demosthenes known for creative name-calling,[32] but he also mockingly draws on Aeschines' secretarial work as a source of invective (18.127, 209, 19.95, 314) and makes recurring gibes about his rival's career as an actor (18.127, 139, 242, 262). Other comic flavourings appear in his speeches, such as the use of scornful diminutives or playful exaggeration, while Demosthenes' sense of humour is revealed by Aeschines who warns judges not to let the orator distract them with "jokes" (γέλωτα, Aeschin. 1.175) or recalls how Demosthenes got "unprecedented" amounts of laughter from jokes told during a diplomatic mission to Pella (2.112). Despite his documented use of humour and personal insults, however, Demosthenes endeavours to depict himself as "moderate and kind" (μέτριος καὶ φιλάνθρωπος, 21.185) or "retiring and timid" (ἄτολμον καὶ δειλόν, 19.206). By his own description, he is someone who repudiates verbal abuse (οὐ φιλολοίδορον ὄντα) and, if he is forced to rely on invective, speaks only what is "absolutely necessary" (τἀναγκαιότατ᾽ εἰπεῖν, 18.126). Demosthenes characterises himself as a sober and rational orator who stands above the mudslinging and insults of other law-court speakers. Squaring this self-portrayal of decency and moderation with the ample evidence for Demosthenes' use of invective is a challenge, though doubtless symptomatic of an ambivalence that surrounded *loidoria*. Verbal abuse – especially when combined with humour – was an effective means of belittling adversaries and, as we have seen, gratifying an audience hungry for entertaining insults. At the same time, a surfeit of invective could come across as uncivilised or bring shame upon the speaker himself.[33] The explicit reticence of litigants (whether feigned or not) to repeat some insults in court attests to a culture in which certain words were thought capable of embarrassing speakers and listeners alike, while the slander law and other possible bans on invective formalised citizens' protection from verbal abuse. From this perspective, insults were to be employed with caution. There was likely a tension, in other words, between wanting to please or entertain the judges with bouts of personal invective, yet also come across as a reasonable and restrained citizen. Experienced litigants, like Demosthenes, would have been aware of the potential benefits, but also the associated risks of using verbal abuse in front of the judges.[34]

---

32 Examples from the sources include "gold-horned" of Aeschines (χρυσόκερων, Aeschin. 3.164) and "Margites" of Alexander (Aeschin. 3.160). For name-calling in comedy, see Kanavou 2011. For nicknames in Roman oratory, see Corbeill 1996, 57–98.
33 Compare the advice in the *Rhetoric to Alexander* not to direct "shameful names" (αἰσχροῖς ὀνόμασι, 35.17–19 = 1441b11–21) at opponents lest in doing so, you besmirch your own character.
34 Kish in this volume discusses the similar need to strike a balance between jokes and discretion, as expressed in Cicero's *De oratore*.

5 Conclusion

The performative nature of the law-courts, the emphasis on a litigant's *ēthos* and the agonistic judicial system all combined in Athens to create an environment fertile for personal invective. Although scattered across diverse sources and spanning a period of almost a hundred years, the evidence gathered and discussed in this contribution suggests that, much like in the comic theatre of Aristophanes, the Athenians of the classical period enjoyed listening to insults also in politico-legal settings and that they could react to this with laughter. Despite sensitivities around, and formal restrictions on verbal abuse, invective (especially when combined with humour) could impress judges and help bring them over to a litigant's side. It did this by denigrating opponents through a combination of character assassination and shame-inducing laughter, as well as by exploiting the basic attraction of hearing other people trade insults. Striking the right balance between satisfying the judges' appetite for *loidoria* and constructing a pertinent and logical case against an adversary would likely have been one mark of a successful public speaker.

Bibliography

Allen, D. (2004), 'Angry Bees, Wasps, and Judges: The Symbolic Power of ὀργή in Athens', in: S. Braund and G. Most (eds.), *Ancient Anger. Perspectives from Homer to Galen*, Cambridge, 76–98.
Apostolakis, K. (2017), 'Pitiable Dramas on the Podium of the Athenian Courts', in: S. Papaioannou, A. Serafim and B. da Vela (eds.), *The Theatre of Justice. Aspects of Performance in Greco-Roman Oratory and Rhetoric*, Leiden/Boston, 133–156.
Bain, D. (1991), 'Six Greek Verbs of Sexual Congress (βινῶ, κινῶ, πυγίζω, ληκῶ, οἴφω, λαικάζω)', in: *Classical Quarterly* 41, 51–77.
Brenne, S. (2002), 'Die Ostraka (487–ca. 416 v. Chr.) als Testimonien (T1)', in: P. Siewert (ed.), *Ostrakismos. Testimonien I: die Zeugnisse antiker Autoren, der Inschriften und Ostraka über das athenische Scherbengericht aus vorhellenistischer Zeit (487–322 v. Chr.)*, Stuttgart, 36–166.
Carey, C. (1999), 'Propriety in the Attic orators', in: F. de Martino and A.H. Sommerstein (eds.), *Studi sull'eufemismo*, Bari, 369–391.
Cohen, D. (1995), *Law, Violence, and Community in Classical Athens*, Cambridge.
Conley, T. (2010), *Toward a Rhetoric of Insult*, Chicago.
Corbeill, A. (1996), *Controlling Laughter. Political Humor in the Late Roman Republic*, Princeton.
Davidson, J. (1997), *Courtesans and Fishcakes. The Consuming Passions of Classical Athens*, London.
Dover, K. (1974), *Greek Popular Morality in the Time of Plato and Aristotle*, Oxford.

Dover, K. (2002), 'Some Evaluative Terms in Aristophanes', in: A. Willi (ed.), *The Language of Greek Comedy*, Oxford, 85–97.
Edwards, A.T. (1991), 'Aristophanes' Comic Poetics: τρύξ, Scatology, σκῶμμα', in: *Transactions of the American Philological Association* 121, 157–179.
Fisher, N. (2001), *Aeschines, Against Timarchos*, Oxford.
Fisher, N. (2017), 'Demosthenes and the Use of Disgust', in: D. Lateiner and D. Spatharas (eds.), *The Ancient Emotion of Disgust*, New York, 103–124.
Fraenkel, E. (1955), 'Neues Griechisch in Graffiti', in: *Glotta* 34, 42–47.
Hall, E. (1995), 'Lawcourt Dramas: The Power of Persuasion in Greek Forensic Oratory', in: *Bulletin of the Institute of Classical Studies* 40.2, 39–58.
Halliwell, S. (1991a), 'Comic Satire and Freedom of Speech in Classical Athens', in: *Journal of Hellenic Studies* 111, 48–70.
Halliwell, S. (1991b), 'The Uses of Laughter in Greek Culture', in: *Classical Quarterly* 41, 279–296.
Halliwell, S. (1995), 'Forms of Address: Socratic Vocatives in Plato', in: F. De Martino and A.H. Sommerstein (eds.), *Lo spettacolo delle voci*, Bari, 89–121.
Halliwell, S. (2008), *Greek Laughter. A Study of Cultural Psychology from Homer to Early Christianity*, Cambridge.
Harding, P. (1994), 'Comedy and Rhetoric', in: I. Worthington (ed.), *Persuasion. Greek Rhetoric in Action*, London/New York, 196–221.
Hatzilambrou, R. (2011), 'The Use of the *ad hominem* Argument in the Works of Isaeus', in: *L'Antiquité Classique* 80, 37–51.
Heath, M. (1997), 'Aristophanes and the Discourse of Politics', in: G.W. Dobrov (ed.), *The City as Comedy. Society and Representation in Athenian Drama*, Chapel Hill/London, 230–249.
Hesk, J. (2014), 'La construction de l'"autre" et la contestation du "soi". L'invective et l'*elenchos* dans l'art oratoire athénien', in: A.Q. Bottineau (ed.), *La représentation négative de l'autre dans l'antiquité. Hostilité, réprobation, dépréciation*, Dijon, 143–160.
Jocelyn, H.D. (1980), 'A Greek Indecency and its Students: Λαικάζειν', in: *Proceedings of the Cambridge Philological Society* 26, 12–66.
Kamen, D. (2009), 'Servile Invective in Classical Athens', in: *Scripta Classica Israelica* 28, 43–56.
Kanavou, N. (2011), *Aristophanes' Comedy of Names. A Study of Speaking Names in Aristophanes*, Berlin/New York.
Koster, S. (1980), *Die Invektive in der griechischen und römischen Literatur*, Meisenheim am Glan.
Lang, M. (1976), *The Athenian Agora XXI. Graffiti and Dipinti*, Princeton.
Lape, S. (2016), 'The State of Blame: Politics, Competition, and the Courts in Democratic Athens', in: *Critical Analysis of Law* 3, 87–113.
Loomis, W.T. (1998), *Wages, Welfare Costs, and Inflation in Classical Athens*, Ann Arbor.
Milne, M.J. and von Bothmer, D. (1953), 'ΚΑΤΑΠΥΓΩΝ, ΚΑΤΑΠΥΓΑΙΝΑ', in: *Hesperia* 22, 215–224.
Ober, J. (1989), *Mass and Elite in Democratic Athens. Rhetoric, Ideology, and the Power of the People*, Princeton.
Olson, S.D. (1998), *Aristophanes: Peace*, Oxford.
Olson, S.D. (2002), *Aristophanes: Acharnians*, Oxford.
Parker, R. (1983), *Miasma. Pollution and Purification in Early Greek Religion*, Oxford.
Peppler, C.W. (1918), 'Comic Terminations in Aristophanes. Part IV', in: *American Journal of Philology* 39, 173–183.

Rosenbloom, D. (2002), 'From *Ponēros* to *Pharmakos*: Theatre, Social Drama, and Revolution', in: *Classical Antiquity* 21, 283–346.
Rowe, G.A. (1966), 'The Portrait of Aeschines in the *Oration on the Crown*', in: *Transactions of the American Philological Association* 97, 397–406.
Rubinstein, L. (2004), 'Stirring up Dicastic anger', in: D.L. Cairns and R.A. Knox (eds.), *Law, Rhetoric, and Comedy in Classical Athens. Essays in Honour of Douglas M. MacDowell*, Swansea, 187–203.
Serafim, A. (2017), *Attic Oratory and Performance*, London/New York.
Spatharas, D. (2006), 'Persuasive ΓΕΛΩΣ: Public Speaking and the Use of Laughter', in: *Mnemosyne* 59, 374–387.
Spatharas, D. (2017), 'Sex, Politics and Disgust in Aeschines' *Against Timarchus*', in: D. Lateiner and D. Spatharas (eds.), *The Ancient Emotion of Disgust*, New York, 125–139.
Todd, S.C. (2007), *A Commentary on Lysias, Speeches 1–11*, Oxford/New York.
Wallace, R. (1994), 'The Athenian Laws Against Slander', in: G. Thür (ed.), *Symposion 1993. Vorträge zur griechischen und hellenistischen Rechtsgeschichte*, Cologne/Weimar/Vienna, 109–124.
Worman, N. (2008), *Abusive Mouths in Classical Athens*, Cambridge.

Kostas Apostolakis
Comic Invective and Public Speech in Fourth-Century Athens

Abstract: This chapter examines fundamental topics of comic invective (including *ēthopoiia* and the language and imagery of abuse) as they appear in fourth-century oratory, both forensic and deliberative. The increasing rivalry between pro-Macedonian and anti-Macedonian orators fomented fierce invective. It appears that Demosthenes, Hyperides, Aeschines and Dinarchus, who played a leading part in the relevant debates of the time, often draw on comic tradition when using invective. The vitriolic attacks they launch against each other as litigants are no less inventive and imaginative than comic methods. The struggle between Demosthenes and Aeschines, in particular, includes jeering attacks which have implications for the personal satire of Old Comedy or patterns that are used in the surviving fragments of Middle Comedy. A close reading of representative speeches composed in the framework of these political controversies offers insights about recurrent aspects of comic invective, e.g. accusations that are trotted out against opponents of deception and bribery, and attacks against their social status and family.

1 Comic and Rhetorical Invective: A Two-Way Relationship

It is well established that invective aims at the public denigration and isolation from the community of an individual, on the basis of existing social preconceptions.[1] The Attic orators, well aware of the function of invective in the courts and the Assembly, did not hesitate to employ a kind of "rhetoric of anti-rhetoric", in order to reprove Athenian audiences for their tendency to enjoy this kind of personal abuse. Demosthenes in his *Third Philippic* criticises his audience for allowing hired men to attack their political opponents and for laughing at those

---

I would like to express my thanks to the editors of this volume and the anonymous referees for their valuable comments on my chapter.

---

1 Cf. e.g. Koster 1980, 38–39.

attacked by the speakers.² At the centre of this critique is the view that, when listeners laugh at the victim of an invective, they unconsciously side with the abuser and establish a kind of "emotional community" with him, estranging the target of the invective from the sustained whole.³

The reason why insults and invectives prevailed in the courts and the Assembly in fourth-century Athens is presumably connected with the entertainment and enjoyment they provided to jurymen and assemblymen, who had an inclination to scurrility and scandal.⁴ This entertainment is often described as not very different from that provided in the comic theatre of Aristophanes and other poets of Old Comedy, where personal abuse prevails. We should also take into account that comic invective is associated with abusive, belittling and socially dividing laughter, what Halliwell calls "consequential laughter",⁵ which invites the listeners to side with the speaker against the person laughed at. This derisive laughter destroys the reputation of the target. Given, therefore, that oratory and comedy often share common targets, such as politicians, it is hardly a surprise that the rhetorical invective engaged in on the rostrum is often fed and enriched by the personal satire (*onomasti kōmōidein*) of Old Comedy, and in turn feeds back to the comic stage.

It seems that, in some cases at least, invective in oratory is more effective when constructed on models of personal abuse well established in comic satire. In other words, when comic language invades oratory, the listeners are invited to receive aspects of the case in the light of a new environment, familiar to them through the comic stage. When dealing, however, with comic invective in Attic oratory, we should always take into account not only the similarities but also the differences between a theatrical and a rhetorical performance. While comic poets are free to introduce invectives against a person whenever they want, in order to entertain the spectators without needing to substantiate their attacks, the orator has to render his invectives relevant to the disputed case, by making them part of an *ad hominem* argument.

---

2 Dem. 9.54; cf. 18.8; 18.138.
3 For this triangular relationship and its performative dynamics: Yunis 2001, 22; Serafim 2020a, 23–42.
4 Dem. 18.3 ἕτερον δ', ὃ φύσει πᾶσιν ἀνθρώποις ὑπάρχει, τῶν μὲν λοιδοριῶν καὶ τῶν κατηγοριῶν ἀκούειν ἡδέως, τοῖς ἐπαινοῦσι δ' αὐτοὺς ἄχθεσθαι, "The second point is simply a matter of human nature: people listen with delight to insults and accusations, but are annoyed by those who praise themselves". All translations of Attic oratory in this chapter follow *The Oratory of Classical Greece* series (edited by M. Gagarin).
5 Halliwell 1991, 279–296.

Surprisingly enough, techniques of invective which are prominent in Aristophanes and Old Comedy mainly survive in the fourth century not in contemporary comedy, but on the rostrum of the courts, especially in cases with a political dimension. A plausible explanation is that comedy production becomes international in the fourth century, also embracing non-Athenian issues and targets, whereas oratory remains Athenian.[6] Given, therefore, that in fourth-century comedy, so-called "Middle Comedy", the *onomasti kōmōidein* declines, it is only to be expected that, at least in some cases, the fierce invective in forensic speeches, which aims at denigrating, abusing and ridiculing the opponent, uses techniques already recognisable in Old Comedy. Nevertheless, political invective sometimes occurs in fragments of the (otherwise less political) Middle Comedy. Timocles, in particular, seems to employ Aristophanic techniques in satirising contemporary politicians.[7]

Comic invective in current bibliography is mostly discussed in a limited number of forensic speeches, especially those of Demosthenes.[8] My chapter has a broader focus, since it examines fundamental topics of comic invective, including comic characterisation, terms of abuse, vocabulary, metaphors and imagery, which appear in fourth-century oratory, both forensic and deliberative. These topics are dealt with under the light of both Old Comedy and the surviving fragments of Middle Comedy, in order to detect possible interplays between the rostrum and the comic stage. I also intend to show that, irrespective of possible direct or indirect influence, rhetorical and comic invectives have a two-way relationship.[9]

2 Invective and Deceptive Rhetoric

2.1 Aeschines as Impostor: Fake Actor, Fake Ambassador, Fake Doctor

When an orator activates comic invective against his opponent, he has to adapt this attack to the subject matter of the debate. He accordingly constructs the

---

[6] For the "internationalisation" of Athenian comic theatre: Konstantakos 2011, 153–162.
[7] Cf. Apostolakis 2019, 9–16.
[8] For comic elements in oratory: Rowe 1966; Harding 1994; Rosen 1988; Miner 2006; Worman 2008, 213–274. Also: Donelan and Serafim in this volume.
[9] Cf. Webster 1956, 47: "it is not always easy to decide whether a comic poet is borrowing from an orator or an orator from a comic poet".

portrait of his opponent, so as to use it as the basis for interpreting his past or future actions.¹⁰ And, although both oratory and comedy make use of deception for their own reasons, they do not fail to blame untrustworthy orators and reveal their deceptive methods. Demosthenes and Aeschines, in particular, exchange fierce invectives against each other in their speeches delivered during the trials concerning the False Embassy (343 BC) and the crowning of Demosthenes (330 BC).¹¹

More specifically, it was Ctesiphon who proposed in 336 BC that the Assembly should bestow a crown on Demosthenes for his services to the city. Aeschines, on his part, attacked this proposal as conflicting with the existing laws. It has often been remarked that in the speech *On the Crown*, tragedy and comedy coexist.¹² Demosthenes reserves to himself the role of a tragic hero, who foresees what will happen but insists on his patriotic policy. Aeschines, on the other hand, is depicted as a fake tragic actor and a true comic *alazōn*.¹³ It is, indeed, in this comic setting that Demosthenes attacks his opponent on the grounds that he has undertaken different duties, but has proven over the course of time to be a charlatan, who performs all these tasks badly. Demosthenes actually depicts Aeschines as a failed tragic actor, one who has occasionally been assigned important tragic roles but destroyed them (Dem. 18.180).¹⁴ However, while Aeschines failed as Cresphontes, Creon or Oenomaus, at the same time he emerges from Demosthenes' speeches as a successful *alazōn* of the comic stage, a man who pretends to have abilities he does not in fact possess.¹⁵

Already in his speech *On the False Embassy*, Demosthenes has described Aeschines as a fake ambassador, who supposedly undertook the duty to promote the Athenian positions in Macedonia, but actually recommended policies completely opposed to Athenian interests and wasted time at the expense of the

---

10 Cf. Miner 2006, 8–16.
11 As Serafim 2020a, 35 notes, "... comic invective is used in the parts of the oratorical script where personal or occupational (i.e. political, ambassadorial) matters are discussed, or where the speaker refers to the private life or affairs of his adversary". For comic invective in Demosthenes and Aeschines: Harding 1994, 200–201; Serafim in this volume on the private speeches of Demosthenes.
12 E.g. Yunis 2001, 12–22.
13 For the comic *alazōn* cf. Whitman 1964, 26–28; Hubbard 1991, 2–5; Rowe 1966, 402–406; Worman 2008, 85.
14 Cf. Dem. 18.209 ὦ τριταγωνιστά and the comic title *Τριταγωνιστής* by Antiphanes, the poet of Middle Comedy.
15 On the evolution of the meaning of the comic *alazōn*: MacDowell 1990, 287–292; Miner 2006, 50–70.

city, due to corruption: Dem. 19.8 "... and that together with Philocrates he took gifts and payments in return for all these services (δῶρα καὶ μισθοὺς εἰληφότα μετὰ Φιλοκράτους)".[16]

Ambassadors being accused of corruption is a common theme in Old Comedy: *Πρέσβεις* is the title of two comedies by Leucon (422 BC) and the comic Plato (ca 390 BC). In Plato's play (fr. 127 K.-A.), Epicrates and Phormisius are said to have received many bribes (πλεῖστα δωροδοκήματα) from the Persian King. In Aristophanes' *Acharnians* (61–72), Theoros and other Athenian ambassadors, recently returned from Thrace, appear on stage (vv. 134–137) as false politicians (ἀλαζόνες) who spend a long time in the court of Sitalces in Thrace in order to draw hefty pay (μισθὸν φέρειν).[17] It is also worth noting that concerning foreign policy, Persian politics in particular, Athenian anti-Macedonian orators participating in diplomatic legations are personally satirised by Timocles, the most "Aristophanic" poet of the fourth century. He employs acerbic personal satire that departs from the norm of his times and is more in harmony with the spirit of Old Comedy. He seems to take up pro-Macedonian positions, since he satirises the most prominent anti-Macedonian orators of the time, Demosthenes and Hyperides. Open prejudice on such matters is expressed in a comic dialogue focusing on the Harpalus affair (324 BC) in his play *Dēlos* fr. 4, where Demosthenes (along with Hyperides and other anti-Macedonians) is said to have got fifty talents. In another play, Hyperides is described as a "hired servant who waters his employer's fields" (μισθωτὸς ἄρδει πεδία τοῦ δεδωκότος, *Ikarioi Satyroi*, fr. 17 K.-A.). Hyperides was probably thought to have been bribed by the Persian King in order to incite war against the Macedonians.[18] The Persian gold, indeed, is a well- established pattern of invective in Attic oratory. Also, Demosthenes, the leader of the anti-Macedonians in Athens, is described by the pro-Macedonian Aeschines and Dinarchus as being corrupted by the king's gold in different circumstances, e.g. the exile of Thebans after the destruction of their city (Aeschin. 3.156), and Demosthenes' involvement in the Harpalus affair (Din. 1.77).[19]

---

16 Cf. Dem. 18.38; 18.52: μισθωτὸν ἐγώ σε Φιλίππου πρότερον καὶ νῦν Ἀλεξάνδρου καλῶ, "but I do call you a hireling, formerly of Philip, now of Alexander"; 19.110: μισθώσας αὐτὸν καὶ λαβὼν ἀργύριον ταῦτ' εἶπε καὶ προὔδωκεν ἐκείνῳ, "he hired himself out and took money to make the speech and betray us to Philip".
17 For more comic material on corrupted ambassadors: Harvey 1985, *passim*.
18 Cf. Apostolakis 2019, 36–44 and 152.
19 Cf. the case of Arthmius of Zeleia: "because he brought the gold from the Medes into the Peloponnese" (Dem. 3.42–43); on this passage: Serafim 2020b, 136.

Moreover, according to Demosthenes, Aeschines is a fake physician, who pretends to attend the sick person but does not actually provide any remedy in time; instead, when the patient dies, he joins the funeral procession and declares, "if the man had only done such and so, he would still be alive" (Dem. 18.243). The figure of the charlatan doctor first appears in fourth-century society, when book-trained doctors displaced traditional physicians who were orally taught medicine by teachers.[20] The quack doctor is a typical character in Middle Comedy, as titles by Antiphanes, Aristophon, Philemon and Theophilus suggest. This comic type, along with boastful cooks and braggart soldiers, is represented on stage as a typical *alazōn*.[21] The comic setting of this passage may also be underlined by the supposed reaction to the quack doctor's words: 18.243 ἐμβρόντητε, εἶτα νῦν λέγεις; The word ἐμβρόντητος, literally "thunderstruck", "demented", is unique in oratory, and mainly occurs in Middle and New Comedy as a form of comic abuse, especially in the vocative case.[22] Given, therefore, that quack doctors in action appear on stage in fourth-century comedy, it is quite possible that Demosthenes, when describing Aeschines' failure to make a diagnosis, is actually introducing a comic character on the platform.

The quack doctor also appears in New Comedy. In Menander's *Aspis*, a play certainly staged later than the date of *On the Crown*, the cunning slave Daos advises an Athenian friend of Chaereas to disguise himself as a quack doctor and diagnose Chaerestratus, Chaereas' stepfather, with a mortal disease.[23] The victim of this stratagem is the aged relative Smicrines, who is expected to be attracted to Chaerestratus' daughter, the supposed heiress (*epiklēros*), after the latter's fake death; so Smicrines will forget the claim on another girl, with whom Chaereas is in love. Daos' deceptive scheme is detailed as follows: "Then a doctor will be called in, someone who weighs up all the symptoms and says the trouble's pleurisy or phrenitis or one of those ailments that carry people off quickly. Ch. And then? Da. Suddenly you're dead. We cry "Chaerestratus is gone" and we beat our breasts outside the door" (339–342). Daos' designation of

---

20 Cf. Dean-Jones 2003, 97–121.
21 And cf. Anaxandrides' *Pharmakomantis* ("Soothsaying Druggist"). It is telling that in fr. 50 K.-A. the speaking character, probably the *pharmakomantis* himself, confesses that he is an *alazōn*, and that his art outdoes all others by far after flattery; cf. Arist. *EN* 1127b, where Aristotle includes as examples of *alazones* men such as seers and physicians: οἷον μάντιν σοφὸν ἢ ἰατρόν.
22 Cf. Men. *Dysc.* 441; Philem. fr. 45 K.-A.; Com. *Adesp.* 258.41 K.-A.; also in nominative, Antiph. fr. 230.4 K.-A.; Men. *Perik.* 522. For the peremptory tone of the vocative without ὦ: Yunis 2001, 244.
23 On this scene: Tommaso 2009, 301–315.

the quack doctor as "something of a charlatan" (374–375 ξενικόν τιν' οἶσθ' ἰατρόν, Χαιρέα, / ἀστεῖον, ὑπαλαζόνα;) is an accurate description of a comic *alazōn*. Finally, since "quack doctor" is a stock character in Greek mime, when Demosthenes describes Aeschines in such terms, he may well have drawn on this subliterary genre. Actually, Sosibius (*FGrHist* 595 F 7=Athen. 14.621d-e) mentions an old type of Doric mime, in which individuals are presented as imitating foreign doctors (speaking in a sophisticated manner; cf. Alexis fr. 146 K.-A.), and stealing fruits (an individual with whom Aeschines is compared in Dem. 18.262).[24]

2.2 Demosthenes as an Impostor: Brave in Words, Cowardly in Deeds

As in legal debates, so too in exchanges of invectives, the principle "who delivered the first unjust blow" is often applied, so that similar responses will seem a justified retaliation. Usually it is the opponent who first started the slanders and has dragged down the level of the contest, obliging the speaker to fight him on the same terms. It is hardly a surprise, therefore, that Aeschines asserts that Demosthenes used slanderous practices to prevent men of sense from giving advice, while he himself sold off the opportunities to make the city secure (Aeschin. 3.225–226). Aeschines also argues that his opponent is a villain and charlatan, who cannot even say something true by accident (2.153). Even worse, unlike other crooks, who attempt to make vague and imprecise statements, Demosthenes is a dangerous braggart (*alazōn*), who makes grandiose claims and deceives the hearers by mimicking people telling the truth (Aeschin. 3.99). Besides, Demosthenes' participation in the embassy to Philip proved to be an utter catastrophe. When his turn came to demonstrate his famous verbal skills in front of Philip, he collapsed and disappointed everybody (Aeschin. 2.34):

> οὕτω δὲ ἁπάντων διακειμένων πρὸς τὴν ἀκρόασιν, φθέγγεται τὸ θηρίον τοῦτο προοίμιον σκοτεινόν τι καὶ τεθνηκὸς δειλίᾳ, καὶ μικρὸν προαγαγὼν ἄνω τῶν πραγμάτων, ἐξαίφνης ἐσίγησε καὶ διηπορήθη, τελευτῶν δὲ ἐκπίπτει τοῦ λόγου.

> With all listening so intently, this creature uttered an obscure prologue in a voice dead with fright, and after a brief narration of earlier events, suddenly fell silent and was at a loss for words, and finally abandoned his speech.

---

24 For the "quack doctor" in Doric mime: Reich 1903, 306–307. On Dem. 18.262: Yunis 2001, 257; Serafim 2015, 105–106.

Aeschines' description has an undeniable theatrical colour, as the use of ἐκπίπτειν indicates.[25] The "mute orator", who is unable to defend his position, calls to mind the Aristophanic portrait of the politician Thucydides, the son of Melesias, who once lost his voice in court: Ar. *Vesp.* 948 ἀπόπληκτος ἐξαίφνης ἐγένετο τὰς γνάθους, "his jaws suddenly set fast". This description also recalls to mind Pericles in Hermippus' *Moirai*, where the Athenian general is presented as uttering brave words, but actually has the soul of a coward (fr. 47 K.-A.). Finally, the word θηρίον (in orators mainly found in Demosthenes, Aeschines and Dinarchus) is an Aristophanic term of abuse (e.g. *Eq.* 273; *Vesp.* 448).

The deceptive power of rhetoric is also exploited on the comic scene of the time, and in particular in the poetry of Timocles. In a fragment from *Hēroes*, a play dated about 341 BC, Demosthenes' rhetoric is fiercely satirised. In 342 BC Philip decided to offer the island of Halonnesus to the Athenians, probably in order to satisfy those who were discontented with the Peace of Philocrates. It was on that occasion that Demosthenes reacted and proposed that Philip's offer be rejected, declaring that the Macedonian king should not give (δοῦναι) the island but return it (ἀποδοῦναι), since it formerly belonged to Athens (Dem. 7.6). This claim, formulated in the form of a *paronomasia*, apparently became a slogan of the time, and is echoed in Timocles fr. 12 K.-A.:

> οὐκοῦν κελεύεις νῦν με πάντα μᾶλλον ἢ
> τὰ προσόντα φράζειν. (Β.) πάνυ γε. (Α.) δράσω τοῦτό σοι.
> καὶ πρῶτα μέν σοι παύσεται Δημοσθένης
> ὀργιζόμενος. (Β.) ὁ ποῖος; (Α.) τὸ Βριάρεως,
> ὁ τοὺς καταπάλτας τάς τε λόγχας ἐσθίων,
> μισῶν λόγους ἄνθρωπος οὐδὲ πώποτε
> ἀντίθετον εἰπὼν οὐδέν, ἀλλ' Ἄρη βλέπων

> (A). I see what you mean; you ask me to tell anything except what is appropriate. (B.) Just the thing! (A). I will do it for your sake. This is the first: Demosthenes will stop being angry with you. (B). Who is Demosthenes? (A) Briareos, who swallows catapults and spears, this hater of discourse, who never used a single antithesis in his speech but has a martial stare.

In the fragment two interlocutors play a game called *antiphrasis*: the basic premise of this ironical game is to describe a person by using the exact opposite

---

25 Cf. Dem. 18.265 ἐξέπιπτες, ἐγὼ δ' ἐσύριττον, "you were hissed offstage, I was hissing" (Demosthenes mocks Aeschines as a failed actor); Arist. *AP* 1456a16–19 (on a failure of Agathon), and Philip's attempt to encourage Demosthenes by calling him not to suppose that he has suffered an absolute catastrophe, like an actor in the theatre (2.35 ὥσπερ ἐν τοῖς θεάτροις). See also Serafim 2017, Ch. 3.

qualities to those this person actually possesses. This game may playfully recall on stage the rhetorical exchanges between Athenian politicians, who are often believed to deceptively project the opposite image to what they actually are (πάντα μᾶλλον ἢ τὰ προσόντα). Interlocutor (A) undertakes to describe Demosthenes in these terms. His description constructs Demosthenes' comic portrait and seems to include material from Old Comedy and political oratory. The bellicose orator is described as a *miles gloriosus*, who utters warlike cries but in fact is a cowardly boaster. This description is compatible with Aeschines' version of the embassy to Philip, where Demosthenes was stated to be a proverbial coward at critical moments.[26]

2.3 Invective, Sycophancy and Deception

Invective is sometimes used against supposed deceptive orators and sycophants. In an emblematic passage in 18.242, Demosthenes fiercely reviles Aeschines as a typical sycophant and a deceptive orator who works against his city's interests:

> πονηρόν, ἄνδρες Ἀθηναῖοι, πονηρὸν ὁ συκοφάντης ἀεὶ καὶ πανταχόθεν βάσκανον καὶ φιλαίτιον· τοῦτο δὲ καὶ φύσει κίναδος τἀνθρώπιόν ἐστιν, οὐδὲν ἐξ ἀρχῆς ὑγιὲς πεποιηκὸς οὐδ' ἐλεύθερον, αὐτοτραγικὸς πίθηκος, ἀρουραῖος Οἰνόμαος, παράσημος ῥήτωρ. τί γὰρ ἡ σὴ δεινότης εἰς ὄνησιν ἥκει τῇ πατρίδι;

> Every sycophant is a depraved character, Athenians, depraved as well as backstabbing and fault finding at every opportunity; and this puny fellow is by nature a rogue. From the beginning he's done nothing useful or generous. He's a real ape on the tragic stage, an Oenomaus of the countryside, a counterfeit politician. What good, Aeschines, has your cleverness done the country?

If we consider the terms of invective in this passage, we will find that most of them are already used, or even established, in Old Comedy, Aristophanes in particular, in reference to deceitful demagogues and politicians. To begin with, the term παράσημος is properly used of coins bearing a false stamp, resembling an official minting-die. The description of Aeschines as a παράσημος ῥήτωρ renders him an untrustworthy and deceitful politician. In the *Acharnians* those who denounce the Megarians for importing goods without paying the duties, and thus kindling the Peloponnesian War, are metaphorically described as

---

[26] For an analysis of this fragment: Apostolakis 2019, 115–123.

"falsely marked" politicians (ἀνδράρια παράσημα).²⁷ Βάσκανος, "sorcerer", as a term of abuse also occurs sometimes in comedy.²⁸

Even more interesting is the kind of invective in which animal names are used to describe human characteristics. Such animals *par excellence* are the fox and the ape, both emblematic of deceptive rhetoric. Concerning κίναδος, this term of invective mainly appears in oratory and comedy. Κίναδος is probably a Sicilian word for fox,²⁹ and its first occurrence is in Sophocles' *Ajax* 102, where Ajax speaks contemptuously of Odysseus (τοὐπίτριπτον κίναδος). This expression, however, is almost exclusively comic.³⁰ The word κίναδος occurs in Aristophanes, always in a context of deceitful rhetoric,³¹ and it is significant that Aeschines in his turn applies this term to Demosthenes in the speech *Against Ctesiphon* (3.167).³²

On the other hand, the ape was the animal most mentioned in comic contexts of mimicry and deception. In the satire on embassies in the *Acharnians* it is Cleisthenes, a beardless, effeminate politician, who appears on stage like a monkey, wearing a fake beard, actually dressed as a eunuch: Ar. *Ach*. 120–121 Τοιόνδε δ', ὦ πίθηκε, τὸν πώγων' ἔχων / εὐνοῦχος ἡμῖν ἦλθες ἐσκευασμένος; Cleisthenes was a politician of the late fifth century, apparently involved in sacred embassies (cf. Ar. *Lys*. 620–624).³³ The most emblematic association of apes and politicians occurs in the *Frogs*, where Aeschylus accuses Euripides of encouraging demagogues to employ deceptive rhetoric against the people's

---

27 Ar. *Ach*. 517–519 ἀλλ' ἀνδράρια μοχθηρά, παρακεκομμένα, / ἄτιμα καὶ παράσημα καὶ παράξενα, / ἐσυκοφάντει; "for men, misminted, worthless, brummagem, and foreignmade, who began denouncing the Megarians' little cloaks".
28 E.g. Ar. *Eq*. 103 (said of Paphlagon); *Pl*. 571; Antiph. fr. 157 K.-A.; Men. *Pk*. 529.
29 Cf. Willi 2008, 37.
30 Cf. Finglass 2011, *ad loc*.
31 *Nub*. 448, in an accumulation of attributes of a fraudulent orator, including εἴρων and ἀλαζών; *Av*. 429–430 πυκνότατον κίναδος, / σόφισμα, κύρμα, τρῖμμα, παιπάλημ' ὅλον, "a most crafty fox, all resourcefulness, a dead shot, an old hand, experience one hundred per cent". For the fox as trickster *par excellence*: Serafim 2020a, 38–39.
32 Cf. Andoc. 1.99 ὦ συκοφάντα καὶ ἐπίτριπτον κίναδος, "you malicious accuser, you damned fox"; Din. 1.40, where Demosthenes and the anti-Macedonian orators are described as rogues (κινάδη) doing nothing of value for the city, but only looking after their own safety and making money anywhere they can. On animal names in invective: Spatharas 2013, 77–95.
33 For other instances of similar invective in the frame of *onomasti kōmōidein* cf. Phryn. Com. fr. 21 K.-A. (with Stama 2014, *ad loc*); Ar. *Ran*. 708–709 οὐδ' ὁ πίθηκος οὗτος ὁ νῦν ἐνοχλῶν, / Κλειγένης ὁ μικρός, "not long with this annoying ape, Cleigenes the tiny" (on Cleigenes, a minor politician of the time). For the monkey in comedy cf. also Ar. *Eq*. 887; *Vesp*. 1290–1291; *Pax* 1065; *Th*. 1133; Eub. fr. 114.4; Lilja 1980; Totaro 2000, 191–192.

interests (1082–1085: Κᾆτ' ἐκ τούτων ἡ πόλις ἡμῶν / ὑπογραμματέων ἀνεμεστώθη / καὶ βωμολόχων δημοπιθήκων / ἐξαπατώντων τὸν δῆμον ἀεί, "So now, because of him our city here is crammed with bureaucratic types and stupid democratic apes who always cheat our people").

Besides, Aeschines' description as an ape is directly relevant to the mimic qualities of dramatic performances. We can refer, for example to Mynniskos, a senior tragic actor, who called his younger fellow actor, Kallippides, an "ape" because of excessive *mimēsis* (Arist. *Po*. 1416b34–35).[34] Kallippides was also satirised in comedy, apparently for the same reason (Ar. fr. 490 K.-A.).[35] It is also worth noting that invective is sometimes considered fictitious, only employed by the orators in order to conceal a collusion. Remarkably enough, this assumption first appears in Antiphanes, the poet of Middle Comedy. In the context of a riddle, the speaking character describes politicians reviling each other on purpose, so that the people take no notice of their corruption: fr. 194. K-A οὗτοι (sc. οἱ ῥήτορες) κεκραγότες δὲ τὰ διαπόντια / τἀκ τῆς Ἀσίας καὶ τἀπὸ Θράκης λήμματα / ἕλκουσι δεῦρο, νεμομένων δὲ πλησίον / αὑτῶν κάθηται λοιδορουμένων τ' ἀεί / ὁ δῆμος οὐδὲν οὔτ' ἀκούων οὔθ' ὁρῶν, "they shout and bring the overseas revenues from Asia and Thrace here. And while they're splitting the money up among themselves and constantly abusing one another, the people sit nearby, hearing and seeing nothing".

This complaint, which was delivered on the comic scene most probably in the mid-360s,[36] is repeated, adapted to a forensic situation, in ca 340 BC (in pseudo-Demosthenes' *Against Theocrines*) and in 323 BC (in Dinarchus' speech against Demosthenes on the Harpalus affair).[37] An almost indispensable aspect

---

34 For interpretative analysis of this passage: Csapo 2010, 117–120.
35 For metatheatrical comments on tragic actors: also Eubulus fr. 134 K.-A.
36 Cf. Konstantakos 2000, 161–180; Olson 2007, 188–189 and 201–203.
37 [Dem.] 58.40 οὐ γὰρ ὀλιγάκις ἑοράκατ' αὐτοὺς ἐπὶ μὲν τῶν δικαστηρίων καὶ τοῦ βήματος ἐχθροὺς εἶναι φάσκοντας ἀλλήλοις, ἰδίᾳ δὲ ταὐτὰ πράττοντας καὶ μετέχοντας τῶν λημμάτων, καὶ τοτὲ μὲν λοιδορουμένους καὶ πλύνοντας αὐτοὺς τἀπόρρητα, μικρὸν δὲ διαλιπόντας τοῖς αὐτοῖς τούτοις συνδεκαδίζοντας καὶ τῶν αὐτῶν ἱερῶν κοινωνοῦντας, "you have, after all, often seen them in the courts and on the speaker's platform claiming they are mutual enemies but in private working together and sharing the profits, at one moment abusing each other and reviling each other with unspeakable slurs, yet after a little while joining in a party with the very same men and sharing the same sacrifices"; cf. Din. 1.99 ... οἱ δὲ (ἡγεμόνες καὶ δημαγωγοὶ) διηλλαγμένοι πρὸς αὐτοὺς ἐν μὲν ταῖς ἐκκλησίαις λοιδορῶνται καὶ προσκρούωσιν ἀλλήλοις ἐξεπίτηδες, ἰδίᾳ δὲ ταὐτὰ πράττωσιν ἐξαπατῶντες ὑμᾶς τοὺς ῥᾷστα πειθομένους τοῖς τούτων λόγοις, "but these men have reached agreement so that they deliberately vilify and attack each other in the Assembly but in private are united to deceive you, and you are too easily persuaded by their speeches".

which renders this deceptive political rhetoric effective is the simplicity and stupidity of the audience. *Euētheia*, "naivety", of the Athenians is a *topos* both in Aristophanes' comedy (the most emblematic expression being *Knights* 1262 Κεχηναίων πόλις, "the city of Open-Mouthenians") and in Demosthenic political speeches.[38]

3 Invective in the Assembly: The Unique Case of Aristomedes

Invective against politicians, who are suspected either of stealing public money or of being involved in bribery when participating in embassies, is typical in forensic speeches composed for public trials, such as Demosthenes' and Aeschines' speeches on the False Embassy. In fact Demosthenes, when speaking as a political adviser (σύμβουλος), reserves all his attacks for Philip and avoids using invective against his political opponents; cf. Plu. *Mor.* 810d "And yet even Demosthenes employs abuse only in his speeches before a court of law; the Philippics are free from all jeering and scurrility". Apparently, however, Plutarch is making a general comment here and has forgotten a passage full of invective from the fourth Philippic, actually the only one in Demosthenes' deliberative speeches. This speech contains a fierce attack on Aristomedes, a minor pro-Macedonian politician of the time. Although in the introductive sentence of the relevant section Demosthenes asserts that he will treat his opponent without taunt, he actually employs abusive language which includes Aristomedes' father and grandfather; thus in Dem. 10.70–73:

> καίτοι λοιδορίας εἴ τις χωρὶς ἔροιτο... ἀλλὰ νὴ Δία παππῴα σοι καὶ πατρῴα δόξ' ὑπάρχει, ἣν αἰσχρόν ἐστιν ἐν σοὶ καταλῦσαι· τῇ πόλει δ' ὑπῆρξεν ἀνώνυμα καὶ φαῦλα τὰ τῶν προγόνων. ἀλλ' οὐδὲ τοῦθ' οὕτως ἔχει· σοὶ μὲν γὰρ ἦν κλέπτης ὁ πατήρ, εἴπερ ἦν ὅμοιος σοί...

> And yet, if one should ask without raillery... But, by Zeus, perhaps you have inherited a good reputation from your grandfather and father, which it would be shameful for you to squander, whereas the deeds of our city's ancestors are obscure and trivial? But that is not the case. Your father was a thief, if he was like you...

---

38 Cf. Ar. *Ach.* 75–76, 114, 133; Dem. 9.10; 19.103. On deception in Athenian politics: Hesk 2000, 219–241.

This personal attack, formulated in the rhetorical figures of *apostrophē* and circular composition, may have been famous.³⁹ Aristomedes' thievery was probably no more true than that of Cleon in Aristophanes' *Knights*, where he appears as Paphlagon to contest with the Sausage-Seller on this matter.⁴⁰ This invective may have been further influenced by the satire of Old Comedy. More specifically, in the archaic tradition one who imitates his forebears in virtues and follows the tradition of his father or grandfather is worthy of praise.⁴¹ Sometimes, however, this *topos* is perversely applied in Aristophanes, i.e. to prove second- or third-generation sycophants and scoundrels. In Aristophanes' *Birds* the Sycophant is determined to continue his family tradition of informing, since he has inherited it from his grandfather: *Av.* 1451 Παππῷος ὁ βίος συκοφαντεῖν ἐστί μοι.⁴² In a similar way, Demosthenes' invective includes the assumption that Aristomedes has inherited thievery from his father and grandfather, and it would be shameful to abandon these arts. The inversion of the *topos* intensifies when Demosthenes argues that it is due to Aristogeiton's corruption that his father would also be considered a thief.⁴³

This invective against Aristomedes, which may well have derived from Old Comedy and Aristophanes, also seems to be exploited on the contemporary comic stage. Timocles, in *Hēroes*, has one of his characters say (fr. 14 K.-A.): "Hermes, the son of Maia, aids in conducting these affairs, on condition that he is eager to do so. He has descended with pleasure, showing favour to Aristomedes the Handsome, so that Satyrus will no longer call him a thief". This fragment probably belongs to a context involving the return of dead politicians from the Underworld. Hermes, as a patron of thieves, is said to have already descended to the Underworld (καταβέβηκεν), in order to rescue his protégé Aristomedes from being slandered by Satyrus. It is remarkable that Satyrus, a highly

---

39 It is revealing that the late rhetorician Hermogenes (*Inv.* 195 Rabe and *Id.* 261.15 Rabe) considers it a perfect model of a κύκλος; see also: Apostolakis 2019, 131.
40 Ar. *Eq.* 296–297 ΠΑ. Ὁμολογῶ κλέπτειν· σὺ δ' οὐχί. / ΑΛ. Νὴ τὸν Ἑρμῆν τὸν Ἀγοραῖον; "*Pa.* I admit I'm a thief; you don't. *Saus. Sell.* I do so, by Hermes of the Markets!"
41 E.g. Hom. *Od.* 24.508; Eur. *Or.* 1154; *Ion* 736–737.
42 Cf. *Eq.* 447–449, where the Sausage Seller attempts to prove that Paphlagon is a tyrannophile, by associating through a false etymology his grandfather with Myrsine, the wife of Hippias.
43 If Aristomedes' family has a tradition in thievery, another litigant of the Corpus Demosthenicum has the insignia of public debtors. Theocrines, who is described as an emblematic sycophant, is vilified as a third-generation scoundrel (πονηρὸς ἐκ τριγονίας, [Dem.] 58.17), since, as his grandfather's heir, he has inherited both his debts and his *ponēria*. Cf. Hyp. *Athen.* Col. 9 οὗτ[ος] δὲ ὁ ἐκ τριγ[ο]νίας [ὢν] μυροπώλης, "this fellow, who is a third-generation perfume seller".

skilled comic actor, was credited with training Demosthenes in speech delivery (*hypocrisis*). Moreover, it has been suggested that Satyrus had impersonated Demosthenes in a previous performance, and it was on that occasion that the famous actor satirised on stage Demosthenes' invective against Aristomedes.[44] If so, this meta-theatrical comment is a piece of refracted satire, i.e. on anti-Macedonians attacking pro-Macedonians, and not a direct satire of a pro-Macedonian politician by Timocles.

4 Athenians as Foreigners: A *Topos* of Political Invective

Personal attack on prejudicial issues (*diabolē*), such as allusions that a citizen is a foreigner or a slave, was a standard *topos* of invective throughout the classical period following Pericles' law in 451 BC stating that only those of Athenian origin from both father and mother were considered citizens.[45] Predictably, taunts associated with a politician's parentage became part of comic invective in Aristophanes and other poets of Old Comedy. In the *Knights,* Cleon is represented as a Paphlagonian slave throughout, but the only association with slave origin is the false etymology from *paphlazein,* "to splash", due to his turbulent rhetoric. Such slanders are also traced in oratory of the fourth century. In the trial concerning the crowning of Demosthenes, Aeschines, *inter alia*, asserts that Demosthenes is not even a citizen, because, supposedly, he is of Scythian origin on his mother's side. A telling passage is in Aeschin. 3.172:

> Οὐκοῦν ἀπὸ μὲν τοῦ πάππου πολέμιος ἂν εἴη τῷ δήμῳ, θάνατον γὰρ αὐτοῦ τῶν προγόνων κατέγνωτε, τὰ δ' ἀπὸ τῆς μητρὸς Σκύθης βάρβαρος ἑλληνίζων τῇ φωνῇ· ὅθεν καὶ τὴν πονηρίαν οὐκ ἐπιχώριός ἐστι.

> So then, from his grandfather he would naturally be an enemy of the people (you condemned his ancestors to death), while on his mother's side he is a Scythian barbarian who speaks Greek. Hence his dishonesty, too, is of foreign extraction.

Demosthenes is accused of being a third-generation barbarian on his mother's side and, therefore, not a full citizen. However, as Carey notes, Demosthenes' mother was apparently born before the restoration of democracy in 403 BC, at a

---

44 Hajdu 2002, 425–438.
45 Cf. Harding 1994, 200–202.

time when Pericles' law on parentage was set aside, and her status was not affected.⁴⁶

The defamatory description "Scythian barbarian who speaks Greek" calls to mind a passage from Aristophanes' *Acharnians* (703–712), where the politician Euathlus, the son of Cephisodemus, is described as "the Scythian desert", an "archer" and, interestingly enough, a "talkative advocate" (λάλος συνήγορος), not unlike Demosthenes, who is a "Scythian-speaking Greek". Both Euathlus and Demosthenes are actually described as third-generation Scythians, Euathlus supposedly on his paternal grandmother's side and Demosthenes on his maternal grandfather's. However, as Olson notes, Cephisodemus might well be a μητρόξενος, i.e. a non-Athenian on his mother's side, without further repercussions, since his mother was apparently born before Pericles' law in 451; most probably, however, she was from the north of Greece or was simply blonde.⁴⁷

Demosthenes, on his part, counter-attacks Aeschines on the grounds that both his father and his mother used to perform humble and servile occupations. He argues that Aeschines' father was an ex-slave working as schoolteacher in the temple of Theseus, wearing heavy fetters and a wooden collar (18.129). Aeschines himself turned his father's name Tromes – supposedly non Athenian – into Atrometus by adding two syllables: 18.130 χθὲς μὲν οὖν καὶ πρώην ἄμ' Ἀθηναῖος καὶ ῥήτωρ γέγονεν, καὶ δύο συλλαβὰς προσθεὶς τὸν μὲν πατέρ' ἀντὶ Τρόμητος ἐποίησεν Ἀτρόμητον, "rather, it was yesterday or the day before that he became an Athenian citizen and politician. He turned his father Tromes into Atrometus by adding two syllables".

This story may well be Demosthenes' invention, in his attempt to support the claim that Aeschines' father was a non-Athenian. It seems more plausible, however, that Tromes was just a concise substitute for the full name Atrometus, and functioned as a nickname constructed on a word play (Mr Trepid/Intrepid). Such slanders have a recognisable comic origin, and indeed they were part of the comic portrait of fifth-century politicians as they were represented in Old Comedy. The best-known case is that of the Athenian politician Hyperbolus, who was almost unanimously satirised by poets of Old Comedy as being of slave origin on both his father's and his mother's side. Interestingly enough, Hyper-

---

46 Carey 2000, 233 n. 194.
47 Olson 2002, 253; Also Hipponicus, the son of Callias, is called Σκυθικός, apparently because he was blond (Cratin. fr. 492 K.-A.; cf. Eup. fr. 20 K.-A.). Denigrating references to Scythian also appear in other genres, the most detailed ones being Hdt. 4.5–82, where their barbaric way of life (concerning language, customs and attire) is compared with that of the civilised Greek world. Cf. Hp. *Aer.* 17 ff., where the Scythian nation becomes target of contempt and ridicule.

bolus himself supposedly used non-Attic Greek spelling, which also included contracted words: Pl. Com. fr. 183 K.-A. ὁ δ' οὐ γὰρ ἡττίκιζεν, ὦ Μοῖραι φίλαι, / ἀλλ' ὁπότε μὲν χρείη 'διητώμην' λέγειν, / ἔφασκε 'δητώμην', ὁπότε δ' εἰπεῖν δέοι / 'ὀλίγον', 'ὀλίον' ἔλεγεν. "O dear Fates, the man [Hyperbolus] just couldn't speak Attic Greek. But when he ought to be saying 'I used to live', he would come out with 'I use to live', and when he should be saying 'just a bit', he would say <'jus' a bit'>".[48] Concerning Hyperbolus' father, the comic influence was so strong that one fourth-century author actually believed his name to be Chremes, a typical comic name (Theopompus, *FGrHist* 115 F 95). But we know from a preserved *ostrakon*, "shell", that his father's name was actually Antiphanes, and his demotic Perithoidae (*PAA* 902050); therefore the comic invective has fabricated all these stories about him.

However, while in Greek and Roman New Comedy courtesans are sometimes revealed in the course of the plot to be marriageable Athenians, in forensic speeches women who were considered Athenian *astai* are said to behave as courtesans, the connotation being that they are not Athenians and their sons are not legitimate citizens. Demosthenes argues that Aeschines attempted to restore his mother's real name Glaucothea, instead of the far better-known nickname Empousa, which alluded to her sexual versatility:[49] 18.130 τὴν δὲ μητέρα σεμνῶς πάνυ Γλαυκοθέαν, ἣν Ἔμπουσαν ἅπαντες ἴσασι καλουμένην, ἐκ τοῦ πάντα ποιεῖν καὶ πάσχειν δηλονότι ταύτης τῆς ἐπωνυμίας τυχοῦσαν, "and (he made) his mother into the very dignified Glaucothea, though everyone knows she was called Empousa, a name she obviously got because she would do anything and allow anything to be done to her". She is also insulted as a cheap whore, who receives her customers not only at night but also in broad daylight: "engaged in midday matrimonies in a shed by the shrine of the hero Calamites" (18.129). This kind of invective supports suspicions of foreign origin, since most prostitutes were non-Athenian immigrants. Such an insult is typical of Old Comedy. Here, again, Hyperbolus' case might be an example; cf. Hermipp. fr. 9 K.-A. ὦ σαπρὰ καὶ πασιπόρνη καὶ κάπραινα, "you old hag, and whore and lewd woman", where the person addressed is most probably Hyperbolus' mother.[50]

---

48 Cf. fr. 182.4–5 K.-A. ὅτι πονηρῷ καὶ ξένῳ / ἐπέλαχες ἀνδρί, †οὐδέπω γὰρ† ἐλευθέρῳ "because you were chosen as an alternate to a nasty foreign person, not yet a free citizen". Cf. Colvin 2000, 285–298, who argues that Hyperbolus' dialect was low-urban rather than "barbarian".
49 For Empousa as a typical nickname borne by prostitutes: Yunis 2001, 187.
50 Cf. Rosenbloom 2014, 306; Comentale 2017, *ad loc.*

Aeschines' parentage was presented as being shameful on both his father's and his mother's side, and his citizenship and capacity to participate in politics is at least brought into question.[51] Concerning the nicknames, Demosthenes uses a kind of invective which seems to reverse the real order: he actually presents those humiliating nicknames as quasi-official forms of address, and blames Aeschines for restoring the original names. Demosthenes is hinting that Aeschines has attempted to get rid of any implication that his parents had occupations unworthy of Athenian citizens, eventually subverting his Athenian origin and ultimately his capacity to speak as a public orator.

Invectives associated with parentage were used not only in political trials, but also in procedures directly associated with citizenship, such as *diapsēphisis*. This legal procedure included a scrutiny of the citizen status of the demesmen of Attica, and the main issue was whether a person was a freeman and whether both his parents were *astoi*. Demosthenes' *Against Eubulides* (Dem. 57) is a forensic speech which deals with contested citizenship in the framework of such a procedure, taking place in 346/5 BC. The speaker is a certain Euxitheus, who is appealing against the decision to eject him from Halimus, his deme. Euxitheus' opponent is Eubulides, who has questioned the speaker's citizen status. Euxitheus' father has been slandered for speaking like a foreigner: Dem. 57.18 Διαβεβλήκασι γάρ μου τὸν πατέρα, ὡς ἐξένιζεν, "They have maligned my father for having a foreign accent". It is worth noting that, while Demosthenes was described by Aeschines as "a Scythian-speaking Greek", the reverse assertion is made here: a (supposed) Greek, who speaks in a foreign accent. In this case, again, Hyperbolus' comic description is recalled; like the fifth-century demagogue, Euxitheus' father is slandered as not using Attic Greek like a native speaker.[52]

---

[51] A woman might also be described as a courtesan in speeches composed for inheritance cases, so that her children appear as illegitimate claimants of the disputed inheritance. For example, in Isaeus' *On Pyrrhus' estate*, the speaker asserts that Phile's mother was a prostitute (3.13, 15), and Phile herself is the daughter of a prostitute (3.6, 24, 45, 48, 52, 55, 70, 71). Moreover, in the speech *On the estate of Nicostratus* (Isae. 4.10) the speaker argues that Chariades attempted to insert in Nicostratus' family both himself and his child by his *hetaera*; on such slanders in Isaeus: Hatzilambrou 2011, 145.

[52] Cf. Eup. fr. 99.25 K.-A. κοὐδ' ἂν ἠττίκιζεν, εἰ μὴ τοὺς φίλους ᾐσχύνετο (probably, but not certainly, said of Hyperbolus); also Plato Comicus in his play *Cleophon* depicts Cleophon's mother talking to him in a foreign tongue. She was said to be a Thracian, and therefore Cleophon himself is satirised as a foreigner (Pl. com. *Cleophon* fr. 61 K.-A. [Schol. Ar. *Ran.* 681] Θρηκία χελιδών). For the case of Eubulides cf. Lape 2010, 199–206.

Moreover, Eubulides is said to have taunted (λελοιδόρηκεν) Euxitheus by questioning the status of the latter's mother; he asserts that she performed humble menial tasks, that of a ribbon-seller (ταινιόπωλις) and a wet-nurse (τίτθη), and implies that she was probably a foreigner or even a slave (Dem. 57.33–34). Women working in the *agora*, especially those who did not have permanent establishments but operated at the edge of the market, were considered to be of low social status.[53] They even were described as foreign metics or slaves, and became a laughing stock in both Old and Middle Comedy. In Eupolis' fr. 262 (from *Prospaltioi*), the citizenship of a prominent politician is apparently questioned on his mother's side, who is described as a Thracian ribbon-seller: μήτηρ τις αὐτῷ Θρᾷττα ταινιόπωλις ἦν.[54] This sort of woman selling goods in the Agora is a common figure in Aristophanes: a "bread-seller" (ἀρτόπωλις) and a "greengrocer" (λαχανόπωλις) are characters in Aristophanes' *Wasps* (238, 497), an ἰσχαδόπωλις, "dealer in figs", in *Lysistrata* (564), an ἀλφιτόπωλις, "seller of barley groats", and a μυρόπωλις, "seller of perfumes", in *Assembly Women* (686, 841), and a λεκιθόπωλις, "peasepudding-seller", in *Wealth* (427). In Hermippus' Ἀρτοπώλιδες Hyperbolus' mother was also probably represented as one of these bread vendors.[55]

In Dem. 57.44–45, Euxitheus manipulates the allegation that his mother, having served in the past as a wet nurse, was not an *astē*. Judges might well be affected by current social stereotypes, depicted and reproduced in comic plays. Nurses were already ridiculed in Old Comedy (e.g. Ar. *Eq.* 716–718). In Middle Comedy, in particular, they are normally represented on stage as old women, slaves or poor foreigners; Eubulus' *Titthai* is one such indicative title.[56] The tradition continues in New Comedy, where wet-nurses as slave attendants are involved in plots including kidnapping and recognition scenes.[57] This comic tradition also survives in terracotta figurines representing nurses bearing a slave mask and holding a child.[58]

---

53 Cf. Dem. 18.127 περίτριμμ' ἀγορᾶς, "man who loafs in the market-place". As Halliwell 2008, 231–232 notes, ἀγορά was considered "a sordid place, associated, in socially elite terms, with the 'crowd' or 'rabble'".
54 Cf. Olson 2016, 352–354, and Eubulus' title Στεφανοπώλιδες, "Women selling crowns".
55 Cf. Comentale 2017, 65–68.
56 Cf. Antiph. fr. 157.4 K.-A. κοὐ μὰ Δία τίτθας εἰσάγουσι (sc. Σκύθαι) βασκάνους.
57 E.g. Plaut. *Poen.* 83 ff., 1120 ff.; Ter. *HT* 614 ff., *Eun.* 807 ff., 913. This stereotype survives even in later authors, such as Aulus Gellius 12.1.17–18; cf. Hunter 1983, 209; Arnott 1996, 648.
58 Cf. Wrenhaven 2013, 138–139.

5 Conclusion

Invective seems to recycle from rostrum to stage and vice versa. Since we do not have sufficient samples of original fifth-century public speeches at our disposal, it is difficult to appreciate how rhetorical invective invaded the territory of comic stage and vice versa during that period. It is easier to substantiate the two-way relationship of comic and rhetorical invective during the fourth century, through forensic speeches with a political dimension and the deliberative speeches of the time, and through the surviving fragments of so-called Middle Comedy.

The comparative study of rhetorical and comic invective in fourth-century Athens reveals that they actually share weapons from the same arsenal. Under a close reading of representative speeches composed in the framework of political controversies, aspects of comic invective often emerge, such as attacks on deception, bribery, social status and family tradition. General political criticism normally occurs in deliberative speeches, where the orators act as advisers, while acerbic personal abuse prevails in the forensic speeches delivered at trials associated with the political situation.

It seems that the strongest invective occurs in forensic speeches which perpetuate a political dispute. The increasing rivalry between pro-Macedonian and anti-Macedonian orators, in particular, often fomented fierce invective. It appears that Demosthenes, Hyperides, Aeschines and Dinarchus, who played a leading part in the relevant debates of the time, often draw on comic tradition when using invectives. The vitriolic attacks they launch against each other as litigants are no less inventive and imaginative than comic methods.

On the other hand, since contemporary political issues are at the center of the debates in the Assembly, it is rather expected that invectives and personal abuses are suppressed in deliberative oratory – at least between Athenian politicians; invective against foreigners, e.g. Philip, is another issue. However, as the case of Aristomedes' and Antiphanes' satire indicates, even in the Assembly invective is possible, although sometimes the orators pretend to avoid it. Besides, we should always take into account that a possible revision of a deliberative speech before publication might account for the absence of abusive personal references. At the same time, although in the Middle Comedy the political satire declines, some comic poets came under the influence of contemporary oratory, which provided them with rich material for parody and invective. Timocles, in particular, is in line with both Aeschines and Dinarchus in transferring aspects of invective from the podium onto the comic stage.

Bibliography

Apostolakis, K. (2019), *Timokles*. (FrC 21), Göttingen.
Arnott, W.G. (1996), *Alexis: The Fragments. A Commentary*, Cambridge.
Carey, C. (2000), *Aeschines*, Austin.
Colvin, S. (2000), 'The Language of Non-Athenians in Old Comedy', in: D. Harvey, J. Wilkins, and K.J. Dover (eds.), *The Rivals of Aristophanes: Studies in Athenian Old Comedy*, London, 285–298.
Comentale, N. (2017), *Ermippo. Introduzione, traduzione e commento* (FrC 6), Heidelberg.
Csapo, E. (2010), *Actors and Icons of the Ancient Theater*, Oxford.
Dean-Jones, L. (2003), 'Literacy and the Charlatan in Ancient Greek Medicine', in: H. Yunis (ed.), *Written Texts and the Rise of Literate Culture in Ancient Greece*, Cambridge, 97–121.
Finglass, P.J. (2011), *Sophocles: Ajax*, Cambridge.
Hajdu, I. (2002), *Kommentar zur 4. Philippischen Rede des Demosthenes*, Berlin/New York.
Halliwell, S. (1991), 'The Uses of Laughter in Greek Culture', in: *Classical Quarterly* 41, 279–296.
Halliwell, S. (2008), *Greek Laughter, A Study of Cultural Psychology from Homer to Early Christianity*, Cambridge.
Harding, P. (1994), 'Comedy and Rhetoric', in: I. Worthington (ed.), *Persuasion: Greek Rhetoric in Action*, London/New York.
Harvey, F.D. (1985), '*Dona Ferentes*: Some Aspects of Bribery in Greek Politics', in: *History of Political Thought* 6.1/2, 76–117.
Hatzilambrou, R. (2011), 'The Use of *ad hominem* Argument in the Works of Isaeus', in: *L'Antiquité Classique* 80, 37–51.
Hesk, J. (2000), *Deception and Democracy in Classical Athens*, Cambridge.
Hubbard, T.K. (1991), *The Mask of Comedy: Aristophanes and the Intertextual Parabasis*, Ithaca/London.
Hunter, R. (1983), *Eubulus: The Fragments*, Cambridge.
Konstantakos, I. (2000), *A Commentary on the Fragments of Eight Plays of Antiphanes*, PhD Dissertation, Cambridge University.
Konstantakos, I. (2011), 'Conditions of Playwrights and the Comic Dramatist's Craft in the Fourth Century', in: *Logeion* 1, 145–182.
Koster, S. (1980), *Die Invektive in der griechischen und römischen Literatur*, Meisenheim am Glan.
Lape, S. (2010), *Race and Citizen Identity in the Classical Athenian Democracy*, Cambridge/New York.
Lilja, S. (1980), 'The Ape in Ancient Comedy', in: *Arctos* 14, 31–38.
MacDowell, D. (1990), 'The Meaning of Alazon', in: E.M. Craik (ed.), '*Owls to Athens*': *Essays on Classical Subjects presented to Sir Kenneth Dover*, Oxford, 287–292.
Miner, J.L. (2006), *Crowning Thersites. The Relevance of Invective in Athenian Forensic Oratory*, Ph.D. Dissertation, The University of Texas at Austin.
Olson, S.D. (2002), *Aristophanes: Acharnians*, Oxford.
Olson, S.D. (2007), *Broken Laughter. Select Fragments of Greek Comedy*, Oxford.
Olson, S.D. (2016), *Eupolis: Heilotes-Chrysoun Genos, frr. 147–325. Translation, Commentary* (Fragmenta Comica 8.2), Heidelberg.
Reich, H. (1903), *Der Mimus. Ein litterar-entwickelungsgeschichtlicher Versuch*, I 1, Berlin.

Rosen, R. (1988), *Old Comedy and the Iambographic Tradition,* Atlanta.
Rosenbloom, D. (2014), 'The Politics of Comic Athens', in: M. Fontaine and A. Scafuro (eds.), *The Oxford Handbook of Greek and Roman Comedy*, New York/Oxford, 297–320.
Rowe, G. (1966), 'The Portrait of Aeschines in the Oration *On the Crown*', in: *Transactions of the American Philological Association* 97, 397–406.
Serafim, A. (2015), 'Making the Audience: *Ekphrasis* and Rhetorical Strategy in Demosthenes 18 and 19', in: *Classical Quarterly* 65, 96–108.
Serafim, A. (2017), *Attic Oratory and Performance*, London/New York.
Serafim, A. (2020a), 'Comic Invective in the Public Forensic Speeches of Attic Oratory', in: *Hellenica* 68, 23–42.
Serafim, A. (2020b), *Religious Discourse in Attic Oratory and Politics*, London/New York.
Spatharas, D. (2013), 'The Sycophant's Farm: Animals and Rhetoric in *Against Aristogeiton* I', in: *Ariadne* 19, 77–95.
Stama, F. (2014), *Phrynichos. Introduzione, traduzione e commento* (FrC 7), Heidelberg.
Tommaso, S. (2009), 'Il falso medico dell' Aspis di Menandro', in: *Rudiae* 20–21, 301–315.
Totaro, P. (2000), *Le seconde parabasi di Aristofane*, Stuttgart.
Vince, J.H. (1964), *Demosthenes III*, Cambridge.
Webster, T.B.L. (1956), *Art and Literature in Fourth Century Athens*, London.
Whitman, C. (1964), *Aristophanes and the Comic Hero*, Cambridge.
Willi, A. (2008), *Sikelismos: Sprache, Literatur und Gesellschaft im griechischen Sizilien (8.-5. Jh. v. Chr.)*, Basel.
Worman, N. (2008), *Abusive Mouths in Classical Athens,* Cambridge.
Wrenhaven, K. (2013), 'A Comedy of Errors: The Comic Slave in Greek Art', in: B. Akrigg and R. Tordoff (eds.), *Slaves and Slavery in Ancient Greek Comic Drama*, Cambridge/New York, 124–143.
Yunis, H. (2001), *Demosthenes On the Crown*, Cambridge.

Andreas Serafim
Comic Invective in Attic Forensic Oratory: Private Speeches

Abstract: This chapter aims to examine the features and functions of comic invective in private speeches, with the purpose of indicating whether or not the generic dichotomy between public and private orations has any impact upon how comicness in the invective is used as a means of influencing the verdict of the judges. The patterns that Serafim explores in private speeches are, specifically: incongruity; inversion of tragedy into comedy; language or vivid descriptions that draw on, or have implications for, the features of stock comic characters; references to the (ab)use of the human body that also point to comic types of figures (e.g. *kolax*); carrying out menial jobs; being sexually deviant or militarily useless. Three conclusions have been drawn: the first is that the patterns of comic invective in private speeches are largely the same as those used in public speeches; the second is that the dichotomy between public and private speeches affects the frequency of using patterns of comic invective; and the third conclusion is that the other generic dichotomy between private defence and prosecution speeches also affects the use of comic invective, but not in a coherent and consistent way in all private speeches: techniques differ from orator to orator.

In my article, "Comic Invective in the Public Forensic Speeches of Attic Oratory", which was recently published in *Hellenica*, I made two statements: one clarifying my goal to examine the features and patterns of comic invective in the institutional contexts of public forensic speaking in classical Athens, and one making a future research promise. My goal, I explained, was "to explore the totality of public forensic speeches to pin down the main features and functions of comic invective that enabled speakers to attack each other and forge a rapport with the judges, as well as to draw some conclusions about the framework – i.e. the means or restrictions – that specific contexts provide to the speakers concerning the use of comic invective in public prosecution and defence speeches".[1] After reading and discussing (salient passages in) 59 speeches of Attic forensic oratory, and drawing conclusions about the use, patterns and

---

1 Serafim 2020a, 23–42.

https://doi.org/10.1515/9783110735536-004

purposes of comic invective,² I made the promise that I would investigate private speeches of Attic forensic oratory, in order to find out the convergences and divergences between public and private speeches with regard to the use of comicness in the attacks against the opponents.

This is exactly what I aim to do in this chapter: to examine comic invective in private speeches, complementing and enhancing the thorough and knowledgeable discussion of the subject in public forensic speeches that the chapter of Kostas Apostolakis in this volume offers. I aim specifically to examine the features and functions of comic invective, with the purpose of indicating whether or not the generic dichotomy between public and private orations has any impact upon how comicness in the invective is used as a means of influencing the verdict of the judges. For, it has long been argued in classical scholarship on the Greek orators that the legal character of the case (e.g. public and private cases) affects the options available to the speakers in terms of the content of their speech, the arguments and the rhetorical strategies.³ In my recently published book, *Religious Discourse in Attic Oratory and Politics*, I suggest, for example, that, beyond some patterns of religious discourse which are used in all three generic categories of orations, i.e. forensic, symbouleutic and epideictic (e.g. references to impiety that is committed by individuals, and to several types of divine intervention in human affairs), there are also patterns that are used in specific categories only (e.g. references to the act of swearing oaths, when signalled by vocatives, particles and prepositions, are made in forensic and symbouleutic orations, but not in epideictic ones).⁴

This is because, as New Institutionalism theory argues, different institutions have different "logics of appropriateness", i.e. rules that dictate the use of patterns and techniques. "An institution is an enduring collection of rules and organised practices, embedded in structures of meaning and resources that are relatively invariant in the face of turnover of individuals and relatively resilient

---

2 I argue, for example, that the speakers attack their opponents by presenting their actions or mishaps in a caricaturish way, which points, in some cases, to a humorous reverse of gender expectations (as in Aeschines 3.209 where Demosthenes is presented as uttering words reminiscent of the *escape songs* that are mostly attributed to women in tragic plays); that invective draws on, or has implications for, comedy as a result of using stock comic characters and language; that comic invective is not placed in the introduction or the peroration of speeches; and that it is used in (the parts of) the speeches where details of the personal life of opponents are discussed.
3 Rubinstein 2004, 187–203; 2005, 129–145.
4 Serafim 2020c, Chapter 2. On the use of religious discourse in varied contexts of Attic oratory, see also: Martin 2009.

to the idiosyncratic preferences and expectations of individuals and changing external circumstances. There are structures of meaning, embedded in identities and belongings: common purposes and accounts that give direction and meaning to behaviour, and explain, justify and legitimate behavioural codes. To act appropriately is to proceed according to the institutionalised practices of a collectivity and mutual understandings of what is true, reasonable, natural, right and good".[5] In other words, rules and practices specify what should be expected and what makes sense within a given context.

The use of comic invective is also affected by the "logics of appropriateness", as scholars argue and ancient theorists indicate. J. Miner, for example, examining four private cases of Demosthenes (speeches 36, 37, 45, 54), points out that "the status of the individual delivering the speech affects the degree to which comic invective is employed against an opponent".[6] This succinct conclusion is true, but a more nuanced approach to the matter needs to be offered on the basis of a greater sample of private speeches of Attic oratory, so that it may be possible to draw overarching conclusions about how comic invective is used in private speeches, how differently it is used in comparison with public speeches, and how the defendant and the prosecutor use comic invective in their orations.

In the pursuit of this goal ancient rhetorical treatises will also be discussed; one of them, the *Rhetoric to Alexander* 1441b24–9, clearly makes the distinction between the role of comic invective in public and private cases. The author of this treatise urges speakers to use (comic) invective sparingly in public orations, preferring to target the character of the opponents through episodes from their life because such accounts are more persuasive and more harmful to the opponents. "In finding fault you must employ irony and laugh at the points of which your adversary prides himself; in private, and in the presence of a few listeners (ἰδίᾳ μὲν καὶ ὀλίγων παρόντων ἀτιμάζειν αὐτόν), you should seek to discredit him, but before the multitude (τοῖς ὄχλοις) you should abuse him by levelling only ordinary accusations against him".[7]

The problem with this statement in the *Rhetoric to Alexander* is that it does not reflect the practices of many orators. The study of public speeches clearly indicates that both prosecutors and defendants in public actions use comic

---

[5] March and Olsen 2005, 4. Further on New Institutionalism: Merton 1938, 672–682; Simon 1965; Pitkin 1967; Meyer and Rowan 1977; Kratochwil 1984, 695–708; Apter 1991, 463–481; Weaver and Rockman 1993; March and Olsen 1995; Egeberg 2003.
[6] Miner 2006, 145.
[7] Forster 1908, 297.

invective to serve a twofold purpose: firstly, to increase the audience's receptiveness to their arguments, as Aristotle's *Rhetoric* encourages them to do, and, secondly, to denigrate their opponents' character. Different priorities and divergent angles of analysis may explain the considerable difference between theory and practice concerning the use of comic invective and derision: it is not only that "rhetorical systematization is more concerned with the impact of laughter upon the speaker's own self-presentation, while speakers seem to do the most out of vituperative laughter".[8] It may also be that philosophers, as Aristotle is, in whose corpus of speeches the *Rhetoric to Alexander* belongs (despite now being attributed to Anaximenes of Lampsacus), are not interested in describing the practice of rhetoric, but rather in theorising prescriptively about its ideal form, i.e. how rhetoric should have been used. The oratorical practices employed by Attic orators, despite going against the remark of the author of the *Rhetoric to Alexander* that comic invective is more appropriate in private than in public speeches, and that foul language should generally be avoided and substituted by allusive language (1441b21–24), confirm his implied conclusion that aspects of the use of comic invective are (thought to be) affected by the nature of the case.

To examine how comic invective is used in private orations, I read the corpus of private speeches that are attributed to Demosthenes (speeches 27–58), Lysias (speeches 1, 10, 11, 17, 23 and 32)[9] and Isaeus.[10] The patterns I explored in private speeches include those used in public forensic speeches, specifically: incongruity; change of tragedy into comedy; language or vivid descriptions that draw on, or have implications for, the features of stock comic characters; references to the (ab)use of the human body that also point to comic types of figures

---

8 Spatharas 2006, 386.
9 There is scholarly dispute about whether or not speech 3, *Against Simon*, is to be considered a public or a private case. For Hansen 1976, 108–110; MacDowell 1978, 124 and Carey 1989, 109 this speech is public; for Todd 2007, 284 the speech is private. I would follow the suggestion of the majority of scholars, taking this as a public speech. Speech 8, *Accusation of Defamatory Speech against the Sunousiastai*, "is not in the strict sense a forensic speech: that is, although it deals with a dispute, there is no indication that it was prepared for a law-suit"; Todd 2007, 543.
10 In the corpus of Isaeus' transmitted speeches, there are private speeches (i.e. 2, 3, 5 and 6), a public defence speech (i.e. 11), while half of them (i.e. 1, 4, 7, 8, 9 and 10) belong to the special category of speeches that present the legal process of *diadikasia*. As Griffith-Williams 2013, 8 argues, "the dynamics of a *diadikasia* were different from those of an adversarial *dikē* or *graphē*, where one party (the prosecutor) was seeking redress for a wrong allegedly done by the other (the defendant)".

(e.g. *kolax* as in Dem. 19.314);[11] carrying out menial jobs; being sexually deviant or militarily useless.[12]

Let us examine salient examples of the use of comic invective in the speeches of all three orators, starting with Dem. 36.41, a private defence speech. The passage reads as follows:

> τοσαῦτα μὲν τοίνυν χρήματ' εἰληφὼς καὶ χρέα πολλῶν ταλάντων ἔχων, ὧν τὰ μὲν παρ' ἑκόντων, τὰ δ' ἐκ τῶν δικῶν εἰσπράττει, ἃ τῆς μισθώσεως ἔξω τῆς τραπέζης καὶ τῆς ἄλλης οὐσίας, ἣν κατέλιπεν Πασίων, ὠφείλετ' ἐκείνῳ καὶ νῦν παρειλήφασιν οὗτοι, καὶ τοσαῦτ' ἀνηλωκὼς ὅσ' ὑμεῖς ἠκούσατε, οὐδὲ πολλοστὸν μέρος τῶν προσόδων, μὴ ὅτι τῶν ἀρχαίων, εἰς τὰς λῃτουργίας, **ὅμως ἀλαζονεύσεται** καὶ τριηραρχίας ἐρεῖ καὶ χορηγίας.

> All these monies he has received; he has debts due him to the value of many talents, which he is collecting, some by voluntary payments, some by bringing action. These debts were owing to Pasio – quite apart from the rent of the bank and the other property which he left; – and these the two brothers have recovered. He has expended upon public services merely what you have heard, the smallest fraction of his income, not to say of his capital; **and yet he will assume a bragging air**, and will talk about his expenditures for trierarchic and choregic services.

The comicness of the jibe that is directed against Apollodorus is based on the assumption that the man is presented as braggart because of the Greek term that is used, ἀλαζονεύσεται (> ἀλαζονεύομαι "to feign"), which attributed to the accused the behavioural mannerisms of the stock comic persona of the *alazōn*,[13] the character who pretends to have worthy qualities that he does not have.[14] What is important to mention is that, in the context of Dem. 36, the (assumed) association of the jibe with comedy is not as clear as it is when speakers, in public forensic orations, attribute the persona and the qualities of an *alazōn* to their opponents (e.g. in Dem. 18.243 where Aeschines is presented akin to the quack doctor). The speaker in Dem. 36 talks about serious matters that have to do both with a series of private monetary misconducts which Apollodorus committed and the lack of state service through liturgies (trierarchy and

---

11 In Dem. 19.314, there is a lively description of Aeschines raising his eyebrows (τὰς ὀφρῦς ἀνέσπακε) and puffing out his cheeks (τὰς γνάθους φυσῶν). As argued in Serafim 2020b, 122, "the presentation of Aeschines' facial appearance indicates his arrogance and snobbery towards his fellow Athenians, corroborating his presentation as a *kolax*, a petty flatterer and a double-faced citizen who pretends to be a patriot, but who fawns on the city's enemies".
12 On the comic dimension of carrying out menial jobs and being sexually deviant: Serafim 2020a, 23–42.
13 See Miner 2006, 148–150.
14 On the character of braggart: Whitman 1964, 26–28; Duncan 2006, 90–102.

chorēgia).¹⁵ For this reason, it is not fully clear how an invitation to the audience to think of the opponent as being a figure somehow related to comedy serves the interests of Phormio, the man who is defended in this case.

Unlike Aeschin. 3.99, where the term ἀλαζονεύηται is also used as part of the speaker's plan to instigate the audience's feelings of hatred towards Demosthenes, who is accused of being a liar and a deceiver,¹⁶ there is no such clear attempt in Dem. 36. That this is the purpose of Demosthenes – to reconstruct the memory of the law-court audience in such a way as to sustain a "You"-"He" adversarial pattern which would enable him to invite the judges and onlookers to express contempt for the (alleged) liar and wrongdoer by voting against him¹⁷– can be taken for granted. But it is the lack of clarity in taking full advantage of the reference to the braggart for the purpose of character assassination that makes the association with comedy a bit loose. By that association I do not mean that that the prosecutor should have attempted to make the judges laugh at Apollodorus; for, as Miner rightly argues, "whereas politicians [i.e. public case speakers] use comic elements to provoke open laughter from the jury at their opponents, private men [i.e. speakers in private cases] tend to use them primarily to shape the character of an opponent".¹⁸ The problem with Dem. 36.41 is exactly that the (what we assume as) comically-flavoured jibe is not exploited to the best rhetorical effect, with the aim of fully undermining the ethos of the prosecutor.

Comic invective is also used in the private prosecution speeches that are included in the corpus of Demosthenes' transmitted speeches. [Dem.] 45.63–66, despite being of dubious authenticity,¹⁹ contains comically-flavoured references to the accused, Stephanos, as being a flatterer, a fawner upon Phormio, an individual who has the behavioural features of the comic *kolax*. In §65, Stephanos is

---

15 Johnstone 1999, 94 is right to note that "defendants recalled such 'actions' both to erode the authority of the prosecutor's story and to construct a relationship between themselves and the judges that did not depend on the vagaries of rhetorical language". For a comprehensive discussion of liturgies in Athens: Kremmydas 2012, 11–23.
16 Aeschin. 3.99: "but Demosthenes, when making grandiose claims, firstly adds an oath to his lies, calling destruction down on himself, and secondly has the nerve to give a date for events he knows will never happen and provides the names of people he has not seen in person, deceiving his hearers and mimicking the manner of people telling the truth. And for this he deserves fierce hatred, because as well as being a criminal, he also obliterates the signs that distinguish honest men".
17 See the Introduction to this volume, on pp. 10–11.
18 Miner 2006, 145.
19 This is considered a pseudo-Demosthenic speech; it is thought to have been pleaded by Apollodorus. See Scafuro 2011, 215, 227–230.

openly accused of being a flatter: "a man, then, who is a flatterer (ἐστὶ κόλαξ) of those in prosperity, and who betrays these same men if they fall into adversity; who out of all the host of good and worthy citizens of Athens deals with not a single one on the basis of equality, but willingly fawns upon people like Phormio". The next reference to Stephanos, in §66, is more biting because the speaker attempts to give a civic/political dimension to a private case: his opponent is accused of being useless to the city because he has refused to undertake a liturgy. The whole enterprise of assassinating the character of Stephanos becomes stronger by the direct comparison Demosthenes makes between the public and the private: Stephanos avoids his obligations towards the city (ἐπὶ τῷ τὴν πόλιν φεύγειν) and, as a result of that, he is successful in increasing his property (ἔχων γὰρ οὐσίαν τοσαύτην). The speaker tries to make a link between Stephanos' (alleged) avoidance of public duties and the increase of his property: the second is presented as being the result of the first, and Stephanos is again castigated at the end of §66 as being a flatterer (κολακεύοντα).

So lively is the description of Stephanos that the speaker offers a physiognomic description of his exertion of *kolakeia* – a theme which, as argued above, can also be found in instances of using comic invective in public forensic speeches. In §63, we read:

> δικαίως τοίνυν, ὦ ἄνδρες Ἀθηναῖοι, τούτων ἁπάντων δοὺς ἂν δίκην, πολὺ μᾶλλον ἂν εἰκότως διὰ τἆλλα κολασθείη παρ' ὑμῖν. σκοπεῖτε δέ, τὸν βίον ὃν βεβίωκεν ἐξετάζοντες. οὗτος γάρ, ἡνίκα μὲν συνέβαινεν εὐτυχεῖν Ἀριστολόχῳ τῷ τραπεζίτῃ, **ἴσα βαίνων ἐβάδιζεν ὑποπεπτωκὼς ἐκείνῳ**, καὶ ταῦτ' ἴσασι πολλοὶ τῶν ἐνθάδ' ὄντων ὑμῶν.

> Now, men of Athens, while he might justly be made to pay the penalty for all these things, he deserves even more to be punished in your court for the rest of his conduct. Observe the kind of a life he has lived, and judge. For so long as it was the lot of Aristolochos, the banker, to enjoy prosperity, this fellow fawned upon him as he walked beside him, **adapting his pace to his**, and this is well known to many of you who are present here.

As I argue in a recently published article on non-verbal communication in Attic oratory, "fawning stigmatises an individual who is presented as having no scruples about undertaking any action, from which he stands to benefit in any way. Whoever fawns upon the most powerful creates for himself the image of someone with unstable morality and dubious values. The purpose of Demosthenes' reference to the adaption of Stephanus' pace when walking next to a financially powerful man is clear: to cast doubts on his behaviour and morality, and to invite the audience to turn against the man who had no hesitation to change his manner, in order to benefit himself".[20] It is important to note that Demosthenes tries, from the beginning of §63, to direct the judges towards the punishment of his opponent, as the phrase πολὺ μᾶλλον ἂν εἰκότως διὰ τἄλλα κολασθείη παρ' ὑμῖν surely indicates. The use of the personal pronoun ὑμῖν points to the attempt of the speaker to create a "You"-"He" pattern of opposition, and exploit the hostile attitude of the Athenians (that is why the judges are addressed by their civic identity)[21] towards the flatterers.[22] As A. Duncan argues, "the evidence from Old Comedy points to a widespread anxiety in fifth-century Athens that some aspiring politicians were using flattery as a means of upward social mobility and political achievement".[23]

Comic invective is also used in Dem. 54, the prosecution against Conon. While throughout the speech comic invective is avoided,[24] in §9 there is a reference to Conon as impersonating the voice and the flight of a crow:

> ὃ δὲ τῆς ὕβρεώς ἐστι τῆς τούτου σημεῖον καὶ τεκμήριον τοῦ πᾶν τὸ πρᾶγμ' ὑπὸ τούτου γεγενῆσθαι, τοῦθ' ὑμῖν ἐρῶ: **ᾖδε γὰρ τοὺς ἀλεκτρυόνας μιμούμενος τοὺς νενικηκότας**, οἱ δὲ κροτεῖν τοῖς ἀγκῶσιν αὐτὸν ἠξίουν ἀντὶ πτερύγων τὰς πλευράς.

> One thing, however, which is an indication of the fellow's insolence and a proof that the whole affair has been of his doing, I will tell you. **He began to crow, mimicking fighting cocks** that have won a battle, and his fellows bade him flap his elbows against his sides like wings.

This impersonation, whether or not accompanied and enhanced by teasing vocal parody on the part of Demosthenes, so that the liveliness and the pictorial effect of the description (*ekphrasis*) is maximised, is argued to have a comic effect.[25] To present an adult mimicking a bird is an example of incongruity:

---

20 Serafim 2020b, 134.
21 On the use of addresses to the audience in Attic oratory: Serafim 2020d, 71–98.
22 On patterns of opposition in social identity theory, see the Introduction to this volume on pp. 11–12.
23 Duncan 2006, 105. On flatterers in Greek literature: Fisher 2000, 355–378; Miner 2006, 152–155 (on Dem. 45 in particular); Duncan 2006, 102–123; Serafim 2017, 93.
24 In his articles "The Uses of Laughter in Greek Culture" and in "Aischrology, Shame, and Comedy", Halliwell argues for the connection of invective with Old Comedy and for its use in oratory as "self-consciously comic" and laughter-provoking; Halliwell 2004, 118. He argues that, in Dem. 54, a private suit for assault and battery, abusive terms (such as §2: ἀσέλγεια; §4: κακῶς λέγειν, ἐχλεύαζον; §5: παροινουμένους) connect with comedy and are designed to provoke "hostile laughter"; Halliwell 1991, 287. Reading through the specific contexts in which these words appear, I do not understand why they are described as having a comic dimension.
25 Miner 2006, 177–178.

since you expect more serious behaviour from an adult, the opposite is designed to cause laughter and provoke mockery. The description in Dem. 54.9 is also reminiscent of comedy: E. Csapo argues that on a calyx krater, preserved at J. Paul Getty Museum Malibu, the two fighting cocks are the actors of Aristophanes' *Birds*, bearing comic costumes.[26]

The problem with this approach – i.e. that the bird impersonation in the speech of Demosthenes has a comic or laughter-inducing effect – is that the reference is situated in a part of the speech where the violent attack of Conon against Ariston is described.[27] The description of Ariston's past mishaps and his maltreatment by Conon, which aims to arouse anger in the audience towards the perpetrator and empathy towards the sufferer, would not be well served by comic or laughter-provoking invective. This is what Ariston himself clearly points out in §13: "he [Conon] will try to divert your attention from the outrage and the actual facts, and will seek to turn the whole matter into mere jest and ridicule". The speaker is presented, through these words, as anticipating the arguments of his opponent, in a way that echoes what Aristotle says that "for jests, since they may sometimes be useful in debates, the advice of Gorgias was good – to confound the opponents' earnest with jest and their jest with earnest" (*Rhetoric* 1419b7). Csapo argues that the description of Conon's impersonation of a crow encapsulates the violent economic, social and sexual contrast between Ariston and Conon: "it was as a form of sexual violence, symbolic buggery, that the Athenian democracy imagined the oligarchic program to disenfranchise the lower classes and reduce them to servile status. The habits of the cock served as an archetypal expression of this fear".[28] But even if this is a case of *consequential* laughter, as Halliwell puts it, i.e. laughter "which exemplifies the qualities of an attack and causes social division",[29] the placement of this jibe makes its use rather risky and clumsy: Demosthenes moves from a harsh attack against Conon that is incorporated in the first part of §9 (and the whole of §8) to an instance of comic invective before going back to another harsh personal attack.[30] This transition from the solemnity of a dramatic description to a comic

---

26 Csapo 2006/2007, 20.
27 See, for example, Dem. 54.8: "they first stripped me of my cloak, and then, tripping me up they thrust me into the mud and leapt upon me and beat me with such violence that my lip was split open and my eyes closed; and they left me in such a state that I could neither get up nor utter a sound".
28 Csapo 2006/2007, 31.
29 See the Introduction to this volume, pp. 2–3.
30 Dem. 54.9 – the last part of the section: "after this some people who happened to pass took me home stripped as I was, for these men had gone off taking my cloak with them. When my

jibe and vice versa deflates the dramatic tone of the description of the maltreatment Ariston received from Conon.³¹ Despite Demosthenes trying to instruct the audience on how to evaluate the reference to bird impersonation, underlining its function as "an indication of the fellow's insolence", his personal debauchery and rapacity, it is rather uncertain whether the audience sees the description purely from this "serious" point of view.

What can be surmised from the above reading of private defence and prosecution speeches of Demosthenes is that, in both of these generic categories, comic invective is used albeit in a constrained,³² and in some cases also risky and awkward, way. This awkwardness, as described above, may indicate that comic invective is largely out of context in private speeches.³³ The scarcity of examples of comic invective in the private orations of Isaeus corroborates this conclusion. Invective is used in Isaeus, of course, but with no comic element. The patterns of invective I found coincide with those suggested by Süss and

---

bearers got to my door, my mother and the women servants began shrieking and wailing, and it was with difficulty that I was at length carried to a bath. There I was thoroughly bathed, and shown to the surgeons".

31 The whole description of Ariston's suffering reminds us of Pittalacos being maltreated by the two lovers, Timarchos and Hegesandros, as this incident is described in Aeschin. 1.59–61 (a description that also includes birds, but without any attempt to present the actions of two lovers as somehow being connected with comedy or as deserving laughter: "they killed the quails and cocks, so well beloved by the miserable man").

32 I also found two mentions in the private speeches of Demosthenes of individuals laughing at their opponents: Mnesicles in 37.11 and Polycles in 50.26. These two references may be seen as attempts to underline the baseness of the perpetrators – thus, to present their ethos in a negative way – but they cannot be taken as patterns of comic invective. There are also references in Dem. 57.34, 35 to the mother of the speaker carrying out the menial job of being a vendor of ribbons because of poverty. This accusation would have acquired a comic dimension in the very speech of Eubulides, who mocks a woman because of the jobs she carried out (there is also a reference in Dem. 57.35 to her being a nurse, which was considered "a lowly thing", as we are told in 57.45). On the comicness of being accused of carrying out menial jobs, see above n. 12. Ironic (but not necessarily comic, i.e. reminiscent of comedy or laughter-provoking) statements can also be found in the private orations of Demosthenes, as in 42.29 where the accused, Phaenippus, is apostrophised and called "my good man" (ὦ βέλτιστε), and 58.32 where the speaker's opponent is called "this worthy fellow" (ὁ χρηστὸς οὗτος).

33 Unlike comic invective, which is used only rarely in the private speeches of Demosthenes, plain invective is used more frequently, with abundant references to the rapacious behaviour of individuals (27.38), their audacity and shamelessness to make invalid statements and lie (28.9, 29.1, 29.13, 31.6, 33.19, 34.20, 39.22, 52.20, 56.19, 56.41), debauchery (38.27), impiety (28.16, 33.10, 42.29 with an accusation of perjury) and their inclination to act contrary to the laws (42.1–2, 42.15, 57.30, 58.14).

cited by Corbeill,[34] i.e. accusations of being indecent towards relatives (e.g. 4.19, 5.39); emotional invective (3.3: "the legal representative of the woman who was suing for the estate had the audacity" – ἐτόλμησε; 8.1);[35] religious discourse (e.g. perjury: 3.4, 4.22, 6.53); accusations of lying (e.g. 3.4 but with no wording pointing to *alazōn*); questions used as a rhetorical means of presenting evidence that incriminates opponents;[36] references to the socio-economic status of individuals (e.g. 5.35) and their refusal to serve the *polis* either by undertaking liturgies (e.g. 5.45) or carrying out military duties (e.g. 5.46).[37] I only found an instance of comic invective in 8.37, which is not a private speech but one following the legal procedure of *diadikasia*. The passage is quite explicit in associating the behaviour of the speaker's opponent with the comic *kolax*; we read, specifically: "so he gradually persuaded Ciron to let him handle all the sums owing to him, and the interest upon them, and to manage his real property, cajoling the old man by his attentions and flattery (κολακείαις) until he had all his estate in his grasp". The purpose of comic invective in this context is clear: to attack the opponent and undermine his ethos – this is *negative ēthopoiia*, a technique expected to have significant impact upon the audience.[38]

Passages with patterns and examples of comic invective are absent from the private speeches of Lysias (plain invective is used, of course, as in the references to the opponent acting as cloak-remover in 10.10 and 11.5). Comicness can only be found in the defence speech 1, *On the Murder of Eratosthenes*. It should necessarily be noted of course that, in this speech, there is no invective *stricto sensu*: Euphiletus, the man who caught Eratosthenes and his wife *in flagrante*, and killed the adulterer, invites the audience to laugh at his naivety, in an attempt to use laughter as a means of brushing aside the suspicion that he committed a calculated homicide. Having this in mind, we can say that there is considerable similarity and distinctiveness in the ways in which comicness is used in the public speeches of Aeschines and Demosthenes, which are examined in my article in *Hellenica*, and in Lys. 1. Stock comic characters are used – the braggart, as in the parallelism of Aeschines' behaviour with that of the quack doctor in Dem. 18.243, and the comic character-type of the cuckolded husband

---

34 See the Introduction to this volume: p. 14.
35 On the use of emotions as a means of attack against opponents: Serafim 2017, 115–116 specifically on referring to audacity.
36 On questions in Attic oratory: Serafim 2020e, 228–249.
37 See also Hatzilambrou 2011, 37–51 on *ad hominem* attacks in Isaeus.
38 On the notion of *negative ēthopoiia*: Serafim 2017, 25–28.

in Lys. 1.³⁹ Incongruity is also evident in Lys. 1, as indeed in the public speeches of Aeschin. 2.34–35, 3.209–210, and of Dem. 18.262.⁴⁰ Instead of being suspicious at his wife's telltale behaviour (§10 ff.), as other males (indeed those in the law-court audience) would have expected him to do,⁴¹ Euphiletus made a laughing-stock of himself by allowing his wife to lock him in his bedroom (§13). In his words, "I behaved so stupidly" (§10: οὕτως ἠλιθίως διεκείμην).

There are, however, different purposes behind the ways in which stock comic characters and laughter-inducing incongruity were used: Aeschines and Demosthenes use both techniques to attack each other and their rivals, i.e. *aggressive use*, while the defendant in Lys. 1 uses them to absolve himself from the accusation of premeditating crime, i.e. *defensive use*. In Lys. 1 patterns and imagery that have the potential to provoke laughter work in the way described by Ariston in Dem. 54.13: to divert the attention of the judges from the facts of the case, create in them a favourable disposition towards the defendant and elicit their sympathy for him, dispersing any outrage caused by his crime.

This chapter has investigated, as promised earlier, three "hows": how comic invective is used in private speeches, how differently it is used in comparison with public speeches, and how the defendant and the prosecutor use comic invective in their orations. Three conclusions have been drawn: the first conclusion is that the patterns of comic invective in private speeches are largely the same as those used in public speeches; these patterns have been identified and discussed above in the context of salient passages. The second conclusion is

---

39 Lysias' description of Euphiletus has affinities with and implications for Ar. *Thesm.* 478–489 and other comic adultery scenarios. See Porter 1997, 421–453.
40 In Serafim 2015, 105–106, I offer an alternative reading of Dem. 262 from the one of Yunis 2001, 257, who argues that the speaker presents Aeschines as being in the country and stealing fruits from fields. In my view, this reading does not underline the mocking power of the jibe against Aeschines, the failed actor. It is important to see that "the derision is underscored by the ironic statement that Aeschines gets more from what the audience threw at him than from prizes for the performances that he acted at the danger of his life. The hostile audience response registered by throwing fruit becomes a total war between Aeschines and the audience and causes wounds (τραύματα) for the hapless actor. This exaggeration is designed to belittle and ridicule not only the acting career, but also the impressive military performance of Aeschines (at least according to what he himself claims in 2.167–169). Demosthenes relocates Aeschines' martial bravery from the battlefield to the theatrical stage and degrades his campaigns against the enemies to a fight against spectators armed with fruit".
41 Mitchell 2015, 168–183 offers a comprehensive discussion of the reasons underpinning men's anxieties about women. The fear of adultery, for example, is caused not only by the loss of honour, but also by issues of inheritance and property: if a woman is seduced, the adulterer may acquire and get access to the husband's wealth.

that the dichotomy between public and private speeches affects the frequency of using patterns of comic invective: there are only a few instances of comicness in the attacks against opponents in private speeches. The third conclusion is that the other generic dichotomy between private defence and prosecution speeches also affects the use of comic invective, but not in a coherent and consistent way in all private speeches: techniques differ from orator to orator. Demosthenes uses comic invective in both private defence and prosecution speeches; Lysias makes use of comicness (not, strictly speaking, invective) in his private defence speech 1; and Isaeus uses comic invective in one *diadikasia* speech only, speech 8 – so neither in defence nor in prosecution orations.

It seems that idiosyncrasy and circumstantial matters (i.e. everything that has to do with specific cases) play an important role in determining the use or not of comic invective. Talking, for example, about will and inheritance matters, as Isaeus did, allowed the least possible space for comic invective, since its use against opponents who were largely unknown to the general public, and thus also to the judges in the law-court, would give the impression these individuals were unable to do harm or seriously transgress the law.[42] This conclusion is corroborated by the fact that comic invective is absent from the inheritance speeches of Lysias (e.g. 10 and 17), as well from his speech 32 about guardianship, where sensitive issues involving children are discussed. The same absence can also be found in the three speeches of Demosthenes against his guardians (i.e. speeches 27–31). It is also evident that circumstances in the case of Lysias 1 make the use of comic invective useful as a means of removing the suspicion that Euphiletos could commit a calculated crime against Eratosthenes. It can certainly be argued, then, that comic invective is tailored to the demands of the circumstances in every case.

This chapter makes a modest step forward in the direction of further investigating the patterns, the use and the purposes of comic invective, as it is deployed in varied texts and contexts of Attic oratory. The analysis that this chapter offers aims to identify specific patterns of invective that are used in attacking the opponents, thus establishing a framework within which invective in other kinds of oratory might be explored. Topics that deserve better, more meticulous and in-depth examination in future research endeavours, may include the use of comic invective on symbouleutic and epideictic orations – in regard to symbouleutic oratory the chapter of Apostolakis in this volume offers perceptive starting insights that would facilitate further research on the matter. Comparison between forensic (both public and private) speeches, on the one hand, and

---

42 Miner 2006, 145.

the other kinds of oratory, on the other, would enable scholars and researchers to better understand the impact that the framework and the "logics of appropriateness" have upon the use of rhetorical stratagems for persuasive reasons.

Bibliography

Apter, D.A. (1991), 'Institutionalism Revisited', in: *International Social Science Journal* 43, 463–481.
Carey, C. (1989), *Lysias. Selected Speeches*, Cambridge.
Csapo, E. (2006/2007), 'The Cultural Poetics of the Greek Cockfight', in: *The Australian Archaeological Institute at Athens Bulletin* 4, 20–37.
Duncan, A. (2006), *Performance and Identity in the Classical World*, Cambridge/New York.
Egeberg, M. (2003), 'How Bureaucratic Structure Matters: An Organizational Perspective', in: B.G. Peters and J. Pierre (eds.), *Handbook of Public Administration*, London, 116–126.
Fisher, N. (2000), 'Symposiasts, Fish-eaters and Flatterers: Social Mobility and Moral Concerns in Old Comedy', in: D. Harvey and J. Wilkins (eds.), *The Rivals of Aristophanes: Studies in Athenian Old Comedy*, Swansea, 355–396.
Forster, E.S. (1908), *De Rhetorica Ad Alexandrum: Translated into English*, Oxford.
Griffith-Williams, B. (2013), *A Commentary on Selected Speeches of Isaios*, Leiden/Boston.
Halliwell, S. (1991), 'The Uses of Laughter in Greek Culture', in: *Classical Quarterly* 41, 279–296.
Halliwell, S. (2004), 'Aischrology, Shame, and Comedy', in: I. Sluiter and R.M. Rosen (eds.), *Free Speech in Classical Antiquity*, Leiden/Boston, 115–144.
Hansen, M.H. (1976), *Apagoge, Endeixis and Ephegesis against Kakourgoi, Atimoi and Pheugontes: A Study in the Athenian Administration of Justice in the Fourth Century BC*, Odense.
Harvey, Y. (2001), *Demosthenes: On the Crown*, Cambridge.
Hatzilambrou, R. (2011), 'The Use of the *ad hominem* Argument in the Works of Isaeus', in: *L'Antiquité Classique* 80, 37–51.
Johnstone, S. (1999), *Disputes and Democracy: Litigation in Ancient Athens*, Austin.
Kratochwil, F. (1984), 'The Force of Prescription', in: *International Organization* 38, 685–708.
Kremmydas, C. (2012), *Commentary on Demosthenes' Against Leptines*, Oxford.
MacDowell, D.M. (1978), *The Law in Classical Athens*, Ithaca/London.
March, J.G. and Olsen, J.P. (1995), *Democratic Governance*, New York.
March, J.G. and Olsen, J.P. (2005), 'Elaborating the "New Institutionalism"', in: *ARENA Centre for European Studies*, Online publication: http://unesco.amu.edu.pl/pdf/olsen2.pdf
Martin, G. (2009), *Divine Talk: Religious Argumentation in Demosthenes*, Oxford.
Merton, R.K. (1938), 'Social Structure and Anomie', in: *American Sociological Review* 3, 672–682.
Meyer, J. and Rowan, B. (1977), 'Institutionalized Organizations: Formal Structure as Myth and Ceremony', in: *American Journal of Sociology* 83, 340–363.
Miner, J. (2006), *Crowning Thersites: The Relevance of Invective in Athenian Forensic Oratory*, PhD Dissertation, The University of Texas at Austin.

Mitchell, A.G. (2015), 'Humour, Women and Male Anxieties in Ancient Greek Visual Cultures', in: A. Foka and J. Liliequist (eds.), *Laughter, Humor, and the (Un)Making of Gender: Historical and Cultural Perspectives*, New York, 168–183.
Pitkin, H. (1967), *The Concept of Representation*, Berkeley.
Porter, J. (1997), 'Adultery by the Book: Lysias 1 (*On the Murder of Eratosthenes)* and Comic *Diegesis*', in: *Echos du Monde Classique/Classical Views* 16, 421–453.
Rubinstein, L. (2004), 'Stirring up Dicastic Anger', in: D.L. Cairns and R.A. Knox (eds.), *Law, Rhetoric, and Comedy in Classical Athens. Essays in Honour of Douglas M. MacDowell*, Swansea, 187–203.
Rubinstein, L. (2005), 'Differentiated Rhetorical Strategies in the Athenian Courts', in: M. Gagarin and D. Cohen (eds.), *The Cambridge Companion to Ancient Greek Law*, Cambridge, 129–145.
Scafuro, A.C. (2011), *Demosthenes, Speeches 39–49*, Austin.
Serafim, A. (2015), 'Making the Audience: *Ekphrasis* and Rhetorical Strategy in Demosthenes 18 and 19', in: *Classical Quarterly* 65, 96–108.
Serafim, A. (2017), *Attic Oratory and Performance*, New York/London.
Serafim, A. (2020a), 'Comic Invective in the Public Forensic Speeches of Attic Oratory', in: *Hellenica* 68, 23–42.
Serafim, A. (2020b), 'Paralinguistics, Community and the Rhetoric of Division in Attic Oratory', in: *Roda da Fortuna. Revista Eletrônica sobre Antiguidade e Medievo* 9, 114–143.
Serafim, A. (2020c), *Religious Discourse in Attic Oratory and Politics*, New York/London.
Serafim, A. (2020d), '"I, He, We, You, They": Addresses to the Audience as a Means of Unity / Division in Attic Forensic Oratory', in: A. Michalopoulos, A. Serafim, A. Vatri and F. Beneventano della Corte (eds.), *The Rhetoric of Unity and Division in Ancient Literature*, Berlin/Boston, 71–98.
Serafim, A. (2020e), 'ΕΡΩΤΗΣΟΝ ΑΥΤΟΥΣ: Questions, Rhetorical purpose and Hypocrisis in Attic Forensic Oratory', in: G. Thür, S. Avramovic and A. Katanceviic (eds.), *Law, Magic and Oratory*, Belgrade, 228–249.
Simon, H.A. (^{2}1965), *Administrative Behavior*, New York.
Sommerstein, A. (2009), *Talking about Laughter*, Oxford.
Spatharas, D. (2006), 'Persuasive ΓΕΛΩΣ: Public Speaking and the Use of Laughter', in: *Mnemosyne* 59, 374–387.
Todd, S.C. (2007), *A Commentary on Lysias, Speeches 1–11*, Oxford.
Weaver, R.K. and Rockman, B.A. (1993), *Do Institutions Matter? Government Capabilities in the United States and Abroad*, Washington.
Whitman, C.H. (1964), *Aristophanes and the Comic Hero*, Cambridge, MA.

Emiliano J. Buis
Rhetorical Defence, Inter-poetic *Agōn* and the Reframing of Comic Invective in Plato's *Apology of Socrates*

Abstract: This chapter identifies the features that are shared by Aristophanic comedy and Plato's *Apology of Socrates*. Those similarities include specific rhetorical arguments employed by the main characters in order to criticise their enemies in front of a civic audience, which is willing to enjoy the pleasures of vituperation and verbal violence. Paying attention to the staging of comic invective in each genre reveals some of the elaborate methods employed by Plato to confront comedy and its influence by means of the consolidation of an efficient "inter-poetic *agōn*". The chapter shows that an examination of the *Apology* based on the importance of the rhetorical construction of Socrates' defence can greatly profit from a comparison with Aristophanes' *Acharnians*. In that regard, while the *Clouds* is often quoted in order to trace the root of the offences included in the judicial indictment against Socrates, a comparative approach to the defence strategies employed in the *Acharnians* can reveal new links and contribute to a better understanding of Plato's verbal hostility towards Socrates' adversaries.

1 Introduction: Socrates and Comic Invective

The proximity between the Platonic dialogues and the extant comedies of Aristophanes has been studied by philologists and historians, who have tried to compare texts in order to discern relationships between the two genres.[1] For the

---

The final version of this chapter has been written in the context of the research project "Pensar las emociones en la Atenas democrática: Diálogo entre la comedia y la filosofía" (Programa Logos de Ayudas a la Investigación en Estudios Clásicos 2019, Fundación BBVA), led by José María Zamora Calvo (Departamento de Filosofía, Universidad Autónoma de Madrid).

1 Born in 428/7 BC, Plato grew up while Aristophanes was already a recognised poet and it is quite possible that, over time, they knew each other personally. It is hard to imagine that Aristophanes' character would have gone unnoticed by a young man interested in poetry and, most particularly, in the comic genre. As it will become clear, however, my interest here is much less biographical than philological.

https://doi.org/10.1515/9783110735536-005

most part, these intellectual explorations have focused on the identification of chronological or thematic associations (by analysing the relationship, for instance, between works composed around the same period and on similar subjects).[2] In other cases, the connections between Plato and Aristophanes have rather been suggested by the presence of a common character, in spite of the years elapsed between their works.

This is the case with Plato's *Apology of Socrates*, whose comic features have often been examined in relationship to Aristophanes' *Clouds*. The connection is not surprising, taking into account that Socrates' legal defence makes explicit reference to the charges laid against him when the *Clouds* was staged two decades before the trial. When it comes to identifying the content of the old charges brought against him, Socrates introduces the attacks of Meletus by reading the indictment (*Ap.* 19b-c):

> Σωκράτης ἀδικεῖ καὶ περιεργάζεται ζητῶν τά τε ὑπὸ γῆς καὶ οὐράνια καὶ τὸν ἥττω λόγον κρείττω ποιῶν καὶ ἄλλους ταὐτὰ ταῦτα διδάσκων.
>
> Socrates is an offender and a meddler, in studying things below the earth and in the sky, and making the weaker argument into the stronger, and instructing other people in these same things.[3]

He then immediately recognises the Aristophanic origins of the offences he was charged with (*Ap.* 19c). The reference to the *Clouds* (218 ff.), where Socrates was brought on stage as a comic character (a ridiculous sophist), shows the nature of Aristophanes' comic invective against him. Many have drawn conclusions about the effect that this humorous presentation of the philosopher could have had on the political charges introduced many years later.[4]

It seems that this traditional reading, which is limited to the explicit presentation of Socrates in the *Clouds*, has obstructed broader interpretations of the nature of the textual links between the *Apology* and Old Comedy in general. I contend that analysing the defence speeches in legal proceedings and the role played by invective within these performances helps to revisit some aspects which have been neglected in the examination of those literary parallels that may be drawn between the *Apology* and Aristophanes' comedies. I focus here on

---

[2] Such is the case, for instance, with the parallels between the *Republic* and the *Assemblywomen*, which have encouraged interesting reflections around the utopian creation of a city and the revolutionary nature of political positions questioning democratic values; cf. Ellis 2015.
[3] Here and elsewhere, the Greek text and – with slight variations – its translation corresponds to Stokes 1997.
[4] Cf. Segoloni 1994, 15–108.

Aristophanes' *Acharnians*, with the purpose of exploring patterns of resemblance between this play and the *Apology*, which have not been sufficiently explored in critical approaches to date. To stress the need of studying these affinities, I will reflect on the ways in which the literary defence of the *Apology* turns to the strategies of comic invective deployed by Aristophanes when drafting Dicaeopolis' rhetorical intervention in the *Acharnians*.

As reframed in the literary texts, comic invective encompasses a whole set of literary strategies, frequently employed by the comic genre, which, being pleasurable or amusing, aim at attacking someone in front of an audience who enjoy both the abuse and vituperation and the subtle criticism of the adversaries. When discussing Aristophanes' comic invective, I refer here to those mechanisms put in place in Old Comedy to publicly denigrate an individual and isolate him from his community. Since Athenian political comedy used to experiment with different levels of mockery and amusement, comic invective did not necessarily have to be funny in modern terms, nor did it entail just jokes or laughter, but it could rather involve a complex set of expressions of disapproval which were constructed in a way which happened to be typical of Old Comedy. It is in this sense that I consider Plato's reframing of comic invective: even if Platonic sources seem to express a certain disdain for laughter,[5] they develop interesting parallelisms that rely on "comic" strategies to blend and parody genres. By replacing vulgar humour with subtle irony and refined hilarity,[6] the *Apology* responds to Aristophanes' caricature of Socrates, and, by means of an elaborated literary amalgamation, establishes its final authority over comedy.

I argue here that the structures of argument presented by Socrates in response to the charges against him in the *Apology* represent another instance of comic invective. They consist of literary initiatives reminiscent of those launched by Aristophanes to confront Cleon and his accusations in 426 BC. By placing comedy in another context, Plato ultimately reframes comic invective and uses it to respond to Socrates' enemies and to reproduce some of the key elements present in Aristophanes' defence politics in the *Acharnians*. These elements enable him to use certain literary features of comedy to construct an inter-poetic *agōn* between genres. In other terms, through the subversion of the theatrical defence, as mastered by Aristophanes, and the reuse of comically-flavoured diatribes, the *Apology* finds new ways of countering the old comic

---

5 Cf. *Rep.* 388e.
6 According to Harding 1994, 201, the initial corrosive aggression which was the landmark of comic invective was progressively transformed into a more sophisticated (and less violent) wittiness.

accusations recorded in the *Clouds*. Plato is able to employ a highly efficient strategy in order to intensify the dramatic role of characters, and, in doing so, he manages to reframe comic invective in such a way as to ensure a poetic victory by discrediting Socrates' accusers in a comically devastating fashion.

2 Comic Invective and Judicial Retaliation in the *Apology*: An Acharnian Connection?

The *Acharnians*, the first complete Athenian comedy that has been preserved, won first place at the Lenaia festival in 425 BC. Confronting the social and political crisis of war, the protagonist of the play – Dicaeopolis (which literally means "Just City") – resolves to conclude a private truce for himself and his family, which leads the farmers of the deme of Acharnai to launch an assault against him. In accordance with the tradition of the genre, Dicaeopolis' response to this attack borrows heavily from tragic sources. After visiting the poet Euripides to ask for a stage costume (the rags of the beggar Telephus) in order to arouse pity from the chorus (*Ach.* 407–479), he pleads his case.

The comedy plays with different identities and overlapping levels of performance. On the one hand, thanks to Euripides, Dicaeopolis plays the role of king Telephus, who, according to the myth, entered the Greek camp disguised as a beggar. The explicit allusion to this story in the *Acharnians* shows Aristophanes' parodic intention. A second degree of representation involves Dicaeopolis becoming the mask of Aristophanes himself. While the protagonist is accused by the Acharnians of having obtained a private peace, the chorus reminds us that the comic poet had also been the target of verbal attacks. Aristophanes, in fact, had been attacked by the demagogue Cleon, who tried to bring him to justice (*Ach.* 628–632):

> ἐξ οὗ γε χοροῖσιν ἐφέστηκεν τρυγικοῖς ὁ διδάσκαλος ἡμῶν,
> οὔπω παρέβη πρὸς τὸ θέατρον λέξων ὡς δεξιός ἐστιν·
> διαβαλλόμενος δ' ὑπὸ τῶν ἐχθρῶν ἐν Ἀθηναίοις ταχυβούλοις,
> ὡς κωμῳδεῖ τὴν πόλιν ἡμῶν καὶ τὸν δῆμον καθυβρίζει,
> ἀποκρίνασθαι δεῖται νυνὶ πρὸς Ἀθηναίους μεταβούλους.

> Ever since our producer has had charge of comic choruses, he has never come forward to the audience to say that he is clever (δεξιός). But having been traduced (διαβαλλόμενος) by his enemies before the Athenians, ever quick to make up their minds, as one who ridi-

cules our city and insults our people (κωμῳδεῖ τὴν πόλιν ἡμῶν καὶ τὸν δῆμον καθυβρίζει), he now desires to make his reply before the Athenians, ever ready to change their minds.[7]

Dicaeopolis presents his defence by resorting to a set of political critiques, blaming the citizens for the war. Aristophanes elaborates his apology on the stage based on elements which are typical to the spirit of comic invective: he mocks the Athenians because of their unfortunate quickness of spirit and criticises demagoguery as a political evil for the *polis*. In both cases, unjust accusations are met with comic responses aimed at waking up the spectators, who seem blind in the face of injustice.

The situation is not too different from the setting of Plato's *Apology*, where Socrates as a character delivers a public speech before the judges (and the Athenians) in order to talk justice and expose the evil intentions of ill-disposed demagogues.[8] Indeed, since the *Acharnians* stages the defence of a just man, unjustly accused by his enemies of making fun of the city and having committed injustices against the people, it is reasonable to postulate a resemblance to the situation of Socrates dragged to court in 399 BC.

The comic accusation reveals the political nature of the indictments against the playwright. The reasons behind these allegations are hard to pinpoint, given the limited evidence that can be collected from the text itself. The information offered by the *Scholia*, especially in the case of line 378, provides us with additional, yet doubtful, features to consider.[9] Cleon, the Athenian *stratēgos*, might have decided to prosecute the poet because, as a result of his staging of *Babylonians* the year before at the Great Dionysia, he had made fun of many (πολλοὺς κακῶς εἶπεν), mocking the magistrates in front of the foreign allies who were attending the theatre. The *Scholia* falsely suggest that, as a consequence of these offences, Cleon initiated a public action (ἐγράψατο) against Aristophanes

---

[7] The Greek text is taken from the edition by Olson 2002. The translations here and elsewhere correspond to Sommerstein ³1992, with minor changes.
[8] There exists a very large bibliography devoted to studying the theatricality of Plato's works. If we add the theatrical nature of legal pleadings, this performative aspect becomes even more significant in the *Apology*. On the isomorphism between the practice of drama and the courts in Athens, see Garner 1987; Ober and Strauss 1990; Hall 1995; and Todd 2005. Papaioannou, Serafim and da Vela 2017 deal extensively with these relations. I have been able to discuss them in greater depth in Buis 2019, 55–63.
[9] The *Scholia* have been transmitted by the manuscripts REΓL. On the *stemma codicum* for the play, see Sommerstein ³1992, 34–36, and Olson 2002, lxxv–xcix.

on the charges of wronging the citizens (ἀδικίας εἰς τοὺς πολίτας) and insulting the people and the Council (ὕβριν τοῦ δήμου καὶ τῆς βουλῆς).[10]

The exact nature of Cleon's *diabolē* against Aristophanes remains unknown, but its political nature cannot be underestimated and can contribute to our reading of the *Apology*. The crime of wronging the people reappears as a recurrent motif in later political proceedings, including the prosecution against the generals at Arginusae and of course Socrates' trial.[11] Indeed, in the latter case, the offences of corrupting the youth and impiety (*asebeia*) involve the disruption or upending of the social, i.e. political, order by means of manipulation of civic instruction. Thus, the reasoning behind the accusations against Aristophanes and Socrates, in spite of the time gap, points to some common ground: as intellectuals, they were both charged with the intention of overthrowing the democratic order established in the *polis*, which at the end of the fifth century BC was considered a serious attack on the integrity of the whole *dēmos*.[12]

Before entering into an examination of humour in the *Apology*, it is necessary to identify the nature of these comic *diabolai*. As suggested, comedy usually resorts to interpersonal violence in order to achieve its goals, and personal invective can be considered a verbal alternative to the frequent representation of physical aggression.[13] For the sake of laughter, Aristophanes makes ample use of direct attacks with the purpose of caricaturing his opponents. The political implications of this negative and exaggerated portrait of his adversaries cannot be underestimated. Through the poetic staging of *loidoria* (i.e. railing, abuse, reproach) against specific targets,[14] Old Comedy creates in-group solidarity and singles out those citizens who should be considered outsiders and deserve hostile treatment.[15] In order to show in what ways this dramatic use of venomous hostility against public rivals is exploited by Plato, a comparison of the accusations formulated against Aristophanes in the *Acharnians*, on the one hand, and those directed at Socrates in the *Apology*, on the other, becomes nec-

---

10 Atkinson 1992, 56. I have examined these arguments and rejected the historical accuracy of these *Scholia* in Buis 2019, 75–109.
11 Olson 2002, 201.
12 Ismard 2017, 127–128.
13 See, for instance, Riess 2012.
14 Saetta Cottone 2005.
15 I am simplifying here for the sake of brevity. Comic violence is of course ambiguous, and I concur with Ruffell 2013 when he claims that verbal attacks in Old Comedy are not necessarily limited to the social exclusion of specific target groups. On the techniques of using comic invective to forge in-group solidarity and out-group hostility, see the Introduction to this volume pp. 10–12.

essary. Both literary trials share interesting commonalities related to the appropriation of comic invective.

Concerning the nature of verbal aggression in comedy, it has been stated that comic invective aims at fostering a relationship between a character (mostly the protagonist) and the public, in opposition to the target of the ridicule. It amounts to the exercise of power of a speaker over his adversary before an audience which is invited to side with one of the two parties of the *agōn*.[16] Aiming to examine the similarities (and dependencies) between Aristophanes and Plato, I will pay attention in this chapter to the literary strategies implemented to create an opposition between contestants. Firstly, I will deal with the self-praise of the speakers (the invective-producers) in the *Acharnians* and the *Apology* (i.e. Dicaeopolis and Socrates). Secondly, I will address in both works the description of those enemies (the invective-receivers) who accuse the main characters (i.e. Cleon and Aristophanes/Meletus/Anytus), in order to focus, thirdly, on the interaction between comedy and political/forensic oratory when resorting to targeting of the "others" on stage. This will lead me to conclude that the *Apology* may have reframed the elements of comic invective in order to provide an efficient forensic justification of Socrates' defence which, far from excluding the humorous seriousness (*spoudaiogeloion*) of Old Comedy, is able to play with its precedent and manipulate it for its own poetic purpose (i.e. Socrates' literary triumph over his comic enemies).

2.1 The Invective-Producers

The usual starting point of comic invective, as stated, is the self-praise of the speaker, who places himself in a position of moral superiority, in order to legitimise his attacks. In this sense, both Dicaeopolis in the *Acharnians* and Socrates in the *Apology* attribute to themselves some positive features which deserve special attention. It has been pointed out that, in spite of the formal environment of legal proceedings, the *Apology* includes a healthy dose of the comic when Socrates describes his own role and builds his dramatic persona in front of the Athenians. According to some critics, Socrates does not seriously face the charges and throws up a mocking defence.[17] His insistence on not knowing, or rather not having self-knowledge, has been understood as a humorous con-

---

16 Serafim 2020, 23–42, who offers a comprehensive description of influential theories on comic invective.
17 Greene 1920, 71–72.

struction,[18] especially since Socrates himself concedes that he could eventually be seen by some judges "as joking" (παίζειν) when describing his reputation as wise (*Ap.* 20d).

This widespread reference to the comical can be easily found throughout his defence. Socrates' frequent comparison of himself to Greek heroes, for example, is ill-fitting and ridiculous, especially when taking into account his alleged modesty, humility and restraint.[19] However, although he displays several characteristics which may serve to identify him as a comic hero (i.e. appearing to be unattractive, unfavourable, infuriating and insolent),[20] there is an insistence on his part to be taken seriously.[21] Thus, when he compares Achilles' reaction to the prophecy of his death with his own future after the trial, he indicates that he fears being laughed at. He explicitly resembles Achilles, who preferred to die than to be mocked (*Ap.* 28d).[22]

But how does Socrates build his "comic" self-esteem? The question cannot be answered if the larger picture, related to the links between comedy and Plato's account of Socrates' last days – already observed by ancient and recent critical literature[23] – is not complemented by a philological approach. Few attempts have been made to prove textual similarities between the Socratic dialogues and aforementioned comic plays, in order to justify Socrates' behaviour as a "comic hero" within that larger framework. I will advocate here that a linguistic, syntactic and stylistic examination of the forensic passages in the *Apology* in the light of the literary strategies employed by Aristophanes in his defence in the *Acharnians* proves useful for understanding the complex ways in which Plato reframes comic invective for the benefit of Socrates' plea.

One of the most fruitful pairs of comparisons deals with the morality attributed to the speaker, which of course falls within the realm of the fictional representation of a morally sound self. In the text of the parabasis of the *Achar-*

---

18 Danielewicz 2015, 148; Tanner 2017, 1.
19 Tanner 2017, 4.
20 Tanner 2017, 12–13.
21 On the *Apology* as "inverted parody" and Socrates' self-presentation as Palamedes (the defendant in Gorgias' famous speech): Feaver and Hare 1981.
22 Naas 2016, 24 acknowledges that this responds to a system of moral values that seems not have changed from Homer to Plato: the coward is identified with the laughable.
23 Wilson Nightingale 2000, 172 has claimed that Plato "is arguably more indebted to comedy than to any other literary genre". On the comic influence on Plato, see Greene 1920 and especially Mader 1977, who provides an interesting bibliographical survey (1977, 72–77). Brock 1990 still remains the most important contribution to the multilayered links between Plato and comedy.

nians, a clear allusion was made to the poet's cleverness (*Ach.* 629). Not surprisingly, this virtue and other similar ones – which belong to a complete set of nouns and adjectives used by Aristophanes to describe his work, his personality and his spectators (such as δεξιός, σοφός, καινός) – also appear in the *Clouds* to identify Socrates and his teaching.[24] Plato resorts to this same vocabulary when getting Socrates to justify his position. As said before, during the defence plea comic emphasis is placed on wisdom, confirmed by the oracle at Delphi (*Ap.* 21a). In the *Acharnians*, the chorus makes a similar reference to a situation of consultation when trying to explain, in a ludicrous manner, Aristophanes' virtues: it is reminded that the Lacedaemonians praised Aristophanes' advice as a reason for Athenian strength (*Ach.* 650–651).

A methodological caveat is needed when tackling these similarities, since it could be contended that the argument of building parallelisms between Socrates and Aristophanes cannot be used to blindly justify the existence of intertextuality. Quite clearly, the threshold for building convincing arguments upon intertextual references in antiquity is high. Since the information available on the circulation of the *Acharnians* is scarce, there is no evidence to conclude unequivocally that there is in the *Apology* a deliberate intention to parody specific verses of Aristophanes' comedy.[25] However, the fact that Plato is clearly aware of the specific content of the *Clouds* (staged in 421 BC, rewritten by 418 BC) constitutes a non-negligible hint to suggest that Cleon's political and legal accusation of the playwright after 426 BC was probably a well-known story at the time of Socrates' trial.[26] Moreover, it is reasonable to argue that the close similarities between the unfounded accusation of an intellectual by influential politicians, as presented in the *Acharnians*, and the situation of Socrates himself would not have escaped the attention of someone like Plato, determined to defend his teacher by responding to charges which originated in Aristophanes' diatribe.

Taking this into account, the proximity in language between the two texts can contribute to a better understanding of the techniques of comic invective.

---

24 Noël 2000, 114.
25 Concerning the circulation of the text of the *Acharnians* in later decades, Michelini 1998, 120–121 has offered strong arguments to indicate that, for example, Isocrates' speech *On the Peace* makes reference to the *Acharnians*. Since the oration was composed at the end of the Social War in 355 BC, these clear allusions show that Aristophanes' play was still circulating – at least among the intellectual elite – in mid-fourth century Athens.
26 The fact that Aristophanes' comedy had won the first prize at the Lenaia is indicative of "his brilliant early success and the fame it brought"; Olson 2002, xxix. Cf. *Vesp.* 1023.

Self-praise, for example, becomes a common ethical stereotype.²⁷ Aristophanes' role as capable of "making men better" (βελτίους γεγενῆσθαι) seems to be close to Socrates' role as described in the *Apology*, when as a reply to the question "but tell me, there is a good fellow, who *makes them better*?" (ἀμείνους ποιεῖ; 24e) the philosopher indeed complains that he is not valued enough (25a). Besides, it was Socrates' σοφία that made him the object of verbal attacks, as revealed in 22e–23a:

> ἐκ ταυτησὶ δὴ τῆς ἐξετάσεως, ὦ ἄνδρες Ἀθηναῖοι, πολλαὶ μὲν ἀπέχθειαί μοι γεγόνασι καὶ οἷαι χαλεπώταται καὶ βαρύταται, ὥστε πολλὰς διαβολὰς ἀπ' αὐτῶν γεγονέναι, ὄνομα δὲ τοῦτο λέγεσθαι, σοφὸς εἶναι.

> As a result of this inquiry, Athenians, I have acquired widespread dislike (ἀπέχθειαι), and of the most troublesome and unpleasant kind. The dislike has given rise to many slanders (διαβολάς), and to my being described by this word, as "wise" (σοφός).

On the basis of common rhetorical *topoi*, the context of the διαβολαί mentioned in this passage reminds us of διαβαλλόμενος in the *Acharnians* (l. 630), and the appeal to hatred (ἀπέχθειαι) points to the presence of those enemies (ἐχθροί) who, according to the testimony of the same verse, attacked the comic poet.²⁸ The analogy also extends to the rhetorical depiction of the Athenians. As argued in what follows, the Athenians who (according to the *Acharnians*) often changed their minds and made quick decisions without thinking about them, are not unlike Meletus or Anytus, who encourage the dispute against Socrates irrationally, in a manner contrary to the spirit and interests of the city.

As I explained, the construction of comic invective is sometimes based on a subtle connection to other genres and texts. In this "carnival of genres" typical of Old Comedy,²⁹ the vulgar humour coexists with intellectual word-plays and sophisticated puns. Therefore, it is not surprising to see that the self-image of the invective-producer is embedded in humour but equally engaged with the gravity of the matter at stake. This conflation of seriousness and hilarity, which was appropriate for a speaker that needed to call for attention in order to attack an adversary, can be better grasped if Plato's strategies in the *Apology* are compared to his presentation of Aristophanes in the *Symposium* (c. 380 BC).

When Plato includes Aristophanes in the *Symposium* as one of the speakers at the gathering organised by Agathon in 416 BC, he presents a very lively image

---

27 On self-praise in oratory: Spatharas 2019, 159–188.
28 On the etymological nexus between both terms: Chantraine 1999, 391, s.v. ἔχθος.
29 As coined by Platter 2007.

of the poet. Already dead for some years, the playwright is represented in a positive light.[30] Acting with the ambiguities of a comic hero, the playwright is described as a *bon vivant*, a lover of the pleasures of good life, such as eating and drinking: just like Socrates in the *Apology*, Aristophanes is depicted as a funny man who, nevertheless, wants to be taken seriously when making his speech on Eros. In his words, which constitute a sophist-style parody of the etiological myth relating to the origins of erotic attraction, a mixture of comic features and seriousness (*spoudaiogeloion*) is exploited by Plato.[31] Aristophanes' statement is strategically situated in the middle of Eryximachus' double request to avoid the comic interpretation of these ideas. Aristophanes asks Eryximachus twice, before and after this conclusion, not to make fun of him: μή μοι (...) κωμῳδῶν τὸν λόγον (*Smp.* 193b) and μὴ κωμῳδήσῃς αὐτόν (*Smp.* 193d). The playwright makes an effort to be taken as one speaking seriously.[32] This "anti-comic" conception of the poet's role in the banquet is complemented by Plato's own comic game: in fact, when resorting to the inclusion of hiccups in order to shift unexpectedly the order of interventions, the philosopher inverts the places granted to humour and seriousness in order to illustrate the way in which literary universes can be transformed and still remain closely connected.[33]

In the *Acharnians*, the figure of the invective-producer also revolves around the need to mingle comedy with serious intent when launching his defensive slander (*Ach.* 497–503):

μή μοι φθονήσητ' ἄνδρες οἱ θεώμενοι,
εἰ πτωχὸς ὢν ἔπειτ' ἐν Ἀθηναίοις λέγειν
μέλλω περὶ τῆς πόλεως, τρυγῳδίαν ποιῶν.
τὸ γὰρ δίκαιον οἶδε καὶ τρυγῳδία.
ἐγὼ δὲ λέξω δεινὰ μὲν δίκαια δέ.
οὐ γάρ με νῦν γε διαβαλεῖ Κλέων ὅτι
ξένων παρόντων τὴν πόλιν κακῶς λέγω.

---

30 Strauss 1966, 5 concluded that "[f]ar from being an enemy of Socrates, Aristophanes was his friend, but somewhat envious of his wisdom". Brock 1990, 42 used the positive image of Aristophanes in the *Symposium* to come to the conclusion that Socrates and Plato were forgiving of the comedic attacks against them.
31 The substance of the praise proposed by Aristophanes is rather linked to the divine punishment of impiety and injustice (*Smp.* 193c-d), which is undoubtedly a serious topic.
32 In spite of these attempts, Neumann 1966, 426 concludes that the comic poet finally does what he most wants to avoid: making himself ridiculous (*Smp.* 189b4–7).
33 Destrée 2015, 362–363 has identified that there is a double verbal pun with Aristophanes' name in *Smp.* 189a7–8, where Ὠγαθέ, φάναι, Ἀριστόφανες, plays with the idea of the comic playwright as the "best" speaker.

> Be not indignant with me, members of the audience, if, though a beggar, I speak before the Athenians about public affairs in a comedy. Even comedy is acquainted with justice; and what I have to say will be shocking, but it will be right. This time Cleon will not allege that I am slandering the city in the presence of foreigners.[34]

Some additional passages in the *Acharnians* and the *Apology*, related to the civic role of intellectuals, can be added to this comparison and help distinguish the defendant from his enemies. When Dicaeopolis attempts to explain the reasons for his actions by claiming that the Spartans are not the only cause of the Athenians' misfortunes, his words could be attributed to Aristophanes himself. This is so because the Coryphaeus speaks directly on behalf of the comic poet when he reminds spectators that his plays have always proven to be beneficial for the people because he has struggled to dismantle the arguments of the demagogues and instruct the people about what is right (*Ach.* 655–658):

> ἀλλ' ὑμεῖς τοι μή ποτ' ἀφῆσθ'· ὡς κωμῳδήσει τὰ δίκαια·
> φησὶν δ' ὑμᾶς πολλὰ διδάξειν ἀγάθ', ὥστ' εὐδαίμονας εἶναι,
> οὐ θωπεύων οὐδ' ὑποτείνων μισθοὺς οὐδ' ἐξαπατύλλων,
> οὐδὲ πανουργῶν οὐδὲ κατάρδων, ἀλλὰ τὰ βέλτιστα διδάσκων.

> But if you take my advice, never you let go of him; for in his comedies he'll say what's right. He says he will give you much good instruction that will bring you true felicity, not flattering you nor dangling rewards before you nor diddling you nor playing any knavish tricks nor drenching you with praise, but giving you the best of instruction.

As in the case of the *parabasis*, Aristophanes hides here behind the Coryphaeus, who immediately continues to use the first person in order to show his attachment to justice and civic values (*Ach.* 659–664):

> πρὸς ταῦτα Κλέων καὶ παλαμάσθω
> καὶ πᾶν ἐπ' ἐμοὶ τεκταινέσθω.
> τὸ γὰρ εὖ μετ' ἐμοῦ καὶ τὸ δίκαιον
> ξύμμαχον ἔσται, κοὐ μή ποθ' ἁλῶ
> περὶ τὴν πόλιν ὢν ὥσπερ ἐκεῖνος
> δειλὸς καὶ λακαταπύγων.

> So let Cleon contrive, let him devise what he will be against me; for right and justice will be my allies, and never shall I be convicted of being, as he is, a cowardly and right buggerable citizen.

---

34 On Dicaeopolis' defence arguments here, see Beta 1999; Ercolani 2002.

The moral role of the comic poet is clear: integrity and justice are presented as his allies in the effort to fight against injustice and lies.[35] Both Dicaeopolis/Aristophanes and Socrates comically build their own personae on moral *ēthos* forged by honesty and frankness, a necessary step in order to justify the poetic retaliation against their accusers. This literary operation should be complemented by an analysis of the rhetorical construction of their respective accusers (the invective-receivers), depicted in opposite terms. Just as Cleon is a coward and a broken citizen who attempts to flatter and deceive the people,[36] Meletus and Anytus would be similarly reproached because of their selfish motivations, unfair spirit and fake integrity.

2.2 The Invective-Receivers

The ambiguous self-praise of Aristophanes in the *Acharnians* and Socrates in the *Apology*, which responds to the nature of comic protagonists, needs to be complemented by the identification of those public figures who stand as the object of verbal attack. Here again, Old Comedy provides us with the practice of ὀνομαστὶ κωμῳδεῖν, i.e. pointing at poetic and political rivals who are criticised by name and become the target of violent insult.[37]

Speaking directly on behalf of the author in an unprecedented way,[38] Dicaeopolis tries in *Acharnians* to unveil the hidden lies of Cleon and explain the motivations behind his ill-founded accusation (*Ach.* 377–382):

> αὐτός τ' ἐμαυτὸν ὑπὸ Κλέωνος ἅπαθον
> ἐπίσταμαι διὰ τὴν πέρυσι κωμῳδίαν.
> εἰσελκύσας γάρ μ' ἐς τὸ βουλευτήριον
> διέβαλλε καὶ ψευδῆ κατεγλώττιζέ μου
> κἀκυκλοβόρει κἄπλυνεν, ὥστ' ὀλίγου πάνυ
> ἀπωλόμην μολυνοπραγμονούμενος.

> And I know about myself, what I suffered at Cleon's hands because of last year's comedy. He dragged me into the council chamber and began slandering me, telling glib-mouthing

---

35 Treu 2013.
36 Here again, a similar line of thought is found at the beginning of the *Apology*, when Socrates resorts to the rhetorical *topos* of sincerity (17d–18a).
37 *Cf.* On the importance of *onomasti kōmōidein* in Aristophanes, see Halliwell 1984; Degani 1993; Carey 1994; Storey 1998; Napolitano 2002; Bierl 2002; Mastromarco 2002; and García Soler 2013.
38 Fisher 1993; Sutton 1998. On Dicaeopolis' overlapping roles in the play, see van Steen 2004, 224.

lies about me, roaring at me like the Cycloborus, bathing me in abuse, so that I very nearly perished in a sewer of troubles.

Through these words, Dicaeopolis (i.e. Aristophanes) insists on the violence of the verbal attacks of Cleon, identified here by his name. The virulence and gravity attributed by Socrates to the accusations of Meletus and Anytus will echo this comic invective, in which the accuser is assimilated to a tough Cycloborus because of his power of destruction. In the beginning of the *Apology*, Socrates launches an assault against his enemies by indicating the lies and fabrication embodied in the indictment (*Ap.* 17a):

> ὅτι μὲν ὑμεῖς, ὦ ἄνδρες Ἀθηναῖοι, πεπόνθατε ὑπὸ τῶν ἐμῶν κατηγόρων, οὐκ οἶδα· ἐγὼ δ' οὖν καὶ αὐτὸς ὑπ' αὐτῶν ὀλίγου ἐμαυτοῦ ἐπελαθόμην, οὕτω πιθανῶς ἔλεγον. καίτοι ἀληθές γε ὡς ἔπος εἰπεῖν οὐδὲν εἰρήκασιν.

> How you, Athenians, have been affected by my accusers, I don't know; but certainly they made even me almost forget about myself, they were speaking so persuasively. And yet they have said virtually nothing true.

Although the image of Cleon's violence is more vivid than in the *Apology* (as expected from a passage of Old Comedy), in terms of the description of the effects of the verbal attacks made by malicious sycophants, the two passages look alike. Just as the diatribe launched by Cleon in the case of the *Acharnians* almost (ὀλίγου) destroys the defendant, in the case of the *Apology*, Socrates almost (ὀλίγου) forgets who he is as a result of the judicial blow. The first-person of the defence is explicit in both passages (αὐτός, ἐγώ and ἐμαυτόν/ἐμαυτοῦ), and so are the indications of suffering (ἔπαθον, πεπόνθατε) and the passive voice pointing to the accusers (ὑπὸ Κλέωνος, ὑπὸ τῶν ἐμῶν κατηγόρων). While in the *Acharnians* the comic hero confesses to know (ἐπίσταμαι) and to have suffered (ἔπαθον) the consequences of the charge, in the *Apology* the philosopher comparably states that, while knowing what he feels, he does not know (οὐκ οἶδα) the suffering (πεπόνθατε) experienced by the judges.[39] I contend that, in this context, the stylistic similarities between both speeches point to the construction of a subtle comic invective capable of making a sharp distinction between an honest defendant and his wicked adversaries in order to create a certain disposition in the audience.

Responding to a well-known *topos* in forensic trials, the recurring reference to the adversary's capacity to lie can also be found both in the *Acharnians* and

---

39 The close relationship between ἐγώ and ὑμεῖς concerning the effects of lying also highlights these literal proximities.

the *Apology*.⁴⁰ In Plato's text, when Socrates is presented as a spokesman for the truth, the purpose is to unmask the accusers and blame them as shameless deceivers (*Ap.* 17b):

> ... τοῦτό μοι ἔδοξεν αὐτῶν ἀναισχυντότατον εἶναι, εἰ μὴ ἄρα δεινὸν καλοῦσιν οὗτοι λέγειν τὸν τἀληθῆ λέγοντα (...) οὗτοι μὲν οὖν, ὥσπερ ἐγὼ λέγω, ἤ τι ἢ οὐδὲν ἀληθὲς εἰρήκασιν, ὑμεῖς δέ μου ἀκούσεσθε πᾶσαν τὴν ἀλήθειαν.
>
> ... this struck me at the very height of their shamelessness – unless after all my opponents give the title of 'clever speaker' to one who tells the truth (...) As I said, then, they have said little or nothing true; but from me you shall hear nothing but the truth.⁴¹

The two apologies take advantage of the rhetorical nature of defence speeches and rely on a series of commonplace expressions, as noted, which serve to describe the litigiousness and falsehood of their respective adversaries. Furthermore, following another *topos* of legal language, both texts included references to malice (φθόνος, *Ach.* 497) and slander (διαβολή, *Ach.* 502). This formulaic pair plays an important role in Socrates' invective against his indicters when he points a finger at them because of their uselessness (*Ap.* 28a):

> καὶ τοῦτ' ἔστιν ὃ ἐμὲ αἱρεῖ, ἐάνπερ αἱρῇ, οὐ Μέλητος οὐδὲ Ἄνυτος ἀλλ' ἡ τῶν πολλῶν διαβολή τε καὶ φθόνος.
>
> This is what will catch me – if indeed it is going to catch me, not Meletus nor Anytus, but the widespread slander and grudging feelings against me.⁴²

Through these linguistic patterns, Plato manages to construct the negative image of Meletus and Anytus in a precise manner. Not only are their accusations against Socrates presented as false, but their own insignificant personalities make them the inevitable object of retaliatory slander.⁴³ Socrates' accusers share common features with those citizens who represented a paradigmatic type of

---

40 According to Socrates, the function of judges consists of determining the justice of his arguments. In his speech (18a), there is a very clear link between what is right (*dikaios*) and what is true (*alēthēs*). In the *Acharnians*, the second semi-chorus establishes this same analogy between truth and justice after having heard Dicaeopolis' intervention (*Ach.* 497–503). This is also a replication of the vocabulary linked to the verb *legein* and to the idea of *dikaion*, which reinforces the parallelism.
41 Shortly afterwards, Socrates presents his own truth as opposed to the lies of enemies once again (24a). Cf. 17c.
42 Cf. also 18d.
43 Greene, 1920, 71–72.

Aristophanic *kōmōidoumenoi*, namely those prominent political figures who were active in the institutions of the *polis* and made use of the courtrooms to act as public prosecutors to their own benefit. These politicians, described by Sommerstein as the "idols of the tribe", are very often the target of Aristophanes' verbal violence: in fact, half of the victims of slander referred to in Old Comedy clearly belong to this group.[44]

One of the most evident reasons for the comic scorn against them is their proneness to corruption and their lack of sufficient ability or experience to participate in the important affairs of the city. According to Plato, both features are found in a figure such as Meletus, who is ridiculed because of his excessive irresponsibility and unruliness.[45] The problem of young age and carelessness becomes a strong motif in order to justify Socrates' defence and his attacks against his amateurish, yet arrogant, rivals.

The lack of maturity, reliability and experience constitute central concepts for understanding the nature of Plato's intellectual diatribe against Meletus and Anytus. In its universal reach, Socrates' defence does not for instance attempt to distinguish between young and old citizens (*Ap.* 30a). The topic of age seems to be ever-present throughout the *Apology*, not only because Socrates himself acknowledges his advanced age ("This is the first time I have to come to court, seventy years old though I am", *Ap.* 17d), but also because he explicitly refuses to behave like a youngster: "it would not indeed be fitting, gentlemen, for a man of my age to come before you as an adolescent, polishing arguments" (*Ap.* 17c). On the contrary, Meletus is represented as being a young man instilled with the rash recklessness of his early age (*Ap.* 26e):

ἐμοὶ γὰρ δοκεῖ οὑτοσί, ὦ ἄνδρες Ἀθηναῖοι, πάνυ εἶναι ὑβριστὴς καὶ ἀκόλαστος, καὶ ἀτεχνῶς τὴν γραφὴν ταύτην ὕβρει τινὶ καὶ ἀκολασίᾳ καὶ νεότητι γράψασθαι.

This man seems to me, Athenians, to be no respecter of persons, and to be self-indulgent, and to have laid this indictment simply in a sort of disrespect and self-indulgence and youthfulness.

In addition, the issue of age is referred to again when Socrates reminds the judges that, when the first charges were brought against him, they were all still too young (*Ap.* 18c). Although the antithesis between the natural impulse of the

---

44 Sommerstein 1996, 329.
45 Although rejecting the derisive element in the *Apology*, and more specifically Socrates' witty role, Howland 2008 agrees that Meletus is the object of comic disdain and could amount to a humorous character.

youth and the moderation of old citizens is frequent in Old Comedy,⁴⁶ I believe that there is ground here for another textual comparison. The specificities of the problem of age gaps in a legal setting, such as presented in Socrates' invective against his enemies, justifies re-reading the *parabasis* of *Acharnians*, where, immediately after the praise of the poet, the chorus includes a public complaint on behalf of the city's elders who suffered unjustly as a result of the judicial denunciations promoted by young prosecutors (*Ach*. 676–684).

In its invective against the Athenian citizens who disrespected war veterans, the chorus resorts to the image of darkness: in the eyes of these old Acharnian charcoal burners with very little experience in court cases, justice is considered to be a void because, in the face of death, they feel nothing. The metaphorical image resembles here the idea of the lack of perceptions also suggested at the end of the *Apology*, where death is compared to a state of sleep in which feelings are suspended (*Ap*. 40c-d): for the dead, death is "like being nothing and having no perception of anything" (40c). The figure of an old man struggling alone without seeing anything in front of the shadows, without being able to identify his adversaries, is also evoked by Socrates when describing his situation (*Ap*. 18d).

In the *Acharnians*, the chorus points to the way in which young lawyers, comfortable with the new mechanisms of justice, shout well-constructed invectives against old men, taking advantage of the circumstances (*Ach*. 685–691).⁴⁷ The comic ending of the passage includes a hilarious legislative proposal: in the opinion of the chorus, the *polis*, in order to restore justice, has to decree (ψηφίσασθε) a legislative reform that would file the cases according to the age of the parties involved in the dispute (*Ach*. 713–718). The political necessity of bearing in mind the differences of age in order to ensure the right balance in judicial proceedings is also taken into account in the *Apology*: by placing emphasis on his old age, Socrates also presents himself as a victim of ruthless accusers. By depicting the negative characteristics of invective-receivers in similar ways, Socrates' defence speech coincides with the main arguments elaborated by the chorus in the *Acharnians*.

All these passages illustrate that, by resorting to specific rhetorical strategies employed in comedy to retaliate against enemies, Plato lays the groundwork for Socrates' line of defence. Firstly, he follows a pattern of abuse and

---

46 On the systematic presence of old men in Aristophanes, especially in the early plays where they are clashing against young men, see Hubbard 1989.
47 I have dealt with these lines from a legal perspective in Buis 2011. On the complaint against the city in the *parabasis*, see Riu 1995.

counterattack similar to the one launched by the young Aristophanes when promoting the need for justice and truth in the face of unethical denunciations. Secondly, he reproduces the pattern of the chorus' complaint in order to condemn the mistreatment of good old citizens at the hands of an ungrateful *polis* which does not care about its elders. In doing so, the elements of comic invective are reproduced and reframed to fit their new context and provide a discursive platform for active retaliation. The defence strategy includes the moral self-construction of the speaker (the invective-producer), represented by a wise, experienced and self-centered intellectual with the right dose of ludicrous complicity, and the disqualification of the accusers (the invective-receivers), represented by unsophisticated politicians who, taking advantage of their public influence, act as unrestrained and childish demagogues in pursuit of their own selfish profit. However, as I will explore in the next section, Plato's reframing of this scheme adds a new layer of complexity: Socrates behaves like Aristophanes opposing his accusers, but, paradoxically, Aristophanes happened to be Socrates' first adversary. This double role played by the comic playwright could explain the final twist in the strategy: in the following section, I shall argue that, in order to confront comedy, Plato incorporates an inter-poetic dimension into the dynamics of comic invective.

3 Reframing Comic Invective: From Aristophanes to Plato and Back

The literary dialogue proposed in the *Apology*, as explored in the previous section, is rich in strategies that can be traced back to comedy. But far from limiting its scope to the allegations against Socrates presented in the *Clouds*, as is generally accepted, a comparative analysis shows that Plato also exploits many of the comic techniques used by Aristophanes in the *Acharnians*.

That being said, under the new circumstances the negative description of political adversaries presented in Old Comedy is transformed in order to suit the distinctive character of Socrates: Meletus and Anytus are in fact presented as targets of a comic diatribe, just like Cleon. But although Socrates can be identified with Aristophanes as being the target of abuse, at the same time Plato needs to stress the difference between them. Since, according to *Apology* 19c, Aristophanes is considered to stand at the very origin of the legal indictment, Plato has to separate Socrates from those accusations in order to differentiate the philosopher from the comic playwright: a quiet man like Socrates, not interested in conflicts or in the affairs of the city, should prevail against another one who laughed at the city while pretending to protect it (*Ap.* 35b):

> ... τοῦτο αὐτὸ ἐνδείκνυσθαι, ὅτι πολὺ μᾶλλον καταψηφιεῖσθε τοῦ τὰ ἐλεινὰ ταῦτα δράματα εἰσάγοντος καὶ καταγέλαστον τὴν πόλιν ποιοῦντος ἢ τοῦ ἡσυχίαν ἄγοντος.
>
> ... You ought to demonstrate this very point, that you will much rather condemn the man who puts on these pitiful dramas and makes the city the butt of jokes than the man of quiet behaviour.

If the old men of the chorus of the *Acharnians* had to vote (ψηφίσασθε, *Ach.* 714) for a proposal in order to reestablish justice, in the *Apology* a similar vote should be cast (καταψηφιεῖσθε) to release Socrates and convict his oldest accuser, Aristophanes, a man who made fun of the city (καταγέλαστον τὴν πόλιν). Needless to say, the vocabulary in this passage once again recalls Cleon's accusation against Aristophanes as described in *Ach.* 631, where the poet explains that he was accused of ridiculing the city (κωμῳδεῖ τὴν πόλιν). Socrates' words, therefore, give rise to an inter-poetic *agōn* in which his own oratory interacts with comedy.

As already signaled, the conflation of literary genres is a technique inherent to Old Comedy, which frequently returns to tragedy to parody it.[48] This overlapping of tragic and comic discourse becomes evident when Dicaeopolis dresses like Telephus pretending to be someone else (*Ach.* 440–444). Thanks to the intersection of identities, Aristophanes remains concealed behind Dicaeopolis, who in turn is camouflaged under the mask of Telephus. The subversion of the tragic subtext constitutes here a rhetorical strategy that introduces an inter-poetic pattern similar to the one set by Plato when performing the literary construction of Socrates in his dialogues.

Behind the dramatic game of masks between authors and characters instituted both in comedy and the *Apology*, the ultimate goal of comic invective seems to be a serious one. In the *Acharnians*, for example, by delivering useful advice to the citizens from the stage, Dicaeopolis/Aristophanes claims for a just return in exchange for the contributions offered to society (*Ach.* 633–635 and 641–645). Similarly, in the *Apology* Socrates requests special treatment from the city. Instead of punishment, he should be granted a meal at the Prytaneum (*Ap.* 36c–d), which was a privilege reserved for honoured citizens and benefactors of the *polis*. Those intellectuals who risk their own life to offer justice, truth and

---

[48] The frequent mention of *trygōidia* shows Aristophanes' blend of comedy and tragedy. Cf. Taplin 1983; Cavallero 2006; Mauduit 2015.

honesty against unjust, deceitful and unethical accusers, require a special protection from the *dēmos*. But in spite of these obvious similarities the contexts of these rewards are radically different: whereas Dicaeopolis is able to tell the truth only by means of a tragic disguise, Socrates refuses to use supplications and artifices to hide his position: he indicates that he never offered advice to the city in public (*Ap.* 31c). The role played by Socrates in politics is therefore explicitly different from the public activities carried out by Dicaeopolis at the assembly at the beginning of the *Acharnians*.

This disparity can be explained if the broader relationship with democracy in both contexts is compared. Whereas Dicaeopolis encourages real popular participation in the middle of the *ekklēsia*, in the case of Socrates the return to a democratic order seems to have been at the origin of his trial; considered to be an enemy of democracy, the philosopher is charged with crimes allegedly motivated by his sympathy for the oligarchic cause. These underlying political differences are better understood if a last element contributing to the effects of comic invective is considered: the treatment of civic *thorybos*. As frequently stated, the use of exhortations as a popular manifestation in the collective institutions of the *polis* was an important landmark of democratic invective in Athens. The association with invective is evident: *thorybos* represents, in political terms, the verbal violence exerted by the outraged *dēmos* when it publicly expresses its indignation against someone who acts wrongfully.[49] In the *Apology*, as mentioned, Socrates does not hesitate to ask the judges not to scream or cry out (μὴ θορυβεῖτε). This explicit rejection of *thorybos* is pervasive in the speech (cf. μὴ θορυβήσητε, *Ap.* 20e),[50] which is not surprising if we consider Socrates' rejection of popular manifestations. In the *Acharnians*, inversely, the status of *thorybos* is different: Dicaeopolis shows his interest in shouting, interrupting and proclaiming during the opening scene (*Ach.* 37–39).

The profound gap in the treatment of civic *thorybos* can also contribute to our modern understanding of Plato's reframing of comic invective. In the *Acharnians*, after trying to speak at the assembly, Dicaeopolis decides to leave the public space in order to sign a personal peace treaty with the enemy, celebrate a private rural festival and inaugurate his own individual *agora*. In the *Apology*, meanwhile, an inverted order is noticed: Socrates claims to have lived away from the public *agora* but explains that he was forced to come back to the tribunal, against his will, in order to defend himself. The movement from public

---

[49] *Thorybos* amounts to any collective vocal expression, such as shouting, addressed to the speaker; cf. Bers 1985 and Thomas 2011, 171–185.
[50] See also *Ap.* 21a, 27b, 30c.

affairs to personal quietness that can be noticed in Aristophanes' play is now overcome by an opposite movement from personal quietness to public affairs.

In spite of these differences, it seems reasonable to argue that the defence rhetoric in the *Acharnians* could have inspired the construction of Socrates' plea when he runs the risk of being convicted. But at the same time, if this was the case, the need to draw a distinction between the philosopher and the playwright may have contributed to a reframing of the original comic invective in order to adapt it to a completely new political environment.

4 Εἰ καὶ γελοιότερον εἰπεῖν (*Ap.* 30e): Conclusive Remarks

I have identified some common features shared by comedy and the *Apology*, including specific rhetorical arguments employed by the main characters in order to criticise their enemies in front of a civic audience willing to enjoy the pleasures of vituperation and verbal violence. In addition, paying close attention to the staging of comic invective in both the *Acharnians* and the *Apology* reveals some of the elaborate methods employed by Plato to confront comedy and its influence.

I tried to demonstrate here that a textual examination of the *Apology* based on the importance of the rhetorical construction of Socrates' defence can greatly profit from a comparison with Aristophanes' comedy. And to that end, while the *Clouds* is often quoted in order to trace the root of the offences included in Meletus and Anytus' indictment, a comparative approach to the defence strategies employed by Aristophanes in the *Acharnians* can reveal new links and contribute to a better understanding of Plato's verbal hostility towards Socrates' adversaries.

When transplanted into Socrates' speech, the invective presented in the *Acharnians* against Cleon seems to serve a new purpose in the context of Plato's dialogues.[51] In terms of judicial diatribe, the *Apology* responds to the old charges fuelled in Aristophanes' *Clouds* by resorting to a defence tactic similar to what Aristophanes himself had put on the comic stage when accused by Cleon after

---

51 This manipulation of comic technique in order to show the inferiority of comedy could be also found in Isocrates, as stated above; cf. Michelini 1998, 128.

his first comedy.⁵² Aristophanic comedy – which since the staging of *Clouds* had been at the basis of the initial invective against *kōmōidoumenos* Socrates – is strongly echoed in the *Apology* by means of similar strategies. In other words, the techniques provided by Old Comedy could have paradoxically paved the way for the composition of Socrates' legal rhetoric against his enemies in the *polis*, who decided to accuse the philosopher on charges that could be traced back to an exercise of comic invective in the first place.

By setting an inter-poetic *agōn* between comic drama and forensic oratory (which responds to a merge of genres typical to Old Comedy), Plato is coherent with his identification of the comic vein in *Philebus* as a *mixture* of pain and pleasure (μεῖξις μία λύπης τε καὶ ἡδονῆς, *Ap*. 50a) which resides in the ambiguities of malicious amusement.⁵³ At the end, however, this generic blending needs to be left aside in order to show Socrates' moral triumph. In spite of all the amusement involved in his staging of his works, at the end of the day, Plato's oratory could resort to wit but should never be confused with the fiction of comedy, where truths are always lies.⁵⁴ The practical utility of comedy ends here, granting Plato his final victory against Aristophanes and Socrates' adversaries.⁵⁵

"Even if the expression is rather comic" (εἰ καὶ γελοιότερον εἰπεῖν), Plato writes in *Ap*. 30e, the truth is that Athens would hardly find anyone like Socrates again. The philosopher himself makes it absolutely clear that, unlike the "comic" Meletus (ἐπικωμῳδῶν Μέλητος, *Ap*. 31d), he is not being funny: "I shall perhaps strike some of you as joking (παίζειν); but you should know that I shall be telling you nothing but the truth" (*Ap*. 20d). By parodying techniques that resemble those implemented in the verbal attacks of the *Acharnians*, could there have been a smarter way for Plato to represent his own comic diatribe against Aristophanes than using a similar invective? In any case, after Socrates' speech, it was the turn of the audience of the *Apology* to perceive and enjoy the

---

52 From Cleon to Dicaeopolis to Aristophanes to Socrates to Plato, in short, it is possible to find a movement from reality to fiction and then back from fiction to reality.
53 Cf. Dem. 18.3. This reference in *Philebus* to pain and pleasure sets the basis of the so-called superiority (or disparagement) theory. According to Applauso 2019, 11, "[h]umour originates from an act of aggression that stirs an ill-natured laughter at the wrongdoings of other individuals considered morally inferior, and thus bestows a sense of superiority". For a larger discussion of this theory, see the Introduction to this volume.
54 Naas 2016, 14 demonstrated that comedy in Plato is always directed towards a very serious end.
55 Interestingly, the story of the dialogue between Plato and comedy does not end here. In fact, apart from many fragments mentioning the Academy, the philosopher will be named fourteen times in the extant remains of fourth-century Attic comedy, as studied by Farmer 2017.

multilayered *agōn* and to finally side, decide and cast its vote in this subtle textual contest.

Bibliography

Applauso, N. (2019), *Dante's Comedy and the Ethics of Invective in Medieval Italy: Humor and Evil*, Lanham/Boulder/New York/London.

Atkinson, J.E. (1992), 'Curbing the Comedians: Cleon versus Aristophanes and Syracosius' Decree', in: *Classical Quarterly* 42(1), 56–64.

Bers, V. (1985), 'Dikastic Thorybos', in: P. Cartledge and F.D. Harvey (eds.), *Crux: Essays presented to G.E.M. de Ste Croix*, Exeter, 1–15.

Beta, S. (1999), 'La difesa di Diceopoli e le arti retoriche di Euripide negli *Acarnesi* di Aristofane', in: *Seminari romani di cultura classica* 2, 223–233.

Bierl, A. (2002), 'Viel Spott, viel Ehr! - Die Ambivalenz des *onomastì komodeîn* im festlichen und generischen Kontext', in: A. Ercolani (ed.), *Spoudaiogeloion. Form und Funktion der Verspottung in der aristophanischen Komödie*, Stuttgart/Weimar, 169–187.

Brock, R. (1990), 'Plato and Comedy', in: E.M. Craik (ed.), *Owls to Athens. Essays on Classical Subjects Presented to Sir Kenneth Dover*, Oxford, 39–49.

Buis, E.J. (2011), '(En)acting Law on Stage: Time, Comic Rhetoric and Legislative Language in Aristophanes' *Akharnians* (vv. 676–718)', in: *Revue Internationale des Droits de l'Antiquité* 5, 13–38.

Buis, E.J. (2019), *El juego de la ley. La poética cómica del derecho en las obras tempranas de Aristófanes (427–414 a.C.)*, Madrid.

Carey, C. (1994), 'Comic Ridicule and Democracy', in: R. Osborne and S. Hornblower (eds.), *Ritual, Finance, Politics: Athenian Democratic Accounts Presented to David Lewis*, Oxford, 69–83.

Cavallero, P.A. (2006), '*Trygoidía*: la concepción trágica de *Nubes* de Aristófanes', in: *Emerita* 74(1), 89–112.

Chantraine, P. (1999), *Dictionnaire étymologique de la langue grecque*, Paris.

Danielewicz, J.R. (2015), *Parody as Pedagogy in Plato's Dialogues*, PhD Dissertation, Ohio State University.

Degani, E. (1993), 'Aristofane e la tradizione dell'invettiva personale in Grecia', in: I.M. Bremmer and E.W. Handley (eds.), *Aristophane*, Vandoeuvres/Genève, 1–49.

Destrée, P. (2015), '"The Allegedly Best Speaker": A Note On Plato On Aristophanes (*Symp.* 189a7)', in: *Classical Philology* 110(4), 360–366.

Ellis, H. (2015), 'The *Ecclesiazusae* and the *Republic*', in: *Vexillum* 10, 30–45.

Ercolani, A. (2002), 'Sprechende Namen und politische Funktion der Verspottung am Beispiel der Acharner', in: A. Ercolani (ed.), *Spoudaiogeloion. Form und Funktion der Verspottung in der aristophanischen Komödie*, Stuttgart/Weimar, 225–254.

Farmer, M.C. (2017), 'Playing the Philosopher: Plato in Fourth-Century Comedy', in: *American Journal of Philology* 138(1), 1–141.

Feaver, D.D. and Hare, J.E. (1981), 'The *Apology* as an Inverted Parody of Rhetoric', in: *Arethusa* 14, 205–216.

Fisher, N.R.E. (1993), 'Multiple Personalities and Dionysiac Festivals: Dicaeopolis in Aristophanes' *Akharnians*', in: *Greece & Rome* 40, 31–47.
García Soler, M.J. (2013), 'La crítica de los políticos en la Comedia Antigua', in: *Humanitas* 65, 55–70.
Garner, R. (1987), *Law and Society in Classical Athens*, London/Sydney.
Greene, W.C. (1920), 'The Spirit of Comedy in Plato', in: *Harvard Studies in Classical Philology* 31, 63–123.
Hall, E.M. (1995), 'Lawcourt Dramas: the Power of Performance in Greek Forensic Oratory', in: *Bulletin of the Institute of Classical Studies* 40, 39–58.
Halliwell, S. (1984), 'Ancient Interpretations of ὀνομαστὶ κωμῳδεῖν in Aristophanes', in: *Classical Quarterly* n.s. 34(i), 83–88.
Harding, P. (1994), 'Comedy and Rhetoric', in: I. Worthington (ed.), *Persuasion: Greek Rhetoric in Action*, London, 196–221.
Howland, J. (2008), 'Plato's *Apology* as Tragedy', in: *The Review of Politics* 70, 519–546.
Hubbard, T.K. (1989), 'Old Men in the Youthful Plays of Aristophanes', in: T.M. Falkner and J. de Luce (eds.), *Old Age in Greek and Latin Literature*, Albany, 90–113.
Ismard, P. (2017), *L'événement Socrate*, Paris.
Mader, M. (1977), *Das Problem des Lachens und der Komödie bei Platon*, Stuttgart.
Mastromarco, G. (2002), '*Onomastì komodeîn* e *spoudaiogeloion*', in: A. Ercolani (ed.), *Spoudaiogeloion. Form und Funktion der Verspottung in der aristophanischen Komödie*, Stuttgart/Weimar, 205–223.
Mauduit, Ch. (2015), 'La « trygédie » des Nuées', in: C. Cusset and M.P. Noël (eds.), *Meteôrosophistai. Contribution à l'étude des Nuées d'Aristophane* (Cahiers du GITA, 19), Besançon, 57–75.
Michelini, A.N. (1998), 'Isocrates' Civic Invective: *Acharnians* and *On the Peace*', in: *Transactions of the American Philological Association* 128, 115–133.
Naas, M. (2016), 'Plato and the Spectacle of Laughter', in: *Angelaki* 21, 13–26.
Napolitano, M. (2002), '*Onomastì komodeîn* e strategie argomentative in Aristofane (a proposito di Ar. *Ach.* 703–718)', in: A. Ercolani (ed.), *Spoudaiogeloion. Form und Funktion der Verspottung in der aristophanischen Komödie*, Stuttgart/Weimar, 89–103.
Neumann, H. (1966), 'On the Comedy of Plato's Aristophanes', in: *American Journal of Philology* 87 (4), 420–426.
Noël, M.-P. (2000), 'Aristophane et les intellectuels: le portrait de Socrate et des «sophistes» dans les Nuées', in: *Actes du 10ème colloque de la Villa Kérylos à Beaulieu-sur-Mer*, Paris, 111–128.
Ober, J. and Strauss, S. (1990), 'Drama, Political Rhetoric and the Discourse of Athenian Democracy', in: J.J. Winkler and F.I. Zeitlin (eds.), *Nothing to Do with Dionysos? Athenian Drama in its Social Context*, Princeton, 237–270.
Olson, S.D. (ed.) (2002), *Aristophanes, Acharnians*, Oxford.
Papaioannou, S., Serafim, A. and Da Vela, B. (eds.) (2017), *The Theatre of Justice: Aspects of Performance in Greco-Roman Oratory and Rhetoric*, Leiden.
Platter, C. (2007), *Aristophanes and the Carnival of Genres*, Baltimore.
Riess, W. (2012), *Performing Interpersonal Violence: Court, Curse, and Comedy in Fourth-Century BCE Athens*, Berlin.
Riu, X. (1995), 'Gli insulti alla polis nella parabasi degli *Acarnesi*', in: *Quaderni Urbinati di Cultura Classica* 50, 59–66.

Ruffell, I. (2013), 'Humiliation?: Voyeurism, Violence, and Humor in Old Comedy', in: *Helios* 40, 247–277.
Saetta Cottone, R. (2005), *Aristofane e la poetica dell'ingiuria. Per una introduzione alla λοιδορία comica*, Rome.
Segoloni, L.M. (1994), *Socrate a banchetto. Il Simposio di Platone e i Banchettanti di Aristofane*, Rome.
Serafim, A. (2020), 'Comic Invective in the Public Forensic Speeches of Attic Oratory', in: *Hellenica* 68, 23–42.
Sommerstein, A.H. (ed.) (³1992), *The Comedies of Aristophanes, vol. 1. Akharnians*, Warminster (¹1979).
Sommerstein, A.H. (1996), 'How to Avoid Being a *Komodoumenos*', in: *Classical Quarterly* 46, 327–356.
Spatharas, D. (2019), *Emotions, Persuasion, and Public Discourse in Classical Athens*, Berlin/Boston.
Stokes, M.C. (ed.) (1997), *Plato, Apology*, Oxford.
Storey, I.C. (1998), 'Poets, Politicians and Perverts: Personal Humour in Aristophanes', in: *Classics Ireland* 5, 85–134.
Strauss, L. (1996), *Socrates and Aristophanes*, Chicago.
Sutton, D.F. (1988), 'Dicaeopolis as Aristophanes, Aristophanes as Dicaeopolis', in: *Liverpool Classical Monthly* 13, 105–108.
Tanner, S.M. (2017), *Plato's Laughter. Socrates as Satyr and Comical Hero*, New York.
Taplin, O. (1983), 'Tragedy and Trugedy', in: *Classical Quarterly* 33, 331–333.
Thomas, R. (2011), 'And You, the Demos, Made an Uproar: Performance, Mass Audiences, and Text in the Athenian Democracy', in: A.P.M.H. Lardinois, J.H. Blok and M.G.M. van der Poel (eds.), *Sacred Words: Orality, Literacy, and Religion*, Leiden/Boston, 161–187.
Todd, S.C. (2005), 'Law, Theatre, Rhetoric and Democracy in Classical Athens', in: *European Review of History* 12, 63–79.
Treu, M. (2013), 'Le poète comique comme maître de vérité: *Les Acharniens* d'Aristophane', *Pallas* 91, 41–47.
van Steen, G.A.H. (2004), 'Aspects of "Public Performance" in Aristophanes' *Akharnians*', in: *L'Antiquité Classique* 63, 211–224.
Wilson Nightingale, A. (2000), *Genres in Dialogue: Plato and the Construct of Philosophy*, Cambridge.

George Kazantzidis
"You are Mad!" Allegations of Insanity in Greek Comedy and Rhetoric

Abstract: This chapter discusses some of the ways in which allegations of insanity across Greek comedy and oratory can be approached as points of convergence between the two genres. Kazantzidis shows that comic slander revolving around the "you are mad!" accusation is worth exploring deeper than we usually do: this is not just random abuse, but it carries with it a complex cultural significance, pointing as it does directly to the world of the Assembly and, along with it, to a masculine trope of abuse detectable in rhetorical settings. At the same time, although insanity in rhetoric can be a tremendously important issue (the accusation that one is "out of his mind", when backed up by sufficient evidence, is no laughing matter), it nonetheless retains a considerably comic charge within it: the idea that madness has no fixed limits and can therefore always surpass itself; the notion that there is no such thing as a definitive diagnosis of madness; the unsettling view that madness can infect entire crowds of people – all these concepts have a distinctively potent presence in comedy and may have passed from there to the delicate prose and word of the Greek orators.

A common feature shared by Greek comedy and rhetoric is that both genres regularly stage characters and speakers accusing their opponents of being mad or out of their mind and (allegedly) insane. This chapter attempts to investigate this common ground in two intersecting and complementary ways: on the one hand, through a close reading of Aristophanes, *Eccl.* 250–251, it proposes to show that some of the instances of comic slander revolving around an opponent's alleged insanity owe a lot, and are designed as sustained allusions, to the practices of contemporary oratory. On the other hand, it explores the possibility that when an orator is resorting to this kind of language, labelling individuals or larger groups of people as "mad", he might be engaging in dialogue with the comic tradition, not necessarily in the sense that he is aiming for a specifically "comic effect" but, more broadly, by virtue of the fact that the discourse of exaggeration attached to madness as well as the idea that madness can be a mat-

---

I would like to thank Andreas Serafim, Sophia Papaioannou and the anonymous reviewers for their valuable comments and feedback.

ter of perspective – something to be debated and be decided by people – are distinctively comic notions.

1 Rhetoric in Comedy

The opening scene of Aristophanes' *Ecclesiazusae* presents us Praxagora rehearsing the speech she is about to give in the Assembly of men and receiving all sorts of compliments from the women who have been gathering under her leadership. At some point, one of those women becomes worried and asks what will happen in case Cephalus offends Praxagora. The female protagonist of Aristophanes' play has the answers ready to hand (241–253):

> Γυ.ᵝ εὖ γ' ὦ γλυκυτάτη Πραξαγόρα, καὶ δεξιῶς.
> πόθεν, ὦ τάλαινα, ταῦτ' ἔμαθες οὕτω καλῶς;
> Πρ. ἐν ταῖς φυγαῖς μετὰ τἀνδρὸς ᾤκησ' ἐν Πυκνί.
> ἔπειτ' ἀκούουσ' ἐξέμαθον τῶν ῥητόρων.
> Γυ.ᵃ οὐκ ἐτὸς ἄρ', ὦ μέλ', ἦσθα δεινὴ καὶ σοφή.
> καί σε στρατηγὸν αἱ γυναῖκες αὐτόθεν
> αἱρούμεθ', ἢν ταῦθ' ἁπινοεῖς κατεργάσῃ.
> ἀτὰρ ἢν Κέφαλός σοι λοιδορῆται προσφθαρείς,
> πῶς ἀντερεῖς πρὸς αὐτὸν ἐν τἠκκλησίᾳ;
> Πρ. φήσω παραφρονεῖν αὐτόν.
> Γυ.ᵃ ἀλλὰ τοῦτό γε
> ἴσασι πάντες.
> Πρ.   ἀλλὰ καὶ μελαγχολᾶν.
> Γυ.ᵃ καὶ τοῦτ' ἴσασιν.
> Πρ.   ἀλλὰ καὶ τὰ τρύβλια
> κακῶς κεραμεύειν, τὴν δὲ πόλιν εὖ καὶ καλῶς.

[WOMAN^B] O darling Praxagora, what amazing speech! Where on earth, my dear, did you learn rhetorical skills? [PRAXAGORA] In the war I lived with my husband on the Pnyx: I used to listen to speakers and learn their words. [WOMAN^A] That explains how you made such a terribly clever speech. We women will now elect you on the spot to be our general and carry out your plans. [*Thinking*] But what if confounded Cephalus shouts abuse? What kind of response will you give him in the meeting? [PRAXAGORA] I'll tell him his mind's all muddled. [WOMAN^A] But everyone knows that already. [PRAXAGORA] I'll say that he's demented! [WOMAN^A] They know that too. [PRAXAGORA] Then I'll say his pottery is dreadful stuff, and his politics are potty![1]

---

1 Translation in Halliwell 1997, 163.

Little attention has been paid by scholars to Praxagora's use of παραφρονεῖν (250) and μελαγχολᾶν (251) in these lines. At first sight, it seems as though Praxagora is randomly picking up idiomatic terms of abuse, exaggerating Cephalus' foolishness and incompetence to the point of (colloquial) insanity. Indeed, a quick look at Aristophanes' comedies reveals a considerable number of characters resorting to this kind of language in contexts of confrontation. We could think, for instance, of the heated disagreement between Pheidippides and Strepsiades in *Clouds* 816–833: exasperated by his father's nonsensical words – αἰβοῖ· τί ληρεῖς; (829) – the son tells him that he must be "mad", letting himself being carried away like this by "lunatics" such as Socrates and Chaerephon (832–833, σὺ δ᾽ ἐς τοσοῦτον τῶν μανιῶν ἐλήλυθας / ὥστ᾽ ἀνδράσιν πείθει χολῶσιν;). Likewise, when in *Wealth* 346–366 Chremylus is accused by Blepsidemus of having stolen gold and silver from the temple, he responds first by saying that his friend is "talking nonsense" (360, παῦσαι φλυαρῶν); as Blepsidemus keeps repeating the accusation, Chremylus, feeling extremely offended by that stage, reciprocates by calling him "completely insane" (366, μελαγχολᾷς, ὦνθρωπε, νὴ τὸν οὐρανόν). Praxagora's handy response could be seen as falling in line with this pattern: if Cephalus insults her, she will insult him back – and a good way for doing this is by declaring in public, in more than one way, if necessary, that he is "out of his mind".

But Praxagora, as she confesses, has been "overhearing" the way men speak on Pnyx (244, ἀκούουσ᾽ ἐξέμαθον τῶν ῥητόρων); and a great deal of what she says, at this point of the play but also subsequently, has to be considered as casting light on a rhetorical discourse which the comedy's female protagonist appears to have processed rather adequately.[2] Just as the disguised women have been said a few lines above to imitate the dress and aspect of men,[3] so does the best among them, Praxagora, move a step further by reproducing successfully the way men "talk". With that in mind, it is by no means a coincidence that Praxagora responds that she will defend herself *by invoking her opponent's insanity*. I would suggest that the reference to insanity here is not incidental, that is to say, it does not appear as a random instance of colloquial abuse,[4] but emerges instead as an echo of the meticulous overhearing Praxagora has been doing: people in the audience, I argue, would have recalled at this point, with a

---

[2] On Praxagora's successful training and the numerous sustained allusions to rhetoric throughout the play, see Rothwell 1990, 77–101; Freydberg 2008, 120; Ruffell 2018, 333. Cf. Hubbard 2007.
[3] See the discussion in Compton-Engle 2015, 75.
[4] As, for instance, maintained by Langholf 1990, 48 and Sommerstein 1998, 161.

smile of recognition, how often the accusation of insanity was actually heard in a public setting.

But what kind of insanity would that be precisely? Praxagora's first immediate reply is designed to cast Cephalus as a παράφρων, a driveling "fool" (250). And when she is told that this will not be enough – "because everyone knows it already" – she essentially adds that in that case she will (go so far as to) call him *properly* insane (251, ἀλλὰ καὶ μελαγχολᾶν). In commenting on μελαγχολᾶν in these lines, Andreas Willi remarks that "in comedy μελαγχολάω is a general term for 'being mad' (e.g. *Av.* 14; *Eccl.* 251, *after the synonym παραφρονεῖν* [emphasis added])".[5] Willi's observation fails to take into account the obvious fact that ἀλλὰ καί in *Eccl.* 251 is meant to add emphasis,[6] by way of introducing a related yet clearly stronger alternative to παραφρονεῖν. It also ignores the fact that, although indeed colloquially distributed across fifth century BC everyday idiom, μελαγχολᾶν nonetheless retains, to a substantial degree, its medical associations in Aristophanes' comedies – as, for example, when we find it being suggestively used by Cario to describe Chremylus' poor mental condition after what seems to be a failed visit to Apollo "the physician" (*Wealth* 12).[7] What is more, references to "bile", χολή, as we have seen above,[8] regularly occur in contexts of escalation, adding an extra layer of (medical) meaning and intensity in cases where a character's sanity is being increasingly contested. At the risk of some generalisation, we could say that when a comic character in Aristophanes wishes to say that someone is "out of his mind" – and to mean this as a figure of speech – it is expected that he will resort to the use of such verbs as ληρεῖν/ φλυαρεῖν, παραφρονεῖν or μαίνεσθαι. But when the point is specifically made that one's behaviour is not just foolish and unreasonable but insane in an exceptional way – almost to the point of calling for a medical cure, as it were – then 'bile' enters the picture.[9]

Praxagora, I submit, is deliberately using in *Eccl.* 251 a stronger, medically coloured term – a product of her overhearing of "men's talk" on Pnyx. Her choice of words echoes the high currency and strategic use of insanity language

---

[5] Willi 2003, 64.
[6] See Ussher 1973, 109.
[7] *Pl.* 11–12: ἰατρὸς ὢν καὶ μάντις, ὥς φασιν, σοφὸς / μελαγχολῶν τ' ἀπέμπεμψέ μου τὸν δεσπότην. There is a calculated contrast between ἰατρός and μελαγχολῶντα in these lines: although Apollo is a reputed physician, Cario complains, he nonetheless let his master go away with a seriously demented state of mind. The joke here is more effective if we assume that the audience would have recognised in μελαγχολᾶν some sort of "clinical" language. Cf. Padel 1992, 24.
[8] See *Clouds* 816–833; *Wealth* 360–366.
[9] Cf. Ar. *Wealth* 66.

in rhetorical contexts where the allegation that someone is "out of his mind" is not thrown lightly, but aims to present the opponent as practically unable to think reasonably. For instance, in the legal context of a trial, to say that someone is "insane" is an extremely serious speech-act which suffices by itself to raise quite a few eyebrows in the audience, leaving the one who is being stigmatised with insanity, or the person who is speaking in defence of the "madman", to explain convincingly why this is not the case. An intriguing parallel to Ar. *Eccl.* 250–251 can be actually found in ps.-Demosthenes, *Against Olympiodorus* 52–56.[10] Towards the end of that speech, Callistratus is mounting an attack against Olympiodorus, his brother-in-law, by notifying the judges that the defendant has been displaying symptoms of insanity – and therefore his decision to spend his money on a courtesan whom he has installed in his house, instead of giving what is due to Callistratus, should be made invalid by law. Callistratus first draws attention to Olympiodorus' bizarre behaviour by saying that "he has lost his wits" and that "his mind has gone astray", ἀλλὰ διέφθαρται, ὦ ἄνδρες δικασταί, καὶ παραφρονεῖ (§52).[11] It is soon revealed that the reason behind this is the courtesan involved, who is leading Olympiodorus "further along the road to madness", ποιοῦσα τουτονὶ περαιτέρω μαίνεσθαι (§53). "For when a man has made an agreement and has contracted willingly with a willing partner and has sworn an oath, isn't it madness (πῶς γὰρ οὐ μαίνεται)", Callistratus asks, "for him to think he is under no obligation to carry out any of it?" (§54). At the end of §55 the question resurfaces: "isn't the defendant manifestly mad and out of his mind" (οὗτος δὲ πῶς οὐ καταφανῶς μαίνεται καὶ παραφρονεῖ) when he decides to waste his life with a courtesan? On the face of it, all these references to madness seem to be rhetorically exaggerated, meaning to slander Olympiodorus and expose him as an unreliable character.

But §56 holds in store an intriguing twist; for in that part of the text Callistratus reminds the judges of Solon's law according to which all transactions made under the influence of a woman should be held invalid, since being under the influence of a woman is a clear sign of madness. For what concerns us here, it is worth observing that, just before reaching the climactic point of invoking Solon's law, Callistratus draws attention, one last time, to the defendant's insanity; and it is in this emotionally intense and highly charged context that μελαγχολᾶν makes its meaningful appearance in the speech (§56):

---

[10] For the ps.-Demosthenic text and Olympiodorus' presumed insanity, see the discussion in Wohl 2010, 173–181.
[11] For the ps.-Demosthenic text I reproduce the translation by Scafuro 2011.

Ὀλυμπιόδωρος μὲν οὑτοσὶ τοιοῦτός ἐστιν ἄνθρωπος, οὐ μόνον ἄδικος, ἀλλὰ καὶ <u>μελαγ-χολᾶν</u> δοκῶν ἅπασιν τοῖς οἰκείοις καὶ τοῖς γνωρίμοις τῇ προαιρέσει τοῦ βίου, καὶ ὅπερ Σόλων ὁ νομοθέτης λέγει, παραφρονῶν ὡς οὐδεὶς πώποτε παρεφρόνησεν ἀνθρώπων, γυναικὶ πειθόμενος πόρνῃ.

Olympiodorus here is this sort of man – not only dishonest but also, in the opinion of all his relatives and acquaintances, *utterly insane* because of the choices he has made in the way he lives; as Solon the Lawgiver says, no madman is ever so out of his mind as the man under the influence of a woman who is a prostitute.

Moments before he draws the speech to a close, Callistratus is clearly doing his best to establish, beyond the shadow of a doubt, that something is not quite right with Olympiodorus, (a) by invoking the opinion of the defendant's relatives and friends and (b) by using precisely the kind of language that should have been meant to sound as medical and technical – and therefore, as conclusive – as it could get.[12] Though obviously linked to παραφρονεῖν, μελαγχολᾶν in the rhetorical text above adds an extra layer of (pathological) significance and is designed in a way to clear out any misunderstandings that Callistratus might have been speaking figuratively up to this point: Olympiodorus is not just "insane", παράφρων, in the common, everyday sense of the term; he is mentally compromised, literally.[13] I suggest that this is exactly the context in which we should place and understand Praxagora's nuanced reference to the two terms in *Eccl.* 250–251: if the claim that Cephalus is "out of his mind" will not be enough, she will then declare him *properly* insane.

So far I have been considering the possibility that Praxagora's insulting and abusive language in *Eccl.* 250–251 is the language of men at court; and I have

---

12 Interestingly, this is the only use of μελαγχολᾶν in the entire corpus of the orators of the fourth century BC.

13 Compare Demosthenes' depiction of Aristogeiton as – literally – a psychopath and a freak who is even said at one point to indulge in cannibalism (*Or.* 25.61): ... ὡς δ' εἰς τοῦθ' ἧκεν, ἀπεσθίει τὴν ῥῖνα τἀνθρώπου. Aristogeiton's unstable nature is conveyed by the use of the word ἀπόνοια (§§33–35): while the term refers to "recklessness" in general, a close reading of the speech reveals that in this specific case it is also meant to describe someone who is mentally unhinged. Aristogeiton is "implacable, restless and unsociable" (ἄσπειστος, ἀνίδρυτος, ἄμεικτος, §52); he makes his way through the market-place "like a snake or a scorpion, with sting erect" (ὥσπερ ἔχις ἢ σκορπίος ἠρκὼς τὸ κέντρον, §52). This is not the place to get into details about Aristogeiton's pathology and to discuss its possible debt to medical descriptions of misanthropy and unsociable behaviour. Suffice it to note that, just as in the case of Olympiodorus (whose insanity is construed through the employment of different "diagnostic" criteria), Aristogeiton's medical profiling appears to involve insanity *in a literal sense*. Demosthenes' insinuation is clearly that the man is not quite right in his mind.

been suggesting that her choice of words serves as an echo of the formal insanity allegation, meaning to present the opponent as mentally incapacitated. If this is the case, we could then speak of an instance of comic invective which allows us a glimpse to how character assassination is working in an oratorical setting. Comedy and oratory intersect at this point through the blurring of different layers of frivolity and seriousness: what appears at first sight as a case of comic slandering ("you are mad!") can have some serious repercussions when it leaves the relatively innocuous space of a private confrontation and enters the context of a crafted speech that is formally delivered in front of others.

I would now like to proceed and explore in more detail the gendered dynamics of Praxagora's pointed emphasis on insanity. There is little doubt that the world of men is one that makes no sense to women, and that when the men assume their formal identity as speakers and orators, the only thing they succeed in is to sound all the more "insane". The "Assembly" is symbolically conceived as a metaphor for masculine lunacy; the decrees of men, as one of Praxagora's female companions puts it early in the play, are "like the ravings of drunkards" (139, ὥσπερ μεθυόντων ἐστὶ παραπεπληγμένα).

In this incomprehensible male world Praxagora participates appropriately, by manipulating insanity rhetorically, and by casting her male opponents as "mad" (thus, in a way, exposing them for what they really are). But her usage of παραφρονεῖν and, especially, μελαγχολᾶν can be taken a step further: I am thinking here of how a woman's boisterous statement that she will formally declare a man insane, in front of other men, would have naturally reminded people in Aristophanes' audience of how often women were linked to madness in contexts of public (legal) disputes since they were regularly cited as evidence that a man, who was acting under their influence, was lapsing to insanity. In contrast to this, Aristophanes' fantasy revolt represents an overturning of the established order: this time a woman emerges from passivity and, rather than being objectified and cited as mute evidence for a male person's insanity, she becomes herself the accuser. In other words, while in a male dominated courtroom a woman is usually the *symptom* of madness, in Aristophanes she becomes the authority who passes the "medical diagnosis".

The ps.-Demosthenic text cited above appeals, as we have seen, to a law decreed by Solon according to which a man with no natural-born legitimate sons of his own was allowed to adopt or bequeath property in a will unless he was "mentally compromised because of old age or drugs or disease, or was under the influence of woman, and was not quite right in his mind due to one of these factors".[14] The text of the law ambiguously – and, certainly, deliberately – blends mental incapacity and a woman's influence within the same conceptual and legal space: men, on the one hand, stand for reason, while women, on the other, are presented as by definition an unsettling factor that compromises male sanity. The legal script that is thereby produced lies intriguingly close to the stuff of comedy. We need only bring to mind here the confrontation between Bdelycleon, the controlling young son, and Philocleon, the "crazy" old father, in Aristophanes' *Wasps*. Philocleon is notoriously suffering from a "strange sickness", a mad obsession with trying cases in the courtroom (more on this below). But as Victoria Wohl has shown, there is also a sexual aspect in Philocleon's lapsing to insanity; in a sense, he "is the father we have come to know from inheritance law. At once impotent and libidinous – a juxtaposition neatly illustrated when he enters at the end of the play, leading a naked flute-girl by his 'rotten rope' – this old man is characterised above all by his immoderate enjoyment".[15]

In the "comedies" presented in the courtroom, young relatives are likewise shaped as restraining figures, casting doubt on the sanity of older men. Women in these cases are virtually absent: we do not get to hear what they have to say, and we encounter them instead as mute, secondary "characters" whose mention only serves as a proof that insanity is at play. It is only when we consider this deeply biased cultural context that we can appreciate the dynamics and potency of Praxagora's claim in *Eccl.* 250–251, a claim made even more effective, as I argue, through the rhetorical resonance of legal overtones: the one who is going to make use of the insanity appeal in Aristophanes' turned-upside-down world is a woman; and she is planning to do it by using precisely the kind of masculine language which orators use in these occasions.[16]

2 Comedy in Oratory

My argument up to this point has built around the hypothesis that comic offensive language involving insanity should by no means be dispensed with as a simple instance of colloquial abuse, but it can be explored instead as throwing light to actual rhetorical practice. I would now like to proceed and examine

---

14 Demosthenes 46.14. Cf. Isaeus 2.14 with Wohl 2010, 171–172.
15 Wohl 2010, 179.
16 Cf. Ruffell 2018, 342: In Aristophanes, adult women do not "accuse individuals of madness: the only exception is when Praxagora is specifically imitating a male speaker".

whether comedy might have helped to shape, at least to some extent, accusations of insanity as these appear in the speeches of the orators.[17] I should stress that I am not so much interested in the potential "comic effect" of such accusations that are used in orations (something that is hard to establish) but, more generally, in the emerging conceptual affiliations between oratorical and comic discourse when it comes to calling someone mad. In the speeches that I explore, insanity is mainly designated with the word μανία which is certainly more charged when compared to the use of ληρεῖν/φλυαρεῖν: while these two words are employed by orators to present an opponent as "talking nonsense",[18] μανία, even when used in a clearly figurative sense, implicates loss of reason in a more pointed and emphatic fashion.

2.1 Way Too Much Madness

Solon's law, briefly discussed above, exaggerates madness by means of presenting it as something quantifiable. While we tend to think of madness in absolute terms (once someone has abandoned the realm of sanity, s/he is considered *in*sane), oratory yields a picture according to which madness comes in different sizes, as it were. So, when we are being reminded by Callistratus of Solon's law, we are essentially invited to think that Olympiodorus is not just a common παράφρων, but a madman who has *exceeded* the regular limits of παραφροσύνη (παραφρονῶν ὡς οὐδεὶς πώποτε παρεφρόνησεν ἀνθρώπων). In a related manner, it is typical among the orators to draw attention to the "quantity" of madness involved in a false and misguided action, usually with the stock phrase τοσαύτη μανία.[19] One of the best examples is provided by Demosthenes, *On the Chersonese* 28: to force Diopeithes to return from Hellespont to Athens so that he will stand trial for misconduct sounds like a reasonable choice, as the speaker observes. By contrast, to waste money and send a second general to Hellespont in order to supervise Diopeithes would make no sense at all: "it would be the height of madness", τοῦτο γ' ἐστὶν ὑπερβολὴ μανίας.[20]

These passages reveal that, while madness has its fixed, identifiable limits (and, therefore, it can be used as a point of reference in comparison to which a

---

[17] For rhetoric turning an eye on comedy, see Harding 1994; for comic *ēthopoiia* and stereotyping in Greek rhetoric, see Serafim 2017, 92–99.
[18] See Kidd 2014, 20–26.
[19] See e.g. Demosthenes, *On the False Embassy* 260; *Against Eubulides* 64; Isaeus, *Cleonymus* 34; Isocrates, *Trapeziticus* 47.
[20] Ὑπερβολὴ μανίας is a hapax phrase in ancient Greek literature.

person's absurd behaviour can be measured and assessed), these limits are essentially open to being extended and revised. The fact that there can be such a thing as a "hyperbole" of madness clearly suggests that certain kinds of behaviour look far-fetched even by the standards of craziness, and that this craziness retains always the potential of becoming expanded.

It is tempting to associate this idea with comedy; for while tragedy presents madness in a more or less conservative way (i.e. as a disease with a predictable pattern of divine cause and effect, and a characteristic set of symptoms through which it manifests itself), Aristophanes' plays toy with the notion that madness occupies an ever-expanding space, constantly absorbing under its clinical register new territories of aberrant behaviour.[21] This is precisely the point in the opening scene of the *Peace* where one of the servants introduces Trygaeus to the audience by saying that his master's madness (feeding a huge dung beetle on whose back he wants to ride and reach the sky) is "brand new", ὁ δεσπότης μου μαίνεται καινὸν τρόπον (54). The servant is focusing here on the *mode* of Trygaeus' madness, but it would be fair to argue that the notion of intensity is also involved: after all, to say that nobody has been mad *this way* before could fairly well be a way of simultaneously pointing to the fact that nobody has been *that* mad before.

Philocleon's "strange disease" (νόσον ἀλλόκοτον, 71) in the *Wasps* invites a similar interpretation. Once more, the opening scene could be read as a delicate comment on how an established list of aberrant behaviours (all of them having as their common denominator the idea of *fixating* on certain things; see esp. 77 (ἀλλὰ 'φιλο' μέν ἐστιν ἀρχὴ τοῦ κακοῦ) could be challenged and (re)opened so as to accommodate new types of madness. As is revealed by Xanthias at 87–88, the old master has been displaying an obsession with the court, the like of which no man has shown before: φράσω γὰρ ἤδη τὴν νόσον τοῦ δεσπότου/ φιληλιαστής ἐστιν ὡς οὐδεὶς ἀνήρ (compare this with the ps.-Demosthenic παραφρονῶν ὡς οὐδεὶς πώποτε παρεφρόνησεν ἀνθρώπων). The emphasis on intensity here is obvious–this is not just a random manifestation of abnormal behaviour, but one which can be only conveyed by means of an overstatement. I argue that such instances of comic overstatement lie at the background of what at a later stage assumes the concrete form of a rhetorical exaggeration of insanity. The effect of this exaggeration, when employed by orators, is not necessarily comic, but its pedigree may well have been.

---

21 For a recent insightful comparison between comic and tragic tropes of madness, see Singer 2018.

2.2 Madness in the Shaping

In *Clouds* 844–846, Pheidippides, feeling at a loss with his father's absurd ideas, asks:

> οἴμοι τί δράσω παραφροῦντος τοῦ πατρός;
> πότερον παρανοίας αὐτὸν εἰσαγαγὼν ἕλω,
> ἢ τοῖς σοροπηγοῖς τὴν μανίαν αὐτοῦ φράσω;
>
> What on earth should I do? My father's lost his wits. Should I get a court order and have him declared insane? Or even prepare for his death and order his coffin?[22]

The important thing to notice in these lines is that the emerging issue of insanity is framed by a question – a question which openly invites the audience to participate, as it were, in the making of the decision as to whether Strepsiades is properly mad or not. Again, a contrast with tragedy would be instructive: while the information that someone has gone mad is normally conveyed by tragic characters in a fairly conclusive and definitive way, madness in comedy is more labile as a notion, its diagnosis being constantly under revision and reshaping (we could think here, for instance, of how certain comic dialogues revolve around two characters accusing each other of insanity[23] – the point being that "mad" behaviour *can* be a matter of perspective, and thus admits of no fixed definition and diagnosis – or how in certain cases we cannot really tell whether a "mad" character has been cured or not).[24] What is more, the audience is not just watching, but is invited to actively ponder[25] who the real madman is, and wherein true madness lies. In this context, there is nothing to guarantee a uniform response; in fact, the comic effect derives in part from the fact that what is considered sane by certain people in the audience (as in the play itself) is deemed insane by others, and vice versa.[26]

The rhetorical space of political and forensic disputes is by definition the place where insanity, even in the austerely clinical sense of the term, transpires to defy a conclusive diagnosis; whether someone has "lost his wits" or not is by no means as concretely identifiable as a physical impairment, and therefore provides a matter for debate: thus, while someone can be dragged to the court

---

22 Translation in Halliwell 2016, 55.
23 See e.g. the dispute between Pheidippides and Strepsiades in *Clouds* 816–819.
24 This is especially the case with Philocleon in the *Wasps*. See Sidwell 1990.
25 Perhaps also shout out an answer, as happens in oratory; cf. Demosthenes 18.52. I owe this observation to Andreas Serafim.
26 Cf. Ruffell 2018, 336.

with the accusation of insanity, on the basis of what is taken by the accuser to be firm, incontestable evidence, may be judged in the end to be sane. This is something that the orators know well and thus they often invite the audience to think *with* them on the issue of whether a certain kind of behaviour could actually qualify as a sign of insanity. Consider, for instance, the following passage from Demosthenes, *Philippic* 3.54: it is impossible, the orator claims, to defeat the enemies of the city until their servants, who reside "within our very walls", have been chastised. "And that", he continues,

> as all heaven is my witness, you will never be able to do; but you have reached such a height of folly or of madness or – I know not what to call it, for this fear too has often haunted me, that some demon is driving you to your doom (ἀλλ' εἰς τοῦτ' ἀφῖχθε μωρίας ἢ παρανοίας ἢ οὐκ ἔχω τι λέγω – πολλάκις γὰρ ἐπελήλυθε καὶ τοῦτο φοβεῖσθαι, μὴ τι δαιμόνιον τὰ πράγματ' ἐλαύνῃ), that from love of calumny or envy or ribaldry, or whatever your motive may be, you clamor for a speech from these hirelings.[27]

Is it just pure stupidity, or some sort of madness, or, worse even, some kind of demonic possession that is ailing you? Demosthenes asks. We are familiar with this escalating mode from comedy, especially from cases where comic characters start with the assumption that nonsensical behaviour is a sign of foolishness, only to soon reach the conclusion that what they are actually dealing with is a case of madness proper.[28] But Demosthenes' wondering is what is most interesting here; for while presenting himself as having reached no clear conclusion as yet – and, therefore, as exploring various possibilities – the orator does not undermine his point but instead he is reinforcing it; and he does so by means of engaging the audience in helping him out, as it were, make up his mind. There is a subtle process here during which madness is being constructed through a direct appeal to the audience's cultural idiom and sensitivities: "I am so bewildered by this foolish behaviour that I wonder whether I should call it madness, wouldn't you do the same?" Demosthenes seems to be asking implicitly.[29] If there is a semantic stretch involved in the (figurative) deployment of the word "madness" here, the orator is perfectly willing to endorse it, with the audience's permission.

---

27 Translation in Vince 1930.
28 See Ar. *Clouds* 816–833; *Wealth* 346–366.
29 Compare the rhetorical question addressed to the audience in Dem. *For Phormio* 48, εἰς τοῦθ' ἥκεις μανίας (τι γὰρ ἂν ἄλλο τις εἴποι;) ὥστε οὐκ αἰσθάνει... and the presentation of madness as an open-ended issue for thought and debate in *Against Meidias* 69, ἐμοὶ δ', ὃς εἴτε τις, ὦ ἄνδρες Ἀθηναῖοι, βούλεται νομίσαι μανίαν (μανία γὰρ ἴσως ἐστὶν ὑπὲρ δύναμίν τι ποιεῖν).

Rhetoric operates in this instance on a comic mode: rather than present madness as a fixed and conclusively defined concept (in the way in which we encounter it, for instance, in tragedy), comedy stages madness instead as an issue open for debate. Pheidippides' question above ("should I get my father certified on grounds of insanity?") is representative, as I pointed out, of a wider comic tendency to present madness as having its meaning under construction, and to involve the audience in the shaping of that meaning.[30] In Aristophanes' world, insanity is not so much a matter of a concretely identifiable mental impairment as it is a social and cultural construction that depends on the perspective through which one is approaching it (women, for example, might find what men do insane at the very same moment that men think of women as mad;[31] a character who gives the impression of a madman might turn out in the end to be perfectly reasonable,[32] and so on). It is precisely this semantically open and fluid environment in which comic madness circulates that allows Aristophanic characters to use it freely, blending it with folly, turning it into a synonym for silliness, exaggerating it rhetorically and ultimately manipulating it conceptually in order to achieve their purposes. This, I suggest, gives rise to an idiom of madness, which orators pick up[33] at a later stage, thereby establishing a further thread of engagement with the comic tradition.

2.3 Madness and the Civic Body

A final point of comparison that I would like to pursue briefly has to do with the (metaphorical) attachment of the label "madness" to larger groups of people, sometimes extending even to the entire civic body. Consider the following passage from Demosthenes, *On the False Embassy* 260:

---

30 For the open-ended nature of comic madness, see Ruffell 2018.
31 Aristophanes' *Lysistrata* (more on which below) is a good example.
32 As, for instance, Chremylus in Aristophanes' *Wealth*.
33 By "picking up" here I do not mean to suggest a one-directional relationship according to which it is only the orators who look at comedy and make use of its concepts of insanity. This dialogue, as I argued in the first section of this chapter, can also work the other way around, when a comedian alludes to the rhetorical use of allegations of insanity. That said, given that our main surviving orators produce their work during the fourth century BC, that is, when comic insanity had already assumed a concrete and clearly identifiable form, it is possible that certain points of convergence could be read as instances where oratory turns an eye on the genre of comedy.

> Yet, this infatuation, this hankering after Philip, men of Athens, until very recently had only destroyed the predominance of the Thessalians and their national prestige, but now it is already sapping their independence, for some of their citadels are actually garrisoned by Macedonians. It has invaded Peloponnesus (εἰς Πελοπόννησον δ' εἰσελθὸν) and caused the massacres at Elis. It infected those unhappy people with such delirious insanity (καὶ τοσαύτης παρανοίας καὶ μανίας ἐνέπλησε τοὺς ταλαιπώρους ἐκείνους) that, to overmaster one another and to gratify Philip, they stained their hands with the blood of their own kindred and fellow-citizens.[34]

"They were all mad to think that Philip would help them!", Demosthenes exclaims; and though what he describes is a series of catastrophic, tragic events, which on the face of it seems to exclude any kind of association – however distant and elusive – with comedy, the way in which madness is eventually presented by the orator, as a spreading disease that infects entire civic bodies, has something comic in it. Once again, I should clarify that by the use of the term "comic" I do not mean to narrowly refer to a comic effect, but rather to establish a line of connection with the way in which madness is distinctively shaped in comedy.

Tragic madness can of course affect large groups of people,[35] but normally it is personalised; it is inflicted upon individuals, isolating them from the community to which they belong and disrupting any meaningful relation between the patient and those surrounding him/her. By contrast, comic madness, precisely by virtue of the fact that it can be semantically stretched so as to absorb folly and (political) incompetence in a broader sense,[36] spreads, fairly often, as a communal evil across the civic body: we could say, that compared to its tragic counterpart, comic madness is far more infectious a disease. So, for example, the women in *Lysistrata* tend to think of men's obsession with war as a sign of madness – one that ails the entire body of male citizens, and groups them all together as equally insane.[37] Here is the exchange between Lysistrata and the *proboulos* at *Lys.* 554–559:

> Λυ. οἶμαι ποτε Λυσιμάχας ἡμᾶς ἐν τοῖς Ἕλλησι καλεῖσθαι.
> Πρ. τί ποιησάσας;
> Λυ.   ἢν παύσωμεν πρώτιστον μὲν ξὺν ὅπλοισιν
>   ἀγοράζοντας καὶ *μαινομένους*.
> Γρ.ᵃ   νὴ τὴν Παφίαν Ἀφροδίτην.
> Λυ. νῦν μὲν γὰρ δὴ κἂν ταῖσι χύτραις καὶ τοῖς λαχάνοισιν ὁμοίως

---

34 Translation in Vince and Vince 1926.
35 For example, the group of Bacchae in Euripides.
36 Cf. Thumiger 2017, 19.
37 See e.g. 342, πολέμου καὶ μανιῶν.

περιέρχονται κατὰ τὴν ἀγορὰν ξὺν ὅπλοις *ὥσπερ Κορύβαντες*.
Πρ.   νὴ Δία. χρὴ γὰρ τοὺς ἀνδρείους.

[LYSISTRATA] Then I believe all Greece will one day calls us Disbanders of Battles. [MAGISTRATE] For what achievement? [LYSISTRATA] If to begin with we can stop people from going to the market fully armed and acting crazy. [OLD WOMAN[A]] Paphian Aphrodite be praised! [LYSISTRATA] At this very moment, all around the market, in the pottery shops and the grocery stalls, they're walking around in arms like Corybants! [MAGISTRATE] By Zeus! A man's got to act like a man![38]

When the men come to take notice of the disorder caused by Lysistrata and her companions, madness once more enters the text, this time as an accusation thrown by men against the women.[39] This and other instances in Aristophanes' plays illustrate how madness turns, in the context of public disputes, into a handy weapon to use against a political enemy, and how, during this process, it can be rhetorically stretched so as to become attached to an entire community of ideological opponents. Such metaphorical inflation in the meaning of madness, with the intent of questioning the actions, motives and arguments of extended communities of people, is typical among the orators of the fourth century BC[40] and suggests a further possible line of engagement with the comic tradition.

3 Conclusion

This chapter has been a modest attempt to explore only some of the ways in which allegations of insanity across Greek comedy and oratory can be approached as points of convergence between the two genres.[41] My intention has

---

38 Translation Henderson 2000, 343–345.
39 See e.g. *Lys.* 387–398 at which point the *proboulos* compares this disorder with the ecstatic rites of Sabazius and Adonis.
40 For the association of warfare and the politics of war with madness in the Greek orators, and the possibility that such an association can be ultimately traced back to Aristophanes, see Ruffell 2018, 340–341. Cf. Worman 2010, 219.
41 For reasons of space I have not been able, for instance, to adequately stress the importance of the distinction between forensic and deliberative oratory, and to explore the diverse ways in which the accusation of insanity might appear in each context. To mention only one notable difference: given that a forensic environment is dominated by personal disputes, insanity is construed through references to the defendant's specific traits of character and to specific incidents of his life. It is, in other words, highly individualised and comes into sharp focus as a

been to show that comic slander revolving around the "you are mad!" accusation is worth exploring deeper than we usually do: this is not just random abuse, but sometimes it carries with it complex cultural significance, pointing as it does directly to the world of the "Assembly" and, along with it, to a masculine trope of abuse detectable in rhetorical settings. At the same time, although insanity in rhetoric can be a tremendously important issue (the accusation that one is "out of his mind", when backed up by sufficient evidence, is no laughing matter), it nonetheless retains a considerably comic charge within it: the idea that madness has no fixed limits and can, therefore, always surpass itself; the notion that there is no such thing as a definitive diagnosis of madness; the unsettling view that madness can infect entire crowds of people – all these concepts have a distinctively potent presence in comedy and may have passed from there to the delicate prose and world of the Greek orators.

Bibliography

Compton-Engle, G. (2015), *Costume in the Comedies of Aristophanes*, Cambridge.
Freydberg, B. (2008), *Philosophy and Comedy: Aristophanes, Logos, and Eros*, Bloomington/Indianapolis.
Halliwell, S. (1997), *Aristophanes: Birds, Lysistrata, Assembly-Women, Wealth*, Oxford.
Halliwell, S. (2016), *Aristophanes: Clouds, Women at the Thesmophoria, Frogs*, Oxford.
Harding, P. (1994), 'Comedy and Rhetoric', in: I. Worthington (ed.), *Persuasion: Greek Rhetoric in Action*, London, 196–221.
Henderson, J. (ed. and trans.) (2000), *Aristophanes: Birds; Lysistrata; Women at Thesmophoria*, Cambridge, MA/London.
Hubbard, T. (2007), 'Attic Comedy and the Development of Theoretical Rhetoric', in: I. Worthington (ed.), *A Companion to Greek Rhetoric*, Malden, MA/Oxford, 490–508.
Kidd, S.E. (2014), *Nonsense and Meaning in Ancient Greek Comedy*, Cambridge.
Langholf, V. (1990), *Medical Theories in Hippocrates: Early Texts and the 'Epidemics'*, Berlin/New York.
Padel, R. (1992), *In and Out of the Mind: Greek Images of the Tragic Self*, Princeton.
Rothwell, K.S. (1990), *Politics and Persuasion in Aristophanes' Ecclesiazusae*, Leiden.

---

concretely established clinical entiry, as a medical fact that should not be disputed. On the other hand, in deliberative oratory the chances are high that insanity becomes attached as a label to large groups of people and communities. This seems to invite a shift to a more metaphorical understanding of it. Each of these environments, the deliberative and the forensic, may be accordingly explored as inviting different kinds of dialogue with the comic tradition. On that difference: Apostolakis, in this volume, gives useful insights; on the different ways in which comic invective is used in public and private speeches: Serafim, in this volume, is useful.

Ruffell, I. (2018), 'Stop Making Sense: The Politics of Aristophanic Madness', in: G. Kazantzidis and N. Tsoumpra (eds.), *Morbid Laughter: Exploring the Comic Dimensions of Disease in Classical Antiquity*, in: *Illinois Classical Studies* 43, 326–350 (special issue).
Scafuro, A.C. (2011), *Demosthenes: Speeches 39–49*, Austin.
Serafim, A. (2017), *Attic Oratory and Performance*, London/New York.
Sidwell, K. (1990), 'Was Philocleon Cured?', in: *Classica et Medievalia* 41, 9–31.
Singer, P.N. (2018), 'The Mockery of Madness: Laughter at and with Insanity in Attic Tragedy and Old Comedy', in: G. Kazantzidis and N. Tsoumpra (eds.), *Morbid Laughter: Exploring the Comic Dimensions of Disease in Classical Antiquity*, in: *Illinois Classical Studies* 43, 289–325 (special issue).
Sommerstein, A.H. (1998), *Aristophanes: Ecclesiazusae*, Warminster.
Thumiger, C. (2017), *A History of the Mind and Mental Health in Classical Greek Medical Thought*, Cambridge.
Ussher, R.G. (1973), *Aristophanes' Ecclesiazusae*, Oxford.
Vince, J.H. (ed. and trans.) (1930), *Demosthenes, Orations, Vol. I*, London/Cambridge, MA.
Vince, C.A. and Vince, J.H. (ed. and trans.) (1926), *Demosthenes, Orations 18–19; De corona; De falsa legatione*, London/Cambridge, MA.
Willi, A. (2003), *The Languages of Aristophanes: Aspects of Linguistic Variation in Classical Attic Greek*, Oxford.
Wohl, V. (2010), *Law's Cosmos: Juridical Discourse in Athenian Forensic Oratory*, Cambridge.
Worman, N. (2010), *Abusive Mouths in Classical Athens*, Cambridge.

Dennis Pausch
Comic Invective in Cicero's Speech *Pro M. Caelio*

Abstract: Cicero's speech *Pro Caelio* is a prime example of the entertaining as well as aggressive use that can be made of a combination between rhetoric and comedy. Cicero enriches his speech with many references and citations from Roman plays. In addition to this, he portrays the persons involved in the trial, above all his client Caelius and Clodia, whom he wants to be seen as the true moving spirit of the accusation, as if they were figures in a comedy. On the one hand, this enables him to play down the importance of the charge. On the other hand, he casts his client in the favourable light of the young lover in a comedy, whereas he assigns to Clodia the role of the prostitute, even alleging an incestuous relationship with her brother Clodius Pulcher. Whereas the speech has been analysed mainly with regard to the strategic use of the elements of comedy, this chapter focuses on the complex invective dynamics between the two genres, but also between the speaker, his opponents and the audience. In doing so, we can also see why our own reactions to *Pro Caelio* are changing, shifting away from the artistry of the speaker towards his victims and their emotional violations.

1 Introduction

After Cicero had decided, in the spring of 56 BC, to take on the defence of M. Caelius Rufus against accusations, amongst other things, of violence (*vis*) that caused dangerous wounding and attempted poisoning,[1] he was not at all displeased when the trial continued into the *Ludi Megalenses*, the celebrations in honour of the *Magna Mater*. This unusual scheduling meant that Cicero had to give his final plea, the last of three in total, on the 4th of April and thus in com-

---

This chapter has been hugely profited from the discussions with my colleagues at the Dresden Classics Department and the Collaborative Research Centre 1285 "Invectivity. Constellations and Dynamics of Disparagement" (among others Hanna Maria Degener, Antje Junghanß, Ken Heuring, Jan Lukas Horneff, Bernhard Kaiser, Christoph Schwameis). I also owe special thanks to Glenn Patten for taking care of the translation of my text into English.

[1] Since the speeches of the prosecutors are lost, the exact charges are difficult to reconstruct: see Dyck 2013, 2–8.

petition with a rich and varied programme of entertainment on the *Forum Romanum*, including, not least, theatrical performances. Cicero addresses this situation himself at some length in the opening lines of the speech and promises in return to entertain the judges and other spectators as well as he can as compensation for the enjoyments they would be missing out on.[2] In so doing, he implicitly acknowledges that this legal plea has many points of contact with the theatre, which he brings to the fore by means of numerous quotations of Roman dramas,[3] the introduction of typical comic characters,[4] and the use of language and literary style in general.[5] At the same time, these borrowings from comedy are a central part of Cicero's strategy to refute the accusations against his client and, in particular, to discredit Caelius' accusers, whose case he represents as a stage play based on intrigues in which the only role left for Clodia is that of the morally questionable courtesan (*meretrix*).[6]

In this interpretation of the *Pro Caelio*, the close connection between comedy and invective observed in the speech appears to have emerged more or less accidentally from the scheduling of the trial in conjunction with the specific tactics Cicero adopted in it. What we see here, however, is no singular encounter of genres, but rather a frequently occurring combination,[7] as indicated not least by the other chapters in the volume at hand. One reason for the close proximity of these two genres or registers is given by Cicero himself in the first part of the speech when he denies the accusations levelled against Caelius and his frivolous lifestyle with the remark that they are merely malicious slander, and that this *maledictio autem nihil habet propositii praeter contumeliam; quae si petulantius iactatur, convicium, si facetius, urbanitas nominatur* ("slander, on the other hand, has no object except of insult. If its character is coarse, it is termed abuse, but if sophisticated, it is termed wit").[8] At the same time, this criticism of

---

2 See esp. Cic. *Cael.* 1: ... *vos laboriosos..., quibus otiosis ne in communi quidem otio liceat esse*; for further detail, see Geffcken 1973, 11–14; Volpe 1977, 313–316, and Leigh 2004, 301–303.
3 E.g. Cic. *Cael.* 18; 36–38; for more details, see further Zillinger 1911, 64–68.
4 E.g. Cic. *Cael.* 37–38.
5 E.g. Cic. *Cael.* 33; 60; 64–67.
6 See esp. Geffcken 1973; May 1988, 105–116; Arcellaschi 1997; Klodt 2003, 82–97, and Leigh 2004, but also Tatum 2007, who argues that Cicero uses the analogies to comedy mainly to distance his own person from it.
7 For the use of comic roles in other speeches by Cicero, see Harries 2007 and Klodt 2003; for the element of theatre inherent to any trial, see e.g. Bablitz 2007 (for Rome); Hall 2014 (for Cicero) and Papaioannou, Serafim and da Vela 2017 (for antiquity in general).
8 Cic. *Cael.* 6 (the Latin text is that of Maslowski 1995, the translation by Berry 2008, here as in the following).

his opponent turns out to be an accurate description of his own strategy: his slanderous attacks on Caelius' accusers are to appear as a version of *urbanitas* and must, therefore, be performed in such a way as to seem as spontaneous and amusing as possible.

We can observe this same desire to justify aggressive language and to amplify its effects by presenting it as an allegedly harmless, impromptu joke, in many other places in Cicero's works, and indeed in ancient rhetoric in general.[9] Even in the invectives that Cicero never actually delivered but only published, such as the *actio secunda* of the *Verrines* or the *Second Philippic* against Marc Antony, we can find numerous examples of this kind of artificial orality or simulated spontaneity.[10] The verbal techniques used for this purpose in these speeches are often closely related to comedy, partly because Cicero keenly invests in humour and comic effect, and partly because the production of immediate reactions also plays an important role on the stage. Viewed in this light, Cicero's speech *pro Caelio* turns out to be less the singular, special case of a generic hybrid than the intensification of tendencies already present that serve both to legitimise and at the same time exacerbate invective speech by borrowing from comedy. In what follows, I aim to explore further this connection in a number of examples from the speech in which Cicero gradually moves from refuting the accusations to a frontal attack on the accusers.[11]

2 Exposing the Accusations as a Typically Comedic Erotic Intrigue

Although the charge had been formally submitted by L. Sempronius Atratinus, who had also given one of the three speeches *in Caelium*,[12] Cicero sees the seventeen-year-old aristocrat as merely a front man and, from the beginning, leaves his audience in no doubt that, as far as he is concerned, the driving forces be-

---

[9] For further discussion, see e.g. Fuhrmann 1990 and Pausch (forthcoming).
[10] See e.g. Cic. *Verr*. 2.4.4–5. A better understanding of this technique is central to our ongoing work on Cicero's invective speeches as part of the Dresden-based Collaborative Research Centre 1285 'Invectivity. Constellations and Dynamics of disparagement'; for further information, see https://tu-dresden.de/gsw/sfb1285.
[11] Cic. *Cael*. 3–69, esp. 30–38.
[12] The others had been delivered by the two *subscriptores*, P. Clodius (most likely not the famous tribune of the *plebs*, but rather a relative of his) and L. Herennius Balba.

hind the trial are P. Clodius Pulcher and his sister Clodia Metelli.[13] This scarcely seems, at first glance, to be a move calculated to do his client any favours, since Clodius Pulcher was a member of the *gens Claudia*, one of the oldest and most successful aristocratic families in Rome, who, further, had been a very successful and thus well-known politician as he had served in 58 BC as tribune of the plebs and in 57 BC, the year before the trial, as curule aedile. At the same time, however, Clodius appears to have been an extremely polarising and scandalous figure, even if our view of him is impaired by the fact that practically all of our information about him comes from Cicero, who saw Clodius as his arch enemy, especially after the latter had forced him into temporary exile.[14]

But in the *Pro Caelio* Cicero does not intend to give to the charge against Caelius extra weight by emphasising Clodius' role; instead, he is pursuing a strategy of μείωσις, i.e. the reduction of the severity of the accusations, as Quintilian noted (*Inst.* 4.1.39).[15] This may offer another explanation about why he reserves the main role for Clodius' sister Clodia. In Cicero's version of events, which aims to win over the judges and the rest of the audience, the real background of the case is neither political nor criminal, but rather erotic: Caelius was for a time Clodia's lover, but then left her, and she, driven by erotic disappointment, set out to revenge herself upon him by making up these accusations. In other words, Cicero turns a political and legal event into an erotic intrigue: this is a central feature of New Comedy, a genre influenced by Greek models and popular on the Roman stage. We will come back in the next section to the consequences for Clodia when Cicero not only accuses her of having had an affair with Caelius, but also assigns her the part of the comedic *meretrix*.

For the moment, we want to consider the linguistic strategies by which Cicero tries to change the charge into a *palliata* plot. The generally close proximity between the role of an orator and that of an actor[16] already becomes apparent in the first part of the speech when Cicero sets out to refute the accusations against Caelius of insufficient *pietas* and points with a sweeping gesture to the latter's parents who, dressed in mourning, are watching the trial from the spectators' benches.[17] This is just as typical an element of many forensic speeches as the alleged moment of realisation when Cicero pretends that he has as his oratorical

---

[13] Cicero alludes to them already at the start, but without naming them: see Cic. *Cael.* 1–2.
[14] On Clodius Pulcher, see Tatum 1999 and Nippel 2000; on the history of their enmity, see Jehne 2020.
[15] See also: Leigh 2004, 302, and Tatum 2007, 165.
[16] On the use of comic language and imagery in Attic oratory: Serafim 2017, esp. 17–20.
[17] See Cic. *Cael.* 3–4; cf. e.g. Stroh 1975, 258–259.

delivery is under way, understood why Clodius' rental expenses have been so high (*nunc demum intellego*). This leads naturally to a jab at Clodius Pulcher: the latter turns out, ironically, to be the owner of the luxury apartment that Caelius had rented and whose allegedly exorbitant cost his accusers had used against him, to insinuate that he was in financial difficulties and so had a motive to be involved in the violent attacks on the Egyptian envoys.[18] The same technique by which an invective remark is presented as a seemingly spontaneous idea or witty afterthought on the part of the speaker (despite the fact that in this case we are dealing not with a live recording, but with the published version of a speech),[19] is employed again later on, when the discussion turns to Clodia.

As the speech develops, Cicero goes well beyond these obvious points of contact between oratory and comedy, that lie, as it were, on the performative level of theatrical play. He elaborates on Caelius' glamorous apartment, which was evidently not only extremely expensive, but also located on the Palatine and thus close to Clodia's residence, a piece of information that Cicero attempts to impress upon his audience as having been crucial to the development of their alleged relationship. He emphasises the geographical proximity further, by quoting the first verses of Ennius' *Medea exul*, in which the nurse (following the example of her counterpart in Euripides) curses the building of the Argo as the beginning of all unhappiness. By employing a Euripidean quotation to introduce the journey of the Argonauts as a parallel to Caelius' move within Rome, Cicero uses a technique frequent in the comic tradition, parody of tragedy.[20] At the same time, our sympathies are no longer meant to be with Medea, who fell in love with Jason, was abandoned by him and is now consoled by her nurse, but rather with Jason himself, who turns out to be no one other than Caelius:[21]

> quo loco possum dicere id quod vir clarissimus, Marcus Crassus, cum de adventu regis Ptolemaei quereretur, paulo ante dixit: 'utinam ne in nemore Pelio...' ac longius quidem mihi contexere hoc carmen liceret: 'nam numquam era errans' hanc molestiam nobis exhiberet 'Medea animo aegro, amore saevo saucia.' sic enim, iudices, reperietis quod, cum ad id loci venero, ostendam, hanc Palatinam Medeam migrationemque <eam> huic adulescentuli causam sive malorum omnium sive potius sermonum fuisse.

> While on this subject I can repeat what the illustrious Marcus Crassus said a little while ago, when he was deploring the arrival of King Ptolemy: 'Would that never in Pelion's for-

---

18 See Cic. *Cael.* 17.
19 For further discussion of this important point, see below pp. 135 ff.
20 See Geffcken 1973, 15–17.
21 Cic. *Cael.* 18 (= Ennius fr. 246; 253; 254 Vahlen = 208; 215; 216 Jocelyn).

est ...' And I could go on with the quotation: 'for never would a wandering woman' have caused us all this trouble, 'Medea, sick at heart, wounded by a wild passion'. For you will find out, gentleman, what I shall show you when I come to that point – that this Medea of the Palatine and the change of residence was the cause of all this young man's difficulties, or rather of all the talk.

The fact that Caelius is, once again,[22] described as *adulescens*, is an essential part of Cicero's defence strategy. Although Caelius is in his early thirties and thus in principle too old for this "role",[23] Cicero repeatedly defines him as such throughout the speech, which inevitably strengthens his identification with his counterpart in the plays of Roman comedy: a youth from a prominent family, of promising talent and, above all, highly likeable, who for hormonal reasons temporarily has walked off the straight path, though eventually he will come to his senses and in due time will become a valuable and respected member of society.[24]

Caelius' portrayal as a reckless *adulescens* is amplified by means of Cicero's artful recollection of Greek myths well-known to the audience from dramatic performances, which feature heroes whose behaviour may be compared to Caelius' own. The quotations from Ennius' *Medea* serve this mission with notable success. It is interesting that the parallel between Caelius and Jason did not originate in Cicero. Rather, Cicero reminds us, as noted earlier, that the speaker for the defence before him, Marcus Crassus, the later so-called triumvir, had quoted the same verses (or at least a part of them) as well, although it is not clear in what context he did so.[25] In fact, this identification appears to have been made first by Caelius' accusers, as a passage in Consultus Fortunatianus, the author of an *ars rhetorica* in Late Antiquity, suggests. Fortunatianus writes that in his opening speech Sempronius Atratinus described Caelius as "pretty-boy Jason",[26] presumably in order to make the accusation of rash adventuring out of craving for the "golden fleece" seem more plausible by means of a mythological parallel.[27] Caelius, who would have understood this identification as invective,

---

[22] See Cic. *Cael.* 1; 3; 6; 7.
[23] Admittedly, Caelius' year of birth is controversial: Pliny the Elder (*NH* 7.765) gives 82 BC, but this does not fit to the dates known for his public career (aedile 50, praetor 48), in light of which the *communis opinio* is in favour of 88 or 87 BC; see e.g. Dyck 2013, 4, but also Austin 1960, 144–146, who argues for 82 BC.
[24] See Leigh 2004, esp. 305–308; 315–326, and Dyck 2013, 61.
[25] See Austin 1960, 68–69, and Dyck 2013, 85.
[26] Fortun. Rhet. 3.7, *Atratinus Caelium pulchellum Iasonem appellat* (p. 124 Halm).
[27] For this understanding of the gibe, see e.g. Wiseman 1985, 73; Jensen 2003, 65–67, and Dyck 2013, 85.

probably responded by calling Atratinus "Pelias with curls", thus assigning him the role of the evil step-uncle and at the same time making fun of his youthful hair; regrettably, Quintilian, who attests to *Pelia cincinnatus* for Caelius, gives no further information about the context.[28]

As a part of the mutual exchange of invective identifications with figures of myth that seems to have marked the course of the trial on both sides,[29] Caelius reportedly[30] described Clodia, in a particularly denigrating remark, as *quadragintaria Clytemnestra*. In doing so, he accused her at once of prostitution at the very cheap rate of a quarter *as* and of murdering her husband.[31] Q. Caecilius Metellus Celer, Clodia's husband and consul in 60 BC, died unexpectedly a year later, in 59 BC, a fact that evidently gave rise to malicious talk about the possible involvement of his widow.[32] In contrast to Agamemnon's violent death in the bath, however, the rumours here were about the use of poison. Against this background, the identification of Caelius with Jason was probably not a very clever move on the part of the accusers, since it gave first Crassus and then Cicero the opportunity to counter the accusation by taking it up and pursuing it to its logical conclusion, in which Clodia became Caelius' alleged lover and could thus be presented as the Roman reincarnation of the unscrupulous poison-mixer Medea.[33]

These slanders against Clodia are certainly the gloomy climax of the speech, but invective that explicitly relates to drama is not limited to them. Let us consider two other telling passages before we finally come to Clodia herself. The first is set immediately after the famous entries of Clodia's ancestor, Appius Claudius Caecus, whom Cicero calls up from the underworld to scold his descendent, and of her brother Clodius Pulcher, who picks up on Appius' scolding.[34] Then, after he has berated Clodia in this way for her promiscuous and extravagant behaviour, Cicero turns to Caelius: he emphasises his client's role

---

28 See fr. 162.37 Malcovati (= Quint. *Inst.* 1.5.61), *Pelia cincinnatus*.
29 See Leigh 2004, 309: "cycle of mythic allusions and banter".
30 His speech comprised at least two more insults, one against Clodia (162.27 Malcovati = Quint. *Inst.* 8.6.52, *in triclinio coam, in cubiculo nolam*) and one against Plotinus Gallus, Atratinus' alleged speechwriter (162.24 Malcovati = Suet. *Rhet.* 2, *subtractoque nomine, hordearium eum rhetorem appellat deridens ut inflatum ac levem et sordidum*), although Cicero highlights other qualities in his brief summary: see Cic. *Cael.* 45.
31 Fr. 162.26 Malcovati (= Quint. *Inst.* 8.6.52); see e.g. Jensen 2003, 67–70.
32 See Schol. Bob. 139.8-10 (... *qui... decesserat infami etiam morte de veneficio, quod ei paratum vel aput Clodium fratrem vel aput uxorem Clodiam videbatur*); cf. e.g. Dyck 2013, 150.
33 See esp. Cic. *Cael.* 59–60; cf. Fyntikoglou 2003.
34 Cic. *Cael.* 33–36; see below pp. 138–139.

as an *adulescens* led astray by an unscrupulous *meretrix* and deserving of leniency by taking on the role of two typical fathers of Roman comedy and quoting some of their lines. As he was doing so, he would certainly have adapted his voice, facial expression and gestures to the given role – Quintilian at least assumes this when he discusses this passage in the *Institutio Oratoria*.[35] In yet another display of performative talent reminiscent of an actor, Cicero pretends that he has difficulty making a spontaneous decision on which character to choose for this purpose in the situation at hand (*sed dubito quem patrem potissimum sumam...* "but I am unsure which father I ought to choose..."). At first, he plays a typical *senex durus* from an unknown comedy of Caecilius, who censures Caelius' behaviour,[36] before adopting next the role of Micio from Terence's *Adelphoe*, an especially well-known example of a *pater clemens*, who is forbearing with his *adulescens*. In embracing the part of Micio, the orator betrays his intention to prefigure the audience's reaction.[37]

The second passage is set towards the end of the speech. There Cicero picks up his opponents' narrative about how Clodia's slaves failed to capture P. Licinius in the baths of the Senia as he was handing over the poison, and turns it into a piece of narrative bravura and a farce in a swimming-pool.[38] In order to prove that the accusers' version, according to which Clodia's slaves set a trap for Licinius by persuading him to bring the poison to them, is implausible, Cicero emphasises the unlikely and scurrilous elements of the scene, amongst other things by presenting them in the style of a parody of epic:[39]

> I am bursting to set eyes on those elegant young men, the friends of a wealthy and noble lady, and on those valiant warriors stationed by their commandress in a fortified ambush at the baths. I intend to ask them how and where they hid themselves, whether it was the famous bath-tub or a Trojan horse that carried and concealed so many invincible heroes waging a woman's war.

As the author of this (in his eyes particularly unrealistic) plot, Cicero names Clodia explicitly as *vetus et plurimarum fabularum poetria* ("an experienced

---

35 Quint. *Inst.* 11.1.39: *utimur enim fictione personarum et velut ore alieno loquimur dandique sunt iis, quibus vocem accomodamus, sui mores; aliter enim P. Clodius, aliter Appius Caecus, aliter Caecilianus ille, aliter Terentianus fingitur*; cf. Geffcken 1973, 17–18.
36 Cic. *Cael.* 37 (= Caecil. fr. 230–242 Ribbeck).
37 Cic. *Cael.* 38 (= Ter. *Adelph.* 120–121); for the relevance of plot of the *Adelphoe* for Cicero's argumentation, see Leigh 2004, 318–322; for Cicero's use of Terence in general, see Manuwald 2014.
38 Cic. *Cael.* 61–67; on the episode as a whole, see e.g. Klodt 2003, 93–95.
39 Cic. *Cael.* 67; see Geffcken 1973, 25–27, and Jensen 2003, 70–71.

poetess with a great many plays to her credit")⁴⁰ – thus accusing her of exactly the same thing he himself does in his speech: presenting the public with a comedy.⁴¹ He then, however, proceeds to associate her acting with that of an actress of a mime, a performance that has no actual plot, nor a proper ending, and as a result collapses in confusion, just as the charges against Caelius have done – (*mimi ergo iam exitus, non fabulae*, "so, then, we have the finale of a mime, not of a proper play").⁴² At the same time, he connects Clodia with a genre that, not least on account of its use of scantily dressed actresses, had always been particularly associated with prostitution. In order to make this association even clearer, Cicero accuses Clodia of having offered herself to the swimming-pool attendant.⁴³ Clodia's acting, in short, reflects her moral degradation, as she evolves from a tragic Medea to a comedic *meretrix* and finally to an actress in a mime.⁴⁴

This debasement of Clodia as a person is accompanied by the exposure of the charge against Caelius, initially, as an epic parody, then, in the long central section, as a foremost comedic plot, and finally, towards the end, as merely the kind of disjointed burlesque typical of the mime. Thus, the different references to the theatre that occur frequently in this speech serve the general strategy of the advocate to play down the accusations made against his client as much as possible, and, in addition, to present that client as the temporarily misled but immensely likeable *adulescens* that his audience knew from the comic stage. But they also make, as I have attempted to show above, an important contribution to the denigration of the people Cicero wants to present as the driving forces behind the charge. This connection of comedy and invective is a more general phenomenon and thus less attached to the specific occasion of this speech than has usually been argued. This will become more apparent when we turn to consider more closely the verbal attacks on Clodia.

---

40 Cic. *Cael.* 64.
41 This is, incidentally, a move typical of both comedy and invective. I am very grateful to Christoph Schwameis (Vienna/Dresden) for this observation.
42 Cic. *Cael.* 65.
43 Cic. *Cael.* 62: ... *nisi forte mulier potiens quadrantaria illa permutatione familiaris facta erat balneatori*; for the pun with *quadrans* (one quarter of an *as*) as the usual entrance fee to the baths and Clodia's alleged charge as low-price prostitute according to Caelius' slur as *quadrantaria Clytemnestra*, see Austin 1960, 124–125, and Dyck 2013, 154–155 (with further references). On the comic dimension of menial jobs, see Serafim in this volume.
44 See Geffcken 1973, esp. 24.

3 The Denigration of Clodia as an Allegedly Notorious *Femme Fatale*

Clodia was the daughter of Appius Claudius Pulcher, consul in 79 BC, the widow of Q. Caecilius Metellus Celer, consul in 60 BC, and the sister of P. Clodius Pulcher, curule aedile in 57 BC, all of whom came from old, wealthy and extremely influential families.⁴⁵ Since women in Rome were not allowed to hold political office themselves, we are essentially reliant on the positions of her closest male relatives for our hypotheses about her position in contemporary society. On this basis, we would normally have to draw the conclusion that Clodia Metelli, as she is called in the secondary literature in order to be distinguished from her sisters, was a leading representative and ideal instantiation of the aristocratic class in the Late Republic. In fact, the opposite is the case. Today, we perceive her as the *femme fatale*, surrounded by scandal – a woman of the highest nobility who used the early and unexpected death of her husband to enjoy her life to the full amongst the *jeunesse dorée* of the Roman capital, and whose string of affairs displayed nothing as much as her lack of taste and discrimination. For those who take Clodia as a perfect example of the moral degeneration bemoaned by many in the last years of the Roman republic, Cicero's attack against a woman like this may seem to contribute to the moral edification of the general public and, as a result, can be reckoned with a certain degree of agreement.⁴⁶

This reading of the *Pro Caelio*, however, is in all likelihood nothing other than a misconception based on the extraordinarily successful reception history of this speech, which first created this image of Clodia as a notorious *femme fatale*.⁴⁷ Admittedly, one must account for the fact that Cicero speaks about Clodia in some of his other writings in much the same terms, particularly in his letters to Atticus,⁴⁸ although we should bear in mind here that his view of the sister of his arch enemy Clodius Pulcher will scarcely have been impartial. The identification of Clodia with Catullus' Lesbia similarly looks back on a long

---

45 For her family background and social standing, see Skinner 2011, esp. 19–95.
46 For a critical reevaluation of this traditional picture, see e.g. Günther 2000; Hartmann 2007, 152–154; Harder 2008, 228–247, and Skinner 2011.
47 For Cicero's overbearing influence on our view of Clodia, see e.g. Stroh 1975, 296–298, and Skinner 2011, 9–18.
48 Cf. esp. Cic. *ad Att.* 2.9.1; 2.10.2; 2.14.1; 2.22.5; 2.23.3 (nicknaming her each time with Hera's epithet as βοῶπις, which may imply an incestuous relationship with her brother); see Harder 2008, 237–238, and Thurn 2018, 146–147. For the quotation of obscene verses against her and her brother in Cic. *ad Q. fr.* 2.3.2, see below p. 137 n. 63.

tradition in scholarship.⁴⁹ But even this identification is ultimately largely based on her image as a promiscuous *demi-mondaine* as portrayed in the *Pro Caelio*.

In light of the above, it seems reasonable to forget for a moment Clodia's negative image and, instead, to imagine that in April 56 BC we are dealing with a respected and honoured member of the Roman upper class who, in a public trial, or at least in the published version of the speech given at it, is accused of having had an affair with a younger man, of prostitution at a bargain price and of incest with her own brother.⁵⁰ The question that arises here is the following: how did Cicero manage to present these outrageous allegations against a woman of the highest circles of society in such a way that they did not arouse the ire of the audience and cause it to fall back upon his head?

Despite the fact the Romans of the late Republic evidently had the impression themselves that they lived in a society addicted to invective – *in tam maledica civitate*, as Cicero says in this very speech⁵¹ – and the enjoyment of mockery appears to have been understood as an element of *urbanitas*, contributing positively to one's own image,⁵² Cicero the advocate, nevertheless, risks much here. For this reason, he goes to considerable verbal lengths to reduce the unfortunate chance that these invectives might be received as a violation of social custom and ultimately turn against him, and he succeeds in his effort not least through the employment of numerous elements typical of comedy,⁵³ which help him present the unheard-of verbal aggression against Clodia, on the one hand, as a series of typically comedic jokes, and on the other, as spontaneous witticisms that have arisen on the spur of the moment. This performance proves successful, and as a result, Cicero not only enhances the effect of the attacks, but also has found a way to justify them socially, at least to a certain extent.⁵⁴

---

49 This goes back to the famous but controversial decipherment of the cryptonyms of four *puellae* of Latin erotic poetry (Lesbia, Cynthia, Delia and Perilla) by Apuleius in the second century AD (*Apol.* 10); for the discussion, see Stroh 1975, 297–298; Skinner 2011, 121–145, and Gräßner 2013.
50 On the scandalous character of these slanders, see e.g. Leigh 2004, 302–305.
51 Cic. *Cael.* 38.
52 That *urbanitas* included competitive and invective elements, is clearly shown by the definition cited by Quintilian and attributed to Domititus Marsus: cf. Quint. *Inst.* 6.3.104; on *urbanitas* in general, see Ramage 1973; Krostenko 2001 and Rühl 2019, 200–306.
53 The risk is stressed also by Tatum 2007, esp. 171–173; he argues, however, that Cicero turns to comedy in order to mark the distance to his own role as a serious and thus trustworthy speaker.
54 On the role of humour in Cicero's invective against Clodia, see Geffcken 1973, esp. 27–28, and Volpe 1977.

As we saw above, Cicero announces right from the beginning that he considers neither the official plaintiff, Sempronius Atratinus, nor the other two speakers on the opposing side to be the driving forces behind the trial, but instead he puts the blame on Clodius Pulcher and, above all, his sister Clodia. She is the focus of Cicero's attacks from the outset, even if the orator initially declines to mention her name and merely makes dark insinuations about the pernicious effects of the erotic passions of a woman,[55] whom he first smugly describes as the "Medea of the Palatine".[56] In this way he creates tension which he will effectively resolve later in the speech when he comes to repudiating the accusations against Caelius.[57] Cicero's repudiation strategy rests, simply put, on making the crimes of which his client has been accused appear to be slanders invented by Clodia, who is using them to avenge herself on him for having ended their affair against her wishes. We cannot, of course, know whether this relationship had actually existed or not; Cicero's insinuations aside, there is not much that speaks for it.[58] But, regardless of how we view this, the public allegations that the daughter of an aristocrat and widow of a consul had an erotic affair with a young man, is already an unheard-of affront.

From the beginning, Cicero strives to make this violation of the social norm appear less harsh and at the same time more damaging by presenting it as though it had an entirely unintentional comic effect of the situation. Thus, the first of the many fast-paced attacks in this section of the speech begins with a characteristic mixture of calculated wit and apparent reticence: *res est omnis in hac causa nobis, iudices, cum Clodia, muliere non solum nobili verum etiam nota; de qua ego nihil dicam nisi depellendi criminis causa* ("In this trial, members of the jury, everything has to do with Clodia, a woman who is not only of noble birth, but notorious. In talking about this woman, I shall say only what I need to say to rebut the charge").[59] By means of this carefully positioned appeal Cicero tries to convince the excited audience attending the trial (and, of course, the readers of the published version of his speech) that he had originally intended to speak with more restraint, but he failed to control his emotions once he

---

55 Cic. *Cael.* 1: *libidinem muliebrem*.
56 Cic. *Cael.* 18: *Palatinam Medeam*.
57 Cic. *Cael.* 30; see Ramage 1984 and Dyck 2013, 12–13.
58 As is convincingly shown by Stroh 1975, 243–298; see further Dyck 2013, 14: "Clodia Metelli was a wealthy widow; as such she may have participated in the round of parties, pleasure-boating etc. associated with Baiae, but there is no need to suppose that her reputation was compromised when the trial began".
59 Cic. *Cael.* 31.

launched his speech: in this way, his invectives against Clodia later on would appear at least in part as spontaneous, and thus justifiable, overreactions.

This double strategy of ostensible reticence and well-prepared punch-lines against Clodia becomes more clearly evident a little later. Cicero once again asserts that he intends to say only as much about her as he must for the defence of his client, but then continues: *quod quidem facerem vehementius, nisi intercederent mihi inimicitiae cum istius mulieris viro – fratre volui dicere; semper hic erro* ("indeed, I would do this more vigorously, were it not for the fact that I am restrained by my personal enmity with this woman's husband, I mean her brother – I'm always making that mistake").[60] By presenting the accusation of incest as a slip of the tongue, Cicero of course only apparently retracts it; in reality, he has sharpened it in two ways, first, by presenting it as an unintentional joke that provokes laughter and thus encourages unintentional assent, then, by making the assertion on which it is based appear so real and obvious that it can cause him to make the mistake against all intention.[61] In this way, he introduces this topic, to which he will return at various points and which belongs, both in rhetorical practice and in the rhetorical handbooks, to the category of standard accusations (*praeteritio*),[62] as something to be taken for granted by his audience.[63]

Immediately after this passage, Cicero repeats the same manoeuvre in almost identical form: he first claims, once again, that he is going to hold back, and then makes another playful attack that, even though not explicitly marked as a spontaneous comment, is nevertheless so loosely connected to the syntax of the preceding phrase that it can easily be received as an afterthought: *nunc agam modice nec longius progrediar quam me mea fides et causa ipsa coget. nec enim muliebris umquam inimicitias mihi gerendas putavi, praesertim cum ea quam omnes semper amicam omnium potius quam cuiusquam inimicam*

---

60 Cic. *Cael.* 32.
61 Cf. Hickson-Hahn 1998, 19–25, esp. 20: "When the accusation of incest is couched in witty language, listeners may focus on the humorous technique rather than on the taboo content and the aggressive hostility. Moreover, there is always the 'only a joke' excuse. Listeners take pleasure in the penalty-free expression of hostility and sexual aggression against the target and are won over to the side of the speaker who has given them that pleasure"; see further Geffcken 1973, 34–36; Williams 2007, 123–124, and Dyck 2013, 111.
62 On this topic, see in general Hickson-Hahn 1998.
63 In a letter to his brother Quintus (2.3.2), Cicero reports that during the trial against Milo in 52 BC the crowd chanted among others *versus... obscenissimi in Clodium et Clodiam*; it is doubtful, however, if this incident can be taken as a proof for the existence of such rumours or if it is rather the result of Cicero's slanders in *Pro Caelio*.

putaverunt. ("I shall treat her gently, then, and go no further than my duty to my client and the demands of the case require. Indeed, I never thought I would be getting involved in quarrels with women, especially with one who is always thought of as every man's friend rather than any man's enemy").[64] By means of these artful double entendres, the ground has been prepared for the main section soon to follow, in which Cicero will explicitly employ theatrical elements both in content and in performance.

The culmination – or, depending on one's perspective, lowest point – of his invective against Clodia consists of Cicero taking on at first the role of one of her ancestors, and then that of her brother Clodius, in order to put his criticism of Clodia's behaviour into their mouths. Both personifications have had a rich afterlife; Quintilian, for example, cites them more than once as classic examples of the rhetorical technique of *sermocinatio* (also known as προσωποποιία).[65] Here, too, Cicero makes an effort to present his approach not as a prepared malicious remark, but as something that has simply occurred to him on the spur of the moment. This time, he even goes so far as to put a question to Clodia directly: *sed tamen ex ipsa quaeram prius utrum me secum severe et graviter et prisce agere malit, an remisse et leniter et urbane* ("But I should like to ask her first whether she would prefer me to deal with her in a stern, solemn, old-fashioned way or in a relaxed, easy-going, modern way").[66] In the published version of the speech, one understands the question for the most part as purely rhetorical. In court the speaker likely paused emphatically at this point as if expecting an actual reaction from Clodia.[67] When he proceeds as planned soon afterwards, and by means of *sermocinatio* addresses Clodia first with old-fashioned sternness and then in a more urbane manner, it becomes evident that this question was just another case of simulated spontaneity.

In order to make his old-fashioned and severe address more effective, Cicero summons up not just any of the morally rigorous *summi viri* of Rome's history, but one of Clodia's own ancestors. Here, too, he pretends that his selection of the most famous representative of her *gens*, Appius Claudius, surnamed *Cae-*

---

64 Cic. *Cael.* 32; see Geffcken 1973, 36: "suddenly as in an afterthought", and Dyck 2013, 111: "There is a simple but effective play on several senses of *amicus/-a* (either 'friend', often with reference to exchange of political and other favors [...] or 'girlfriend, lover' or, especially since it is limited with *omnium*, 'prostitute')...".
65 Quint. *Inst.* 3.8.54; 9.2.29–32 and 12.10.61, see further e.g. Lausberg 1960, §§ 820–825.
66 Cic. *Cael.* 33.
67 Catherine Steel has convincingly questioned the view that the orator was always able to control the court and argued for a stronger consideration of the unforeseen elements and reactions during a trial; see Steel 2017.

cus,⁶⁸ who died in 273 BC, has only been made at the last minute, and this because, as a blind man, he would be spared the sight of Clodia: *existat igitur ex hac ipsa familia aliquis ac potissimum Caecus ille; mininum enim dolorem capiet qui istam non videbit* ("Let me therefore summon up a member of her own family – and who better than the famous Caecus? He, any rate, will be the least shocked at her, since he will not be able to see her").⁶⁹ Cicero brings Appius Caecus, known both for his political successes and for his steadfastness to his principles, back from the dead, so to speak, in order to use him as a *persona*, that is, as a mask or a role (as he says himself explicitly afterwards⁷⁰) through which to rebuke Clodia and shame her publicly.⁷¹

For Quintilian, who cites the personifications in the *Pro Caelio*, as we have seen, as classic examples of the use of this rhetorical technique, it seems obvious that the speaker in these cases alters his voice, facial expressions and gestures like an actor, in order to perform the character being personified.⁷² Since we have no video recording of the trial, we must rely on stylistic analysis of the text for conclusions about performative aspects. The diction of the speech, however, as Geffcken has shown, is not homogenous, but rather alternates between a venerable, dignified tone, such as one would expect from the real Appius Claudius, and a colloquial register – an oscillation which corresponds exactly to the expectations one would have of a parody of a great historical figure in a comedy.⁷³

The comedic elements become even stronger when Cicero soon afterwards takes on the role of Clodia's brother, Clodius, and most likely imitates his voice, facial expressions and gestures. Given that Clodius was both alive and well-known at the time, this impersonation would presumably have been a challenging one; had Cicero carried it off reasonably well, he would have scored even more highly with his audience. Here too, he prefaces his performance by presenting the following malicious remarks, including among other things the repeated accusation of incest, as thoughts that have simply occurred to him spontaneously:⁷⁴

---

68 On this prominent figure in Rome's historical imagination, see e.g. Linke 2000 and Humm 2005.
69 Cic. *Cael.* 33; see Klodt 2003, 88–89.
70 Cic. *Cael.* 35, *iam enim ipse tecum nulla persona introducta loquor*; see Geffcken 1973, 17.
71 Cic. *Cael.* 34; for the historical and literary allusions, see Dyck 20113, 113–116.
72 Quint. *Inst.* 11.1.39 (see above note 35).
73 See Geffcken 1973, 18–19.
74 Cic. *Cael.* 36.

> *sin autem urbanius me agere mavis, sic agam tecum. removebo illum senem durum ac paene agrestem. ex his igitur tuis sumam aliquem ac potissimum minimum fratrem, qui est in isto genere urbanissimus, qui te amat plurimum, qui propter nescio quam, credo, timiditatem et nocturnos quosdam inanes metus tecum semper pusio cum maiore sorore cubitavit. eum putato tecum loqui.*
>
> You may, on the other hand, prefer me to deal with you in a smart, modern way; if so, this is what I shall do. I shall get rid of that harsh and almost rustic old man, and choose instead a different member of your family: your youngest brother. He is the very model of smart, modern manners, and he is exceedingly fond of you. Indeed, when he was a little boy, being, I assume, of a somewhat timid nature and inclined to be frightened at night for no reason, he always used to sleep with you, his elder sister! So imagine what he would say to you.

Once the preface is over, Cicero addresses Clodia in the persona of her bother. The advocate gives the impression that he rebukes Clodia's behaviour overall, but in truth his criticism is set to expose the particular fact that his addressee is so upset because Caelius has allegedly broken up with her – the entire affair is, we recall, in all likelihood Cicero's invention, and a trivial one, since Clodia could easily replace Caelius with another lover. As it becomes apparent not least in the verses Cicero puts into his mouth right from the outset,[75] Clodius' speech calls to mind a set of characters from the stage, both comic and tragic: he reminds of another character of the *fabula palliata*, the advisor (a friend or a clever slave) of the love-struck *adulescens amans*, who offers erotodidactic instruction and encouragement while at the same time calling for caution (the character of Palinurus in Plautus' *Curculio* comes to mind); or of the older and more experienced courtesan who advises a younger one on how to treat potential lovers/customers (the character of Syra in Terence's *Hecyra* is an outstanding example of the type). At the same time, the identification of Clodia with Medea reaches back to Apollonius' treatment of the story, which sets at the beginning of Medea's infatuation with Jason an animated conversation between the heroine and her sister, Chaliciope, who offers Medea erotic advice (and who, in turn, draws on the character of the tragic nurse of Phaedra, the stepmother in love with her stepson in Euripides' *Hippolytus*). Seen in this light, Cicero's offering erotic advice to Clodia in the character of her brother, who in turn impersonates a series of famous "stage experts" on the matter, portrays Clodia, not least on account of her gender, in a way that is hardly flattering:[76]

---

[75] The trochaic septenarius is not known otherwise, but is usually attributed to Caecilius: see Dyck 2013, 119.
[76] Cic. *Cael.* 36; see Geffcken 1973, 20–22, and Leigh 2004, 310–311.

"quid tumultuaris, soror? quid insanis? 'quid clamorem exorsa verbis parvam rem magnam facis?' vicinum adulescentulum aspexisti; candor huius te et proceritas, vultus oculique pepulerunt, saepius videre voluisti: fuisti non numquam in isdem hortis. vis nobilis mulier illum filium familias patre parco ac tenaci habere tuis copiis devinctum, non potes, calcitrat, respuit, repellit, non putat tua dona esse tanti: confer te alio. habes hortos ad Tiberim ac diligenter eo loco parasti, quo omnis iuventus natandi causa venit. hinc licet condiciones cotidie legas. cur huic qui te spernit molesta es?"

What's all this fuss about, sister? Why have you gone mad? Why do you protest so much, and make so much of nothing? You happened to notice a boy who lives nearby. You were attracted by his fair complexion, his tall figure, his face, his eyes. You wanted to see him more often. You sometimes spent some time with him in the same pleasure-gardens. You are a noble lady and he has a stingy, parsimonious father. You want to keep him tied to you with your money, but you can't: he kicks against the goad, spurns and rejects you, and thinks nothing of your presents. Try somewhere else, then! You own pleasure-gardens on the Tiber, and you have carefully established them where all the young men like to come for a swim. You can pick up whatever you fancy there, any day you like. So why go on bothering this man who is not interested in you?

After this, Cicero turns once again to the defence of Caelius proper, but he continues to draw inspiration from comedy by taking, one after the other, the roles of the strict and the lenient father, as we have seen above. By the time he reaches the end of his direct attack on Clodia, Cicero has gone to considerable lengths to create an extremely negative image of her as a notorious *femme fatale*. Even if the tactical advantages of this strategy for the trial are obvious – in particular for discrediting her statements against Caelius[77] and at the same time making her alleged affair with him seem more plausible – the level of verbal violence is astonishingly high, despite the fact that the moral disqualification of opponents or witnesses was very common and played a significant role in Roman forensic practice in general, and that *ad hominem* arguments were often more significant than arguments based on the evidence at hand.[78] This unusual and potentially risky aggressiveness is constrained and at least in part legitimated by Cicero's repeated appeals to seemingly spontaneous humour and constant alluding to comedy. These techniques make Clodia's denigration seem justified and at the same time more effective. Let us turn, then, to the last aspect of the case and thereby remind ourselves of the specific circumstances of the trial.

---

77 On this point, see Dyck 2013, 13: "It is relevant here that prostitutes as a class were burdened by *infamia* and explicitly excluded from testifying under the *lex Iulia de vi* (...); Cicero's attack would thus have created strong prejudice against her testimony".
78 On this difference between the modern and ancient court system, see May 1988, esp. 1–12, and Thurn 2018.

4 Conclusion: Asserting Agreement with the Audience as a Resource of the Speaker

Until now we have primarily focused on an analysis of the text of the speech, and we have spoken little about the circumstances surrounding Caelius' trial and Cicero's performance on the 4th of April 56 BC on the *forum Romanum*. This makes sense not least because, apart from a few general notions of how such a trial was normally conducted according to the *lex Plautia de vi* (a presiding magistrate, a jury of 75 judges and, given the prominence of the individuals involved, presumably a large audience of spectators),[79] we are entirely dependent for the details on the information contained in the published speeches. How one might determine the relationship of the published versions to the speeches as they were actually delivered, has always been one of the most difficult issues in scholarship.[80] In this particular case, it is even more difficult to reach safe conclusions because we do not know whether Cicero revised and published the speech himself, or whether the publication was only undertaken posthumously on the basis of *commentarii* left in his estate.[81] That Cicero would have wished to make his success against Clodia known to a wider public has been adduced as his reason for a publication by his own hand.[82] More recently, however, the extremely acid invective character of the speech has been used as an argument against its prompt publication.[83]

In either case one can assume that the written version at the very least allows the readers of the *Pro Caelio* to reconstruct mentally the situation during the trial and as closely as possible to the intentions of the speaker and author. This holds not least for the reactions of the other participants in the trial, which

---

[79] For a concise overview, see Dyck 2013, 1–2; on the usual size and the rather active role often played by the audience, see Rosillo López 2017.
[80] See esp. Humbert 1925; Stroh 1975, 31–54; Powell/Patterson 2004, 52–57; Steel 2013; La Bua 2019, 33–42.
[81] The latter was argued especially by Norden 1913, with regard to supposed inconsistencies in the structure of the speech; for a convincing refutation of Norden's assumption, see esp. Stroh 1975, 243–298.
[82] See e.g. Austin 1960, 158–161, esp. 161: "But it is much more probable that the speech was published at once; this was Cicero's usual custom (...), and he was most unlikely to have delayed putting on record as soon as possible his triumph over Clodia, or to have been indifferent to what is a most brilliant and amusing speech, which some scholars have held to be the best he ever composed".
[83] See esp. Loutsch 2007, 68–71; for a review of the discussion and further references, see Dyck 2013, 25–28.

here, in contrast to the situation in the Verrines, are not explicitly described, but are left to the imagination of the reader. This applied above all to the laughter on the part of the judges and audience whom Cicero's performance would certainly have provoked; laughter plays a major role as an indication of spontaneous assent and as an important means by which Cicero would infuse the situation he describes with credible realism.[84]

How Clodia reacted to the invective against her in this speech is hard to say. Her presence during the trial is suggested by the fact that Cicero pretends, as we saw above, to invite her response in the course of his speech. Whether she was really present or not is impossible to tell with certainty. Most likely this is a simulated face-to-face situation of the kind that invective speech acts frequently evoke in order to strengthen their effectiveness.[85] In other words, we have absolutely no way of knowing whether Clodia was physically present or she was merely a comedic figure in the imagination of the speaker.

One thing, however, we can say a little more about is how successfully Cicero in this speech used his mastery of argumentation techniques in general, and his borrowings from comedy in particular, not only to increase the effectiveness of his verbal aggression in its power to hurt, but also to make it appear socially acceptable. It is not without significance that, on account of these techniques, readers in later times also have the feeling that they are joining in the laughter of the original audience and side with their verdict on the situation.

It may be that in our day, which is generally marked by a more sensitive approach to verbal violence, especially when such violence is directed towards women, we have developed a different sense of appreciating this speech. Even so, it is difficult to read Cicero's defence speech *Pro Caelio*, which is in large part an invective *in Clodiam*, simply as an entertaining example of forensic rhetoric. But one could safely state that the different reactions to this speech in the course of time may serve as a guide towards understanding social change better – but that would be a topic for another article.

---

84 For many similar reactions to the speech way by modern readers, see e.g. Austin 1960, 91 ad § 33: "Cicero's tactics here are masterly; even by the end of § 38 he must have known that he had won his case, with Clodia being laughed out of the court".
85 A better understanding of this important invective technique is part our project at Dresden; see above note 10.

Bibliography

Arcellaschi, A. (1997), 'Le *Pro Caelio* et le théâtre', in: *Revue des Études Latines* 75, 164–172.
Austin, R.G. (³1960 [¹1933]), *M. Tulli Ciceronis pro M. Caelio Oratio*, Oxford.
Bablitz, L. (2007), *Actors and Audience in the Roman Courtroom*, London.
Berry, D. (²2008 [¹2000]), *Cicero: Defence Speeches, Translated with Introductions and Notes*, Oxford.
Butler, H.E. (1922), *Quintilian. With an English Translation, vol. 4*, London.
Dyck, A.R. (2013), *Cicero: Pro Marco Caelio*, Cambridge.
Fuhrmann, M. (1990), 'Mündlichkeit und fiktive Mündlichkeit in den von Cicero veröffentlichten Reden', in: G. Vogt-Spira (ed.), *Strukturen der Mündlichkeit in der römischen Literatur*, Tübingen, 53–62.
Fyntikoglou, V. (2003), 'Caecus, Clodia, Metellus: Theatre and Politics in *Pro Caelio*', in: *Studies in Latin Literature and Roman History* 11, 186–198.
Geffcken, K.G. (1973 [²1995]), *Comedy in the Pro Caelio. With an Appendix on the In Clodium et Curionem*, Leiden.
Gräßner, C.A. (2013), 'Clodia', in: P. von Möllendorff et al. (eds.), *Historische Gestalten der Antike. Rezeption in Literatur, Kunst und Musik,* Stuttgart, 311–318.
Günther, R. (2000), 'Sexuelle Diffamierung und politische Intrigen in der Republik. P. Clodius Pulcher und Clodia', in: T. Späth and B. Wagner-Hasel (eds.), *Frauenwelten in der Antike. Geschlechterordnung und weibliche Lebenspraxis*, Stuttgart, 227–241.
Hall, J. (2014), *Cicero's Use of Judicial Theater*, Ann Arbor.
Harders, A.-C. (2008), Suavissima Soror. *Untersuchungen zu den Bruder-Schwester-Beziehungen in der römischen Republik*, Munich.
Harries, B. (2007), 'Acting the Part: Techniques of the Comic Stage in Cicero's Early Speeches', in: J. Booth (ed.), *Cicero on the Attack: Invective and Subversion in the Orations and Beyond*, Swansea, 129–147.
Hartmann, E. (2007), *Frauen in der Antike*, Munich.
Heinze, R. (1925), 'Ciceros Rede pro Caelio', in: *Hermes* 1960, 193–258.
Hickson-Hahn, F. (1998), 'What's so Funny? Laughter and Incest in Invective Humor", in: *Syllecta Classica* 9, 1–36.
Humbert, J. (1925), *Les plaidoyers écrits et les plaidoiries réelles de Cicéron*, Paris.
Humm, M. (2005), *Appius Claudius Caecus: la république accomplie*, Rome.
Jehne, M. (2020), *Freud und Leid römischer Senatoren. Invektivarenen in Republik und Kaiserzeit,* Karl-Christ-Preis für Alte Geschichte 4, Göttingen.
Klodt, C. (2003), 'Prozessparteien und politische Gegner als *dramatis personae*. Charakterstilisierung in Ciceros Reden', in: B.-J. Schröder and J.P. Schröder (eds.), *Studium declamatorium: Untersuchungen zu Schulübungen und Prunkreden von der Antike bis zur Neuzeit*, Leipzig, 35–106.
Krostenko, B.A. (2001), *Cicero, Catullus and the Language of Social Performance*, Chicago.
La Bua, G. (2019), *Cicero and Roman Education: The Reception of the Speeches and Ancient Scholarship*, Cambridge.
Linke, B. (2000), 'Appius Claudius Caecus - ein Leben im Zeitalter des Umbruchs', in: K.-J. Hölkeskamp and E. Stein-Hölkeskamp (eds.), *Von Romulus zu Augustus. Große Gestalten der römischen Republik*, Munich, 69–78.

Lausberg, H. (1960), *Handbuch der literarischen Rhetorik. Eine Grundlegung der Literaturwissenschaft*, 2 vol., Munich.
Leigh, M. (2004), 'The *Pro Caelio* and Comedy', in: *Classical Philology* 99, 300–335.
Loutsch, C. (2007), 'Remarques sur la publication du *Pro Caelio* de Cicéron', in: *Parole, media, pouvoir dans l'occident romain: hommages offerts au Professeur Guy Achard*, Lyon, 53–71.
Malcovati, E. (1967), *Oratorum Romanorum Fragmenta liberae rei publicae*, vol. 1, Turin.
Manuwald, G. (2014), 'Cicero, an Interpreter of Terence', in: S. Papaioannou (ed.), *Terence and Interpretation*, Newcastle upon Tyne, 179–200.
Maslowski, T. (1995), *M. Tulli Ciceronis scripta quae manuerunt omnia Fasc. 23: Orationes in P. Vatinium testem; pro M. Caelio*, Stuttgart.
May, J.M. (1988), *Trials of Character: The Eloquence of Ciceronian Ethos*, Chapel Hill.
Møller Jensen, B. (2003), 'Medea, Clytemnestra and Helena. Allusions to Mythological Femmes Fatales in Cicero's *Pro Caelio*', in: *Eranos* 101, 64–72.
Moretti, G. (2006), 'Lo spettacolo dello pro Caelio: oggetti di scena, teatro e personaggi nel processo contre Marco Celio', in: G. Petrone and A. Casamento (eds.), *Lo spettacolo della giustizia: le orazioni di Cicerone*, Palermo, 139–164.
Nippel, W. (2000), 'Publius Clodius Pulcher - "der Achill der Straße"', in: K.-J. Hölkeskamp and E. Stein-Hölkeskamp (eds.), *Von Romulus zu Augustus. Große Gestalten der römischen Republik*, Munich, 279–291.
Norden, E. (1913), 'Aus Ciceros Werkstatt', in: *Sitzungsberichte der Königlich Preußischen Akademie der Wissenschaften*, Berlin, 2–32.
Papaioannou, S., Serafim, A. and da Vela, B. (eds.) (2017), *The Theatre of Justice. Aspects of Performance in Greco-Roman Oratory and Rhetoric*, Leiden.
Pausch, D. (forthcoming), 'Ars invectiva und artifizielle Mündlichkeit: Schmähungen in Rom zwischen Schulbuch und scheinbarer Spontaneität', in: A. Dröse, M. Münkler, F. Prautzsch and A. Sablotny (eds.), *Invektive Gattungen. Formen und Medien der Herabsetzung*, Dresden.
Powell, J. and Patterson, J. (2004), 'Introduction', in: J. Powell and J. Patterson (eds.), *Cicero the Advocate*, Oxford, 1–57.
Ramage, E.S. (1973), *Urbanitas. Ancient Sophistication and Refinement*, Norman, OK.
Ramage, E.S. (1984), 'Clodia in Cicero's *Pro Caelio*', in: D.R. Bright et al. (eds.), *Classical Texts and Their Traditions: Studies in Honor of C.R. Trahman*, Chico, CA, 201–211.
Riggsby, A. (1999), *Crime and Community in Ciceronian Rome*, Austin.
Rosillo López, C. (2017), 'The Role and Influence of the Audience (*corona*) in Trials in the Late Roman Republic', in: *Athenaeum* 105, 106–119.
Rühl, M. (2019), *Ciceros Korrespondenz als Medium literarischen und gesellschaftlichen Handelns*, Leiden.
Serafim, A. (2017), *Attic Oratory and Performance*, New York/London.
Skinner, M.B. (2011), *Clodia Metelli. The Tribune's Sister*, Oxford.
Steel, C. (2013), 'Cicero, Oratory and Public Life', in: C. Steel (ed.), *The Cambridge Companion to Cicero*, Cambridge, 160–170.
Steel, C. (2017), 'Speech without Limits: Defining Informality in Republican Oratory', in: S. Papaioannou, A. Serafim and B. da Vela (eds.), *The Theatre of Justice. Aspects of Performance in Greco-Roman Oratory and Rhetoric*, Leiden, 75–89.
Stroh, W. (1975), *Taxis und Taktik. Ciceros Gerichtsreden*, Stuttgart.
Tatum, W.J. (1999), *The Patrician Tribune: P. Clodius Pulcher*, Chapel Hill.

Tatum, W.J. (2007), 'Invective Identities in *Pro Caelio*', in: C. Smith and R. Covino (eds.), *Praise and Blame in Roman Republican Rhetoric*, Swansea, 165–179.

Thurn, A. (2018), *Rufmord in der späten römischen Republik. Charakterbezogene Diffamierungsstrategien in Ciceros Reden und Briefen*, Berlin.

Volpe, M. (1977), 'The Persuasive Force of Humor: Cicero's Defense of Caelius', in: *Quarterly Journal of Speech* 63, 311–323.

Williams, H. (2007), 'Cicero, *pro Caelio*: What was it that Most Undermined Clodias' Case - Her Character, the Prejudices of Roman Men, the Skills of Cicero or ...?', in: *Akoterion* 52, 121–127.

Winterbottom, M. (1970), *M. Fabi Quintiliani institutionis oratoriae libri XII*, Oxford.

Wiseman, T.P. (1985), *Catullus and his World*, Cambridge.

Zillinger, W. (1911), *Cicero und die altrömischen Dichter*, Würzburg.

Hanna Maria Degener
How to Start a Show: Comic Invectives in the Prologues of Terence and Decimus Laberius

Abstract: This chapter examines the patterns and functions of comic invectives in the prologues of Roman theatrical performances, while also paying attention to the spectrum of possible applications of comic invectives for the *captatio benevolentiae*, when the aim is to win over the target audience. The prologues of two Roman theatre playwrights, Terence and Decimus Laberius, are rich in content for this purpose. Terence's prologues can be used to trace the narratological construction of a conflict that extends over a long period of time. Decimus Laberius uses *auto-invective*, i.e. self-deprecation that aims to evoke an emotional reaction from the audience, by creating positive images for the invector, while scathingly criticising Caesar's actions and presenting him as the enemy of the existing social order. The chapter, finally, proposes some answers to the question of what risk Terence and Laberius expose themselves to by using comic invective in their speeches.

Some scholars associate invectives with the sophisticated degradations in the Greek and Roman judicial systems, in which the speaker has the opportunity not only to vilify and discredit his opponent, but also to distinguish himself as a rhetorical artist. However, similar demands are also made of an actor.[1] Both the orator and the actor strive to win over an audience for their cause and to convince them of the facts presented.[2] In both forensic and dramatic speeches, the *captatio benevolentiae* and the *narratio* are used for this purpose.[3] In this con-

---

I would like to thank my colleagues at TU Dresden for their kind remarks on this chapter, especially Martin Jehne, Franziska Luppa, Katja Schulze, Dennis Pausch and Jan Lukas Horneff, and the editors of the volume for their remarks and effort. I owe special thanks to Peter P. Krüger for taking care of the translation into English.

1 A fine compilation of some of the points can be found at Barbiero 2020, 393. The connection between the figure of the orator and the actor has already been analysed with different focal points and approaches.
2 Cic. *De orat.* 1.143, *ante quam de re diceremus, initio conciliandos eorum esse animos, qui audirent* [...].
3 Sharrock 2009, 84.

text, emotions can serve as a key element for success. The use of humour and skilful wit is said to have been particularly appealing to an audience.[4] Thus, a good orator, according to Cicero, must have, among other things, the words of a writer, the voice of a tragedian and the gestures of a performer.[5]

This chapter focuses on the Roman playwrights as designers of invectives in units that are decidedly rhetorical, namely evocative of oratorical delivery. The Roman theatre forms a space for public praise, blame and disparagement of individuals and groups on and off stage. In what follows, we shall examine which elements contribute to the visualisation of the comic in invectives that feature in the prologues of Roman theatre plays. The aim is to highlight those aspects that strengthen the comic potential of the stage productions. Reference is made to two distinct examples: on the one hand, the prologues of the six pieces of Terence, and on the other hand, a fragment by Decimus Laberius often quoted as a prologue. The selected texts have one thing in common: both authors use the prologue as a platform to get back at another competitor or political figure for wrongful behaviour, but in different ways. The various functions and strategies of the use of comic invectives in the prologues shall be demonstrated based on these examples. Finally, an attempt will be made to assess the potential of playwrights as actors of the invective triad (invector – invectee – audience).[6]

1 Comic Invectives as Part of *Ludi Scaenici*

Theatre plays were an integral part of Roman festive culture and as such played an important role in the formation of social norms, the development of literature and language. The performances took place in a variety of festival scenarios, most of which were organised annually at fixed times and included not only

---

[4] Cic. *De orat.* 2.216.
[5] Cic. *De orat.* 1.128. At the same time there is also criticism of the supposedly excessive theatricality of the speakers. See the chapter by Dennis Pausch in this volume on Cicero's use of theatrical elements in *Pro M. Caelio*.
[6] Invective communication comprises three (groups of) agents: the one who vilifies (the invector); the one who is vituperated (the invectee) and the audience of this spectacle. The reaction of the audience is key to the anticipated outcome of a performed invective. This is not limited to the theatre, but it can also be transferred to other venues. In the Roman theatre, however, the spectators play a special role due to their mass, composition of all demographic groups, their seating arrangements and their ability to comment on current social and political developments.

scenic performances, but also events such as gladiatorial games or sporting competitions. In addition, there were mostly one-off situational games, for example in the context of triumphal processions, funerals or votive games. In the late republic a mixed form emerged, the *ludi victoriae* of Sulla and Caesar. On some occasions certain performative genres were preferred, such as the *mimus* at the *Floralia*. The individual genres, which evolved over time, were subject to certain traditions, which the poets could interpret independently. Although the works of Plautus and Terence are both attributed to the *fabulae palliatae*, the style of the two authors is very distinct, for instance when one looks at the use of comedy. The proximity between humour and the disparagement of others is established by Quintilian:

> [...] The cause of laughter is uncertain, since laughter is never far removed from derision. For, as Cicero says, laughter has its basis in some kind or other of deformity or ugliness and whereas, when we point to such a blemish in others, the result is known as wit, it is called folly when the same jest is turned against ourselves.[7]

Invectives can be found on various levels within the framework of *ludi scaenici*. On the one hand, insults, disparagement and verbal violence are part of the inner dynamics of the pieces. This has been investigated extensively, especially with regard to certain social groups or lines of tradition between different authors.[8] Particularly notable is the dissertation by Hans Bork, who uses the works of Plautus to expound the performative character of insults in Roman plays.[9] In this process, he directs attention not only to sociolinguistics, but also to the evaluation of vituperation on the basis of previously established relationships within the constellation of characters in the play as well as with the audience. On the other hand, Roman theatre offered the opportunity to express criticism of public figures and their actions in a number of instances. This could occur due to lack of respect during the greeting, through riots, disturbances or direct

---

7 Quint. *Inst.* 6.3.7–8, [...] *anceps eius rei ratio est, quod a derisu non procul abest risus. Habet enim, ut Cicero dicit, sedem in deformitate aliqua et turpitudine, quae cum in aliis demonstrantur, urbanitas, cum in ipsos dicentes recidunt, stultitia vocatur.*
8 A good example is Richlin's research, which addressed both the question of sexuality and degradation in Roman comedy and the role and function of slaves in Roman theatres as figures and spectators, especially after the Punic Wars: Richlin 1992 and 2014. Iurescia examines impoliteness and social dynamics in quarrels in the plays of Plautus: see Iurescia 2019.
9 Based on the attribution as thief (*fur*) Bork tries to reconstruct the interpersonal dynamics. This is supplemented by an exposé on the comedy of physical violence: Bork 2018.

insults.[10] In many cases, parts of the actual play were also re-contextualised, for example through gestures.[11] This form of abuse was given weight, among other things because it took place in asymmetrical situations. The audience played a defining role, which, through the reaction to the invective, ascribed a value to the utterance and gave it significance. The audience's demand for repetition of certain invectives, for example, could also underline the social dynamics of these degrading processes. What both forms had in common was that, on the one hand, they were subject to certain norms of the arena in which they were performed and, on the other hand, that certain theatrical elements accentuated the comical character. The presentation includes a composition of linguistic, auditory and visual stimuli.

There are a few aspects of the Roman theatre that underline and emphasise the comic character of invectives on stage. The first nucleus of visual elements revolves around the creation of a low-status or ludicrous invector. Four types of paraphernalia can contribute to this design: masks,[12] costumes,[13] names and props. Costumes that deviate from the norm[14] are mostly associated with stock

---

10 Disputes arose regarding the lawful enforcement of seating arrangements (Schol. *Juv.* 5.3), silence as an expression of protest and disdain (Cic. *Att.* 2.19.2–3), whistling and physical violence (Cic. *Sest.* 116–117), negative acclamations (Dio Cass. 74.2.2–3, SHA *Alex. Ser.* 6.3; SHA *Comm.* 18.5). Those affected were magistrates, senators and also the later Roman emperors. A systematic investigation is conducted at the Collaborative Research Centre 1285 "Invectivity. Constellations and Dynamics of Disparagement". In subproject A "Invectivity in Arenas of Ritualised Communication during the Roman Republic and Imperial Era" led by Martin Jehne, my dissertation on invectives in the theatre, amphitheatre and circus is being prepared.
11 This seems to be the opposite of the attested "Humour without laughter", that Meister discusses by focusing on instances in the political sphere of the imperial period. In this case, the association with a specific person or instance needs further controlling – and the laughter of the audience is crucial: see Meister 2014.
12 A lengthy research debate revolves around the question of the use of masks in the *palliata*. The ancient evidence for this is not unequivocal. In his commentaries, Donatus says that masked actors appeared in the productions of Terence's *Eunuchus* and *Adelphoe*. Don. *Praef. ad Eun.* 6; ibid. Don. *Praef. ad Ad.* 6. For an overview, see Saunders 1911.
13 Manuwald suggests that swift role changes make practical and simple costumes more likely, yet more elaborate and expensive costumes were used in the late Republic and early Imperial period. With reference to Hor. *Epist.* 2.1.204–7: Manuwald 2011, 76.
14 Corbeill makes the connection between these characters and the masks that had distorted or deformed facial features. Physical abnormalities served as indications of internal reprehensibility. Cicero's attack on the witness Vatinius can serve as one of countless other examples. However, this becomes problematic due to the imposing stature of Piso. Here, the accusation is that Piso tries in a malicious way to deceive the Romans with his beautiful appearance and to hide his inner deviance: Corbeill 1996, 37 and chapter 4.

characters such as eunuchs or foreigners. In the style of Greek costumes, padding could be used for some characters, which in certain cases may have followed the tradition of including an artificial *phallus*.[15] While there is scope for differentiation in the way the masks are depicted and equipped,[16] the visual design of the masks and costumes can still be seen as ascribing a recognisable social status.[17] In addition, some roles in Roman comedy are an allusion to marginalised groups of people, such as slaves, pimps and parasites.[18] Clarke identifies the reversal of normative social roles and their licenses to speak as one of the bases for humorous allusions in the Saturnalia, triumphal processions and also the *Floralia* productions.[19] The names of the characters can also unfold an invective potential.[20] The ridicule attached to the *persona* that reviles another character underlines the comic effect and may have added to the humiliation, especially if it contradicts the current social norms.

The second nucleus, around which the comic character of the invective in the Roman theatre is shaped, is defined by the recontextualisation of verses through gesture, body language and music. On the one hand, the adherence to a rhythm in case of negative acclamations strengthened the enforceability even with such a large group as the audience at imperial theatre plays.[21] On the other hand, attention must be paid to the choice of words and music, which can help to add a humorous note to what is said.[22] Impersonation and mimetic mockery can serve as good examples on how gesture and a specific way to move and talk

---

15 Marshall argues here for dramaturgical reasons in reference to Greek role models and confines this to the *palliata*. Marshall 2006, 62–65. According to Marshall, the additional padding makes the use of physical violence more likely, and even invites it. Marshall 2006, 66.
16 Marshall explicitly supports Duckworth's thesis that we should speak of a differentiation and not an individualisation of the stock character in relation to the masks: Duckworth 1952, 270; Marshall 2006, 138.
17 On the closeness and differentiation to ancestral masks, see Wiles 2007 and Flower 1996. Clarke examines the similarity between the graphic representation of masks in the theatre and pictorial graffiti and caricatures: Clarke 2007, 44–49.
18 Corbeill 1996, 41. Terence's *Hecyra* distinguishes himself by skilfully breaking with the expectations of the stock character and making them behave differently than expected: Gruen 2014, 612–613. Brown previously analysed the connection between masks, names and stock characters as well as the playful handling of the breaks in attribution: Brown 1987.
19 Clarke 2007, 22.
20 For the use of (nick-)names as a form of disparagement see the corresponding chapters in Corbeill 1996, 57–98 and Rosillo-López 2017.
21 Aldrete 1999, 134–135.
22 See further Moore 2013 and Vincent 2013, esp. 71–81 and 84–87; as well as Beacham 1995, 131–132.

are used as a source for comic invective on stage.[23] Besides juggling and dance, performance practice was strongly influenced by expressive gestures and mimics, like caricatures.

Common to all kind of gestures is the attempt to underline what is said, or rather its meaning, and to stir up the audience's emotions.[24] It should be emphasised, however, that in the ancient works on oratory, a difference is drawn between theatricality and intensity of gestures in actors and orators.[25] Aldrete points out that numerous great speakers of Roman antiquity used actors as inspiration for their own performances.[26] Gestures can also contextualise what is said and thus become an invective against those present. The following is a representative example of this practice: Suetonius recounts an incident between the actor Datus and Emperor Nero during a performance in a theatre. Datus is said to have uttered the words "Oh Father! Oh, Mother!" with drinking and swimming gestures to indicate the potential poisoning of Claudius and the shipwrecking of Agrippina prior to her death.[27] Nero would not utter any boasts on the spot – as Suetonius reports – so as not to fuel further attacks. The actor was subsequently banished from Italy. In other cases, Nero responded with vituperative lines and gestures towards his opponents.[28]

---

[23] For example the imitation of Phaedria by Parmeno in Terence's *Eunuchus*.
[24] Luc. Salt. 35.
[25] In his *Institutio Oratoria*, Quintilian describes some gestures which, due to their vulgarity and theatricality, are not suitable for the speaker and are to be shown exclusively on stage. Quint. *Inst.* 11.3.102, 103, 104, 123, 125. Cicero imposes the requirement of restraint in gestures on the speaker, so that the comparison to the actor, and especially to the pantomime, is not made. Cic. *De orat.* 2.237–252. This would entail a loss of dignity for the speaker. Although Quintilian notes that over time some gestures have been seen as unproblematic, he too urges us to maintain the distinction. That the degree of differentiation is complex is shown by Aldrete in Quintilian's treatises on gestures: Aldrete 1999, 70–71. For a closer look on Cicero's argumentation in *De oratore* see the chapter by Kish in this volume.
[26] For an overview: Aldrete 1999, 67–73. Conversely, Roscius and Aesopus are said to have watched Hortensius in order to adapt his gesture for the stage. Val. Max. 8.10.2.
[27] Suet. *Ner.* 39. Immediately afterwards, the actor is supposed to draw attention to Nero's proscriptions with a gesture.
[28] Idib. 42. Nero is supposed to have observed and analysed the gestures of the *plebs urbana* with a view to possible abuses: Dio Cass. 62.15.2; Cf. Aldrete 1996, 92.

2 Prologues and Invectives

The prologues of some plays by Roman authors are a rich source of information about the staging of the *ludi scaenici*. Four forms of comedy prologues are derived from the fragments of Donatus:[29] firstly, the prologue can be used as a stage for praising the poet and his work (*commendativus*). The second function is to attack rivals or win over the audience (*relativus*). In addition, there are those elements that refer to the upcoming plot and introduce it (*argumentativus*). Finally, Donatus refers to a mixed form (*mixtus*).

In the prologues of Plautus, for example, there is not only information about the plot and the roles of the ensuing play, but also repeated references to the audience. These include the request for silence and attention, the advice that those who come late should not be assigned a seat, or that it is easier to concentrate on the play with a full stomach. These forms of meta-theatre can be found both in the prologues and in the course of the performance. Prologues usually initiate the events on stage, and as such they need to attract the attention of the audience. Besides appeals and petitions, an interaction with the audience can also be staged. The beginning of the performances could be initially marked by unrest and lack of attention. It sometimes required the active involvement of the audience by the prologue-speaker to draw them in. Richlin illustrates well the fluidity of the interaction between actors and the audience, which makes it possible for infamous actors to comment on contemporary political discourses and to insult socially superior individuals.[30] This is substantiated by two assumptions that she formulates with regard to the use of humour in reference to Scott:

> Two principles from the theory of humour reinforce Scott's arguments: (1) that the conventional structure of jokes acts as a shield to protect the joketeller from a hostile reaction; (2) that audience members who belong to a group ridiculed by a comedian take the comedian to be referring to group members other than themselves [...].[31]

In what follows, two examples serve to illuminate the spectrum of functions that invectives have in prologues. An attempt is made to take a special look at how the use of invectives can extend our current understanding, since they

---

29 Dunsch 2014, 513.
30 Richlin 2017, 139–141.
31 Richlin 2014, 178.

seem to appear less aggressive in the prologues than, for example, in the *carmina* of Catullus.

2.1 Terence's Feud with the Spiteful Old Playwright

Six plays by Publius Terentius Afer, one of the most famous poets of the *palliatae*, have survived today, which were originally performed between 166 and 160 BC. The so-considered former slave from North Africa, probably collaborated closely with a permanent acting troupe, led by Ambivius Turpio as *impressario*. Terence's style was characterised, in contrast to Plautus', by restraint as it lacked the exaggerated comical theatricality observed in his predecessor.

The rhetorical artistry of the prologues of Terence has been widely recognised by the research community. My analysis focuses on the accusations made by Terence and the strategies for dealing with the conflict between himself and a competitor. The *opinio communis* is that the nameless opponent in Terence's prologues is indeed Luscius Lanuvinus.[32] Little is known about this author of *palliata*.[33] Two plays are attributed to him: *Phasma* and *Thesaurus*, both adaptations of Menandrian plays, of which only about ten words have survived.[34] Terence always refers to him as "the old poet", without calling him by his actual name. If one considers this to be invective communication, even fictitious, one must ask the question how and for what purpose this is staged. In addition to the invector identified as Lanuvinus, there are also references to a group of people who made accusations against Terence. Beside the complex ways in which the agents involved in this exchange of allegations and the expressed accusations are related, it is important to consider the narrative lines constructed. For this purpose an overview of the emergence and development of Terence's rivalry across his prologues is in order.

The prologue to *Andria* (*ludi Megalenses* 166 BC)[35] starts abruptly. A resentful old poet (*malevoli veteris poetae*, *An. Prolog.* 6) compels Terence to write a

---

[32] Terence himself, in his criticism of his nameless accuser, identifies him as the author of the two plays that are attributed to Lanuvinus. Donatus makes the connection to the first reference to the accuser in *Andria* in his commentary on Terence.

[33] Here, reference must be made to Garton's comprehensive attempt to investigate the relations and every possible proof of Lanuvinus: Garton 1972, especially 41–72; also Duckworth 1952, 62–65.

[34] Kruschwitz 2002, 26 n. 9 with reference to Lefèvre.

[35] The *didascalia* indicate the year and context of the performance. Because the author's debut would be rather unusual, some researchers assume that the prologue might belong to a

prologue, which should not be simply expository, but it needs to take a stand (*maledictis respondeat, An. Prolog.* 7). The accusation was that Terence had added elements from *Perinthia* to the Menandrian text of the *Andria* and thus contaminated it (*contaminari non decere fabulas, An. Prolog.* 16). He was reproached for this by several persons (*vituperant* [...] *atque in eo disputant, An. Prolog.* 15). Terence extends this accusation by placing himself in a traditional line with Plautus, Naevius and Ennius. He would rather be associated with their carelessness than with the pedantry (*obscuram diligentiam, An. Prolog.* 21) of the attackers. Then he adds a warning: "therefore, I advise them to be quiet in the future, and to cease to slander; that they may not be made acquainted with their own misdeeds" (*An. Prolog.* 22–23).

Terence thus broaches the issue of accusations that have been made against him previously. Although these allegations are made by several people, the slander of the spiteful old poet is the reason for arranging his argument in the prologue in this way.[36] Terence seems intent on invalidating the accusations and putting his own character into perspective through comparison.[37] He designs the prologue like a forensic speech.[38] Although the counter-attacks are not particularly harsh, they show Terence's rhetorical abilities. The identity of the old poet initially remains blurred. It is conceivable that he belongs to the group of people accused of unintelligibility (*faciuntne intellegendo ut nil intellegant?, An. Prolog.* 17) and pedantry. Goldberg puts forward the argument that Terence may have modelled himself on Cato in his choice of words, style and metres, yet in the precise, short prologues he shows that he has forged his own style, one that goes beyond the previously established forms of comedy.

No prologue of the first performance of *Hecyra* (*ludi Romani* 165 BC) has been preserved. Three years after the performance of *Andria*, the conflict does not seem to have been resolved. In *Heauton Timōrumenos* (*ludi Megalenses* 163 BC) two lines of argument in the prologue refer to the conflict that still haunts the poet. On the one hand there is a renewed reference to a group of malevolent people who spread rumours (*rumores distulerunt, Heaut. Prolog.* 16). The accusa-

---

later performance. On the fictionality of the debate drafted in the prologue, see Gilula 1989; Gruen 1992.

36 In this volume, Buis emphasises the comic poets' strategy of self-praise that aims to justify retaliation against one's opponent.

37 Germany argues that the prologue already introduces topics that are important for the later course of the event: Germany 2013, 230–233.

38 Goldberg analyses the prologue as a complete rhetorical speech consisting of the following sections: *exordium* (1–8), *narratio* (9–16), *argumentatio* (17–23) and *conclusio* (24–27): Goldberg 1983, 209.

tion pertains to the contamination of the Greek models with external additions, hardly resulting to the production of an original composition (*multas contaminasse Graecas dum facit / paucas Latinas, Heaut. Prolog.* 17–18.). Terence does not deny the accusation, but once again mentions the parallel approach of well-known role models. In contrast to the first example, however, the active involvement of the audience is more prominent in this instance. Terence stages the event, on the other hand, as a court case, even before the above-mentioned accusations are addressed: Turpio, the prologue-speaker, is supposed to act as a lawyer (*oratorem esse voluit me, non prologum, Heaut. Prolog.* 11–12.),[39] the spectators are appointed as judges (*vostrum iudicium fecit, Heaut. Prolog.* 12). Turpio makes it evident that these are not his words but those of the author (*sed hic actor tantum poterit a facundia / quantum ille potuit cogitare commode / qui orationem hanc scripsit quam dicturus sum, Heaut. Prolog.* 13–15).

He also adopts an invective of the old poet, who asserts that Terence's success is not based on his own talent but rather on that of his friends (*repente ad studium hunc se adplicasse musicum, / amicum ingenio fretum, haud natura sua, Heaut. Prolog.* 23 f.). Terence does not take a stance on the accusations; instead, he turns to flattering the audience, whose members, he confidently asserts, will judge wisely (*arbitrium vostrum, vostra existumatio / valebit, Heaut. Prolog.* 25 f.) and will not "let the words of the prejudiced have more weight than the words of the unprejudiced" ([...]*ne plus iniquom possit quam aequom oratio, Heaut. Prolog.* 27). Subsequently, Terence criticises one of Lanuvinus' plays and entices the audience to inquire why they should follow a madman[40] (*insano, Heaut. Prolog.* 32). The invective against his opponent is more explicit and includes personal elements, while Lanuvinus' accusations receive no further discussion. Terence, however, is concerned to win over his audience and convince them that, contrary to Lanuvinus, he does not lie. He concludes with the warning that he will publish further mistakes (*peccatis plura, Heaut. Prolog.* 33) in front of a large audience, should the old poet not refrain from his insults, implying that he knows so much more.

In 161 BC, two plays were performed, *Eunuchus* in April and *Phormio* in September. In the prologue to *Eunuchus* (*ludi Megalenses*) Terence arranges the

---

39 Quintilian makes a clear distinction between proper rhetorical and theatrical gestures. One might learn the art of expression from an actor, but not all theatrical gestures are appropriate in another context. See the well-designed overview of Fritz Graf on this topic: Graf 1991. In this case, Turpio's mimicry of a lawyer in a staged court could emphasise the comic character of the scene.

40 See Kazantzidis' chapter in this volume on allegations of insanity in comedy and their relationship with oratory.

parts of his speech in reverse order. First, he speaks to the audience and describes himself as a good person who has no interest in offending anyone. Criticism of excessive attack on his part is unjustified, he says, because he can point to previous escalations. Then, he critisises the staging of his opponent: he, Lanuvinus, was a bad author who ruined the good Greek originals.[41] Terence mentions examples from *Phasma* and *Thesaurus*. And he refers to inconsistencies during recent performances of the respective plays. The next part of the prologue speech includes a reference to further insults, which the author originally had kept to himself, but now is willing to share in front of a crowd. He then goes on to discuss the context in which the attack provoking this invective took place. The old poet had crept in before the magistrates during the rehearsal, and in their presence insulted Terence by calling him a thief (*furem*), who stole the characters of the parasite and braggart soldier from Naevius and Plautus. In Terence's reporting of the incident we can catch a glimpse of previous invectives. The incident itself – as serious as the impact on Terence's career can be – also holds comic potential. The subsequent defence aims at three points: first, if he actually took the characters of the parasite and braggart soldier from his Latin predecessors, he did so unintentionally. The audience may form an opinion about this while attending the play. Second, Terence does not deny that the two characters were taken from Greek originals. But he goes on to say that reusing comic material should not raise objection. If this rule were to be applied strictly and consistently, most of the stock characters from New Comedy would have to be left out. Finally, he directs the focus on the old poet's transgressions and incompetence, and the way he describes them makes Lanuvinus' true intentions come out clear.

In the performance of *Phormio* (*ludi Romani* 161 BC) the conflict seems to have reached a peak. The first half of the prologue is devoted to the placement of the accusations in the development of the argument and Terence's response.[42] Contrary to the earlier prologues, the audience here is reduced to silent listeners. The old poet had not succeeded in his previous attempts to eliminate Terence as an author. Lanuvinus needs to invent something novel in order to discredit his opponent as a playwright. Nevertheless, Terence counter-attacks and deflects the charge by pointing instead to the alleged weakness of Lanuvinus' plays. He also observes that the uncontested success of the play should be

---

[41] The closeness to the formulation in *Heauton Timōrumenos* is interesting: *multas contaminasse Graecas dum facit / paucas Latinas* vs *ex Graecis bonis Latinas fecit non bonas*, Heaut. Prolog. 8.

[42] Phorm. Prolog. 1–23.

attributed solely to the talent of the stage director. For this reason, the poet does not know what justifies his opponent to launch such vitriolic criticism. Terence points out twice that he is merely reacting to the invective of his opponent; that he only wishes to respond, not fight back. Lanuvinus' intention, on the contrary, is very different: the older poet is set out to drive Terence into a state of destitution.

Dealing with criticism is placed prominently in the prologue to *Adelphoe* (*ludi funebres* 160 BC). Once again, the playwright points to indignities that predate the prologue. He refers to opponents (*iniquis; adversarios, Ad. Prolog.* 2) who criticise the piece to be performed and tear it up in advance. More significant than accusation seems to be the casting of the audience as judges, who are supposed to cast verdict on whether Terence has recoursed to plagiarism. Their task becomes further complicated because certain "ill-wishers" (*malevoli*) do not hesitate to use the young poet's ties to Scipio and Laelius against him and his artistic reputation. Once again, Terence turns abuse and defamation into praise. In contrast to *Heauton Timōrumenos*, however, the emphasis in *Adelphoe* is on the praise of Scipio and Laelius. If one takes the context of the performance, the funeral games of Aemilius Paullus, into account, one reaches the conclusion that the intended invective offers Terence the pretext to stress the greatness of his friends. The prologues to the second and third performances of *Hecyra* deal above all with the challenging performance circumstances that cause the staging of the play to be interrupted twice.

In conclusion, behind Terence's reaction to Lanuvinus' attack, one may discern the effort and the need to publicly justify and defend oneself against attacks from colleagues. Terence was a relatively young author who, although well connected, had to win over the audience and gain their approval of his work. And he needed to stand out next to other writers as well as to other forms of public entertainment. The attacks of Lanuvinus gave him an opportunity to take advantage of the possibility to use invective to his advantage as a means of winning success. In the character of the prologue-speaker, he tries to create a *persona* that is appealing to the audience. This technique of creating *ēthos* that is credible and invokes empathy in the audience aims, at the same time, at excluding the invectee from the community and building a sense of solidarity with the audience.[43] In the argumentation strategy of the prologue-speaker Terence evokes court tactics. In this way, he attempts to convince those who have already heard of the accusations against Terence to compare the latter's work

---

[43] On communication-building in oratory Papaioannou, Serafim and Demetriou 2020, 5 with reference to the lines of argumentation in Aristotle and Demosthenes.

with the plays of Lanuvinus. Since the organisers of the *ludi* as well as their potential successors were also present, the argumentation of the prologue-speaker may have influenced them in view of the next occasion they will have to decide on the plays to be chosen for performance in the *ludi*.[44] The complex function of Terence's prologues as illustrated above suggests that it is necessary to differentiate between the play and the prologues, even though there may be overlaps of themes or roles.[45]

Another interesting aspect is the long duration of the conflict as recorded in the prologues. From prologue to prologue, accusations are repeated, new ones are added, threats are made. Sharrock claims that the repetitive character of these introductory sections, allusions and all, offered a comic way of introducing a performance in a programmatic way that appealed to the audience.[46] Germany argues that Terence created his own stock characters in his prologues through the predictable appearance of the same set of agents (the old, envious poet, some other unnamed slanderer, the prologue-speaker, the young poet who breaks with the tradition).[47] Still, the exchange of blows between the two rival playwrights and the threats of a sequel seem to have dragged on over the years. Terence takes a stand on the accusations, involving the audience in the conflict as judges. Attacks, notably, concern only the opponent's artistry and never become personal. This applies to both sides: apart from being accused to have accepted help from his noble friends in the writing process, the accusations against Terence revolve around plagiarism and the correct handling of the Greek originals. It is not the person of Terence that is being disparaged, but his

---

44 There are indications that the choice of plays for performances at public games was based less on content than on the poet's name and connections. Manuwald 2011, 51–52.
45 By no means does this suggest that Terence's prologues are not connected to the rest of the play. Germany, for example, puts forward the thesis that in *Andria* there are connections between the accusations in the prologue and the plot in the rest of the play. In his opinion, however, these do not necessarily have to be thematic, but can also be linked narratologically: Germany 2013, in particular 228–229. He sees the *obscura diligentia* mentioned in the prologue as the key to understanding the play. Just as unexpectedly as the spectators are drawn into the conflict between the writers, they must independently form an opinion about the characters in the play and discover the differences to their Greek counterparts. Earlier research has already alluded to the fact that the prologues may have been more closely associated with the specific performance context, and mentions as an example the sudden start in the prologue to *Andria*: Klose 1966, 42–43.
46 Sharrock 2009, 63.
47 Germany 2013, 228–229.

talent as an author.[48] The same applies to Terence's attack on Luscius Lanuvinus. Several times he is called the envious old poet. Thrice, Terence refers to mistakes in Lanuvinus' own adaptation of plays and their inferior artistic composition. The name of the invector himself is not mentioned. It is also impossible to verify whether Lanuvinus is one of the opponents collectively referred to as such in the plural. Beacham detects an intensification of the conflict in the prologue to *Phormio*, where the intention of the attacker is revealed: to discredit Terence as an author so that he may no longer exercise this profession and be reduced to starvation.[49] Already in *Eunuchus*, which was performed earlier the same year, there seems to be some escalation. Terence justifies his attack against his rival on the grounds that Lanuvinus has already launched a bitter attack against Terence. It is questionable whether a levelling off of the intensity is connected with the solemn occasion of the funeral games for Aemilius Paullus, during which *Adelphoe* and *Hecyra* were brought to stage.[50]

Terence deploys invective in the prologues primarily for two reasons: to elaborate and convey his own understanding of literature,[51] and to involve the audience in the overall experience. By appointing the audience as judges[52] in this conflict, he does not only flatter them, but also puts them in charge of following the play attentively and enables them to form their own opinions. He draws the attention of the audience not only to what is going to happen on stage, but also to how the writer arranged it.[53] Terence's strategy in dealing with his opponent's attacks is twofold: he tries to revert and sometimes even stylise

---

48 The colourful *topoi* of invective motifs used in other contexts offer great entertainment value. This limitation may indicate that the invective motifs are only a narratological pretext. Moreover, it would only be of limited use to make forms of character assassination identifiable to a larger audience, especially since they are not so easily refuted.
49 Beacham 1995, 51.
50 Moreover, the accusations included in this prologue are all written in the plural. This may indicate that the conflict with Lanuvinus eventually receded into the background or that the opponent here is some other than Lanuvinus. In the case of *Hecyra* there is a need to negotiate the repetition of his performance and to justify the failed attempts.
51 See in details Papaioannou 2013. Franko recognises a skilful play in the successful balancing act between defending against the accusations and promoting the coming play: Franko 2013, 37.
52 This scenario is also found in the prologue of Cato's *De agricultura*. Sharrock points out that it was possibly a popular motif at the time: Sharrock 2009, 84–85.
53 Lefèvre sees the purpose of the expository prologues of New Comedy in giving the audience the opportunity, through the information provided, to concentrate more on the *how* than on the *what*: Lefèvre 1974, 41. However, the two are not mutually exclusive, hence the statement can only be understood as a general claim of the poet turning attention to both.

degradations as praise, yet at the same time uses the invectives as a strategy for legitimising his own attacks.

2.2 Auto-Invectives Against the Giant. The Case of Decimus Laberius

Decimus Laberius, a Roman knight, was one of the foremost mime poets of the first century BC. In total, however, only about 150 lines and 44 titles of the author's work were preserved. Among the fragments, there are 27 continuous lines of a single fragment, known as the prologue, which are handed down to us by Macrobius.[54] Laberius is introduced to us in the prologue as a harsh and blunt speaker.[55] He has been invited by Caesar to act in a mime for a fee of 500,000 sestertii. According to Macrobius, however, due to Caesar's position, this invitation was not voluntary. In his prologue,[56] Laberius uses a different strategy than Terence, a strategy that is centred on his own supposed auto-invective. At the beginning, Laberius turns to Necessitas to draw attention to his tragic fate: he, a Roman knight of impeccable reputation, had never let himself be tempted by ambition, money or pressure, nor would he jeopardise his own reputation. Now things are different; simple words of a great man, spoken gently and calmly, have brought him down: "me, a human, refusing him to whom the very gods have not been able to refuse anything?"[57] Caesar's prominent position after the death of Pompeius, combined with the subtle allusions to his person, made the audience aware of the current political situation no matter the way it was presented (with seriousness or sweeping exaggeration). Laberius, who possibly wore the costume of a slave in the prologue, clarifies the absurdity of his performance and the evident disparity in the status of power between Caesar and himself. The 60–year-old Laberius instead of enjoying his fame has to stomach the loss of his social status, since being in a forced performance as a mime, an infamous comic agent, degrades him beyond doubt. This degradation happens

---

54 Macr. *Sat.* 2.7.1–3.
55 Apart from Caesar, there are said to have been brief arguments with Cicero and Clodius Pulcher, which testify to the poet's trenchant tongue. Sen. *Controv.* 7.3.9; Macr. *Sat.* 2.6.6.
56 It is possible to date it to the *ludi victoriae* of 46 BC. Then the prologue would be part of the competition organised by Caesar between the poet Laberius and the mime actor Pubilius Syrus. Panayotakis rules out any such linkage of the fragments in favour of a staging at the plebeian games in 47 BC: Panayotakis, 40–56. Manuwald at least considers Macr. *Sat.* 2.7.1–4 as a unit: Manuwald 2011, 275.
57 Macr. *Sat.* 2.7.1, 10–11.

at an advanced age when he is neither physically resilient nor has much to offer to the theatre world: neither voice nor presence, form or flair. All that now remains is his name.

Such a prologue must have won the audience for Laberius and against Caesar. The apparent ease with which the social status of this Roman knight was destroyed, let alone his suitability for the stage, unveils the dangers tied to Caesar's unlimited exercise of power. Laberius enacting his dramatic self-deprecation might have intensified the public disparagement of Caesar and exposed his outstanding power to the audience. In fact, Macrobius tells us that Laberius kept along this line of invective and took revenge on Caesar several times during the performance.[58] Disguised as a flogged slave, he exclaimed that they are losing their freedom (*porro, Quirites! Libertatem perdimus*). And a little later he made the following striking comment: "he whom many fear must inevitably fear many",[59] explicitly directing the audience to contextualise these statements and digest the fact that they apply to Caesar. Unwilling to risk decline in his popularity, Caesar, who had endured Laberius' denigrations and hostile glances during the performance, promptly elevated Laberius back into the knighthood after the conclusion of the latter's performance. When, however, the elderly knight moved to take a seat in the reserved rows, he was met with rejection by his peers.

3 Playwrights as Invectors

Terence as well as Laberius are staging their prologues as rhetorical pieces meant to be performed before an audience. Nevertheless, a subtle distinction must be made between the use of comic invectives in the prologues of Terence and those in court. The theatre is an arena that demands performers to follow its own codes, norms and expectations – what New Institutionalism calls "logics of appropriateness".[60] Terence's attacks, for example, focus on the actions of the invectee instead of his physical appearance or family origins. Additionally, some aspects of the staging in the theatre underlines the specific comic character of the invectives.

---

58 Macr. *Sat.* 2.7.4.
59 Macr. *Sat.* 2.7.4.
60 This applies both to the use and purpose of invectives and to the composition of the argumentation. On the theory of New Institutionalism: Serafim in this volume, pp. 66–67.

The employment of invectives is not risk-free and has to be considered on two levels. The invective must be staged properly and skilfully. Success is not always guaranteed, especially on the comic stage. Regardless of the author's personal style, humour, according to theory, functions on four levels, which the invector may not always fully control: social frame, cognitive mechanism, affective response and expression through body language.[61] The social frame illuminates the setting in which comedy takes place and influences the relationships between performer, audience and target.[62] Three factors are to be emphasised here: firstly, it makes sense not only to look at individual jokes, but to assess them in the context of a longer narrative. The contextualisations, in the later stages of Laberius' play, are easier to identify, considering the accusations in the prologue. The invective also initiates a change of perspective that transforms Caesar from the jester who mindlessly plays with the social status of Laberius, to the enemy of democracy and thus of the audience in attendance. In the case of Terence's response to Lanuvinus a kind of running-gag may have developed that caused laughter and inevitably affected the perspective through which to consider the serious charges of plagiarism.[63]

Secondly, attention must be paid to the identity of the invectors in the prologues of Terence and Laberius. It can hardly be assumed that Terence himself entered the stage and recited the prologue.[64] This was partly due to the social status of the actor. Sharrock surmises that the use of another speaker gave Terence the opportunity to reject the charges against his work more effectively and to highlight his talents without any accusation of *hubris*.[65] Thus, in the prologue the speaker assumes the role of the defender of the poet in the staged conflict. This part of the defender is undertaken by Ambivius Turpio on behalf of Terence. Performing on stage may have benefited from techniques observed in court performances, and this likely affected the staging of the invective in the prologue. At the same time, the actors might also face the risk of later retribution, especially considering their social status and the attendant rights. The lack of rhetorically-informed performance skills might have made the performance of Laberius much more pitiful and perhaps funny.

---

[61] Lowe 2007, 7–8 following the theories of Attardo 1994 and Raskin 1985.
[62] Lowe 2007, 7.
[63] Sharrock imagines that the recurring appearance of the topic has already caused some viewers to burst into laughter: Sharrock 2009, 63.
[64] Livius Andronicus, who is said to have played in his own pieces, is an exception: Manuwald 2011, 83.
[65] Sharrock 2009, 66.

Thirdly, the staging of the prologue as part of the play is disrupted and deviates from a normative pattern. In the prologue to *Hecyra II*, Turpio tells us this much: "I come before you as an orator in the guise of the prologue".[66] The same applies to the speaker in the *Heauton Timōrumenos*: "He (the author, HMD) wanted me to be an orator, not a prologue-speaker".[67] Not only does Terence use this specific form of the prologue, but he also sets the prologue-speaker apart from the play by presenting him as an orator. Whether or not this was linked to a visual separation, e.g. the speaker did not wear a mask or a costume that associated him with a certain role, cannot be conclusively clarified.[68] It would be possible to stage a production that underlined both the dissociation of actor from role, and the exact opposite, the interfusion of the two, which would generate laughter. It can be presumed that the uttering of the invective would have been accompanied by gestures. In addition, the actors' well-formed figure as well as their skilled agility and stage presence would have impacted on the performative effectiveness of the invective. The case of Laberius is different. Should one accept the proposed reconstruction of the fragments, it is conceivable that Laberius stood in front of the audience in the costume of a slave throughout his delivery of the prologue. The costume illustrates the difference in status due to his role as an actor. At the same time, however, the slave in New Comedy is granted a special license to defame his masters, as Lefèvre demonstrates with examples from Plautus' plays.[69] The poet's old age would have made the staging of his social degradation and loss of prestige even more disgraceful. Since no masks were used in the mime, the performance may have appeared even more personal.

The invectors accept the risk of a counterattack. This is true of Laberius as well as of Terence, since the prologue-speakers of the latter's plays specify that they report *his* words; that Terence himself wrote the prologues. Goldberg considers it less of a risk to use invectives in general, compared to placing them in the prologues.[70] He refers to the use of arcane literary polemics in Aristophanes' *parabaseis*, which however – and this is where Aristophanes differs from Terence – are placed in the middle of the comedy; by then, they have already achieved audience involvement. The emphatic placement of the invectives in

---

66 Ter. *Hec.* 9.
67 Ter. *Heaut.* 11: *oratorum esse voluit me, non prologum.*
68 In reference to Lefèvre, Kruschwitz referring to Menander's adaptation of *Andria* observes that it is possible that Terence used prologue-speakers who had no impact on the progression of the play: Kruschwitz 2004, 165.
69 Lefèvre 1974, 44–46.
70 Goldberg 1986.

the prologues, and the presentation therein of a situation that is not clearly in favour of the playwright before the audience had had the chance to get sympathetic and emotionally involved, may not serve Terence's purposes as desired.

In the case of Laberius, the invectee must endure the personal attacks in a stoic manner. The use of auto-invectives by Laberius and the legitimation of Terence' attacks as a mere reaction to earlier invectives by Lanuvinus seem to be two possible strategies to enhance the invective potential of their attacks. What they have in common is the emotional impact on the audience. Even if Lanuvinus were present, there is nothing to suggest that he was spotted among the spectators; besides, the prologue-speaker would not have missed the chance to point at him. Since the prologues attest to an ongoing feud, Lanuvinus would probably have come prepared and brought some supporters. The conflict, if it did occur, was carried out on multiple occasions and over a longer period of time. It is conceivable that the incident at the rehearsal of *Eunuchus* may have been discussed in certain circles. This attack by Lanuvinus in front of important members of the elite may have contributed to the escalation of the invective in the prologues, if we assume that it was not merely a rhetorical gimmick. Yet, even in this case, the poet would use a credible scenario to convince the audience and employ the impact of invectives to his advantage. A close collaboration between poet and *dominus gregis* founded on mutual trust, as is the case of Terence and Ambivius Turpio, may open up many creative possibilities.

Bibliography

Attardo, S. (1994), *Linguistic Theories of Humor*, Berlin/New York.
Aldrete, G.S. (1999), *Gestures and Acclamations in Ancient Rome*, Baltimore/London.
Barsby, J. (ed.) (1999), *Terence: Eunuchus*, Cambridge.
Beacham, R.C. (1995), *The Roman Theater and its Audience*, London.
Bork, H.S. (2018), *A Rough Guide to Insult in Plautus*, Los Angeles.
Barbiero, E.A. (2020), '*Alii rhetorica tongent*: Plautus and Public Speech', in: G.F. Franko and D. Dutsch (eds.), *A Companion to Plautus*, Hoboken, 393–406.
Brown, P.G. McC. (1987), 'Masks, Names and Characters in New Comedy', in: *Hermes* 115(2), 181–202.
Beare, W. (1964), *The Roman Stage: A Short History of Latin Drama in the Time of the Republic*, London.
Clarke, J.R. (2007), *Looking at Laughter. Humor, Power and Transgression in Roman Visual Culture, 100 BC - AD 250*, Berkeley.
Corbeill, A. (1996), *Controlling Laughter. Political Humor in the Late Roman Republic*, Princeton.
Dodwell, C.R. (2000), *Anglo-Saxon Gestures and the Roman Stage*, Cambridge.

Dunsch, B. (2014), 'Prologue(s) and Prologi', in: M. Fontaine and A.C. Scafuro (eds.), *The Oxford Handbook of Greek and Roman Comedy*, Oxford/New York, 498–515.
Duckworth, G.E. (1952), *The Nature of Roman Comedy: A Study in Popular Entertainment*, Princeton.
Franko, G.F. (2013), 'Terence and the Tradition of Roman New Comedy', in: A. Augoustakis and A. Traill (eds.), *A Companion to Terence*, Malden, MA, 33–51.
Flower, H.I. (1996), *Ancestor Masks and Aristocratic Power in Roman Culture*, Oxford.
Garton, C. (1972), *Personal Aspects of the Roman Theatre*, Toronto.
Germany, R (2013), 'Andria', in: A. Augoustakis and A. Traill (eds.), *A Companion to Terence*, Malden, MA, 223–242.
Gilula, D. (1989), 'The First Realistic Roles in European Theatre: Terence Prologues', in: *Quaderni Urbinati di Cultura Classica* 62, 95–106.
Goldberg, S.M. (1983), 'Terence, Cato, and the Rhetorical Prologue', in: *Classical Philology* 78, 198–211.
Goldberg, S.M. (1986), *Understanding Terence*, Princeton.
Graf, F. (1991), 'Gestures and Conventions: The Gestures of Roman Actors and Orators', in: J.N. Bremmer and H. Roodenburg (eds.), *A Cultural History of Gesture*, Ithaca/New York, 36–58.
Gruen, E.S. (1992), *Culture and National Identity in Republican Rome*, New York.
Gruen, E.S. (2014), 'Roman Comedy and the Social Scene', in: M. Fontaine and A.C. Scafuro (eds.), *The Oxford Handbook of Greek and Roman Comedy*, Oxford/New York, 601–614.
Iurescia, F. (2019), *Credo iam ut solet iurgabit. Pragmatica della lite a Roma*, Göttingen.
Klose, D. (1966), *Die Didaskalien und Prologe des Terenz*, Freiburg.
Kruschwitz, P. (2004), *Terenz*, Hildesheim.
Lefèvre, E. (1974), 'Die römische Komödie', in: M. Fuhrmann (ed.), *Römische Literatur*, Frankfurt a. M., 33–62.
Lowe, N.J. (2007), *Comedy. (Greece and Rome. New Surveys in the Classics 37)*, Cambridge.
Manuwald, G. (2011), *Roman Republican Theatre*, Cambridge.
Marshall, C.W. (2006), *The Stagecraft and Performance of Roman Comedy*, Cambridge.
Meister, J.B. (2014), 'Lachen und Politik. Zur Funktion von Humor in der politischen Kommunikation des römischen Principats', in: *Klio* 96, 26–48.
Moore, T.J. (2013), 'Meter and Music', in: A. Augoustakis and A. Traill (eds.), *A Companion to Terence*, Malden, MA, 89–110.
Panayotakis, C. (2010), *Decimus Laberius: The Fragments*, New York.
Papaioannou, S., Serafim, A. and Demetriou, K. (2020), 'The Hermeneutic Framework: Persuasion in Genres and Topics', in: S. Papaioannou, A. Serafim and K. Demetriou (eds.), *The Ancient Art of Persuasion across Genres and Topics*, Leiden, 1–16.
Papaioannou, S. (2013), 'The Cultural Poetics of Terence's Literary Comedy', in: *Logeion. A Journal of Ancient Theatre* 3, 1–20.
Richlin, A. (1992), *The Garden of Priapus: Sexuality and Aggression in Roman Humor*, New York.
Richlin, A. (2014), 'Talking to Slaves in the Plautine Audience', in: *Classical Antiquity* 33(1), 174–226.
Rosillo-López, C. (2017), 'Popular Public Opinion in a Nutshell: Nicknames and Non-elite Political Culture in the Late Republic', in: L. Grig (ed.), *Popular Culture in the Ancient World*, Cambridge, 91–106.
Saunders, C. (1909), *Costume in Roman Comedy*, New York (reprint 1966).
Sharrock, A. (2009), *Reading Roman Comedy: Poetics and Playfulness in Plautus and Terence*, Cambridge.

Vincent, H. (2013), '*Fabula Stataria*: Language and Humor in Terence', in: A. Augoustakis and A. Traill (eds.), *A Companion to Terence*, Malden, MA, 69–88.

Wiles, D. (2007), *Mask and Performance in Greek Tragedy: From Ancient Festival to Modern Experimentation*, Cambridge.

Part II: **The Cultural Workings of Invective**

Thomas K. Hubbard
Comic Somatisation and the Body of Evidence in Aeschines' *Against Timarchus*

Abstract: Several distinctive stylistic features in Aeschines 1 mark a rhetorical strategy that focuses on the corporal appearance of the defendant Timarchus in a manner that echoes comic treatment of politicians' bodies. Although Aeschines claims that Timarchus is now wasted due to sensual over-indulgence, T.K. Hubbard argues that, at age 45, Timarchus was still in fact physically impressive, much younger in appearance than his age peer Misgolas, a successful adulterer, athletic in his gestures and delivery. By calling upon the judges to scrutinise Timarchus' body (which for his age was probably well-preserved), Aeschines encourages them to imagine how attractive he must have been when he was really in his prime, and thus how likely he was to have taken advantage of his good looks in a way that Aeschines frames as immoral and disqualifying. As an experienced actor and new orator, Aeschines relied on dramatic techniques of characterisation to make up for the weakness of his case in regard to both evidence and law. The *dokimasia rhētorōn* on which he relies for his prosecution was never a formal law used by other orators or whose text Aeschines could cite, and the law on *hetairēsis* only applied to certain limited public offices.

1 Timarchus' Body

Aeschines' infamous prosecution of Timarchus is notable for its lack of real evidence of the defendant's alleged prostitution,[1] but Aeschines' rhetoric effectively deploys Timarchus' physical appearance as demonstrative of his guilt. The judges' gaze is repeatedly directed toward Timarchus' presence in the court through deictic demonstratives, starting in the very first paragraph of the speech: ὑπὸ Τιμάρχου τουτουί (1.1), a locution later repeated in multiple forms. Sometimes Timarchus is simply pointed to without a name as οὑτοσί (as in 1.95), or more pejoratively as ὁ μιαρὸς οὑτοσί in 1.54. Aeschines uses the deictic demonstrative to focus on Timarchus no less than 21 times in this speech. In contrast, Aeschines uses the same device in his other two speeches only once with respect to his antagonist Demosthenes, though certainly not out of any

---

[1] For the weakness of Aeschines' factual case: Harris 1995, 103–105.

https://doi.org/10.1515/9783110735536-009

respect or love lost.² The insistent repetition of the strongly deictic iota-demonstrative here indicates a rhetorical strategy distinctive to this speech, for which the physical habitus of the opponent's body on public display is central.

Similarly, our eyes are drawn toward Timarchus by vocative addresses to the defendant at climactic points in the oration, as immediately before Aeschines' first introduction of the law debarring men who have prostituted themselves from holding political offices (1.18–19):

> ἐπειδὰν δ' ἐγγραφῇ τις εἰς τὸ ληξιαρχικὸν γραμματεῖον, καὶ τοὺς νόμους εἰδῇ τοὺς τῆς πόλεως, καὶ ἤδη δύνηται διαλογίζεσθαι τὰ καλὰ καὶ τὰ μή, οὐκέτι ἑτέρῳ διαλέγεται, ἀλλ' ἤδη αὐτῷ, ὦ Τίμαρχε. καὶ πῶς λέγει; ἄν τις Ἀθηναίων, φησίν, ἑταιρήσῃ, μὴ ἐξέστω αὐτῷ τῶν ἐννέα ἀρχόντων γενέσθαι...

> But once he is entered in the deme register and knows the city's laws and is now able to determine right and wrong, the legislator from now on addresses nobody else but at this point the individual himself, Timarchus (ἀλλ' ἤδη αὐτῷ, ὦ Τίμαρχε). And what does he say? If any Athenian (he says) prostitutes himself, he is not to have the right to serve as one of the nine archons...

Note how the vocative is placed in the unusual position at sentence end, as if to invite the judges trying the case to turn around and look at no one else but "the man himself, you Timarchus!" We see the same emotional effect with the vocative address to Timarchus at the end of a pointed rhetorical question in 1.75:

> οὐκοῦν τὸν αὐτὸν τρόπον προσήκει ὑμᾶς καὶ περὶ Τιμάρχου ἐξετάζειν, καὶ μὴ σκοπεῖν εἴ τις εἶδεν, ἀλλ' εἰ πέπρακται τούτῳ ἡ πρᾶξις. ἐπεὶ πρὸς θεῶν τί χρὴ λέγειν, Τίμαρχε; τί ἂν εἴποις αὐτὸς περὶ ἑτέρου ἀνθρώπου ἐπὶ τῇ αἰτίᾳ ταύτῃ κρινομένου; ἢ τί χρὴ λέγειν, ὅταν μειράκιον νέον, καταλιπὸν τὴν πατρῴαν οἰκίαν, ἐν ἀλλοτρίαις οἰκίαις νυκτερεύῃ, τὴν ὄψιν ἑτέρων διαφέρων.

> So you should investigate Timarchus in the same way and not ask whether anyone saw him but if this man has engaged in the practice. For by the gods, what is one to say, Timarchus? What would you yourself say about another person who was being tried on this charge? What is one to say when a young lad leaves his father's house and spends his nights in the homes of others, a lad of unusual beauty.

After conjuring up the image of the unfortunate youths who prostitute themselves openly in brothels, Aeschines notes that they at least have the modesty to do their business behind closed doors, but no one is unaware of the trade they practice. So also in Timarchus' case, we need not see the act itself to interpret

---

2 Demosthenes, for his part, was fond of the iota-deictic form and used it frequently against Aeschines in his speeches *On the False Embassy* and *On the Crown*. See Serafim 2017, Chapter 5.

the signs. By then immediately switching to the second person, after gaining everyone's attention with his oath to the gods, Aeschines asks the judges to focus on Timarchus himself theatrically as well as logically. As they look at the man standing before them in the court, they are invited to imagine the same man as a *meirakion neon*, spending his nights in other men's houses, a youth of appearance distinguished from others, a youth who attends lavish dinners without ever paying for himself, enjoys gambling and purchases flute-girls or *hetairai* while another pays on his behalf.

Aeschines' argument that this entertainment of Timarchus was equivalent to a prostitution contract is entirely a matter of inference based not on real evidence, but on what he claims as a collective memory that everyone in the dicastic panel surely had of some elegant pretty boy, whether it was Timarchus or another whose name they now scarcely remember. By asking them to look at the now much older Timarchus present before them, he invites them to visualise this man in the role of the wastrel and unrestrained youth whom we all once knew, whatever his name. Timarchus' mere presence seems to be proof enough. Sissa argues powerfully against Foucauldian anti-identitarianism that Timarchus is characterised as a recognisable "type" of person, not just a prostitute nor a sexual passive, but a man who is sexually and particularly homosexually excessive, and that the Athenian masses would regard such behaviour as pervading a man's complete personality and character in every aspect of his life, thus constituting it as a "sexual identity".[3] Today, we would call such a person "promiscuous" or "hypersexual" and associate their body with transmissible disease, but the more usual term in antiquity was *kinaidos*.[4]

After imagining the defence of a man truly innocent of these charges, based on the purity of his entire lifestyle, Aeschines again uses a vocative address to Timarchus to contrast this with the niggling defence that Timarchus and Demosthenes have actually made against the indictment (1.122). As in the other two passages we just analysed, the vocative directs the judges toward the man's presence standing before them, as if it is proof enough of the lifestyle he led twenty or more years earlier.

---

[3] Sissa 1999, 153–157.
[4] Curiously, this word is never actually applied to Timarchus in this speech, but only to his ally Demosthenes (1.131, 181), to whom it was also applied in the speech on the false embassy (2.88, 99, 151). It may be that Timarchus actually did not have whatever the Greeks imagined as the physique of the stereotypical *kinaidos* as much as the thin, weak-voiced, delicately clothed Demosthenes. See Fisher 2001, 48; and Donelan in this volume (p. 31).

Timarchus' behaviour is throughout characterised as an "offense against his own body", again calling attention to the man's corporeal presence before the court. The word σῶμα is used 29 times in this speech,[5] far more than anywhere else in the corpus of the Attic orators.[6] He committed *hamartia* toward his body as a boy (1.39, 1.94). He is *hybristēs* toward his body (1.108, 1.116). A male in body, he has committed the *hamartia* of a woman (1.185). His defenders are those who have not used their own bodies well (1.194). He has sold himself "in his body" (1.52 ἐπὶ τῷ σώματι; cf. 1.154) and "to the shame of his body" (1.87 ἐπὶ τῇ σώματος αἰσχύνῃ); he is not "pure with respect to his body" (1.188 καθαρὸς τὸ σῶμα).

The degradation of Timarchus' body is exhibited by the fact that it was once very beautiful and desirable, but is now visibly wasted through drink and debauchery. In his youth, he was "at his prime" (1.126 ὡραῖος), "fair-skinned" (1.41 εὔσαρκος) and "exceptional in appearance" (1.75 τὴν ὄψιν διαφέρων). Now, these terms are all negated: he is "painful in appearance" (1.61 ἀργαλέος τὴν ὄψιν) and "past his prime" (1.95 ἔξωρος). Aeschines attributes his faded looks directly to his drunkenness and disgusting behaviour (1.26 ὑπὸ μέθης καὶ βδελυρίας). Aeschines compares Timarchus to other youths who ruined their once considerable beauty through disreputable lives, such as Diophantes or Cephisodorus the son of Molon (1.158). Aeschines may here be tapping into the well-attested notion that sexual excess, particularly in men, leads to a depletion of vital bodily fluids and thus ill health; hence the sexual abstinence of athletes before competition.[7] Later Roman poetry, such as Catullus, Martial and the *Priapea*, is full of graphic descriptions of libertines and courtesans whose bodies have become diseased or wasted from sexual over-indulgence.[8]

In fact, Timarchus was probably still rather attractive, as suggested by his supposed success as an adulterer (1.107) and the pains Aeschines takes to argue that his companion Misgolas was considerably older (1.49), even though Timarchus' service on the Council in 361 proves that Timarchus was probably at least

---

[5] See also Carey 2017, 267 n. 8 for this observation.
[6] The body plays little role as a metaphor in Aeschines' two other extant speeches, where Demosthenes was his principal opponent. Instead, as Worman 2004, 5–14 argues, the focus of sexual innuendo in those speeches is specifically on the unclean mouth.
[7] For the fullest exposition of this doctrine, see Aretaeus, *De causis et signis acutorum morborum* 2.5.4 and Philostratus, *Gymnastica* 52. That some athletes practiced a strict sexual regimen to enhance performance is attested for the classical period by Plato's praise of Iccus of Tarentum and "many others" (*Laws* 839e–840c). For other examples: Scanlon 2002, 227–234.
[8] See Catullus 6.4–5, 57; *Priapea* 46, 50; Juvenal 2.9–13; Martial 1.77, 6.37, 6.93. For discussion of these texts, Ice 2003, 51–64.

45 (i.e. the same age as Misgolas) at the time of this trial in 346, since he needed to be no younger than 30 when he served on the Council fifteen years earlier.[9] Timarchus' distinctive style of unrestrained oratorical gestures also suggests a still vigorous and even athletic constitution.[10] Indeed, Aeschines ridicules Timarchus for exposing too much of his body, in contrast with both the proper bodily display (εὐεξία) of still fit athletes (1.189) and the dignified sobriety of ancient orators who kept their arms tightly wrapped beneath their cloaks (1.26):

σκέψασθε δή, ὦ ἄνδρες Ἀθηναῖοι, ὅσον διαφέρει ὁ Σόλων Τιμάρχου καὶ οἱ ἄνδρες ἐκεῖνοι ὧν ὀλίγῳ πρότερον ἐπεμνήσθην. ἐκεῖνοι μέν γε ᾐσχύνοντο ἔξω τὴν χεῖρα ἔχοντες λέγειν, οὑτοσὶ δὲ οὐ πάλαι, ἀλλὰ πρώην ποτὲ ῥίψας θοἰμάτιον γυμνὸς ἐπαγκρατίαζεν ἐν τῇ ἐκκλησίᾳ, οὕτω κακῶς καὶ αἰσχρῶς διακείμενος τὸ σῶμα ὑπὸ μέθης καὶ βδελυρίας, ὥστε τούς γε εὖ φρονοῦντας ἐγκαλύψασθαι, αἰσχυνθέντας ὑπὲρ τῆς πόλεως, εἰ τοιούτοις συμβούλοις χρώμεθα.

Now observe, men of Athens, the enormous difference between Solon and those great men whom I mentioned a little earlier in my speech and Timarchus. While they for their part thought it shameful to speak with their hand outside of their robe, this man here, not some time ago but just the other day threw off his robe and cavorted like a pancratiast in the Assembly, stripped, in such a vile and shameful physical condition on account of drunkenness and disgusting abuse (βδελυρίας) that decent men covered their faces out of shame for the city if we use such men as advisors.

Timarchus' self-confident style of corporal gesture is thus focalised as tangible proof of his bodily shamelessness. Sissa has called attention to Aeschines' repeated use of the ugly word *bdelyros* and cognates in this speech to provoke visceral and emotional "disgust" at the bodily presence of the defendant in the present court.[11] Characterised as nakedness, Timarchus' habitus is assimilated to the corporal self-display one might expect of a man who allowed his body to be abused in the most brutal and disfiguring of all contact sports, the *pancrati-*

---

9 See also Harris 1988, Lane Fox 1994, 136–137. Davidson 2007, 453–454 assumes a scribal error with regard to Misgolas' age. Lape 2006, 148–149 argues for Timarchus' enduring attractiveness on other grounds.
10 The phrase "large Timarchus-like prostitutes" (πόρνους μεγάλους Τιμαρχώδεις) that Aeschines (1.157) cites from a recent comedy may also suggest that Timarchus was a man of impressive physical stature.
11 Sissa 1999, 159–161. *Bdelyros* and related words are recognisably comic language, occurring 28 times in the extant work of Aristophanes, Eupolis and Cratinus (including the major character Bdelycleon in *Wasps*) but only twice in Tragedy. On the uses of "disgust" in this speech: Spatharas 2016, 125–140.

um,[12] and who by extension might also have become accustomed to using his body to impress and seduce clients in a more private setting.

2 Comedy as Theatre of the Body

Aeschines' strong voice and earlier career as a dramatic actor have occasioned critical comment as key factors in his self-confident delivery, against which Demosthenes warns juries.[13] He is usually thought to have been a tragic actor, but we cannot discount the possibility that he also performed in comedies. At one point in the oration, he cites the anapestic phrase "large Timarchus-like prostitutes" (1.157) from a recent comedy performed at the Rural Dionysia in the deme of Collytus,[14] so we know at the very least that Aeschines was an avid fan of Comedy, even to the extent of travelling out to the demes to see performances. I would argue that much of Aeschines' technique of characterisation in this oration derives from comic models, especially his insistent focus on the spectacle of his opponent's physical body.

Aeschines adopted from Comedy an essentialising discourse on sexuality. Knowing a man's sexual habits was to know the man's whole character. If a man had been sexually passive in his youth, he was sufficiently manipulative and shameless that he was destined to become a successful politician, as some-

---

[12] On the metaphorical character of the pancratiast here, see the discussion of Carey 2017, 272–274. On the particularly strenuous demands of the *pancratium*, which mixed boxing and wrestling, allowed kicking, strangling and twisting of limbs and fingers, and banned only biting and eye-gouging: Gardiner 1910, 435–450; Harris 1964, 105–109; Poliakoff 1987, 54–63. It is more than likely that a long career in this particular event would leave a man disfigured by middle age.

[13] Demosthenes (18.129, 180, 242, 262, 265; 19.200, 246–250, 337) repeatedly refers to Aeschines' tragic roles, but dismisses him as a tritagonist in a minor troupe. On this leitmotif: Easterling 1999; and Worman 2004, 11–13, 20–21.

[14] Collytus was also the site of Aeschines' own tragic acting (Dem. 18.180). This comic reference has entered into debates about the precise date of Timarchus' trial: Harris 1985; Wankel 1988; Fisher 2001, 7–8, 57–58, but it is entirely possible that this reference was something Aeschines added to the published version of the speech and did not form part of the original trial. I have elsewhere argued that published speeches of Aeschines and Demosthenes served as political pamphlets revisiting famous trials with supporting evidence and rebuttals not yet possible at the time of the original trial (Hubbard 2008). In this case, that could mean that the comedy's derogatory reference to Timarchus was inspired by the trial rather than the other way around, but Aeschines is only too glad to incorporate it into the published version of his speech as confirmation that Timarchus' past was a matter of general knowledge.

one predicted when he saw the young Agoracritus stealing sausage and hiding it in his crotch (*Knights* 417–428). As Greater Argument was forced to admit in *Clouds* 1088–1094, all the advocates and political leaders in Athens were *euruprōktoi* ("with dilated anus"). It is no surprise that Plato chose Aristophanes as the appropriate guest at Agathon's symposium to voice an imaginative myth of hereditary sexual identity based on humanity's descent from three ancestral types.

The hypersexual wastrel was also a comic type. Aristophanes lampoons the sophist Ariphrades, who pays female prostitutes to let him pleasure their private parts with his ever-active tongue (*Knights* 1280–1289).[15] In the parabasis of *Wasps* (1025–1028) Aristophanes dissociates himself from obsessive pederasts who bribe comic poets to ridicule uncooperative boyfriends. The fabulously wealthy Callias was known as πορνομάνης ("whore-mad") and consumed his vast estate in dissipation, as portrayed in Eupolis' *Flatterers*.[16] According to Andocides (1.124–129) Callias married the daughter of Ischomachus, but within a year of that marriage made the girl's mother his mistress, and the two of them are alleged to have driven the daughter out; he then married the mother and subsequently tired of her, publicly denying that the son to whom she gave birth was his own, but later, after her return to favour, acknowledging the boy. He also maintained pederastic interests, most famously involved with the young athlete Autolycus, whose Panathenaic victory he celebrated with an extravagant party in Xenophon's *Symposium*; Eupolis satirised the relationship in plays named after the boy.[17]

Fourth-century comedy was even more inclined to presentation of this type: men who spend extravagantly on exquisite varieties of fish, prostitutes, flatterers and boys, as well as the mercenary predators and parasites who supply their

---

[15] For what little can be surmised about this otherwise obscure figure: Hubbard 1991, 85 n. 58.
[16] On Callias: Davidson 1997, 184–186. On Eupolis' characterisation of him: Carey 2000b, 423–425, and Storey 2003, 180–184. Frr. 171, 172.3-4, 174, 184 K.-A. highlight the sexual delights on offer at Callias' house, both male and female.
[17] The sexual subtext is pronounced in the fragments from the play, which was presented in two different versions (the second perhaps incorporating new scandals): see especially frr. 54–57, 65–68, 72 K.-A. Fr. 50 refers to squandering an inheritance on a beloved, fr. 51 calls someone a "ruined old man" (ἐξώλης γέρων) with urinary incontinence, and fr. 60 also seems to be from a lover's quarrel between a younger partner who is accused of being godless and an older one who is too inclined to women. On this play, see Fisher 2000, 375, and Storey 2003, 81–94. The allusion to the boy in Euripides, fr. 282 *TGrF* (on the uselessness of athletes) also indicates his notoriety.

appetites.[18] In an extended fragment from Antiphanes' *Fisherwoman* (fr. 27.9–18 K.-A.), various species of expensive fish are likened to famous courtesans on whom their lovers consume fortunes:

ὑμᾶς δ' ἔταξα δεῦρο πρὸς τὰ δεξιά,
τρίγλας, ἔδεσμα τοῦ καλοῦ Καλλισθένους· 10
κατεσθίει γοῦν ἐπὶ μιᾷ τὴν οὐσίαν.
καὶ τὸν Σινώπης γόγγρον ἤδη παχυτέρας
ἔχοντ' ἀκάνθας τουτονὶ τις λήψεται
πρῶτος προσελθών; Μισγόλας γὰρ οὐ πάνυ
τούτων ἐδεστής. ἀλλὰ κίθαρος οὑτοσί, 15
ὃν ἂν ἴδῃ τὰς χεῖρας οὐκ ἀφέξεται.
καὶ μὴν ἀληθῶς κιθαρῳδοῖς ὡς σφόδρα
ἅπασιν οὗτος ἐπιπεφυκὼς λανθάνει.

You red mullets, I've put you over on the right for handsome Callisthenes to devour; he's already devouring his estate for one of you, you know. And here's an eel with a wider back than Sinope; who will be the first to come and eat it? Misgolas, you see, is not a connoisseur of these, although he'll make a grab for this lyrefish here as soon as he sees it. The man's really keen on his secret attachments to all players of the lyre.

It does not surprise us to see Timarchus' lover Misgolas make an appearance here as a man not in the market for eels like Sinope, but only lyrefish (sympotic lyre-playing being the domain of attractive male youths). Our wealth of evidence from the fourth century for fish mania and men lavishing fortunes on demanding courtesans need not indicate that this behaviour was more common at that time, but it is when these elite phenomena became a matter of intensified discursive elaboration and public censure, as reflected in Comedy and forensic oratory.

Whereas the late fifth-century audience might be expected to have some vicarious sympathy for the glutton Heracles or the healthy outdoor hedonism of agrarian protagonists like Dicaeopolis or Trygaeus, fourth-century Athenians would have viewed such self-indulgence through a more moralistic lens, particularly as it characterised the privileged classes. In the context of the relatively straitened economic circumstances of Athens during most of that period and the lower standard of living most Athenians experienced, conspicuous consumption and profligate waste by the hereditary 1% must have seemed especially

---

18 For a compilation of such material, mostly from the fourth-century and Hellenistic eras: Davidson 1997, especially 183–205. On flatterers and parasites: Fisher 2000; Apostolakis and Serafim in this volume. It is also to the mid-fourth century that we owe Archestratus of Gela's *Gastronomy*, a satirical hexameter poem extolling rare fish with gusto and enthusiasm.

galling from the standpoint of the idealised common-man audience to which Comedy generically played.

Comedy was from its origins a theatre of the body, shamelessly advertising and celebrating characters' appetites for unrestrained food, drink and sexual fulfilment, and even displaying onstage crudity, nudity, farting, belching and excreting (e.g. *Ecclesiazusae* 311–330). The padded costuming and prominent leather phallus emphasised the human body as an exaggerated and distended form. Prominent statesmen and characters about town would have their features distorted by grotesque portrait masks[19] or be repeatedly ridiculed for any anatomical irregularity, like Pericles' onion-shaped head (Cratinus, fr. 73 K.-A.),[20] Cleonymus' excessive girth and ravenous appetite (*Acharnians* 844; *Knights* 1294–1299; *Birds* 288–290, 1477), Cleisthenes' beardlessness (*Clouds* 355; *Thesmophoriazusae* 574–654), Chaerephon's withered paleness (*Clouds* 503–504, *Birds* 1296, 1564, fr. 584 K.-A.), "squint-eyed" Archedemus (*Frogs* 588; Eupolis, frr. 9, 298.3–4 K.-A.)[21] or "skinny-legged" Laispodias (Eupolis, fr. 107 K.-A.). The body image symbolised the man: Pericles' narrow-mindedness, Cleonymus' military unfitness and greed, Cleisthenes' effeminacy, Chaerephon's non-athletic intellectualism, Archedemus' lack of vision, Laispodias' ineffectiveness as general. Gesture and bodily deportment were significant markers of class status in Comedy, with rapid and excited motion characteristic of slavish or lower-class personages;[22] with an actor's experience of tragically dignified and comically undignified bearing,[23] Aeschines' lurid depiction of Timarchus' athletic gestural style appeals to these comic stereotypes.

It is within this context of comic somatisation (the reduction of people to their gross physical embodiment and all-consuming corporal appetites) that we should understand Aeschines' insistent focus on the body of his opponent Timarchus, on which the Athenian public is invited to espy the faded traces of a once-impressive physique, like an aging *pancratiast* who bears the marks of past abuse after having been through one bout too many.

---

19 On portrait masks: Aristophanes, *Knights* 230–233; also: Dover 1967; Varakis 2010, 28–29.
20 For other comic attacks on Pericles' *schinocephaly*, see the collection of fragments in Plutarch, *Pericles* 3.3–7.
21 Archedemus provides another case of Comedy influencing oratory, in that Aristophanes' epithet γλάμων is picked up by Lysias 14.25, where Archedemus is depicted as the lover of Alcibiades the Younger.
22 See Green 1997 for a tentative analysis of comic gestural technique, gait and bearing.
23 For Demosthenes' repeated allusions to Aeschines' stage presence and attention to dramatic gesture: Carey 2000a, 10.

3 The Supposed Law on Prostitution

His rhetorical bluster and techniques of comic characterisation not only make up for the weakness of Aeschines' actual evidence concerning youthful prostitution, but also the emptiness of his legal case that such behaviour, even if it in fact had occurred, statutorily barred Timarchus from speaking before the court. Rather than being based on an actual "law", Aeschines' prosecution appeals to a collective memory and cultural codification of the principles behind demagogic attacks on handsome elite opponents whose pederastic histories made them easy targets for invidious claims of mercenary motives or questionable adherence to the "citizen" values of most common people who had no personal experience of pederasty.[24]

Within a ubiquitously monetised and commodified economy, any relationship between a man and youth could become suspect of prostitution, particularly in cases where there was a significant difference in class, age or access to resources. Any youth who enjoyed the company of multiple men, as Timarchus apparently did, would also be suspect. This is not to say that a clear dividing-line really exists between the gift-giving depicted on older Attic vases and gifts of a more fungible nature.[25] A society in which the two kinds of gifts were indistinguishable was also a society in which all pederasty was vulnerable to attack by both comic poets and demagogic politicians as prostitution and training in corruption.

The very term *hetairēsis* vaguely associated the sympotic and pederastic culture of the aristocratic *hetairia,* so well preserved for us in the aphoristic elegies of the Theognid tradition, with implications of rearing the young elite to become the male equivalent of a *hetaira,* coyly lisping as self-consciously seductive teens (Aristophanes, *Clouds* 977–983) and then turning out as shamelessly glib young orators prosecuting their elders with verbal snares (*Acharnians* 676–

---

[24] On popular suspicion of pederastic liaisons among Athens' elite, as illustrated in this speech and others, as well as Old Comedy, see Hubbard 1998. For some qualifications of my view, but still supporting the notion that pederasty was perceived as a marker of class habitus, see Shapiro 2015.

[25] Lear and Cantarella (2008, 78–86) argue that there is little iconographic difference between pedagogical gifts and mere sacks of money, suggesting that the latter was not necessarily judged as shameful during the period when pederastic vases were popular (the late sixth and early fifth centuries). The equivalence of the two types of gifts is also the point of Aristophanes, *Wealth* 149–159; on which, see Hubbard 1998, 52.

718).²⁶ Already in the 420s, Aristophanic comedy exploited popular prejudice against elite homosexuality as a weapon against attractive young orators prosecuting elder statesmen and speaking to older judges (see also *Knights* 1373–1383, *Wasps* 686–690, 1060–1070), and it may be from this source, rather than any deep legal tradition, that Aeschines derived the idea of utilising this meme to defend himself against the once (and perhaps still) handsome Timarchus. As Aeschines learned from Comedy, rhetorical attacks on an opponent's *hetairēsis* could readily become a convenient tool to disqualify any elitist opponent who had ever been involved in a close personal relationship with an older political mentor, reducing their pedagogical, ideological and personal alliance to mercenary motives.

As van't Wout has argued in a 2011 article, *atimia* was a vague legal concept enforced only sporadically. Only two previous speeches in our extant corpus of oratory cast opponents as deserving *atimia* due to self-prostitution, Andocides' *On the Mysteries* (100–101) and Demosthenes' *Against Androtion* (22.21–32), but in both, the matter is a digression meant to assail the opponent's *ēthos*, not a point of sustained legal contention in the present case.²⁷ That such a charge had seldom been a matter of actual prosecution is indicated by the procedural arguments over which court would even have jurisdiction in such a matter, with Androtion contending (Dem. 22.21–29) that any such charge should have gone before the Thesmothetai, who would normally examine official qualifications,²⁸ and Diodorus (for whom Demosthenes wrote this speech) claiming that any court could act on the matter.

---

26 Andocides 1.100 even puns on the two senses of the word: he defends himself for his associations with a *hetairia* by accusing his opponent of being a *hetairos*, utilising the same technique of confrontational second-person address as Aeschines: "you, of all people, talk to me about the issue of political association (ἑταιρεία) and cast aspersions upon certain men? You? You yourself, after all, have 'associated' (ἡταίρησας) not just with one man (that would be fine), but used to offer pretty cheap rates for anyone who wanted".

27 Andocides' reference is brief and seems largely contrived for the sake of the witty pun referenced in n. 26 supra. Since Androtion was a much-despised tax collector who had been active in Athenian politics for 30 years before his prosecution, it is surprising that no one thought to prosecute him on this basis before, if there were any truth to the charge and such a law actually existed. The real motive in including this accusation may have been to characterise Androtion as a man who rose from penurious origins in his youth (which few at this point could remember very accurately) to great wealth and prominence in virtue of his ruthlessness as a tax contractor.

28 Harrison 1968–1971, II:15–17, 205. The Thesmothetai would certainly be the officials before whom an *endeixis* of an *atimos* would occur; Hansen 1976, 11–17; MacDowell 1978, 75.

The existence of a law barring former male prostitutes from any civic participation has long been assumed as an anchor principle for the evaluation of ancient attitudes toward homosexual liaisons.[29] It has also been assumed as valid by most legal historians.[30] But the evidence for such a broad law or its common use is actually quite thin. Since Aeschines is the first to make this issue the focus of his case, let us examine carefully his presentation of the *graphē hetairēseos* (1.19–20):

> ἄν τις Ἀθηναίων, φησίν, ἑταιρήσῃ, μὴ ἐξέστω αὐτῷ τῶν ἐννέα ἀρχόντων γενέσθαι, ὅτι οἶμαι στεφανηφόρος ἡ ἀρχή, μηδ' ἱερωσύνην ἱερώσασθαι, ὡς οὐδὲ καθαρεύοντι τῷ σώματι, μηδὲ συνδικησάτω, φησί, τῷ δημοσίῳ, μηδὲ ἀρξάτω ἀρχὴν μηδεμίαν μηδέποτε, μήτ' ἔνδημον μήτε ὑπερόριον, μήτε κληρωτὴν μήτε χειροτονητήν, μηδὲ κηρυκευσάτω, μηδὲ πρεσβευσάτω, μηδὲ τοὺς πρεσβεύσαντας κρινέτω, μηδὲ συκοφαντείτω μισθωθείς, μηδὲ γνώμην εἰπάτω μηδέποτε μήτε ἐν τῇ βουλῇ μήτε ἐν τῷ δήμῳ, μηδ' ἂν δεινότατος ᾖ λέγειν Ἀθηναίων. ἐὰν δέ τις παρὰ ταῦτα πράττῃ, γραφὰς ἑταιρήσεως πεποίηκε καὶ τὰ μέγιστα ἐπιτίμια ἐπέθηκεν.

> If any Athenian (he says) prostitutes himself, he is not to have the right to serve as one of the nine archons (the reason being, I think, that these officials wear a sacred wreath), nor to undertake any priesthood (since his body is quite unclean); and let him not serve (he says) as advocate for the state (*syndikos*)[31] or hold any office ever, whether at home or abroad, whether selected by lot or elected by a vote; let him not serve as herald, nor as envoy (nor let him bring to trial people that have served as envoys, nor let him act as a sycophant for pay), nor let him voice any opinion in the Council or the Assembly (not even if he is the cleverest speaker in Athens). (If anyone acts against these provisions, he has allowed for indictments for prostitution and imposed the most severe penalties).

A number of very specific offices are listed here, but Aeschines is clearly interpolating into that list his own explanatory glosses, as for instance when explaining why it is unsuitable for an archon or priest to have led an impure life.[32]

---

29 Dover 1978, 20–30; Foucault 1985, 217–219; Winkler 1990, 54–64; Halperin 1990, 94–95; Cantarella 1992, 48–53; Davidson 2007, 451–453.
30 Harrison 1968–1971, I:37–38, II:171–172, 204–205; MacDowell 1978, 126, 174; Cohen 1991, 176, 181; Harris 1995, 102; Carey 2000a, 19–21.
31 On this office, see MacDowell 1978, 61–62; Todd 1993, 92; Rubinstein 2000; Fisher 2001, 145. This may originally have been a specific state-appointed function to audit and examine public officials, equivalent to the board of ten *synēgoroi*, later expanded to include special prosecutors chosen by the Assembly or Boule. As with a Special Prosecutor in the American system, the appointment would go to only the most highly respected jurists with unimpeachable reputations for integrity. However, Aeschines meant to extend the law's relevance to any prosecutor in a case of political significance.
32 See Dover 1978, 24–25.

Similarly, the parenthetical "nor let him bring to trial people that have served as envoys, nor let him act as a sycophant for pay" is a transparent attempt to bring into the reach of this law Timarchus' present political activity, which is not as an archon, priest, *syndikos*, herald or envoy, but a private citizen bringing a prosecution against Aeschines' own diplomatic service. "Sycophant for pay" is certainly not an official state office, but implies that Timarchus' present prosecution was itself undertaken for mercenary motives like the prostitution that he supposedly performed in his youth. It is unclear whether the bit about speaking in the Council or Assembly was part of the actual law or merely another extension that Aeschines inserts into his paraphrase, although the charges against Androtion (Dem. 22.24) may lend support to the idea that addressing the Assembly was off limits. What Aeschines claims about the "most severe penalties" (usually construed as execution) was probably a gloss rather than anything specified in the actual decree.[33] Since the text of the law that appears in the next paragraph is, like most such texts within the corpus of the orators, probably a later editorial insertion based on Aeschines' paraphrase,[34] it does not help us. However, the only explicit prohibition concerning participation in the courts pertains to a *syndikos*, i.e. a state-appointed prosecutor; if the law applied to all speakers in the court, there would have been no need of specifying this particular office.

Since this law by itself does not quite cover Timarchus' status as a private prosecutor, Aeschines must invoke a second procedure, which he calls the δοκιμασία ῥητόρων and proceeds to expound in paragraphs 28–32. It is significant that the other two extant forensic speeches that invoke a charge of the opponent's prostitution (Andocides 1 and Demosthenes 22) never refer to any such procedure, suggesting that the phrase may be Aeschines' invention. He says that there are four categories of men who should be excluded from speaking in the courts: those who abuse their parents, who have failed to perform required military service (or who have discarded their armour in the heat of battle), who have prostituted themselves, and who have squandered their inheritance. What should be noted here is that unlike all the other laws Aeschines cites in this

---

33 Dover 1978, 26–29 shows that Aeschines' claims about "severest" penalties for legal infractions are inconsistent and contradicted by other evidence. Although Demosthenes (19.284) acknowledges that Timarchus was disenfranchised after Aeschines' prosecution, he says nothing to imply that he was dead; indeed, the future verb ἠτιμώσεται almost certainly implies he is still very much alive.

34 Drerup 1898. Dover 1978, 26 acknowledges that the document purporting to record Misgolas' testimony (1.50) must be a later forgery, which suggests doubts about all the other documents inserted into this speech. See also Carey 2000a, 27 n. 14.

oration, he does not ask the court clerk to read the text of this law. Instead, Aeschines immediately shifts in paragraphs 33–35 to discussion of a quite separate law concerning fines for speakers who propose decrees out of order in the Assembly and Council. That Aeschines never asks the clerk to read a law on *dokimasia rhētorōn* raises the question whether it is in fact an actual law. I would propose that it is instead something much more informal – an ethical standard for what one should expect of a public speaker, something like a general Code of Ethics for members of the bar.[35] By calling it a *dokimasia*, Aeschines likens it to the physical inspection of a young man's naked body that regularly took place when he was registered with his deme at the age of majority (Aristophanes, *Wasps* 578; Aristotle, *Ath. Pol.* 42.1–2), and thus appropriate to the intense scrutiny of Timarchus' past and present body (and character) to which Aeschines repeatedly invites the jury in this trial.[36]

As such, this passage is rather more in the character of rhetorical appeals that demand the highest standards of conduct for generals and orators in regard to all legal and social obligations: I would cite as a parallel Dinarchus 1.71, which makes an issue of Demosthenes claiming as legitimate children those who were not. Similarly, Isocrates, *Panathenaicus* 139–142, lists disgraceful conduct with one's body and squandering one's inheritance as among the attributes that should debar one from being taken seriously as a leader of the state; however, the context does not speak of formal laws so much as Athenian discretion in choosing leaders; that Isocrates includes self-prostitution among the disqualifying attributes may be due to Timarchus' recent condemnation scarcely four years before the *Panathenaicus*.

Failing to support one's parents, squandering one's inheritance, and discarding one's armour in battle were all violations of the kind of common morality enshrined in ἄγραφοι νόμοι.[37] Thucydides 2.37.3 cites Pericles as associating

---

35 Although skeptical of Aeschines' invocations of Athenian law: Lane Fox 1994, 147–151 nevertheless does give some credence to the *dokimasia rhētorōn* based on the reference to such a procedure in Lycurgus (Harpocration s.v. δοκιμασθείς), but this attestation is later than Aeschines' speech and possibly influenced by its success in positing such a procedure. Lane Fox also cites Lysias 10.1, referring to Lysitheus' unsuccessful prosecution of Theomnestus as unqualified to speak based on having discarded his armour in battle, but nothing in that passage refers to a *dokimasia*. It more likely involved traditional arguments about behaviours that deserve *atimia*. Lane Fox does believe the law was not genuinely Solonic and was likely dormant or little used by the mid-fourth century.
36 On this procedure for inducting new citizens, see Rhodes 1981, 496–502; Robertson 2000.
37 Honoring one's parents is specifically listed as such by Socrates in Xenophon, *Mem.* 4.4.20. Antigone notably considered the obligation of kin to provide proper burial an eternal unwritten

unwritten laws with the Athenians' sense of "shame" (αἰσχύνη) and thus more fundamental than any formal decree. Discarding one's gear in battle suggests a failure to fulfill one's commitments as a citizen; Aristophanes repeatedly ridicules Cleonymus for throwing his shield away at the battle of Delion (*Knights* 1372; *Clouds* 353–354; *Wasps* 15–20, 592, 822–823; *Peace* 673–678; *Birds* 289–290, 1473–81; cf. Eupolis, fr. 352 K.-A.), but so far as we know, he had a long political career (epigraphically attested as author of decrees in 426, making a proposal concerning the sacrileges in 415 [Andocides 1.27], and still mentioned by Aristophanes in 411 BC), so the charge seems not to have prevented him from speaking to either the courts or Council.[38]

Prostitution is a bit different, in that it was not illegal or immoral behaviour *per se*, but it was seen as unfittingly servile for a citizen, and thus more worthy of a slave or marginalised metic.[39] Our earliest reference to a charge of prostitution being used to declare someone a non-citizen is Aristophanes' claim that Cleon "erased" Grypus out of jealousy, because he did not want competition for his own services (*Knights* 875–880).[40] Dated to 424 BC, this reference suggests that the original context for charges about a politician's earlier self-prostitution was to allege non-citizenship by birth, not to punish a legitimate citizen with *atimia*. With the growth of Athens' empire and prosperity in the mid-fifth century, Athenians increasingly came to value citizen privileges exempting them from the physical toil and banausic pursuits of slaves and metics. Pericles' citizenship law of 451 was an attempt to regulate who was entitled to citizen privi-

---

law and derived it from the gods (Sophocles, *Antigone* 450–460). Plato (*Laws* 7.793a-c) and Aristotle (*Rhetoric* 1.10.3) both suggest some unwritten laws were universal, but Aristotle acknowledges some are also specific to an individual polity. Plato sees them as the ultimate divinely inspired authority on which all written laws rested; Aristotle (*Rhetoric* 1.13.2) and Demosthenes 18.275 see them as the laws of Nature. Plutarch (*Lycurgus* 13.1) claimed the Spartans had only such basic unwritten laws. For the most complete discussions of the "unwritten laws": Hirzel 1903; Flumene 1925.

38 For Cleonymus' career: see the evidence collected in Storey 1989, 255–256; Dunbar 1995, 238. Storey 1989, 256–261 thinks the allusions to shield-tossing were a metaphor for failure to serve as a hoplite.

39 On the metic status of most *hetairai/oi*: Dover 1978, 31–34.

40 Winkler (1990, 54–55) sees this text as reflecting the same law invoked by Aeschines, but the reference to "erasing" Grypus from some written archive like the deme or phratry register does not suggest *atimia* so much as one of the many cases of challenging citizenship by birth, as Cleon notoriously, but unsuccessfully tried with Aristophanes himself by charging him with being Aeginetan (Σ *Ach.* 378; *Vita Aristophanis* XXVIII, 20–30 Koster; see Schrader 1877, 389–394). The phrase "dragged me into the Council-chamber" (*Ach.* 379) makes Cleon's charge sound like a formal *eisangelia*.

leges, and in its wake politically motivated charges of non-citizenship were common.[41] Prostitution especially was a form of labour inconsistent with citizen status, as emphasised in Apollodorus' ugly attacks on Neaera and Phano in a case that was explicitly about citizenship claims. In this context, one can readily imagine Cleon citing Grypus' self-prostitution as grounds for considering him a metic, since he was engaged in a trade otherwise associated with metics. I suspect that it is to this period's acute concern with who deserved the rights and privileges of citizenship that we also owe the origins of the *graphē hetairēseos*. Only one year before the present trial all Athenian citizens had been required to undergo a renewed scrutiny by their demes due to suspicions that too many metics were claiming citizenship corruptly (Demosthenes 57.49), an event to which Aeschines specifically alludes (1.77–79) as a parallel for his challenge to Timarchus' good citizenship. He appeals to the same citizen anxieties as motivated the *diapsēphisis* of 347 BC.[42]

By embedding such a rhetorical exercise within a much longer section citing actual laws relevant to sexuality, Aeschines succeeds in confusing the jury into thinking that the *dokimasia rhētorōn* had equal legal authority to the *graphē hetairēseōs*. It is therefore hazardous to attribute much credibility to Aeschines' contentions here. In a culture where most citizens were either illiterate or deficient in their memory of legal history, and in a legal system where presiding judges had no authority to rule on matters of law, it is easy for skilled forensic orators to mingle general ethical denunciation with actual legal text in ways that can mislead and manipulate the judges. Having once been a clerk in various city archives (Dem. 19.249), probably including that of the Metroon, where all public documents were stored (Dem. 19.129), Aeschines was adept in reciting (and tendentiously glossing) legal texts;[43] by reciting too many laws (mostly irrelevant to the legal issue at hand), Aeschines can dazzle his audience with a patina of legal expertise and escape the notice of all but the most erudite in presenting as text what may be mere "emanations of the penumbra" of the law. Andrew Ford has illuminatingly demonstrated how Aeschines uses his

---

41 For Pericles' citizenship law as primarily a matter of sharpening status distinctions relative to metics and slaves, see Hunter 2000, 20–21; Wallace 2010.
42 On this event, see Fisher 2001, 62, and Lape 2006, 142–143. Just as in the wake of Pericles' citizenship law, this scrutiny became an opportunity for politically motivated attacks and even extortion. Aeschines accuses Timarchus of challenging Philotades' citizenship by claiming that he was once his own slave, but then dropping the challenge after receiving a bribe from Philotades' brother-in-law (1.114–115).
43 On the rhetorical usefulness of Aeschines' archival experience: Fisher 2001, 12–13.

hermeneutic technique in expounding literary texts as a positive model for how to apply legal text in equally creative and rhetorically expedient ways.[44]

If I am right that the sanctions of the *dokimasia rhētorōn* were more informal than formal, it may explain why the topic of self-prostitution is sometimes mentioned in passing, but seldom actually prosecuted, as we have already noted with regard to Andocides' charge against his accuser Epichares and Diodorus' charge against the tax-collector Androtion. Although the *graphē hetairēseōs* may well have had the status of a formal law with narrow application to a few specific offices, it gradually became stretched into something like the *dokimasia rhētorōn* that Aeschines invokes. The Law is always an evolving organism that reflects the historical contingencies of its time, as established through the remembered outcomes of case law like the present sensational trial.[45] Textual originalism had even less salience in the practice of Greek law than in contemporary Western jurisprudence.

Critics have recognised that Comedy was informed by a detailed knowledge of Athenian legal procedure, inasmuch as it reflected and satirised a perpetually litigious society.[46] But administration of the law was also penetrated by the influence of Comedy, as Socrates recognised in Plato's *Apology*. The prosecution of Timarchus was the first court case tried by Aeschines,[47] whose verbal skills were honed in the theatre, not by long forensic practice. With little solid evidence and a dubious legal theory, the former actor instead relied upon habits of characterisation he had learned from comic drama, where facts and details mattered but little. The rostrum becomes a stage, and he presents to his audience an entertaining spectacle of titillating gossip, an Old Comic *agōn* between himself, a peace-loving protagonist Everyman of normative sexual tastes and citizen values (a Dicaeopolis), and his antagonist, a stereotypical comic wastrel and sexual deviant, an *euruprōktos* just like the ambitious elite youths Aristophanes repeatedly attacked as corrupting parasites to the body politic, schem-

---

[44] Ford 1999. As he notes, Aeschines twice claims to be "teaching" the law to the democratic jury (1.8, 1.196).

[45] Lape 2006, 140: "prosecutors urged jurors to consider themselves actual lawmakers rather than simply judges of a single case (Lycurgus 1.9, Lysias 14.4)".

[46] For an overview of legal terminology and allusions in Old Comedy: Buis 2014, 321–334. Some insights can also be found in Apostolakis in this volume. Scafuro 1997 focuses on New Comedy.

[47] Aeschines himself admits this at the opening of his speech (1.1–2). For his reasons not to have pursued a forensic career earlier: Harris 1995, 36–37.

ing to befuddle their elders with clever legal tricks.[48] By insistent reference to his opponent's body as a physical presence under the judges' scrutinising gaze, Aeschines transcends his role as actor to become producer and director staging a courtroom comedy that will annihilate any serious defence with pre-emptively focalised laughter. Whatever the truth of the allegations and the law, Timarchus did not stand a chance.

Bibliography

Buis, E.J. (2014), 'Law and Greek Comedy', in: M. Fontaine and A.C. Scafuro (eds.), *The Oxford Handbook of Greek and Roman Comedy*, New York, 321–339.
Cantarella, E. (1992), *Bisexuality in the Ancient World*, New Haven.
Carey, C. (2000a), *Aeschines*, Austin.
Carey, C. (2000b), 'Old Comedy and the Sophists', in: D. Harvey and J. Wilkins (eds.), *The Rivals of Aristophanes: Studies in Athenian Old Comedy*, London, 419–436.
Carey, C. (2017). 'Style, Persona and Performance in Aeschines' Prosecution of Timarchus', in: S. Papaioannou, A. Serafim and B. da Vela (eds.), *The Theatre of Justice: Aspects of Performance in Greco-Roman Oratory and Rhetoric*, Leiden, 265–282.
Cohen, D. (1991), *Law, Sexuality, and Society: The Enforcement of Morals in Classical Athens*, Cambridge.
Davidson, J.N. (1997), *Courtesans and Fishcakes: The Consuming Passions of Classical Athens*, London.
Davidson, J.N. (2007), *The Greeks and Greek Love: A Radical Reappraisal of Homosexuality in Ancient Greece*, London.
Dover, K.J. (1967), 'Portrait-Masks in Aristophanes', in: R.E.H. Westendorp Boerma (ed.), *ΚΩΜΩΙΔΟΤΡΑΓΗΜΑΤΑ: Studia Aristophanea Viri Aristophanei W. J. W. Koster in Honorem*, Amsterdam, 16–28.
Dover, K.J. (1978), *Greek Homosexuality*, Cambridge, MA.
Drerup, E. (1898), 'Über die bei den attischen Rednern eingelegten Urkunden', in: *Jahrbuch für klassische Philologie* 24, 221–366.
Dunbar, N. (1995), *Aristophanes: Birds*, Oxford.
Easterling, P. (1999), 'Actors and Voices: Reading Between the Lines in Aeschines and Demosthenes', in: S. Goldhill and R. Osborne (eds.), *Performance Culture and Athenian Democracy*, Cambridge, 154–166.
Fisher, N. (2000), 'Symposiasts, Fish-eaters and Flatterers: Social Mobility and Moral Concerns in Old Comedy', in: D. Harvey and J. Wilkins (eds.), *The Rivals of Aristophanes: Studies in Athenian Old Comedy*, London, 355–396.
Fisher, N. (2001), *Aeschines: Against Timarchos*, Oxford.

---

[48] *Acharnians* 676–718; *Knights* 1373–1380; *Wasps* 686–695, 1067–1070. The plot of *Clouds* is premised on Strepsiades sending his son to Socrates to be educated in such techniques, only to see them turned against him.

Flumene, F. (1925), *La legge "non scritta" nella storia e nella dottrina etico-giuridica della Grecia classica*, Sassari.
Ford, A. (1999), 'Reading Homer from the Rostrum: Poems and Laws in Aeschines' *Against Timarchus*', in: S. Goldhill and R. Osborne (eds.), *Performance Culture and Athenian Democracy*, Cambridge, 231–256.
Foucault, M. (1985), *The Use of Pleasure: Volume 2 of the History of Sexuality*, New York.
Gardiner, E.N. (1910), *Greek Athletic Sports and Festivals*, London.
Green, J.R. (1997), 'Deportment, Costume and Naturalism in Comedy', in: *Pallas* 47, 131–143.
Halperin, D.M. (1990), *One Hundred Years of Homosexuality and Other Essays on Greek Love*, New York.
Hansen, M.H. (1976). *Apagoge, Endeixis and Ephegesis against Kakourgoi, Atimoi, and Pheugontes: A Study in the Athenian Administration of Justice in the Fourth Century BC*, Odense.
Harris, E.M. (1985), 'The Date of the Trial of Timarchus', in: *Hermes* 113, 376–380.
Harris, E.M. (1988), 'When Was Aeschines Born?', in: *Classical Philology* 83, 211–214.
Harris, E.M. (1995), *Aeschines and Athenian Politics*, New York.
Harris, H.A. (1964), *Greek Athletes and Athletics*, London.
Harrison, A.R.W. (1968–1971), *The Law of Athens*, Oxford.
Hirzel, R. (1903), Ἄγραφος Νόμος = *Abhandlungen der philologisch-historischen Classe* 20.1, Leipzig.
Hubbard, T.K. (1991), *The Mask of Comedy: Aristophanes and the Intertextual Parabasis*, Ithaca.
Hubbard, T.K. (1998), 'Popular Perceptions of Elite Homosexuality in Classical Athens', *Arion* 6(1), 48–78.
Hubbard, T.K. (2008), 'Getting the Last Word: Publication of Political Oratory as an Instrument of Historical Revisionism', in: E.A. Mackay (ed.), *Orality, Literacy, Memory in the Ancient Greco-Roman World*, Leiden, 183–200.
Hunter, V. (2000), 'Introduction: Status Distinctions in Athenian Law', in: V. Hunter and J. Edmondson (eds.), *Law and Social Status in Classical Athens*, Oxford, 1–29.
Ice, J.L. (2003), 'Disease and Transmission: Roman Erotic Poetry, Epigram, and Inscription as Evidence for Ancient Knowledge of the Sexual Transmission of Disease", M.A. Thesis, University of Texas at Austin.
Lane Fox, R. (1994), 'Aeschines and Athenian Democracy', in: R. Osborne and S. Hornblower (eds.), *Ritual, Finance, Politics: Athenian Democratic Accounts Presented to David Lewis*, Oxford, 135–155.
Lape, S. (2006), 'The Psychology of Prostitution in Aeschines' Speech *Against Timarchus*', in: C.A. Faraone and L.K. McClure (eds.), *Prostitutes and Courtesans in the Ancient World*, Madison, 139–160.
Lear, A. and Cantarella, E. (2008), *Images of Ancient Greek Pederasty: Boys Were Their Gods*, London.
MacDowell, D.M. (1978), *The Law in Classical Athens*, Ithaca/London.
Poliakoff, M.B. (1987), *Combat Sports in the Ancient World: Competition, Violence, and Culture*, New Haven.
Rhodes, P.J. (1981), *A Commentary on the Aristotelian Athenaion Politeia*, Oxford.
Robertson, B.G. (2000), 'The Scrutiny of New Citizens at Athens', in: V. Hunter and J. Edmondson (eds.), *Law and Social Status in Classical Athens*, Oxford, 149–174.
Rubinstein, L. (2000), *Litigation and Cooperation: Supporting Speakers in the Courts of Classical Athens*, Stuttgart.

Scafuro, A.C. (1997), *The Forensic Stage: Settling Disputes in Graeco-Roman New Comedy*, Cambridge.
Scanlon, T.F. (2002), *Eros and Greek Athletics*, New York.
Schrader, H. (1877), 'Kleon und Aristophanes' Babylonier', in: *Philologus* 36, 385–414.
Serafim, A. (2017), *Attic Oratory and Performance*, New York/London.
Shapiro, J. (2015), 'Pederasty and the Popular Audience', in: R. Blondell and K. Ormand (eds.), *Ancient Sex: New Essays*, Columbus, 177–207.
Sissa, G. (1999), 'Sexual Bodybuilding: Aeschines' *Against Timarchus*', in: J.I. Porter (ed.), *Constructions of the Classical Body*, Ann Arbor, 147–168.
Spatharas, D. (2016), 'Sex, Politics, and Disgust in Aeschines' *Against Timarchus*', in: D. Lateiner and D. Spatharas (eds.), *The Ancient Emotion of Disgust*, Oxford, 125–140.
Storey, I.C. (1989), 'The 'Blameless Shield' of Kleonymos', in: *Rheinisches Museum* 132, 247–261.
Storey, I.C. (2003), *Eupolis, Poet of Old Comedy*, Oxford.
Todd, S.C. (1993), *The Shape of Athenian Law*, Oxford.
Van't Wout, P.E. (2011), 'From Oath-Swearing to Entrenchment Clause: The Introduction of ἀτιμία-Terminology in Legal Inscriptions', in: A.P.M.H. Lardinois, J.H. Blok and M.G.M. Van der Poel (eds.), *Sacred Words: Orality, Literacy, and Religion*, Leiden, 143–160.
Varakis, A. (2010), 'Body and Mask in Aristophanic Performance', in: *Bulletin of the Institute of Classical Studies* 53, 17–38.
Wallace, R.W. (2010), 'Tecmessa's Legacy: Valuing Outsiders in Athens' Democracy', in: M. Rosen and I. Sluiter (eds.), *Valuing Others in Classical Antiquity*, Leiden, 137–154.
Wankel, H. (1988), 'Die Datierung des Prozessus gegen Timarchos (346/5)', in: *Hermes* 116, 383–386.
Winkler, J.J. (1990), *The Constraints of Desire: The Anthropology of Sex and Gender in Ancient Greece*, New York.
Worman, N.B. (2004), 'Insult and Oral Excess in the Disputes between Aeschines and Demosthenes', in: *American Journal of Philology* 125, 1–25

Nathan Kish
Comic Invective, Decorum and *Ars* in Cicero's *De Oratore*

Abstract: This chapter explores how the discussion of the limits of oratorical humour in Cicero's *De Oratore* (55 BC) sheds light on the roles of *ars* and *natura* in oratorical success. Although Cicero was criticised by both his contemporaries and later authors for being inappropriately funny, in *De Oratore* he addressed the importance of decorum and restraint in oratorical humour at some length. In the dialogue the character Julius Caesar Strabo espouses a markedly aggressive brand of humour that accords well with the often turbulent and violent political climate of the Late Republic. Nevertheless, Caesar emphasises that an orator should preserve his dignity and not strive to be funny in the manner of a mime (*mimus*) or a buffoon (*scurra*). Caesar attributes success in maintaining such decorum to *natura* rather than to *ars*, a reflex of a general question about the role of these elements in the training of an orator which is addressed elsewhere in the dialogue. Caesar's emphasis on *natura*, however, obfuscates the fact that for him humour often involves bending or warping how people and things would "naturally" appear through the artful use of language.

1 Introduction

Near the beginning of his *synkrisis* between Demosthenes and Cicero, Plutarch undertakes a comparison of their oratorical styles, proceeding to note that the character (τὸ ἦθος) of each man can be inferred from his speaking style. Whereas, for Plutarch, Demosthenes' style evinced a bitter and gloomy temperament (πικρία τοῦ τρόπου καὶ στυγνότης), Cicero's was characterised by his fondness for humour: "But Cicero, who often was carried away to buffoonery through his mockery, and who in pleading law cases subjected matters that were worthy of serious consideration to laughter and amusement in an ironic vein out of necessity, neglected decorum" (Κικέρων δὲ πολλαχοῦ τῷ σκωπτικῷ πρὸς τὸ βωμολόχον ἐκφερόμενος, καὶ πράγματα σπουδῆς ἄξια γέλωτι καὶ παιδιᾷ κατειρωνευό-

---

I would like to thank the editors, Andreas Serafim and Sophia Papaioannou, for the invitation to contribute to this volume and for their understanding and patience in the midst of a pandemic, as well as the reviewers.

μενος ἐν ταῖς δίκαις εἰς τὸ χρειῶδες, ἠφείδει τοῦ πρέποντος, *Comp. Dem. et Cic.* 1.4). According to Plutarch, humour was not just a defining element of Cicero's style: he indulged in it excessively, violating the all-important rhetorical and philosophical virtue of decorum (τὸ πρέπον). To support this assertion, Plutarch describes two speeches that are especially notable for the humorous manner in which Cicero dealt with his opponents. He claims that in the *Pro Caelio* (56 BC) Cicero made the argument that it was not strange for a young man who was surrounded by luxury and extravagance to enjoy some pleasures, especially when certain philosophers found happiness in pleasure. Those familiar with this speech will recall that by 'pleasures' Plutarch is referring to Cicero's contention that Caelius (as a young man is wont to do) was merely enjoying the lascivious favours offered by the effective prostitute Clodia, who becomes the target of biting invective in the course of the speech. Turning to the speech Cicero delivered while consul in 63 BC in defence of L. Murena, Plutarch writes that when clear laughter swept down from those observing the trial to the judges, Cato the Younger, one of the prosecutors and an object of mockery in Cicero's speech for his Stoic leanings, with a smile said quietly to those next to him, "How funny a consul we have, gentlemen" (ὡς γελοῖον, ὦ ἄνδρες, ἔχομεν ὕπατον, *Comp. Dem. et Cic.* 1.5).[1] In referring to Cicero's office in this quip, Cato seems to be implying that Cicero's humorous speech is inappropriate for his rank.

And yet it was not just the philosophically inclined such as Plutarch and Cato who believed that Cicero, while funny, could go too far in his witticisms. In Book 2 of Macrobius' *Saturnalia*, the character Symmachus suggests that no one who has read the books of Cicero's jokes compiled by his freedman Tiro could be ignorant of Cicero's ability in this field, and yet he also acknowledges that Cicero had his detractors: "Who likewise does not know that he was wont to be called the consular buffoon by his enemies? Vatinius even set this down in a speech" (*Quis item nescit consularem eum scurram ab inimicis appellari solitum? quod in oratione etiam sua Vatinius posuit, Sat.* 2.1.12). In this reproach we can once again identify a perceived discrepancy between Cicero's use of humour and the behaviour that was expected of him as a *consularis*. Whereas Cato pointed to Cicero's current consulship to suggest that Cicero's behaviour during

---

[1] Plutarch also relates this incident at *Cat. Mi.* 21.7–8. On the meaning of Plutarch's γελοῖον, see Krostenko 2001, 224–225, who claims that the quip would have been "more pungent" if Cato's original statement were *quam facetum* or *quam lepidum habemus consulem* rather than the "purely dismissive" *quam ridiculum*. Krostenko credits the suggestion to Leeman 1963, 61, who asserts that the "crushing" *habemus facetum consulem* would be "an oxymoron in Roman ears!"

the trial of Murena was undignified, such criticism apparently was appropriated by Cicero's enemies, who saw a perpetual incongruity that a man who had held the highest office in the Roman state would be so habitually inclined to cracking jokes.[2] Moreover, it would seem that under the charge of *consularis scurra* lay a politically motivated manifestation of class bias: as the *scurra* was something of a parasitic professional jester who would earn his place at a patron's table through his joking ability,[3] the implication of Vatinius' phrase could be that Cicero secured his position in the state by peddling jokes.

While such accusations by both contemporaries and later authors might suggest that Cicero paid little heed to decorum in the use of wit, the opposite is true: Cicero addressed the importance of decorum and restraint in oratorical humour at some length in his three-book dialogue *De oratore* (55 BC).[4] In an extended discussion of the kind of humour that is appropriate for an orator (the so-called *excursus de ridiculis*, *De orat.* 2.216–290; cf. Monaco 1968), the character of Julius Caesar Strabo is prevailed upon by the other discussants to set forth what he knows about eliciting laughter, a subfield of oratory he is said to be a specialist in.[5] One of the five headings under which his lengthy exposition on laughter (*de risu*) is arranged is *quatenus* ("how far"), that is, what are the limits for an orator who wants to make jokes in his speeches? (*De orat.* 2.237–247).[6]

---

[2] In his *Cicero*, Plutarch says that Cicero used his wit immoderately (κατακόρως) and acquired a reputation for malevolence (κακοήθεια, *Cic.* 5.6). Note that while Cicero's contemporaries refer to his political position, Plutarch seems to disapprove of Cicero's excessive humour categorically. Cf. also *Cic.* 27.1. Quintilian reports that Cicero was considered to strive too much for laughter (*habitus est nimius risus adfectator*, *Inst.* 6.3.3).
[3] On the *scurra*, see Grant 1924, 91–96.
[4] Cicero briefly returned to the topic nine years later in the *Orator* (46 BC), a work that features a more developed treatment of *decorum* (70–74) but a much shorter discussion of humour (88–90). In his final philosophical work, *De Officiis* (44 BC), Cicero addressed the virtue of *decorum* at greatest length (1.93–151). Although Cicero does not specifically deal with oratorical humour when treating *decorum* from a philosophical perspective in this work, the treatise can be productively taken into account when approaching the discussions in the rhetorical works. Cf. Guérin 2019.
[5] See Dugan 2005, 112–113 n. 135 for further references to Caesar's wit in Cicero's corpus.
[6] Caesar makes his division at *De orat.* 2.235, *de risu quinque sunt quae quaerantur: unum quid sit; alterum unde sit; tertium sitne oratoris velle risum movere; quartum quatenus; quintum quae sint genera ridiculi* ("With regard to laughter, there are five topics to consider: 1) What is laughter?; 2) From where does it arise?; 3) Is it suitable for an orator to wish to provoke laughter?; 4) To what extent?; 5) What are the types of the laughable?"). Caesar deals with the first three headings very briefly (2.235–236), and after covering the fourth at greater length (2.237–247), the bulk of his discussion is devoted to the fifth (2.247–289), in which Caesar runs through (with supporting examples) the types of jokes that depend on a word (*in verbo*, 2.248–263) and

Caesar, noting that this issue must be considered very carefully (*perquam diligenter*, 2.237), deals in this section with issues pertaining to decorum. He claims an orator should refrain from making jokes about certain targets and should limit the frequency of his jokes, and he also demarcates the kinds of humour that are appropriate for an orator from those that are associated with mimes (*mimi*) and buffoons (*scurrae*). In comparison to those two types of lower-status jokesters, the orator should practice restraint, resorting only to such jokes that are suitable to his elevated social standing and dignity. And so, far from being oblivious to the socially determined limits as to what was appropriate, Cicero made decorum a key element in his theorising on oratorical humour. Accordingly, the fact that some of his contemporaries as well as later readers believed that Cicero had exceeded the bounds of proper taste in his use of jokes raises an intriguing question: What can the theoretical advice on the limits of oratorical humour in *De oratore* teach us about Cicero's alleged violations of it?

This is the question that will guide the remainder of this paper, which falls into three parts. After exploring the aggressive nature of humour that Caesar espouses (2), I consider the limits on humour that Caesar deems appropriate for an orator (3). Lastly (4), I address how Caesar's discussion of the limitations of humour relates to the roles that nature (*natura*) and art (*ars*) play in oratorical success, a fundamental question that surfaces at various points in *De oratore* and is brought to the fore when the conversation turns to humour.

2 The Aggressive Nature of Humour in *De Oratore*

De oratore features the earliest extant extended Roman theoretical discussion of humour, and is perhaps the first general work on rhetoric to include an expansive discussion of it.[7] Within the dramatic frame of the dialogue, the exposition

---

those for which the humour is contained in the matter (*in re*, 2.264–289). On the structure of Caesar's discussion, see Pinkster 1995. For the text of *De oratore* I have used Kumaniecki's Teubner edition (1969, reprinted 1995). Translations are mine unless noted.

[7] Clarke 1996, 59–60. Discussions of Cicero's account of rhetorical humour in *De oratore* include Grant 1924; Leeman, Pinkster and Rabbie 1989, 172–333; Corbeill 1996, 20–30; Krostenko 2001, 202–232; Fantham 2004, 186–208; Dugan 2005, 105–107, 112–129, 145–147; Rabbie 2007; Beard 2014, 107–123; Guérin 2019. The earliest commentary on Cicero's work can be said to be Quintilian's lengthy discussion of laughter in the *Institutio Oratoria* (6.3), as there is considerable overlap between Cicero's and Quintilian's accounts, including shared jokes. Cf. Kühnert 1962 on the relationship between the two works. Good starting points for *De oratore* are May/

on humour (2.216–290) is entrusted to C. Julius Caesar Strabo Vopiscus,[8] who, according to Marcus Antonius, one of the two principal interlocutors, excels all others in jokes and humour (2.216).[9] Like the rest of the dialogue, Caesar's discussion of humour aims to be non-technical – and he takes his start from the claim that humour cannot be taught by an art (*ars*), a point he returns to in the course of his treatment – although several schematic divisions, characteristic of school rhetoric, are fundamental for its structure. Cicero's own gift for humour shines through in Caesar's exposition: many of the jokes and anecdotes that Caesar includes illustrate clearly the type of joke he is explaining and pack a punch.[10]

The nature of the humour that Caesar promotes in *De oratore* is generally mordant and aggressive, and its principal goal seems to be to expose an ugliness in the target of the joke to the delight and ridicule of the third-party audience.[11] While invective could aim to make the audience angry at a target, the emotions that the rhetoricians discussed were not all harsh and violent. Laughter effected through humour, wit and insult could be an effective way for orators to attain their ends, since by means of comic invective an orator could reduce his opponent to an object of ridicule. Indeed, derision was an essential element of Roman oratorical humour, and in Caesar's discussion (the examples for

---

Wisse 2001 and Fantham 2004, as well as the five-volume commentary begun by Leeman and Pinkster and completed by Wisse, Winterbottom and Fantham.

8 On the significance of Caesar as the speaker of the *excursus* see Dugan 2005, 105–107, 117–118.

9 Nevertheless, both Caesar (2.220, 227) and Antonius (2.228) go on to claim that L. Licinius Crassus is the most successful orator in his use of humour, and Antonius specifically says that he is jealous that Crassus, at whose estate in Tusculum the conversations are set, is the most pleasant and urbane as well as the most dignified and austere speaker. The tradition of identifying Cicero with Crassus in *De oratore* can be traced back at least to Quintilian (*Inst.* 10.3.1; cf. 10.5.2); see Dugan 2005, 87, 92 for references, discussion and bibliography. While acknowledging that Cicero gives special care to shaping the words of Crassus, the dialogue's "protagonist", Dugan himself argues that Cicero uses the whole cast of interlocutors in his self-fashioning project (2005, 92–93; cf. also 148, 150–151).

10 Quintilian in several instances uses as examples the same jokes that Cicero does but his versions are often less pointedly delivered. Cf. Clarke 1996, 112: "the grave Quintilian, one feels, was not a great humourist".

11 Richlin 1992 treats the intersection of invective and humour in Roman culture generally, while Corbeill 1996 focuses on its role in a range of Cicero's works, especially the speeches. Beard 2014, who devotes a chapter to the orator (99–127) within a wider study of laughter in ancient Rome, questions how aggressive Roman oratorical laughter was (106–107, 120–123).

which are taken to a large extent from Roman orators)[12] humour primarily consists of wittily pointing out the faults of others, who would then be laughed at. The success of the orator's attack, then, depends on the speaker uniting the audience with himself against the ridiculed target, who in effect has been, to a greater or lesser degree, stigmatised by the community.[13] If Caesar's discussion of humour is representative of Republican oratorical practice, a speaker would principally deploy humour to hurt his adversaries and defend himself.

The large roles of invective and derision in humour in *De oratore* arise in part from Caesar's understanding of the field of subject matter appropriate to *risus*, which he takes up as his second topic for discussion.[14] This, Caesar claims, is confined to the unseemly and the ugly: "but the location and, so to speak, province of the laughable – for that is our next topic of investigation – is delimited by the unseemly and a certain kind of ugliness. For those jokes which mark and point out something unseemly in no unseemly way produce the greatest degree of laughter, if they are not the only jokes to produce laughter" (*locus autem et regio quasi ridicule – nam id proxime quaeritur – turpitudine et deformitate quadam continetur. haec enim ridentur vel sola vel maxime, quae notant et signant turpitudinem aliquam non turpiter*, 2.236).[15] Given this interpretation of the subject matter of laughter, it is understandable that most of the jokes in Caesar's discussion entail picking on another's stigmatised attribute or action and thereby bringing this party into derision and ridicule. A significant component of Caesar's definition is *notare*, "to note", which can also mean "to brand", "to stain" and, for a Roman censor, "to express official condemnation of a citi-

---

[12] Three jokes (2.255, 279, 285) come from Novius, the first-century BC author of Atellan farce, and these are much less insulting and derisive than the jokes of the orators. Cf. Fantham 2004, 196–199 on where Caesar's jokes came from.

[13] For the Freudian triangular model of the persons involved in jokes – a protagonist, an antagonist and a spectator – see Richlin 1992, 60–61. On the potential of humour to create a community and forge proximity between the performer/humour-maker and the audience/humour-receiver, see the Introduction to this volume, pp. 11–12.

[14] See n. 6 above for the topics that Caesar sets out for himself.

[15] Near the beginning of his discourse on laughter, Quintilian (*Inst.* 6.3.8) refers to this with approval, adding that when ugliness and unseemliness are pointed out in others, it is called urbanity (*urbanitas*), but when they recoil upon the one speaking, stupidity (*stultitia*). Cf. Arist. *Po.* 5 (1449a32–34) for comedy consisting of "imitation of lower people" (μίμησις φαυλοτέρων), as laughter is a part of ugliness (τὸ αἰσχρόν). Cf. also *De orat.* 2.248 in connection with the claim that "dignified statements" (*graves sententiae*) can arise from the same situations as jokes: *tantum interest, quod gravitas honestis in rebus et severis, iocus in turpiculis et quasi deformibus ponitur*.

zen".[16] Notably, Caesar here emphasises that the speaker is to mark out the unseemly in no unseemly way: while revealing a man's social ineptitude, unseemly character or physical ugliness, the speaker himself in no way is to be stained by the ugliness of his target.[17] On the contrary, the joker emerges as a man of taste and discerning judgment as he is able to recognise the faults of others and expose them to the community in a clever way.

In the arenas of public life, then, humour was a weapon (even if not the most violent one) that an orator could use to wound his adversaries and heighten his own standing. This is especially apparent in the jokes in *De oratore*, which provides a window onto the competitive world of Roman Republican politics. The first joke that Caesar recounts sets the tone for the rest of his discussion by illustrating the quarrelsome nature of oratorical humour. It comes from an exchange between L. Marcius Philippus and Q. Lutatius Catulus, Caesar's half-brother and one of the participants in the dialogue. In response to Philippus' question, "What are you barking at?" Catulus said, "I see a thief!"[18] In this example of thrust and parry, or attack and counterattack, both statements are meant to make the other party appear ridiculous. *Latrare*, "to bark" was used to describe unpleasant-sounding orators, and by asking Catulus what he is barking at, Philippus implies that Catulus, like a dog, speaks in a noisy and irritating manner.[19] What gives this particular joke a sharper edge, however, is that it plays upon the name Catulus, which is also the Latin word for "puppy". Philippus thus belittles Catulus by saying that he acts like a puppy and cleverly uses Catulus' own name as support for this. In his "comeback", Catulus, caps the initial provocation and turns the jest back upon Philippus, claiming that, like a good watchdog, he is barking at a thief.[20] In using Philippus' joke against

---

16 *OLD noto* 1b, 3, 4. Cf. Antonius' use of *notare* when discussing the oratorical genre of *vituperatio* proper (*De orat.* 2.349).
17 On "staining": cf. p. 223 with n. 49 below.
18 *De orat.* 2.220, *quid enim hic meus frater ab arte adiuvari potuit, cum a Philippo interrogatus quid latraret, furem se videre respondit?* The context for this exchange has unfortunately been lost. Cf. Leeman, Pinkster and Rabbie 1989 *ad loc.* Caesar uses it, however, to emphasise that the sharp, intermittent type of humour that he labels *dicacitas* has no need of art (*De orat.* 2.219–220).
19 For *latro*, see Cic. *De orat.* 3.138, *Brut.* 58, Quint. *Inst.* 11.3.31, and Val. Max. 8.3.2 on Gaia Afrania, a first-century BC woman who often brought suits and spoke on her own behalf in the Forum. Cf. also Plut. *Cic.* 5.6.
20 Quintilian includes this joke as an example of not denying something that is obviously false when it offers material for a good response (*Inst.* 6.3.81).

him, Catulus deflects the blow and wounds Philippus – and he does so with style.

Such an exchange resembles a verbal duel in which each participant attempts to outmanoeuvre and "out-insult" the other.[21] Verbal duelling is an important component of the jokes that Caesar relates as many of them are responses to something someone has said. While such rapid verbal repartee would be especially valuable for *altercationes* in which senators or legal advocates and witnesses would dispute with one another in the senate or the court,[22] it underlies the institutionalised practices of forensic and deliberative oratory in which men compete with one another in speech. Moreover, as with a wide variety of violent competitive activities both ancient and modern, such combative oratorical exchanges could give pleasure to the observer.[23] Caesar returns to Catulus' response to Philippus later in his discussion to illustrate playing upon an equivocal word (*ambiguum*) and there describes it in more violent terms: "this is most agreeable when in a dispute a word is ripped away from the adversary and is used, as Catulus did against Philippus, to hurl something against the one who has goaded him" (*De orat.* 2.255). In his analysis here, Caesar uses language appropriate to the battlefield: words become missiles. Significantly, Caesar regards such an exchange as "most agreeable" (*venustissimum*), which shows that an altercation such as the one between Catulus and Philippus that resembles a violent conflict can be pleasurable for the audience.[24]

The emphasis on humour as a weapon in *De oratore* could be due in part to the fact that Caesar is specifically discussing *oratorical* humour. The political

---

21 For verbal dueling, see Pagliai 2009, with further bibliography. Cohen 1995, 78–79 considers verbal dueling in fourth-century Athenian oratory; Richlin 1992, 74–75 and 2017, 151–184 in Roman culture and Plautine comedy in particular, including its connections with *flagitatio*. Fantham 2004, 186–199 touches on verbal dueling productively in her study of Caesar's *excursus* on humour.
22 For *altercatio*, see Quint. *Inst.* 6.4. In a letter to Atticus, Cicero proudly relates an *altercatio* with Clodius in the senate in which he landed many shots (1.16.10). Cicero's fragmentary speech *In Clodium et In Curionem* may also preserve some of this *altercatio*; see Crawford 1994, 229, 232, 252.
23 On the importance of pleasing the audience in verbal dueling, see Pagliai 2009, 80.
24 In the dialogue such an appreciation is not attributed only to Caesar. During an early pause in Caesar's discussion, Antonius claims that things said in response are "altogether more agreeable" (*omnino probabiliora*) than those said in provocation: as Antonius explains it, "a greater quickness of mind" (*ingenii celeritas maior*) is evident in responding (*in respondendo*), and "response is a human characteristic" (*humanitatis est responsio, De orat.* 2.230). Cf. Quint. *Inst.* 6.3.13, *sunt enim longe venustiora omnia in respondendo quam in provocando*, "for all things said in response are far more attractive than in provocation".

assemblies and law courts in which the agonistic oratorical disputes that resemble verbal dueling took place were civic institutions that functioned, among other things, as venues for conflict resolution wherein community-sanctioned punishment could be meted out. To use a hypothetical example, Marcus believes that Gaius has wronged him and is aggrieved; rather than walking up to Gaius and slugging him, however, Marcus prosecutes him before the community in a court of law, hoping the community representatives will side with him and punish Gaius accordingly. Nevertheless, the immediate physical violence that is deferred onto the court system can manifest in verbal violence when a speaker aims to hurt his adversary by the things he says. And so, the language a speaker uses to attack an opponent both could be violent in itself and could use its violent character to persuade fellow members of the community to inflict real harm upon an individual.

This is especially relevant for *De oratore*, as the backdrops to the conversation and the work as a whole are civil discord at Rome. The characters in the dialogue have retired to Crassus' Tusculan villa during the *ludi Romani* in September 91 BC in part to recuperate from the conflicts between the same Philippus, one of the consuls, and M. Livius Drusus, a tribune of the plebs, that had caused tumult in Rome during the year (*De orat.* 1.24–27). Yet, in setting the stage for the dialogue, Cicero foregrounds the political concerns of the interlocutors. In introducing the two youngest members of the party, P. Sulpicius Rufus and C. Aurelius Cotta, Cicero, even before he relates their names, notes that they are on the closest terms with Drusus (*Drusi maxime familiares*, 1.25). Additionally, the discussion on oratory that is purportedly recorded in *De oratore* began the day after the participants arrived, as they are said to have deplored the current political situation and divinely predicted the disasters that would befall the state until late on the first day (1.26). Accordingly, as the first joke in Caesar's discussion is taken from an altercation between Philippus and Catulus (who, along with Caesar, arrived at Crassus' villa at the beginning of Book 2, when the second day of the conversation about oratory begins), the reader is prompted to recall the troubled political context in which the dialogue is set.[25] And the events that followed from the discord between Philippus and Drusus illustrate how momentous such conflicts could be. Drusus died before the year was out (Appian reports that he was stabbed in the thigh, *BC* 1.36–37). In the aftermath, several of Rome's Italian allies revolted, which led to the Social War, which in turn helped pave the way for the civil wars between Marius and Sulla in the 80s.

---

25 It is noteworthy that at *De Officiis* 1.108 Cicero briefly compares Crassus, Philippus and Caesar with respect to their *lepos* ("humour").

In the preface to Book 3, Cicero laments the deaths of the characters in the dialogue, most of whom died at the hands of Marius or Sulla (*De orat.* 3.9–12); Crassus himself, however, died within ten days of the dramatic date of Books 2 and 3, after he fell ill following a particularly vehement confrontation with Philippus at a senate meeting that had been convened by Drusus (3.2–6).[26] For his part, Cicero, who claimed that he learned of the conversation at Crassus' villa from Cotta, composed *De oratore* in 55 BC during his own retreat from Roman politics: forced to the political sidelines by the First Triumvirate, he laments the disordered state of the Republic in the prefatory addresses to his brother, Quintus (*De orat.* 1.1–4, 3.13–14). And yet, while the relevant historical contexts and Caesar's own discussion of humour suggest that a sharp and ready tongue would be particularly valuable for a Roman orator in the turbulent political climate of the Late Republic,[27] a critical question remains: What limits should an orator observe when ridiculing an opponent?

3 Decorum and the Limits of Humour in *De Oratore*

Caesar discusses the proper limits for oratorical humour when he comes to address the fourth of the five headings that he had set out for himself: "but as for how far the orator must go in treating the laughable, the topic that we had put in the fourth place, we must consider this very carefully" (*De orat.* 2.237). The first topic that Caesar takes up under this heading is the appropriate targets, noting that neither outstanding wickedness (*insignis improbitas*) nor outstanding wretchedness (*miseria insignis*) are suitable sources for laughter, and that one must also be sparing when it comes to the esteem that people hold (*caritati hominum*, *De orat.* 2.237). This leads Caesar into making a general pronouncement on moderation as a guiding principle for oratorical humour (*De orat.* 2.238–239):

> (238) *haec igitur adhibenda est primum in iocando moderatio. itaque ea facillime luduntur quae neque odio magno neque misericordia maxima digna sunt. quam ob rem materies omnis ridiculorum est in iis vitiis, quae sunt in vita hominum neque carorum neque calamito-*

---

26 For the relation of Crassus' death to the dramatic date of the dialogue, see Mankin 2011, 102.
27 Accordingly, it should not be surprising that the derisive nature of humour is more pronounced in Cicero's treatment than in Quintilian's comparable account. On this point, cf. Beard 2014, 124.

sorum neque eorum qui ob facinus ad supplicium rapiendi videntur; eaque belle agitata ridentur. (239) *est etiam deformitatis et corporis vitiorum satis bella materies ad iocandum.*

(238) Therefore moderation must be exercised especially when making jokes. And so, those things are most easily mocked which are deserving of neither great hatred nor the utmost pity. For this reason, all material for jokes is located in those faults which are found in the way of life of people who are neither cherished nor miserable nor who seem fit to be dragged off to punishment on account of their wickedness, and these things, when they are nicely assailed with derision, are laughed at. (239) There is even sufficiently pretty material for jokes in ugliness and the faults of the body.

Caesar's emphasis on *moderatio* and avoiding excess gives a Peripatetic cast to his entire discussion, and in general his understanding of both the possibilities and the limits of oratorical humour is ethically oriented.[28] Since the material that can most easily produce laughter is found in those faults that are located in an individual's way of life (*in iis vitiis quae sunt in vita hominum*), derisive jokes can be used by an orator as a means to shine light on his target's character, as an individual's habits and way of life are a result of his character.[29] The orator himself also needs to practice moderation in his criticisms, which if executed properly can play an important role in the management of his ἦθος or character.[30] In his own humorous formulation at the end of this passage, Caesar ironically claims that attractive material (*bella materies*) can arise from physical ugliness. A speaker can make ugliness pleasing by ridiculing it at the expense of the target, and so Caesar's observation illuminates both the speaker's cleverness and his tendency to mordancy. Part of an audience's enjoyment in a joke could come from momentarily taking pleasure in what is usually unattractive, and this could earn approbation for the speaker, who would appear as clever for finding the pretty in the ugly.

Yet, as I noted above in discussing the material that was the source of humour (*De orat.* 2.236), the orator needs to handle the ugly in such a way that he himself does not become stained by it. And so, having reaffirmed that the proper source for jokes resides in the ugly, Caesar doubles down on the question "how far?" (*sed quaerimus idem, quod in ceteris rebus maxime quaerendum est, quatenus*), and states that an orator not only must take care that he does not say something foolishly (*insulse*), but even if he is able to say something in a very funny way (*perridicule*), he must avoid making the types of jokes that are char-

---

28 Cf. Grant 1924, 76–87.
29 Cf. May 1988, 6 on the Roman understanding of character.
30 Cf. Antonius at *De orat.* 2.182–184 on the manner in which a speaker should comport himself in order to secure the goodwill of the audience.

acteristic of a buffoon or a mime (*vitandum est oratori utrumque, ne aut scurrilis iocus sit aut mimicus, De orat.* 2.239). This point determines the structure of Caesar's ensuing discussion of the limits of oratorical humour, as he will expand upon how the orator must differ in his humour from both the mime (*mimus*) and the buffoon (*scurra*).[31] In the case of each, the limit is related to a fundamental distinction Caesar draws between what he designates as the two types of humour (*Duo sunt enim genera facetiarum, quorum alterum re tractatur alterum dicto, De orat.* 2.239). Of these, the first (*res*), based on matter and found in narration and imitation, corresponds to the humour employed by the mime; the other (*dictum*), which arises from the force of a single word and shows up in quick responses and one-liners, recalls the quick wit that is often displayed by the buffoon.[32]

Caesar's distinction between the types of humour at this juncture recalls an earlier distinction he had made between the kind of humour that is spread out equally in a whole speech and the kind that is very sharp and brief, noting that the ancients called the former *cavillatio* and the latter *dicacitas* (*De orat.* 2.218).[33] Caesar had introduced this classification in the course of his preliminary discussion (*De orat.* 2.217–227) in which his principal objective was to confirm Antonius' claim that humour cannot be taught through art (*ars*) but is a product of nature (*natura, De orat.* 2.219):

> *sed cum in illo genere perpetuae festivitatis ars non desideretur – natura enim fingit homines et creat imitatores et narratores facetos adiuvante et voltu et voce et ipso genere sermonis – tum vero in hoc altero dicacitatis quid habet ars loci, cum ante illud facete dictum emissum haerere debeat, quam cogitari potuisse videatur?*

> But as art is not called for in that type of sustained pleasantry (for nature fashions individuals and creates witty imitators and story-tellers, with one's countenance and voice and manner of speech playing a helping role), truly, then, what place does art have in that other type, the mordant joke, since a bon-mot missile ought to stick into its target sooner than it seems to have been able to be thought of?

Caesar's discussion at this earlier stage in the conversation helps to clarify how the two types of humour of *res* and *dictum* correspond respectively to the *mimus* and the *scurra*. *Perpetua festivitas* (or *cavillatio*) relies on playing a part, essen-

---

31 On the relation of the *mimus* and the *scurra* to the discussion of humour in *De oratore*, see Grant 1924, 88–96.
32 On this point, see Guérin 2019, 136, who claims that the *scurra* and the *mimus* demonstrate a "corrupt version" of *dicacitas* and *cavillatio*, for which see the following paragraph.
33 For the relationship between these two distinctions, see Fantham 2004, 189, 193.

tially, and demands a performance from the orator that includes animation of his face and inflecting his voice; *dicacitas* is pointed and piercing and has some resemblance to violence.[34]

Returning now to Caesar's discussion of the limits of oratorical humour, let us deal first with *res*, which Caesar divides into *narratio* and *imitatio*. Caesar illustrates the former by referring to a story that Crassus, the leading speaker in the dialogue, had told about C. Memmius (*trib. pl.* 111 BC), claiming, however, that Crassus' narrative, funny as it may have been, had nevertheless been completely invented (*salsa ac tamen a te ipso ficta tota narratio*, *De orat.* 2.240).[35] Yet it seems that it was successful because Crassus brought the scene to life, executing the various performative tasks that Caesar notes an orator should focus on when telling a humorous story: "but this is the excellence of this type of humour, that you demonstrate the deeds, that you express the character, voice and all the facial expressions of the person about whom you are telling a story, so that to those listening the things being recounted seem to be done and happen right before their eyes" (*De orat.* 2.241). Accordingly, we can imagine Crassus, when recounting, or really performing this story, acting out the roles of the various characters and mimicking their attributes in order to subject the whole affair to laughter.

As for *imitatio*, Caesar claims that which can be introduced from a kind of distorted imitation can be funny (*in re est item ridiculum, quod ex quadam depravata imitatione sumi solet*, *De orat.* 2.242), and he proceeds to illustrate this by again using Crassus as a model. But yet, Caesar warns, while this type of humour can be very funny, it must be handled with great caution (*cautissime tractandum sit*, *De orat.* 2.242):

> mimorum est enim et ethologorum, si nimia est imitatio, sicut obscenitas. orator surripiat oportet imitationem, ut is qui audiet cogitet plura quam videat; praestet idem ingenuitatem et ruborem suum verborum turpitudine et rerum obscenitate vitanda.

> For if there is an excessive amount of imitation, then it belongs to mimes, just as lewdness does. The orator, on the other hand, ought to undertake *imitatio* surreptitiously, so that the audience conceives of more things in their minds than they see. The orator should exhibit noble-mindedness and his sense of shame, avoiding ugliness of words and lewd actions.

---

34 Indeed, in order to illustrate his claim about the nature of *dicacitas*, Caesar proceeds to relate the exchange between Philippus and Catulus (*De orat.* 2.220) that I discussed above in terms of verbal dueling.
35 On this passage see Hughes 2002.

These words of caution situate Caesar's discussion firmly in the discourse of decorum: the orator should only do and say what is appropriate to his position, which is much different than that of a mime actor. And so, in place of the obscenity and excessive imitation that is characteristic of the mime, it seems that the orator needs to strive for a highly suggestive form of ἐνάργεια ("vivid description"). That is, he should not only attempt to represent vividly whom he is imitating or telling a story about, but should do so in such a way that the audience imagines even more than is being represented.[36] Indeed, in doing just enough to prompt the audience to conceive of what is ugly in their own minds, the orator remains free of any stain that would have resulted from saying or doing anything that is not in agreement with his elevated status.[37]

In turning to the other type of humour, *dictum*, Caesar primarily sees a distinction between the quick-tongued orator and the *scurra* insofar as the former operates with greater care and control. The humour of the *scurra*, on the other hand, lacks precision and purpose, which Caesar illustrates by recounting insulting jokes that were either inopportunely delivered, lacked a specific target, or were uttered simply for raising a laugh, which Caesar says is the most insignificant reward for a clever mind (*vel tenuissimus ingeni fructus*, De orat. 2.247).[38] An orator, on the other hand, whose practice in this vein is governed by an assessment of the moment (*temporis ratio*), moderation of his wit (*dicacitatis moderatio*), self-control (*temperantia*) and a lack of frequency in his sayings (*raritas dictorum*), speaks with a reason, not in order to seem funny, but to accomplish something (*De orat.* 2.247). It seems that for Caesar the issue revolves around the question of timing: "therefore we will measure the timing by means of judgment and dignity – for which I wish we had some system! But the mistress is nature" (*De orat.* 2.247). This is the final sentence in Caesar's discussion of the limits of oratorical humour, and in it he emphasises the need for the orator to remain measured and in control, being guided by discretion and a sense of dignity. While pertaining specifically to *dicacitas*, such advice would seem to apply to both types of humour, as in his treatment of each Caesar devotes his efforts to explaining how one can be funny without exceeding the bounds of decorum. Ultimately, however, Caesar ends on the point that no *ars* is available to teach

---

36 Cf. *De orat.* 2.357, 3.160–161 on sight as the keenest (*acerrimus*) of the senses. Cf. also Webb 2009, 87–106 on Quintilian's discussions in the *Institutio Oratoria* of *enargeia* (Latin *evidentia*), "the quality of language that appeals to the audience's imagination" (87–88).

37 On this issue see the Introduction to this volume, pp. 11–12.

38 Cf. Arist. *EN* 2.7 (1108a 24–25), 4.8 (1128a 33–1128b 1) on the buffoon (βωμολόχος), as well as the Introduction to this volume, p. 12.

an orator how to remain within the proper limits of the behaviour that was considered socially acceptable, and one must rather look to *natura*.

4 *Natura* and *Ars* in Oratorical Humour

Before Caesar's extended treatment of humour, Antonius, in passing the baton off to him, says that Caesar is so distinguished in his use of humour that he will be able to bear witness that no art of wit (*ars salis*) exists, or, if does exist, that he will be able to teach it to the others (*De orat*. 2.216). In the phrase *ars salis*, Antonius understands *ars* as a field of activity governed by rules that can be taught and learned.[39] The preliminary portion of Caesar's discussion of humour (2.217–227) is in part a response to this question, and after citing numerous examples of humour and wit (mostly drawn from the speeches of Crassus), Caesar concludes that it is not possible to learn such humour and witticisms from art (*eas arte nullo modo posse tradi*, *De orat*. 2.227; cf. Caesar's response to Sulpicius' attempt to get him to say more about humour in the interlude that follows his preliminary discussion: '*quid, si*' inquit Iulius '*adsentior Antonio dicenti nullam esse artem salis?*' 2.231). And as we have just seen, this is reiterated at the conclusion of Caesar's treatment of the limits of oratorical humour, as Caesar claims that an orator must discover proper timing for making jokes from *natura* since there is no *ars* through which it can be learned (*De orat*. 2.247).

On the one hand, Caesar's interpretation here is a reflex of a more general understanding of oratory that is articulated elsewhere in *De oratore*. When embarking upon his long discourse at the beginning of Book 2, Antonius, the principal speaker in this book, emphasises that oratory, which is concerned with opinions and not with knowledge, is not an *ars* (*De orat*. 2.30–33).[40] On the other hand, when introducing the topic of humour, Antonius declares that even if all other aspects of oratory are able to be learned by art, humour certainly is pecu-

---

39 *OLD* s.v. 9 a, b. Cf. *BNP techne*.
40 Nevertheless, as Antonius proceeds with his discussion, it becomes clear that it is organised around the five *partes rhetorices* or *opera oratoris* (*inventio*, *dispositio*, etc.) as well as other divisions that are found in ancient rhetorical textbooks, and so his tendency to dismiss the role of art in learning oratory becomes complicated to some extent, if not ironic. For other discussions of rhetoric as an *ars* in the dialogue, see *De orat*. 1.84–133, 145–147 (as well as 1.137–145 for Crassus' cursory treatment of a number of basic precepts of ancient rhetorical theory); May and Wisse 2001, 27; Fantham 2004, 81–82. On the question of rhetoric as an *ars* more generally, see Quint. *Inst*. 2.17.

liar to nature and does not require any art (*De orat.* 2.216).⁴¹ In this interpretation, humour becomes the particular product of natural ability.⁴² It follows, then, that consummate skill in using humour offers proof of a specially endowed or gifted individual, and thus can be a means for attaining high social status. As Cicero, however, is the hand behind Antonius, Caesar, and especially the figure in the dialogue who is alleged to be the wittiest, Crassus, an understanding of humour that sees it as an indication of superior ability would allow Cicero to bolster his own oratorical reputation. Furthermore, if a theoretical treatment of oratorical humour at such length was an innovation on Cicero's part, the *excursus* could also be a way for him to educate his critics and justify his own practices, as he makes the case not only that humour can be a fundamental weapon in an orator's arsenal, but that the leading orators of the previous generation believed as much.⁴³

And yet such a simple distinction between *ars* and *natura* cannot fully explain the workings of oratorical humour in either Caesar's *excursus de ridiculis* or Cicero's own practice. In his discussion of the limits on the type of humour that is based on matter (*res*), Caesar suggests that the orator's task involves considerable artistry. With regard to *narratio*, for instance, in addition to claiming that Crassus invented the story about Memmius, Caesar makes the more fundamental point that *narratio* is very suitable to an orator, whether he has an actual story that he is able to narrate – which nevertheless must be sprinkled with little fibs (*mendaciuncula*) – or he invents one.⁴⁴ For Caesar, then, fiction is

---

41 Crassus does not necessarily voice this same opinion, but when Caesar implies to Sulpicius that he agrees with Antonius that there is no art of wit, Crassus discusses the usefulness of precepts as guidelines for understanding what is either right or wrong (*De orat.* 2.232). This gets the discussion of humour to move forward, but it could also be interpreted as contributing to a consensus in the group that there is, in fact, no art of wit.
42 Cf. Dugan 2005, 167 on Crassus' discussion of metaphor in *De oratore* Book 3: "metaphor, like the performance of humour, cannot be taught".
43 Cf. Krostenko 2001, 224–227; Dugan 2005, 106 (quoting Krostenko 2001, 225), 117; Beard 2014, 121–122 is less certain about this interpretation.
44 *De orat.* 2.241, *perspicitis genus hoc quam sit facetum, quam elegans, quam oratorium, sive habeas vere quod narrare possis, quod tamen est mendaciunculis aspergendum, sive fingas.* Caesar returns to humorous *narratio* when he comes to the kinds of joke in which humour is located in the matter (*in re*), and notes that the things that are vividly presented to the audience should both have the appearance of truth and be somewhat disgraceful (2.264, *in quibus est narratio, res sane difficilis. exprimenda enim sunt et ponenda ante oculos ea quae videantur et veri similia, quod est proprium narrationis, et quae sint, quod ridiculi proprium est, subturpia*). Cf. Quintilian on the *narratio* section of a speech: "for there are very many things that indeed are true but yet are not very plausible, just as false things frequently resemble the truth. For which

a basic component of a successful *narratio*.⁴⁵ Furthermore, it would seem that an orator would need to go to some lengths to exaggerate or caricature the individuals in the story if he wished to satirise them in order for his retelling to be quite humorous. The same also appears to be a basic component of comic *imitatio*, as Caesar notes the humorous can result from "a kind of distorted imitation" (*quaedam depravata imitatio*). By this Caesar presumably means using caricature to bring out the ugly in someone or something, which, according to him, is the font of the ridiculous (*De orat.* 2.236, discussed above, pp. 200–201).

In all of these instances, it appears that the orator is using *ars* in the sense of (human) skill (cf. *OLD* s.v. 1–2) to "bend" or transform nature. In this respect, the speaker's humorous rhetoric resembles funhouse or carnival mirrors (and, now, certain filters on smart-phone cameras) that display whacky, unnatural, and sometimes uglier images of the figures they reflect.⁴⁶ Although Caesar advises that one should follow *natura* as she is the mistress, rhetoric is a practice of controlling nature, so to speak, and of manipulating the minds of an audience.⁴⁷ This is apparent in Caesar's comment that an orator should stealthily make use of *imitatio*, the result being that the members of the audience see more in their mind's eye than they do with their physical eyes. The rhetorical

---

reason we must not put any less effort into our attempts to get the judge to believe what we say truly than what we invent" (*Inst.* 4.2.34). Quintilian also speaks of a *ficta narratio* ("fictitious narrative"), which he says can, among other things, be used to relax the judges with wit (*urbanitas*, *Inst.* 4.2.19). Cf. *De orat.* 2.240, discussed above, p. 203.

45 For an excellent discussion of the 'fictional element' in Cicero's oratory, see Harold Gotoff's aptly titled "Oratory: The Art of Illusion" (1993).

46 Cf. Quintilian's bold claim in his discussion of jokes that are made through suggestion (*per suspicionem*): *et hercule omnis salse dicendi ratio in eo est, ut aliter quam est rectum verumque dicatur* ("And believe me, the entire nature of speaking wittily consists in this, namely, to speak of something in a way that is different from how it rightfully and truthfully is", *Inst.* 6.3.89). Such a "funhouse-mirror" conception of discourse stands in stark contrast to the requirements that Lucian sets for the historian in *How to Write History* (51, transl. Marincola 2017, 389): "above all he is to bring to the task a mind like a mirror [κάτοπτρον]: undisturbed, gleaming and accurate in its focus, and whatever the forms of the deeds he receives are the forms in which he should show them, not distorting, colouring or reshaping them in any way. For historians do not write like orators".

47 The concentration of the public speaker on appearance and probability as opposed to truth is a significant component of Socrates' critique of rhetoric in the *Phaedrus* (see e.g. 259e-260a, 267a-b, 272d-e), a work which *De oratore* is conspicuously in dialogue with (the conversation in Book 1, for instance, takes place under a plane tree (*De orat.* 1.28–29) and Book 3 ends with a brief discussion of Hortensius (3.228–230), which is modeled on the turn to Isocrates at the end of the *Phaedrus*). For an account of Cicero's position in the 'quarrel between rhetoricians and philosophers', see May and Wisse 2001, 20–26.

figure of *occultatio* (also known as *praeteritio*) relies on a similar tactic: an orator introduces a topic only to declare that he is going to pass it over (another fiction), sometimes with the accompanying explanation that he is not going to discuss it because he cannot do so decently (cf. e.g. Cicero, *Phil.* 2.47). As is evident from both Caesar's advice on *imitatio* and the figure *occultatio*, the orator's preservation of decorum, of not doing and saying things that would be beneath his dignity, must be balanced against the need to exaggerate nature and expose the unseemly (and sometimes even to invent it), as these are fundamental aspects of humour. Although the remarks of Cicero's critics suggest that in practice he might have gone too far in his joking and thereby compromised his dignity, the *excursus de ridiculis* in *De oratore* suggests that Cicero had considerable insight into the workings of humour and was well attuned to the inherent artistic difficulties of simultaneously maintaining decorum and distorting nature in order to provoke laughter.

Bibliography

Beard, M. (2014), *Laughter in Ancient Rome: On Joking, Tickling, and Cracking Up*, Berkeley/Los Angeles.
Clarke, M.L. (1996), *Rhetoric at Rome*. Third Edition. Revised with a New Introduction by D.H. Berry, London.
Cohen, D. (1995), *Law, Violence, and Community in Classical Athens*, Cambridge.
Corbeill, A. (1996), *Controlling Laughter: Political Humor in the Late Roman Republic*, Princeton.
Crawford, J.W. (ed.) (1994), *M. Tullius Cicero: The Fragmentary Speeches*. Second Edition, Atlanta.
Dugan, J. (2005), *Making a New Man: Ciceronian Self-Fashioning in the Rhetorical Works*, New York/Oxford.
Fantham, E. (2004), *The Roman World of Cicero's De Oratore*, Oxford.
Gotoff, H. (1993), 'Oratory: The Art of Illusion', in: *Harvard Studies in Classical Philology* 95, 289–313.
Grant, M.A. (1924), *The Ancient Rhetorical Theories of the Laughable: The Greek Rhetoricians and Cicero*, Madison.
Guérin, C. (2019), 'Laughter, Social Norms, and Ethics in Cicero's Works', in: P. Destrée and F.V. Trivigno (eds.), *Laughter, Humor, and Comedy in Ancient Philosophy*, Oxford, 122–144.
Hughes, J.J. (2002), '*Kairos* and *Decorum*: Crassus Orator's Speech *de lege Servilia*', in: P. Sipiora and J.S. Baumlin (eds.), *Rhetoric and Kairos: Essays in History, Theory, and Praxis*, Albany, 128–137.
Krostenko, B.A. (2001), *Cicero, Catullus, and the Language of Social Performance*, Chicago.
Kühnert, F. (1962), 'Quintilians Erörterung über den Witz', in: *Philologus* 106.1, 29–59; 106.3, 305–314.
Leeman, A.D. (1963), *Orationis Ratio: The Stylistic Theories and Practice of the Roman Orators, Historians and Philosophers*, Amsterdam.

Leeman, A.D., Pinkster, H. and Rabbie, E. (eds.), (1989), *M. Tullius Cicero, De Oratore Libri III: Kommentar, 3 Band: Buch II. 99–290*, Heidelberg.
Mankin, D. (ed.) (2011), *Cicero, De Oratore, Book III*, Cambridge.
Marincola, J. (ed. and trans.) (2017), *On Writing History: From Herodotus to Herodian*, London.
May, J.M. (1988), *Trials of Character: The Eloquence of Ciceronian Ethos*, Chapel Hill/London.
May, J.M. and Wisse, J. (2001), *Cicero on the Ideal Orator*, New York/Oxford.
Monaco, G. (ed.) (1968), *Cicerone: L'excursus de ridiculis (de or. II 216–290)*, Palermo.
Pagliai, V. (2009), 'The Art of Dueling with Words: Toward a New Understanding of Verbal Duels across the World', in: *Oral Tradition* 24.1, 61–88.
Pinkster, H. (1995), 'The Structure of Cicero's Passage on the Laughable in *De Oratore* II', in: D. Longrée (ed.), *De Vsu: Études de syntaxe latine offertes en hommage à Marius Lavency*, Louvain-la-Neuve, 247–253.
Rabbie, E. (2007), 'Wit and Humor in Roman Rhetoric', in: W.J. Dominik and J. Hall (eds.), *A Companion to Roman Rhetoric*, Malden, MA, 207–217.
Richlin, A. (1992), *The Garden of Priapus: Sexuality and Aggression in Roman Humor*. Revised edition, New York/Oxford.
Richlin, A. (2017), *Slave Theater in the Roman Republic: Plautus and Popular Comedy*, Cambridge.
Webb, R. (2009), *Ekphrasis, Imagination and Persuasion in Ancient Rhetorical Theory and Practice*, Farnham/Burlington.

Jan Lukas Horneff
No Decorum in the Forum? Comic Invective in the Theatre of Justice

Abstract: This chapter examines the performative role of humour and invective in Roman forensic interaction. An orator taking centre stage was expected to provide entertainment and demonstrate his dominance in the "theatre of justice". He had to craft the better gibes and portray his opponent as an inferior comic character, exploiting social and sexual stereotypes in Roman gender discourse. Thus, presenting a case had much in common with staging a comedy. We find evidence of this in the correspondence of the philosopher and rhetorician Fronto with his friend and pupil Marcus Aurelius. In a remarkable letter, Marcus Aurelius anticipates that Fronto would very likely ridicule and defame the philosopher Herodes Atticus, also a friend and teacher of Marcus Aurelius, and Fronto's opponent in a forthcoming trial. While the adequacy of personal attacks is never questioned in principle, Marcus Aurelius asks Fronto for moderation in this specific case. From a few hints in Fronto's letters, we can conclude that he had planned to portray Herodes Atticus as an effeminate intellectual, a *cinaedus*. This kind of mockery was widespread in antiquity and apparently had the potential to entertain the public: it was the perfect ingredient for comic invective in the theatre of justice.

1 Introduction

Sometime in the early 140s AD, young Marcus Aurelius was in a very uncomfortable position: his two highly esteemed teachers and close friends, Herodes Atticus and Marcus Cornelius Fronto, were about to clash in court.[1] This prompted Marcus Aurelius to write a letter to Fronto, triggering a small correspondence back and forth.[2] Marcus Aurelius obviously assumed that his teachers would violently insult each other, and therefore he asked both of them to be

---

[1] For the debate on the case and the context: Davenport and Manley 2014, 47–48. Neither is it certain in what role Herodes and Fronto would appear in court, nor what the charges were. An exact date for the letters and the lawsuit can also not be determined, but there are good reasons to date it between 140 and 142 AD. Cf. van den Hout 1999, 95–97 *ad* 36.1–39.20.
[2] Front. *Ad M. Caes.* 3.2–6. Cf. the introduction and commentary of Davenport and Manley 2014, 49–56.

https://doi.org/10.1515/9783110735536-011

respectful and control their behaviour: he had already asked Herodes (as we learn from his letter to Fronto) to refrain from abusing his opponent. Yet unsure whether this would suffice, he also advised Fronto not to hit back in the likely event of a verbal retaliation.[3] In his answer, Fronto promised his former pupil to abstain from any abuse that had nothing to do with the case. Nevertheless, he wrote, there was one thing he could not be denied, and that would not hurt too much:

> You may, indeed, as I said, rest assured of this, that I shall not go outside the case itself to speak of his character and the rest of his life (*nihil extra causam de moribus et cetera eius vita*). But if you think I must do the best for my case, I warn you herewith that I shall not even use in a disproportionate manner (*immoderate*) the opportunity my case gives me, for savage charges are made and must be savagely spoken of (*atrocia enim sunt crimina et atrocia dicenda*). Those in particular which concern the robbing and injuring of freemen shall be so told by me as to smack of gall and spleen (*ut fel et bilem sapiant*): if I chance to call him a Greekling and unlearned, it need not mean war to the knife (*sicubi graeculum et indoctum dixero, non erit internecivum*).[4]

In this chapter, I aim to examine a few points from the correspondence that tellingly expose Roman forensic invectivity and the role of the comic in it:[5] first, in all of the letters we observe a great awareness of the imminent risks of heavy polemics in legal interactions (Section 1). Second, we learn that Fronto planned to give his speech a very specific key, *bitter* and *venomous*. As a part of that, he

---

[3] Cf. Front. *Ad M. Caes.* 3.2. On the close relationship between Fronto and Marcus Aurelius, cf. Richlin 2006, who in her selection of letters (regardless of whether one follows her argument for an erotic relationship) has gathered enough evidence for an extraordinarily close bond, which explains why it must have been so difficult for the future emperor to say "no" to Fronto. In addition, as the cautious tone of the letters indicates, a very stable relationship of trust would have been a mandatory requirement for such a delicate request in a friendship of equals. On the paradoxical demands of a patrimonial monarchy posing as a noble republic and the resulting double-bind communication: Winterling 2008, 305–308.

[4] Front. *Ad M. Caes.* 3.3: *Illud quidem, ut dixi, firmum et ratum habeto, nihil extra causam de moribus et cetera eius vita me dicturum. Quodsi tibi videbitur servire me causae debere, iam nunc admoneo ne me immoderate usurum quidem causae occasione, atrocia enim sunt crimina et atrocia dicenda; illa ipsa de laesis et spoliatis hominibus ita a me dicentur, ut fel et bilem sapiant; sicubi graeculum et indoctum dixero, non erit internecivum.* Transl. Haines 1919.

[5] The concept of invectivity (on further information and definition: Jehne 2020), that goes beyond invective speech, seems apt to describe the entire spectrum of disparagement, including its performative dynamics. The central idea here is not to view invective practice as a dyadic conflict (one opponent attacking the other), but as a form of triadic communication, primarily aimed at the public or audience. A similar approach is described in the Introduction to this volume, see pp. 5–8.

intended to *stage* his contempt, presumably in a rather theatrical manner (Section 2). In particular, he announced his intention to describe his opponent as a *Graeculus*, arguably a variant of the *cinaedus*, a popular (comic) stock figure for effeminacy in Rome (Section 3). The entire procedure, i.e. the lively performance of invective reproach and the framing of Herodes as the laughable protagonist in a shameful play, did not necessarily result from extraordinary hatred but was merely a promising legal strategy. Staging comic invective in court was compatible with the role expectations for a forensic speaker and was not generally considered indecorous (Section 4).

2 Invectives and the Court

Marcus Aurelius seems to have been particularly afraid that his teacher would not limit himself to pertinent matters.[6] But why was he worried? A search for traces in the fragmentary sources from Roman court proceedings reveals a multitude of bizarre allegations, which give an idea of what Marcus Aurelius might have feared. To start with a case not too far removed in time, Apuleius of Madauros and his *Apologia* (158/159 AD), the only completely preserved court speech from the Imperial era, can serve as an example for the abusive practices of this genre.[7] Apuleius begins his defence by describing the accuser as a forgetful old nagger, continues by mocking the other side's "barbaric" heritage and education, their inadequate knowledge of Latin and Greek or their lack of filial piety, and in between he insinuates in shorter swipes that one witness is an alcoholic and another near illiterate.[8] Some of these allegations have a direct connection to the case and are logically embedded in his argument. But others are purely mean insults with no such connection, used only for defaming and associated with the case artificially, if at all.[9] For example, when he runs his mouth about the prosecutor's future father-in-law, Apuleius does not spare anyone in the whole family – and in all likelihood, what we see here is just the

---

6 Cf. Front. *Ad M. Caes.* 3.3 and 3.6.
7 For background information: Hunink 1997.
8 On then strikingly frequent taunts against age-related defects and the constant bickering of Sicinius Aemilianus cf. Apul. *Apol.* 1.1–4, 10.8, 36.2, 53.3, 64.2; on barbaric or African heritage and deficient language skills, see 9.1, 30.9, 66.8, 98.8; on filial piety, 100; on drunk witnesses, 57.2, 59, 60.4; and a varied collection of invective motifs is found in 98.
9 Of course, this does not mean that they serve no purpose or are done out of pure malice. For the effectiveness of proof of character defects in forensic reasoning, cf. below p. 227, esp. n. 69.

kind of slander that Marcus Aurelius and Fronto had in mind when speaking of matters *extra causam de moribus et cetera eius vita*:

> [Herennius Rufinus] is the contriver of every lawsuit, the fabricator of every lie, the hand behind every pretense, the seedbed of every wickedness, and at the same time the center, the haunt, the brothel of lecheries and debaucheries, generally known for every vice from his earliest age. As a boy long ago, before that baldness of his ruined his looks, he complied with every unspeakable wish of those who made a eunuch of him (*emasculatoribus suis*); [...] Moreover, now at his present age [...] his whole house is a brothel, the whole family degraded: he himself is shameless, his wife a whore, his sons no different. [...] In person, he contracts with many men about nights for them to spend with his wife. [...] However, his wife, now almost a worn-out hag, at last gave up these insults to the family. Their daughter, though, they passed around among some rich youths, whom her own mother invited in, but to no effect, and they also gave her over to certain suitors for trial.[10]

Clearly none of this directly refutes the charges (of magic and hexing his wife) that Apuleius had to repel.[11] Even if Herennius Rufinus, broadly reviled with many other allegations in the surrounding passages, was himself directly relevant for the trial, as Apuleius insisted that he was pulling strings in the background, his sex life was not. And even less that of his wife or children. In a case like that, one could expect the opposing lawyer to protest and claim that this kind of slander had no place in legal proceedings.[12] Indeed, Cicero made just that kind of declaration in his defence of Caelius:

> All the other matters complained of are not accusations, but slanders (*non crimina sed maledicta*); they smack rather of vulgar vituperation than of a court of justice (*iurgi petulantis magis quam publicae quaestionis*). To call Caelius an adulterer, a lewd fellow, a dealer in bribes, is abuse (*convicium*), not accusation (*accusatio*); there is no foundation for these charges, no ground; they are insulting taunts (*voces contumeliosae*) hurled at

---

10 Apul. *Apol.* 74.6–76.2: *Est enim omnium litium depector, omnium falsorum commentator, omnium simulationum architectus, omnium malorum seminarium, nec non idem libidinum ganearumque locus, lustrum, lupanar; iam inde ab ineunte aevo cunctis probris palam notus, olim in pueritia, priusquam isto calvitio deformaretur, emasculatoribus suis ad omnia infanda morigerus.* [...] *In hac etiam aetate qua nunc est – qui istum di perduint! Multus honos auribus praefandus est – domus eius tota lenonia, tota familia contaminata; ipse propudiosus, uxor lupa, filii similes.* [...] *Cum ipso plerique – nec mentior! – cum ipso, inquam, de uxoris noctibus paciscuntur.* [...] *Ceterum uxor iam propemodum vetula et effeta totam domum contumeliis adnuit. Filia autem per adulescentulos ditiores invitamento matris suae nequicquam circumlata, quibusdam etiam procis ad experiundum permissa* [...]. Transl. Jones 2017.
11 On the charges: Hunink 1997, 12–14.
12 Not to mention the omnipresent elements of hate speech in this passage, which is extraordinarily vitriolic even for ancient conditions. To a more empathic modern recipient this kind of language has no place anywhere.

random by an accuser who is in a rage and who speaks without any authority (*ab irato accusatore nullo auctore*).[13]

On the other hand, it is precisely Cicero himself who used so many of these *maledicta, convicia* or *contumeliae* in his speeches (and not only in his forensic ones) that one could write whole chapters about every single defamatory *topos* in the Ciceronian oratorical corpus; Anthony Corbeill was merely following the ancient judgements when he called him the "most notorious practitioner" of defamation.[14] The use of invectives and the classical *topoi* in Cicero's speeches have been researched and discussed so thoroughly that further elaboration appears unnecessary here.[15] There is also plenty of evidence for violent insults, *ad hominem* attacks and the perception of the court as little more than a mudslinging contest outside of Cicero.[16] Nonetheless, the (obviously fake) outrage in Cicero's defence shows us that, although we know that invectives were indeed an omnipresent part of forensic practice and the speakers were well aware of this fact, it was neither entirely self-evident nor undisputed that this was the way to go. The Roman discourse enabled a separation between appropriate communication in court and abuse – and thereby an invective of invectivity itself.[17] Even Apuleius' highly invective *Apologia* started with criticism of the allegedly indecent abuse of his person, that was not appropriate in a trial.[18]

---

13 Cic. *Cael.* 13.30: *Omnia sunt alia non crimina sed maledicta, iurgi petulantis magis quam publicae quaestionis. "Adulter, impudicus, sequester" convicium est, non accusatio. Nullum est enim fundamentum horum criminum, nullae sedes; voces sunt contumeliosae temere ab irato accusatore nullo auctore emissae.* Transl. Gardner 1958. Cf. ibid. 6.

14 Corbeill 2019 in his review of Thurn 2018. The latter provides the aforementioned detailed overview of Cicero's use of allegations from all areas and the well-ordered *topoi* of defamation in question. For exemplary assessment of our sources cf. Macr. *Sat.* 2.1.10–13, discussed below.

15 Craig 2004 offers an exemplary case study on *Pro Milone*, Pausch (in this volume) discusses comic invective in *Pro Caelio*, and Nisbet 1961, 192–197 treats invectives extensively in his commentary to *In Pisonem*. On comic invective and *decorum* in *De oratore*: Kish in this volume. Powell 2007 focuses on when exactly such things occurred in Ciceronian practice. Cf. also the other articles in Booth 2007. Arena 2007, 159–160 provides an annotated bibliography on (mostly) Ciceronian invectivity.

16 Cf. the short and concise treatment at Nisbet 1961, 198 with further examples from Early Roman orators and a contextualisation in ancient invective cultures.

17 It is surely no coincidence that most of the speeches known under the term invective are preceded by an excuse for their invective character, which in turn is based on the invective character of the opponent's previous speech. Cf. e.g. (Ps.-)Sall. *Inv. Cic.* 1; (Ps.-)Cic. *Sall.* 1–3; Cass. Dio 46.1.1–2.

18 Apuleius extensively criticises not only the invective character of the speech given against him, but also the slander that happened before the trial. Cf. Apul. *Apol.* 1–2.2.

Thus, it can certainly be said that the Roman notion of what was appropriate in court was very different from what they practised.[19] There is a generally accepted explanation for this, which has been applied not only to the Roman, but also to the Greek court: the opposing party was to be defamed, deprived of group affiliation, excluded from the circle of decent people, and – particularly fatal in a society dominated by men – emasculated.[20] In this chapter, the validity of this explanation shall by no means be questioned. Instead, I shall focus on other aspects of invective communication: on its connection with *urbanitas* so valued by the Romans, on its entertaining effect on the audience (especially the judges) and on the momentum that it produced in the forensic performance.[21]

3 The Theatre of Oratory and the Comedic Stage

Unfortunately, Fronto indicates only briefly how he wanted to perform his speech, but his words are very suggestive: with a bitter and venomous taste (*ut fel et bilem sapiant*). Although Fronto did not tell his pupil what specific facial expressions and gestures he wanted to use to support his invective, we can safely assume that he generally intended to give a lively performance. He also knew that *quid dixerit* was important, but *quemadmodum* mattered as well, as he shows in a later letter, addressed to one of his other apprentices:

> Yours has been a happier lot, my lord brother, for you have felt nervous for your son on the spot, than mine, who have had to endure my nervousness at home. For your nervousness was easily allayed with the completion of the pleading, while I did not cease to be nervous until all my pupil housemates had brought me news of the success with which our orator had conducted the case. And you, indeed, at each separate triumph of the speech (*ad singulos orationis successus*), as each sentence evoked applause, were filled with joy, while I, sitting at home, was tortured with continuous anxiety, conscious as I was of the difficulties before the pleader, yet unable to share in the praises of his pleading. Then you carried away manifold advantages besides, for you not only heard, but also saw the performer, and were delighted not by his eloquence (*eloquentia*) only, but by his look

---

19 What is meant here is, first of all, the general idea of the judicial system as a space with a certain *decorum*. But the relationship between rhetorical theory and practice is also extremely complex. Cic. *De orat.* 2.252 for example calls *obscenitas, non modo non foro digna, sed vix convivio liberorum*, but seems to refer more to the explicit language than to the content. Cf. Richlin 1992, 13–18 and Kish in this volume.
20 On invectives in Athenian forensic performances and especially on its sexual or gender-based content: Serafim 2020, 23–42; Donelan in this volume; and on Rome: Arena 2007.
21 On performance in court: Tempest 2013; and (esp. in an Attic context) Serafim 2017, 15–26.

(*vultu*) and gesture (*gestu*). For me, though I know what he said (*quid dixerit*), yet I do not know how he said it (*quemadmodum*). [---] He went down to the Forum noble by birth, he came back from it more noble by eloquence than by lineage (*eloquentia quam genere nobilior*).[22]

Here, Fronto not only takes into account the need to amplify speeches with the right tone and gestures; he also highlights the reaction of the audience, which finally and audibly decided whether an orator was allowed to leave the arena as a *winner* in the competition for the best forensic performance.[23] When Fronto regrets that he could not be present, he is making a correct observation: a speech in court – and this makes it particularly difficult for us to assess – cannot be fully evaluated by simply reading the transcript (just as theatre critics should not just have a manuscript sent to them). It would be wrong to understand the trial only as a series of legal arguments that everyone assesses for himself, as the younger Pliny recaps when asked to recite one of his speeches:

> I know very well that speeches when read lose all their warmth and spirit, almost their entire character, since their fire is always fed from the atmosphere of court: the bench of magistrates and throng of advocates (*celebritas advocatorum*), the suspense of the awaited verdict (*exspectatio eventus*), reputation of the different speakers (*fama non unius actoris*), and the divided enthusiasm of the public; and they gain too from the gestures of the speaker as he strides to and fro, the movements of his body corresponding to his changing passions. [...] Such a disparity shocks, but it exists; for in general a bench of magistrates and an audience have very different demands (*aliud auditores aliud iudices exigent*), though a listener should really be influenced most by what would convince him if he were called on to pronounce judgement.[24]

---

22 Front. *Ad amic.* 1.25: *Tibi, domine frater, commodius evenit, qui pro filio nostro praesens trepidaveris, quam mihi, qui trepidaverim absens. Nam tua trepidatio pro eventu actionis facile sedata est; ego, quoad mihi ab omnibus contubernalibus nuntiatum est, quo successu noster orator egisset, trepidare non destiti. Et tu quidem ad singulos orationis successus, prout quaeque sententia laudem meruerat, gaudio fruebare; at ego domi sedens perpetua sollicitudine angebar, ut qui periculum actoris recordarer, laudibus actionis non interessem. Tum praeterea multiplicis tu fructus abstulisti: Non enim audisti tantum, sed et vidisti agentem; nec eloquentia sola, sed etiam vultu eius et gestu laetatus es. Ego tametsi quid dixerit scio, tamen ignoro, quemadmodum dixerit.* [---] *nam in forum descendit natalibus nobilis, de foro rediit eloquentia quam genere nobilior.*
23 On the power of the audience: Hall 2014. Bablitz 2007, 133–136 assembles the audience's options for participation. Exclamations and shouts were the main ways of expressing applause, and, though there was probably no clapping, the audience must have felt much like it did in the theatre. On audience-interaction in the theatre: Marshall 2006, 73–82.
24 Plin. *Epist.* 2.19.2–6: *Neque enim me praeterit actiones, quae recitantur, impetum omnem caloremque ac prope nomen suum perdere, ut quas soleant commendare simul et accendere*

Just like Fronto, Pliny points out that every trial was an *event*, which the interaction with an audience could render particularly lively. The audience, in turn, might not necessarily favour clever handling of the law but valued being entertained. We have to imagine performative aspects like gestures and voice, the *corona* of listeners around the orators and their interaction to better understand the trials.[25] Legal arguments undoubtedly played an important part in the outcome of legal matters.[26] But for a rhetor, a trial was not only about the judgment (which is not even mentioned in Fronto's letter).[27] He wanted to impress the audience not only in order to win the case for his client, but also to enhance his own *celebritas* (from which of course a client could benefit in turn).[28] Or, as Fronto put it in his letter: success as a rhetor was a potential gateway to nobility.[29] It was also a potent one, since legal procedures in Rome did not take place behind closed doors – they were forensic and thus played an important part in

---

iudicum consessus, celebritas advocatorum, exspectatio eventus, fama non unius actoris, diductumque in partes audientium studium, ad hoc dicentis gestus incessus, discursus etiam omnibusque motibus animi consentaneus vigor corporis. [...] *Est quidem omnino turpis ista discordia, est tamen, quia plerumque evenit ut aliud auditores aliud iudices exigant, cum alioqui iis praecipue auditor affici debeat, quibus idem si foret iudex, maxime permoveretur.* Transl. Radice 1969.

25 If the orator failed on the level of performance, his case and reputation were in danger: cf. e.g. Cic. *Brut.* 276–278. On the *corona*: Rosillo-López 2017b, esp. 112–113. Regarding the client's participation in a claque cf. Bablitz 2007, 136–139. On spontaneity in the *altercatio*: Iurescia 2019, 138–145, on improvisation in Roman comedy cf. Marshall 2006, 272–279. On staging beyond Cicero: Hall 2014, 129–152.

26 Cf. Powell and Paterson 2004, who emphatically call attention to this (in their opinion, too often neglected) fact and warn against understanding Cicero's speeches only as works of literary art and the trial as a "contest of rhetorical strength" (Powell and Paterson 2004, 4). Pliny's letter cited above also seems to imply that judges (at least in imperial times) were more focused on legal arguments than the audience. On the other hand, Cicero himself emphasises (right in the middle of a court speech!) the representative role and the rhetorical skills of the orator in opposition to mere judicial expertise. Cf. Cic. *Cluent.* 57.

27 This is probably nowhere expressed as explicitly as in Quint. *Inst.* 2.17.23–24: *noster orator arsque a nobis finita non sunt posita in eventu; tendit quidem ad victoriam qui dicit, sed cum bene dixit, etiam si non vincat, id quod arte continetur effecit.*

28 *Celebritas* means not only abstract *fame*, but literally *popularity* which manifests itself in followers: both those brought into a trial as well as the fan base gained during it – available for the next trial. On the connection between good oratorical entertainment and the formation of a *corona*, cf. Quint. *Inst.* 12.10.74.

29 Cf. Front. *Ad amic.* 1.25. The fact that rhetorical achievements were honoured in ways comparable to military ones can be seen as early as Polyb. 6.53.

shaping the public opinion and winning popularity for the speakers.[30] Being public, legal procedures had additional societal functions, as Ronald Syme observed: "the law-courts were an avenue for political advancement through prosecution, a battle-ground for private enmities and political feuds, a theatre for oratory".[31] Setting the audience in turmoil with a speech, emerging victorious from the arena of the courts, and triumphing over every contestant, all this created the symbolic capital of victory and superiority – in Roman discourse it was directly connected with the strongest concept of value, virility. The opposite, the impression of weakness and inferiority, and thereby effeminacy, could arise from failure, which could develop its own suggestive power and pull effect.[32]

A good example of how to make use of this dichotomy is provided by Cicero's speech for Cluentius (66 BC). In three earlier suits (74 BC), Cluentius had successfully prosecuted Fabricius, Scamander and his own stepfather Oppianicus for attempting to poison him, and was now himself being accused by the latter's wife, Cluentius' mother, Sassia, of having poisoned her husband. While the logical sequence of Cicero's reasoning in the trial of 66 was far too complicated and far-fetched to form a persuasive argument, his strategy served well to associate his case with victory and superiority, and to link the opponents to the defeats in the three earlier trials.[33] In his speech, Cicero recounts one of these

---

[30] On the localities of Roman jurisdiction: Bablitz 2007, 48–70. On the importance of the *fora* for the formation of public opinion: Rosillo-López 2017a, 52–64. For the modern use of forensic legal procedures and its implication for the aesthetics of a performance: Frieze 2019, 6–8.

[31] Syme 1939, 149, italics not in the original. Although Syme is referring to the Late Republic, Fronto and Pliny (and Gellius to an extent) show that the same generally applies to Imperial times as well.

[32] Regarding the Roman gender construct that generally differentiates between the independent, active (penetrating) and superior part (male) and the passively receptive, pathic and subordinate part (female): e.g. Richlin 1992, Williams 1995, 519–521 and Corbeill 1996, 128–173.

[33] Alexander 1990, N° 147; 148; 149; 198. Cicero's main concern was to prove that Cluentius had not bribed the judges in the prosecution of Oppianicus – using the argument that Cluentius would have won the case anyway, because the abysmal performance of Fabricius' defence made the defeat of Oppianicus in the subsequent trial predictable and bribery unnecessary. Cf. Cic. *Cluent.* 59. To make matters even more complicated: in his defence of Cluentius, Cicero, who had defended the co-conspirator Scamander unsuccessfully in the first of the earlier trials, defused the piquant connection to himself by attributing his failure not to his own performance in court but to the serious incriminating evidence against his client that could not be refuted. Cf. Cic. *Cluent.* 50–53.

trials, the prosecution of Fabricius, and, evoking the alleged performative nadir of the defence, lays it out like a comedy.³⁴

The "scene" starts with a juxtaposition of the lawyers involved, Cannutius (for Cluentius) and Caepasius (for Fabricius). Cicero takes his listeners right into the middle of the situation, using staccato-like sentences and *tempus praesens* to build tension and suspense:

> Well, Fabricius is summoned (*citatur reus, agitur causa*); Cannutius opens the prosecution with a short speech, for he holds the case prejudged. The elder Caepasius embarks on a long and far-fetched exordium.³⁵

As we can see, the dominance of Cluentius' case is anticipated right from the beginning by Cannutius' self-confident certainty of victory, which is also underlined by Cicero's curt and precise language (*paucis verbis accusat ut de re iudicata Cannutius*). On the other side, Caepasius seems long-winded and boring (*incipit longo et alte petito prooemio respondere maior Caepasius*), and thus arguably a bit comic.³⁶ Cicero adds a second facet to his portrayal of Cluentius' opponents as comic characters, when he describes how in the beginning all of them completely misjudged Caepasius' impact on the audience:³⁷

> At first his speech had an attentive hearing: Oppianicus began to raise his drooping and dejected spirits: Fabricius began to feel happy: he did not realize that what was impressing the judges was not the eloquence of the pleader but the effrontery of the plea.³⁸

---

34 Quint. *Inst.* 6.3.39 refers to this passage as *narrare [...] salsa* and produces it as a prime example of arousing laughter in court. Cf. also Quint. *Inst.* 4.2.19.

35 Cic. *Cluent.* 58: *citatur reus, agitur causa; paucis verbis accusat ut de re iudicata Cannutius; incipit longo et alte petito prooemio respondere maior Caepasius*. Transl. Hodge 1927 [modified].

36 How quickly inappropriate style can generate unintentional hilarity, is remarked by Cic. *Part.* 54. Already in the introduction of this little comedy Caepasius is characterised as one of those who are "disposed to regard any chance which they were given to plead as a compliment and a favour" (Cic. Cluent. 57: *eo animo ut quaecumque dicendi potestas esset data in honore atque in beneficio ponerent*). This hint to his desire to speak points to one of the most popular comic stock figures. Cf. e.g. Theophr. *Char.* 7 (Λαλιᾶς). Cicero later in his *Brutus* mocks the style of the Caepasius brothers as *oppidanus*, i.e. falling short of the *urbanitas* that distinguishes humorous style. Cf. Cic. *Brut.* 242.

37 The violation of the Delphic maxim "know thyself" by self-overestimation is the epitome of τὸ γελοῖον already in Plat. *Phil.* 48–50.

38 Cic. *Cluent.* 58: *primo attente auditur eius oratio. erigebat animum iam demissum et oppressum Oppianicus; gaudebat ipse Fabricius; non intellegebat animos iudicum non illius eloquentia sed defensionis impudentia commoveri.*

Up to this point the focus was on Fabricius and Oppianicus, and their unawareness of the improper performance of Caepasius, but Cicero next concentrates entirely on the latter, as he describes how he got tangled up without noticing:

> Coming to the defence proper, Caepasius gratuitously inflicted fresh wounds on a case which was maimed at the outset, until, though he was doing his best, he seemed at times not to be defending his client but to be acting in collusion with the prosecutor.[39]

This shift of attention is necessary to highlight the failed dramatic performance of Caepasius as strongly as possible:

> For instance, he thought he was pleading very cleverly, and produced from the secrets of his stock-in-trade these weighty words: "Look back, gentlemen, upon the lot of mortal man; look back upon its changes and chances; look back upon the old age of Fabricius!" After frequent repetitions of the phrase "Look back", by way of ornamenting his speech, he finally looked back himself: and lo! C. Fabricius had left his seat with hanging head. Thereupon the court burst out laughing.[40]

In this episode and its introduction, Cicero effectively and rather vividly creates a loser type.[41] It is difficult to imagine him giving this description of gestures without using his own body at all. That is to say, Cicero will have acted like Caepasius to a certain extent, doing his best to act out a bad performance. This piece of comedy in the middle of his reasoning was not only entertaining, but also an integral part of his argument: Cicero wanted to prove that Cluentius had no need to bribe the judges in the trial against Oppianicus, simply because they were already inclined to favour him since the case was already won, as had been demonstrated beforehand in the trial against Fabricius. The only evidence Cicero could provide to back up his strongest argument, the court's disposition in the former trial, seems to be the reaction his (re)enactment elicited in the current case. While exploiting the suggestive power of being right on the level of content (by demonstrating that Cluentius had had no need to bribe the judges),

---

39 Cic. *Cluent.* 58: *postea quam de re coepit dicere, ad ea quae erant in causa addebat etiam ipse nova quaedam volnera ut, quamquam sedulo faciebat, tamen interdum non defendere sed praevaricari videretur.*

40 Cic. *Cluent.* 58–59: *itaque cum callidissime se dicere putaret et cum illa verba gravissima ex intimo artificio deprompsisset: 'respicite, iudices, hominum fortunas, respicite dubios variosque casus, respicite C. Fabrici senectutem' — cum hoc 'respicite' ornandae orationis causa saepe dixisset, respexit ipse. at C. Fabricius a subselliis demisso capite discesserat. hic iudices ridere* [...].

41 On the introduction (Cic. *Cluent.* 57) cf. n. 36 above. For the persuasive value of these topical characters in Aristotle's rhetoric cf. Serafim 2017, 25–26.

he simultaneously generates an even stronger dynamic on the performative level: the self-enforcing impression of impending victory. His performance invited the current audience to join in the laughter of the virtual audience and thus reproduce the decision *pro Cluentio*.[42] In ridiculing the lawyer of Fabricius, Cicero simultaneously transferred the taint of failure to the whole case of the prosecution against Cluentius.[43] Here, in such a masterful display of oratorical *comedy*, success and failure, superiority and inferiority can unfold their *autopoietic* character.

4 The Right Villain for the Stage

Back to Fronto. In his letter, he seems already to have had a very clear idea of what to do with his adversary in the upcoming case: he would portray him as a comic figure, a *Graeculus* – an intention that seems to have required no further explanation to be understood by the recipient of the letter. It is not difficult to understand why it was an obvious choice for Fronto to exploit the associations of Greekness for the characterisation of the (phil)hellenic Herodes Atticus.[44] Those associations could be manifold: the positive spectrum ranged from high education through a cultivated and urban way of life to philosophical grandeur. This contrasts with the negative associations of moral decadence, insidiousness and weakness, which resulted in the equation of Greek and effeminate that we find in the work of both Roman and Greek authors.[45] When Fronto announced that he would portray Herodes as an uneducated Greekling, he implicitly ex-

---

42 Cicero considered this a complete success in manipulating the judges, as Quint. *Inst*. 2.17.21 reports. On the in- and exclusive function of laughter: Corbeill 1996.
43 For a similar performance-based attack on the opposing lawyer: cf. Aeschin. 1.131, discussed in n. 67 below.
44 For the explicitly *Greek* origin and identity of Herodes: Stebnicka 2015. On the stereotypes surrounding *Greekness* in Roman comedy: Segal 1987, 37–39. In general: Hunger 1987. On the *Graeculus*: cf. n. 50 below.
45 Cf. McDonnell 2006, 259–265. Although the reputation of Greece certainly might have changed quite a bit in the second century AD, the existing prejudices remained relatively constant. In Plaut. *Most*. 22; 64, this condescending look at excessive Greek (banquet) behaviour is expressed in the word *pergraecari*, which also seems to have belonged to Fronto's vocabulary. Cf. Isid. *Orig*. 15.2.46. Cf. van den Hout 1999, 624 *ad* 273.15. Against the very common but overly simplistic idea of a concrete practice associated with "Greek love" cf. Williams 1995.

cluded the positive spectrum.⁴⁶ We can therefore surmise that he wished to frame him as weak and effeminate.⁴⁷ Another passage of the letter provides further indication of this intention:

> If your Herodes be an honourable and moral man (*pudicus*), it is not right that such a man should be assailed with invectives by me; if he is wicked (*nequam*) and worthless (*improbus*), my fight with him is not on equal terms, nor do we stand to lose the same. For any contact with what is unclean (*polluto*) contaminates (*commaculat*) a man, even though he come off best. But the former supposition is the truer, that he, whom you count worthy of your patronage, is a virtuous man (*probum*).⁴⁸

The words *pudicus* and *improbus*, as criteria of integrity, and especially the idea of pollution by contact (*commaculatio*), can have strong sexual overtones – especially when taken together and in the context of Roman invective practice.⁴⁹ By activating a sexual register, and by belittling Herodes' ethnicon while simultaneously (and explicitly) negating the educational aspects, Fronto certainly shows his intention to portray his opponent as a *vir mollis* and to reduce

---

46 The combination with *indoctus* initially may seem surprising, given the high level of education that Herodes is considered to have had. This incongruity seems to have been intended to enhance comic effect. Perhaps Fronto is alluding to the combination of Greek and (over-)educated, which was used typically as a derogatory characterisation, as attested, e.g., in Plut. *Cic.* 5.2, which tells us that Cicero was mocked as Γραικὸς καὶ σχολαστικός. This combination, which Marcus Aurelius might have expected to hear, might have been understood to have comic connotations, because *indoctus* is an ambiguous word in ancient times, if not an openly negative one (i.e. "pedant"); cf. the jokes about Σχολαστικοί in the Philogelos. Also, Cicero himself (*De orat.* 1.221) warns against over-emphasising one's own intellect in a speech, to avoid being perceived as *ineptum et Graeculum*. There is also an example of ironic usage of the same combination in Cicero, who in *Verr.* 2.127 calls his opponent *eruditus homo et Graeculus* – and in the same breath says that he cannot even read Greek letters. Here, too, Fronto demonstrates wit by not simply exaggerating a familiar figure, but by inverting it.
47 *Framing*, the creation of a normatively charged image by selective emphasis on certain associable aspects was achieved in forensic oratory by skilful characterisation and by constructing a narrative to present the case in a manner favourable to one's own interests. That this practice (under the term of *colores*) was part of an orator's training is documented in the *Controversiae* of the elder Seneca and Quintilian's *Declamationes*. Cf. Zinsmaier 2009.
48 Front. *Ad M. Caes.* 3.3: *Sive sit iste Herodes vir frugi et pudicus, protelari conviciis talem a me virum non est verum; sive nequam et improbus est, non aequa mihi cum eo certatio, neque idem detrimenti capitur. Omnis enim cum polluto complexus, tametsi superes, commaculat. Sed illud verius est, probum virum esse, quem tu dignum tutela tua iudicas.*
49 On the sexual overtones of *pudicus* and *(im)probus*: Richlin 2006, 57, nn. 5, 7. On the idea of staining: Richlin 1992, 27–31. On the invective potential: Arena 2007, 156–157.

Herodes' Greek *habitus* to a penchant for enjoyment and extravagance.[50] In short, Fronto evokes what was perhaps the most commonly evoked character in the ancient toolkit of defamation: the *cinaedus*.[51]

There was a wide variety of effective ways to publicly render a man effeminate and portray him as a *cinaedus* famous for his philosophical education. A good example of such a portrayal is the invective against Piso, which Cicero constructs around his adversary's philosophical attitude. Cicero was apparently dealing with a man renowned for his dignified and educated manner, so he built his strategy on that, by declaring Piso's serious face a deceptive facade and reducing his inclination towards epicurean philosophy to a cover for his lust.[52] Even the mere association with philosophical *habitus* alone could be connected with effeminacy in many ways. For example, the motif of a philosopher who appears very masculine on the outside, but in truth lusts after his students, is also dealt with in Lucian's satire *Eunuchus*, where it is mentioned as a socially well-established prejudice.[53] In Juvenal, we even find an expressive label for the stereotype: *cinaedus Socraticus*.[54] The famous sophist Favorinus, a contemporary of Fronto, appears highly effeminate and fulfils all clichés of the *vir mollis* in a number of sources, a portrayal that certainly helped entrench the effeminate image of philosophers.[55] As we can see, Fronto was able to invoke a whole

---

[50] For the direct association of the *Graeculus* with sexual deviance and terms like *cinaedus*, *vir mollis* and *pathicus* cf. the characterisation of the *Graeculus esuriens* in Juv. 3.58–123, cit. 17 and Mart. 2.86, where *Graecula echo* is set parallel to *Sotaden cinaedum* and *mollem galliambon*. Among other things, Dio has Calenus call Cicero Γραίκουλε in his great invective, and then directly insults him by calling him an anointed man attired in feminine clothing. Cf. Cass. Dio 46.18.1–3. The *Graeculus* of Cic. *Pis*. 71 is also clearly a "softened" man. In Min. Fel. 21.5, we find the combination *Graeculus et politus*. In Plin. *Paneg*. 13.4, a *Graeculus magister* serves as polar opposite of a decorated veteran, who is considered to be extremely manly. Julian was insulted by his soldiers as *Graeculum et fallacem, et specie sapientiae stolidum*; cf. Amm. 17.9.3. This common association with *mollitia* is nicely supported by a play of words if one hears *Graeculus*. That this overtone was present at least in *culina* is argued by Keller 1891, 179. For a comparable reception of a wordplay in court, cf. Macr. *Sat*. 2.2.6 (discussed below).
[51] On the *cinaedus* in general: Olson 2017, 135–136; Gleason 1995, 62–67; Corbeill 1996, 135–139.
[52] Cf. Cic. *Pis*. 1; 70. On Piso's portrayal by Cicero as a *vir mollis* in disguise: Meister 2009. The implied craving for pleasure is a sign of lack of self-control (*moderantia*) and thus of unmanliness. On the topical accusation of excessive behaviour (esp. *vinulentia*), cf. Thurn 2018, 167–191. Cf. more general Nisbet 1961, 192–197. In Cic. *Pis*. 69–71, another *Graeculus* appears, an educated youth who was tricked by Piso's serious face.
[53] Cf. Luc. *Eun. passim* and esp. 9.
[54] Iuv. 2.9–10. Cf. Obermayer 1998, 120–123.
[55] Cf. Gleason 1995, 132–138.

range of associations and stereotypes if he wanted to satirise the educated Greek Herodes as *graeculum et indoctum*.[56]

5 Orators between Character Assassination and Stand-up Comedy

Someone mainly familiar with modern legal proceedings might well wonder what place a comic character has in court at all. An attentive reader of Cicero's speeches, on the other hand, will hardly be surprised, since Cicero discusses explicitly the use of characters from comedy as examples in court.[57] In a certain sense, the same applies vice versa, since comedy mostly deals with *crimina*.[58] Nevertheless, the relationship between comedy and forensic speech is not limited merely to the reception of one by the other. For Quintilian, a comedic performance was part of a good speech – if delivered with moderation.[59] And in his introduction to the witticisms of the ancients, Macrobius identifies Plautus and Cicero as the two most important authors of witticisms, making a direct connection between comedy and oratory:

> [...] the comic writer Plautus and the orator Tully, were both second to none in the charm of their jokes. [...] Similarly, who doesn't know that [Cicero's] enemies used to call him

---

56 On the paradox use of *indoctus* here cf. n. 46 above. The *cinaedus-topoi* included (in addition to the more general idea of debauchery and deviant behaviour) certain movements and signs that an orator could use in a theatrical way during his performance. For example, the "scratching the head with the finger", with which Clodius perfected his denunciation of Pompeius (Plut. *Pomp.* 48). More signs are mentioned in Sen. *Epist.* 52.12: *inpudicum et incessus ostendit et manus mota et unum interdum responsum et relatus ad caput digitus et flexus oculorum. Inprobum risus, insanum vultus habitusque demonstrat.* ("The lecherous man is revealed by his gait, by a movement of the hand, sometimes by a single answer, by his touching his head with his finger, by the shifting of his eye. The scamp is shown up by his laugh; the madman by his face and general appearance". Transl. Gummere 1925). Cf. Corbeill 1996, 151–169 and Gleason 1995, 64.
57 E.g. Cic. *S. Rosc.* 46–48. Cf. in detail Harries 2007.
58 Ov. *Trist.* 2.508. On shared character types in comedy and court: Corbeill 1996, 128–130.
59 Quint. *Inst.* 11.3.181: *regnare maxime modum: non enim comoedum esse, sed oratorem volo*. Read in context, Quintilian does not mean that the orator should not be comedic, but that he should not over-act it. Furthermore, it is telling that Quintilian compares *comoedi* and *oratores* at all, obviously seeing some common ground. On the relationship between (forensic) rhetoric and comedy in general: Leigh 2004, 326–333. On its limits, see the caveat in the Introduction to this volume.

"the consular wag" (*consularem scurram*)? In fact, Vatinius even used the phrase in a speech. And if it wouldn't take too long, I'd tell you about the cases in which he was defending clients who were dead guilty but nonetheless got them off with his jokes: take the case of Lucius Flaccus, for example, whom Cicero got off with a timely joke when he was on trial for extortion and his crimes were as plain as black and white.[60]

As we can see, Macrobius saw no need to explain why one could win a lawsuit with jokes.[61] He does not give us an example of a joke Cicero brought up in a court speech, but he does elaborate on one a shoemaker used against Lucius Munatius Plancus. His explanation clarifies the mechanism of (comic) forensic invectives. Plancus had tried to "destroy" his opponent by mocking his profession.[62] But the attempt backfired because the witness managed to redirect the ridicule to the sexual behaviour of Plancus with a funny retort:

> When Plancus happened to be defending a friend in court and wanted to undermine (*destruere*) a troublesome witness, he asked him (knowing him to be a shoemaker) what craft he practiced to support himself. The man replied smoothly (*urbane*), "I grind the gallnut (*gallam*)", referring to a thing shoemakers use, which he wittily exploited to cast a reference to adultery in Plancus' face: for Plancus' reputation was suffering because of Maevia Galla, to whom he was married.[63]

We see here that the invective and the comic were closely related, and that *comic invectives* had their established place in trials.[64] It seems a reasonable assumption that the primary purpose of Plancus' attack was to perform character assassination (*testem destruere*, as Macrobius put it), and therefore the response

---

60 Macr. Sat. 2.1.10–13 [...] *comicum Plautum et oratorem Tullium, eos ambos etiam ad iocorum venustatem ceteris praestitisse.* [...] *quis item nescit consularem eum scurram ab inimicis appellari solitum? quod in oratione etiam sua Vatinius posuit. atque ego, ni longum esset, referrem in quibus causis, cum nocentissimos reos tueretur, victoriam iocis adeptus sit, ut ecce pro L. Flacco, quem repetundarum reum ioci opportunitate de manifestissimis criminibus exemit.* Transl. Kaster 2011.
61 In much the same way, Val. Max 8.1. abs. 8 reports without further explanation how someone was able to obtain an acquittal by simply reading before the court his accuser's frivolous poems.
62 On the ambiguous social standing of shoemakers: Burford Cooper 2001, 269–270.
63 Macr. *Sat.* 2.2.6: *Plancus in iudicio forte amici, cum molestum testem destruere vellet, interrogavit, quia sutorem sciebat, quo artificio se tueretur. ille urbane respondit: "gallam subigo". sutorium hoc habetur instrumentum, quod non infacete in adulterii exprobrationem ambiguitate convertit. nam Plancus in Maevia Galla nupta male audiebat.*
64 The same applies to almost all of the examples for *dicta* given in Macr. *Sat.* 2.2. On comic invective in Athens: Serafim 2020, 24–27.

was apt to do the same.⁶⁵ The underlying idea is that for the Romans bad character was good evidence for guilt (*probabile ex vita ante acta*).⁶⁶ Actually, Gellius provides an excellent example for this palpable nexus of bad character, especially effeminacy, and violation of the law subject to condemnation:

> Scipio's words are these: "For one who daily perfumes himself and dresses before a mirror, whose eyebrows are trimmed, who walks abroad with beard plucked out and thighs made smooth, who at banquets, though a young man, has reclined in a long-sleeved tunic on the inner side of the couch with a lover, who is fond not only of wine but of men – does anyone doubt that he does what wantons (*cinaedi*) commonly do?"⁶⁷

Some scholars approach invectives primarily as a way of marginalising an enemy and making him appear morally reprehensible.⁶⁸ And of course, for the Romans the character of a person was anything but irrelevant distraction from the case.⁶⁹ Cicero explicitly points out that even vices that have nothing to do with the issue at stake can serve to weaken someone's position in court.⁷⁰

Such views run the risk, however, of reducing the theatre of justice to the level of judicial reasoning (i.e. inferring guilt from bad character) and ignoring the performative character of the process. This aspect has to be considered if we wish to understand the great variety of invectives, their function and especially

---

65 It seems very important to emphasise here that the effect of this attack is not the permanent social death of the party subjected to invective, but the acute performative momentum it delivers to the agent of invective, which successfully sets the audience in motion. Cf. van der Blom 2014, esp. 39 and Arena 2007. Thurn 2018 is an example of a different view. In her detailed treatment of the abuse Cicero inflicted (cf. esp. 25–29), she elaborates on the permanent damage Ciceronian attacks could do to people's reputation, in some cases to this day.
66 Val. Max. 8.5.6 demonstrates this influence of reputation in court on two levels: as *gravitas* that could tip the scales in favour of a given testimony and as a burden of bad renown for the accused. Cf. also Riggsby 2004.
67 Gell. 6.12.5: *Verba sunt haec Scipionis:* "*Nam qui cotidie unguentatus adversum speculum ornetur, cuius supercilia radantur, qui barba vulsa feminibusque subvulsis ambulet, qui in conviviis adulescentulus cum amatore, cum chiridota tunica interior accubuerit, qui non modo vinosus, sed virosus quoque sit, eumne quisquam dubitet, quin idem fecerit quod cinaedi facere solent?*" Transl. Rolfe 1927. An invective of Aeschines (in 1.131) works in a very similar way: Aeschines attributes ἀνανδρία and κιναιδία to Demosthenes, declaring none of the judges could say whether his clothes were those of a man or a woman.
68 Cf. n. 65 above.
69 Cf. Riggsby 2004, 176–177. In the case of the *laudatio iudicialis*, for example, a character witness was at least on occasion a formal part of Roman trials. However, its function was more usually to demonstrate social support through weighty representatives than to make one of the parties seem believable. Cf. Rees 2011, esp. 96.
70 Cf. Cic. *Inv.* 2.33.

the humour that usually goes along with them. For example, if we ignore the performativity of Roman manliness, we cannot understand why the shoemaker in our first example was (playfully) alluding to adultery, which (if he had actually committed it) would have rendered him a morally reprehensible criminal.[71] But that is not the point! He turned the tables, and he did this in a quick-witted and eloquent manner – so *urbane* that it found its way into the Macrobian collection: on the symbolic level, he declared himself capable of penetrating the sphere of Plancus, subordinating him and thereby inverting the social hierarchy.[72] Even intellectually, the man of lower status duped the well-connected senator who had tried to portray him as a simple person.[73] Scipio in our second example also insulted his opponent on the sexual level for his effeminate Greek styling and (banquet) culture.[74] And he too was keen to produce laughter, which becomes clear in his little play on words (*non modo vinosus, sed virosus*). Finally, the performative level should not be underestimated when he, a man *omni virtute praeditus*, probably pointing to the elegant clothing of his counterpart and certainly speaking with a bitter and venomous taste, contrasted the virtuous Roman with the *homo delicatus*, the *cinaedus*, the dissolute *Greekling*.[75] A good forensic invective usually tried to combine all these aspects: it told a dramatic story that mixed the accusation of serious violations of the norms, which in Rome typically were sexually charged, with comic insertions that entertained the audience and made them laugh. The prime example of an invective defence speech, the *Apologia* of Apuleius, also shows "many touches of comedy", for example when he spices up his family-sex-life-invective (chapter I) with a comic narration of how Herennius Rufinus pranked his wife's suitors.[76]

In closing, let us return to Fronto one final time. Unlike Cicero, whose inability to restrain himself finally led to his ruin, Fronto was able to pull himself

---

[71] In fact, not considering Roman sexual hierarchies and their functions (cf. n. 32 above), has often led to confusion regarding this passage. E.g. Watkins 2019, 12 offered a different reading, making Maevia Galla a married woman (*nupta*), and Plancus the adulterer, because for him it seems difficult to imagine that an *adulterii exprobratio* would be directed not against the adulterer but against the cuckold.
[72] The episode is reminiscent of the classic joke (Val. Max. 9.14 ext. 3 and Macr. *Sat.* 2.4.20) of a powerful man meeting a low man who resembles him like a brother. He therefore suggests that the low man's mother had something with the powerful man's father, but then gets an answer implying that it was the other way around.
[73] On Plancus' status and connections: Watkins 2019, 25–34.
[74] On Greek style of dress being associated with effeminacy: Olson 2017, 75. On Greek banquet: cf. n. 45 above.
[75] Gell. 6.12.4. On effeminate appearance cf. Olson 2017, 138–145.
[76] Citation Hunink 1997, 26. On comedy in the *Apologia*: Hunink 1998.

together.⁷⁷ A second, and clearly more explicit request from Marcus Aurelius was required, but ultimately Fronto agreed to stick to the case:⁷⁸

> I will act, my Lord, as to these counts and as to my whole life in the way I see you wish me to act; and I pray and beseech you never to forbear mentioning what you wish done by me [...]. But if we proceed with unbroken speeches (*perpetuis orationibus*), though I go no step outside the case (*extra causam nihil progrediar*), my glance must needs be somewhat keen, and my voice vehement, and my words stern (*tamen et oculis acrioribus et voce vehementi et verbis gravibus*), and I must shew anger with a gesture here and a finger there (*utendum hinc autem nutu hinc digito irato*); and this your man ought to bear with composure (*modeste ferre decet*).⁷⁹

As we see, Fronto promised not to go *extra causam*, in all likelihood to not make fun of his opponent's lifestyle, and to refrain from declaring him a pseudo-philosopher and from depicting his sexual deviance in all its colours. The only thing he insisted on was that he be allowed to give a spicy performance. Being limited to mimicking the strict disciplinarian was certainly not half as entertaining and successful as an unfettered comic invective, but it made it possible to meet the minimal role expectations and thus save face.⁸⁰ Marcus Aurelius, on the other hand, was able to avoid the uncomfortable situation that two well-known men closely associated with him would publicly defame each other in a way that might have rubbed off on him.⁸¹ Especially when we recall that the two men about to confront each other were considered his teachers – a relationship that was a common target for attacks.⁸²*

---

77 Although we do not know the content of the actual speech that was actually delivered in the end, twenty years later Fronto used the dispute with Herodes as an example of surmountable differences. Cf. Front. *Ad Verum Imp.* 2.9.
78 Cf. Front. *Ad M. Caes.* 3.5.
79 Front. *Ad M. Caes.* 3.6: *Ita faciam, quod ad haec nomina, quod ad vitam, ut te velle intellexero faciam; teque oro et quaeso ne umquam quod a me fieri volueris <taceas>. [...] Quodsi agemus perpetuis orationibus, licet extra causam nihil progrediar, tamen et oculis acrioribus et voce vehementi et verbis gravibus utendum <hinc> autem <nutu> hinc digito irato, quod <modeste> hominem tuum ferre decet.*
80 It was part of the theatricality of trials that opponents exhibited personal hostility against each other; cf. Criste 2018, 126–132.
81 On the invective potential of contact with infamous persons: Thurn 2018, 236–257.
82 On typical invectives against philosophers and their relationship to their students: cf. p. 224 above. As an illustrative example for invectives based on a student-teacher relationship, cf. (Ps.-)Sall. *Inv. Cic.* 2, *aut scilicet istam immoderatam eloquentiam apud M. Pisonem non pudicitiae iactura perdidicisti?*
* χάριν ἔχων τῷ γεωργῷ τῷ εν-τάφρῳ
 τῷ ἱππεῖ καρυο-βροντο-ποιῷ.

Bibliography

Alexander, M.C. (1990), *Trials in the Late Roman Republic 149 BC to 50 BC*, London.
Arena, V. (2007), 'Roman Oratorical Invective', in: W.J. Dominik and J. Hall (eds.), *A Companion to Roman Rhetoric*, Oxford, 149–160.
Bablitz, L. (2007), *Actors and Audience in the Roman Courtroom*, London.
Booth, J. (ed.) (2007), *Cicero on the Attack, Invective and Subversion in the Orations and Beyond*, Swansea.
Burford Cooper, A. (2001), s.v. 'Schuster', in: *Die Neue Pauly* 11, 268–270.
Corbeill, A. (1996), *Controlling Laughter, Political Humor in the Late Roman Republic*, Princeton.
Corbeill, A. (2019), 'Review of Thurn (2018)', in: *Bryn Mawr Classical Reviews* 08.44.
Craig, C. (2004), 'Audience Expectations, Invective and Proof', in: J. Powell and J. Paterson (eds.), *Cicero the Advocate*, Oxford, 187–213.
Criste, C. (2018), *Voluntas auditorum, Forensische Rollenbilder und emotionale Performanzen in den spätrepublikanischen Quaestiones*, Heidelberg.
Davenport, C. and Manley, J. (2014), *Fronto: Selected Letters*, London.
Frieze, J. (2019), *Theatrical Performance and the Forensic Turn*, New York.
Gleason, M.W. (1995), *Making Men, Sophists and Self-presentation in Ancient Rome*, Princeton.
Hall, J. (2014), *Cicero's Use of Judicial Theater*, Ann Arbor.
Harries, B. (2007), 'Acting the Part: Techniques of the Comic Stage in Cicero's Early Speeches', in: Booth 129–147.
Hunger, H. (1987), *Graeculus perfidus - Ἰταλὸς ἰταμός. Il senso dell'alterità nei rapporti greco romani ed italo-bizantini*, Rome.
Hunink, V. (1998), 'Comedy in Apuleius' Apology', *Groningen Colloquia on the Novel* 9, 97–113.
Hunink, V. (ed.) (1997), *Apuleius of Madauros pro se de magia (Apologia)*, Vol. I, Amsterdam.
Iurescia, F. (2019), *Credo iam ut solet iurgabit: Pragmatica della Lite a Roma*, Göttingen.
Jehne, M. (2020), 'Invectivity in the City of Rome in the Caesarian and Triumviral periods', in: F. Pina Polo (ed.), *The Triumviral Period: Civil War, Political Crisis and Socioeconomic Transformations*, Zaragoza, 209–228.
Keller, O. (1891), *Lateinische Volksetymologie und Verwandtes*, Wiesbaden.
Leigh, M. (2004), 'The Pro Caelio and Comedy', in: *Classical Philology* 99, 300–335.
Marshall, C.W. (2006), *The Stagecraft and Performance of Roman Comedy*, Cambridge.
McDonnell, M. (2006), *Roman Manliness, Virtus and the Roman Republic*, Cambridge.
Meister, J.B. (2009), 'Pisos Augenbrauen Zur Lesbarkeit aristokratischer Körper in der späten römischen Republik', in: *Historia* 58, 71–95.
Nisbet, R.G.M. (1961), *M. Tulli Ciceronis In L. Calpurnium Pisonem*, Oxford.
Obermayer, H.P. (1998), *Martial und der Diskurs über männliche "Homosexualität" in der Literatur der frühen Kaiserzeit*, Tübingen.
Olson, K. (2017), *Masculinity and Dress in Roman Antiquity*, New York.
Powell, J. and Paterson, J. (2004), 'Introduction', in: J. Powell and J. Peterson (eds.), *Cicero the Advocate*, Oxford, 1–57.
Powell, J.G.F. (2007), 'Invective and the Orator, Ciceronian Theory and Practice', in: Booth 1–24.
Rees, R. (2011), 'The Whole Truth? *Laudationes* in the Courtroom', in: C. Smith and R. Covino (eds.), *Praise and Blame in Roman Republican Rhetoric*, Swansea, 83–98.

Richlin, A. (1992), *The Garden of Priapus, Sexuality and Aggression in Roman Humor*, 2nd ed., Oxford.
Richlin, A. (2006), *Marcus Aurelius in Love*, Chicago.
Riggsby, A.M. (2004), 'The Rhetoric of Character in the Roman Courts', in: J. Powell and J. Paterson (eds.), *Cicero the Advocate*, Oxford, 165–186.
Rosillo-López, C. (2017a), *Public Opinion and Politics in the Late Roman Republic*, Cambridge.
Rosillo-López, C. (2017b), 'The Role and Influence of the Audience (*corona*) in Trials in the Late Roman Republic', in: *Athenaeum* 105, 106–119.
Segal, E. (1987), *Roman Laughter, The Comedy of Plautus*. 2nd ed., Oxford.
Serafim, A. (2017), *Attic Oratory and Performance*, London.
Serafim, A. (2020), 'Comic Invective in the Public Forensic Speeches of Attic Oratory', in: *Hellenica* 68, 23–42.
Stebnicka, K. (2015), s.v. 'Herodes Attikos', in: P. Janiszewski, K. Stebnicka and E. Szabat (eds.), *Prosopography of Greek Rhetors and Sophists of the Roman Empire*, Oxford.
Syme, R. (1939), *The Roman Revolution*, Oxford.
Tempest, K. (2013), 'Staging a Prosecution: Aspects of Performance in Cicero's Verrines', in: C. Kremmydas, J. Powell and L. Rubinstein (eds.), *Profession and Performance. Aspects of Oratory in the Greco-Roman World*, London, 41–72.
Thurn, A. (2018), *Rufmord in der späten römischen Republik Charakterbezogene Diffamierungsstrategien in Ciceros Reden und Briefen*, Darmstadt.
van den Hout, M.P.J. (1999), *A Commentary on the Letters of M. Cornelius Fronto*, Leiden.
van der Blom, H. (2014), 'Character Attack and Invective Speech in the Roman Republic: Cicero as Target', in: M. Icks and E. Shiraev (eds.), *Character Assassination Throughout the Ages*, Basingstoke, 37–57.
Watkins, T.H. (2019), *L. Munantius Plancus, Serving and Surviving in the Roman Revolution*, London. 2nd ed.
Williams, C.A. (1995), 'Greek Love at Rome', in: *Classical Quarterly* 45, 517–539.
Winterling, A. (2008), 'Freundschaft und Klientel im kaiserzeitlichen Rom', in: *Historia* 57, 298–316.
Zinsmaier, T. (2009), 'Zwischen Erzählung und Argumentation: «colores» in den pseudo quintilianischen «Declamationes maiores»', in: *Rhetorica* 27, 256–273.

Part III: **Invective in Ancient Socio-political Contexts**

Ioannis Konstantakos
Political Rhetoric and Comic Invective in Fifth-Century Athens: The Trial of the Dogs in Aristophanes' *Wasps*

Abstract: Old Attic comedy includes plenty of invective against the political leaders of Athens. The comic poets rework rhetorical elements from the public discourses of Athenian statesmen and thus provide indications about the practices and commonplaces of fifth-century political oratory. In this chapter the interaction between comic ridicule and political speeches is analysed through a particular case-study, the mock-trial of the two dogs in Aristophanes' *Wasps* (826–1008). This episode parodies the confrontation between two ideologically opposed statesmen, the arch-demagogue Cleon and general Laches, in the last years of the Archidamian War. The Aristophanic text reflects rhetorical devices, propagandistic statements and ideological tenets drawn apparently from the public discourses which the opposed parties held in the context of their conflict. The presentation of Cleon and Laches in the form of dogs is a grotesque scenic materialisation of a rhetorical metaphor which Cleon used in his own harangues. The motifs of animal imagery and fable, which permeate the episode of the trial, may have been inspired by the use of Aesopic fables as persuasive examples in the speeches of the two opponents. The humorous character portraits of the two dogs reverberate with ideological principles and stereotypes that are familiar from the political debates between radicals and moderates in Athenian public life.

1 Old Comedy, Invective and Political Oratory

One of the greatest losses of ancient Greek literature is the failure to preserve the authentic texts of the political speeches of fifth-century Athens. I have in mind especially the orations held in the Assembly or in public court cases during the celebrated age of Pericles and the agitated years of the Peloponnesian War, at the time of the great acme of the classical Athenian democracy. We would have immensely liked to read the genuine speeches which Pericles delivered, for example, at the beginning of the Samian War, or when he passed the infamous Megarian Decree, or while he tried to support the morale of the Athenian people after the first Spartan invasion under Archidamus. The same applies to Cleon's harangues against his opponents in the *ekklēsia*, his authentic words before and after the maverick expedition of Sphacteria, or his discourse at the nearly fatal Assembly meeting which decided the fate of the revolted Mytilenaeans. The greatest marvel, of course, would be to discover the true orations pronounced by Alcibiades and Nicias at the debate about the Sicilian campaign – a worthy fifth-century counterpart to the analogous pair of speeches by Demosthenes and Aeschines regarding the embassy to Philip of Macedon. Further specimens of the Athenian demagogues' populist rhetoric would also have been welcome: the low-brow eloquence of Hyperbolus, the jingoistic outpourings of Cleophon, the prosecutors' cunning speeches at the trial of Thucydides son of Melesias. But they should have been counterbalanced by rhetorical products of the opposite ideological faction, such as Antiphon's impassioned *apologia* after the failed coup of the Four Hundred or Theramenes' notorious doublespeak.

All these treasures of Attic public oratory are, alas, irretrievably lost for posterity, since the habit of publishing and circulating the written texts of political discourses had not been established in the fifth century, as it was later in the fourth.[1] *Faute de mieux*, the scholar must acquire some idea of fifth-century political rhetoric via intermediary historical and literary sources. Thucydides' famous *dēmēgoriai*, even though they are exercises in historical imagination, provide important first-hand testimonia for the ideological contents, oratorical mannerisms and lines of argument pursued by several Athenian statesmen of the time.[2] Another valuable repository is Old Attic comedy, especially the politicised strand of comic theatre, as cultivated by Aristophanes and like-minded dramatists, which focused on Athenian public life and included acrid invective against political leaders.[3]

In the extant plays and fragments of Old Comedy the prominent statesmen of Periclean and post-Periclean Athens, especially the populist demagogues, are regularly ridiculed. The comic texts thus reflect, even though in a burlesque and exaggerated manner, not only the policies and ideological tenets of the satirised politicians, but often also their public statements, manner of speech and characteristic rhetorical gimmicks. Especially comic passages of invective[4] may rework elements from the actual discourses of Athenian leaders in political fo-

---

[1] On this point cf. the Introduction to this volume.
[2] See e.g. Hornblower 1987, 45–72; Harris 2013; Kremmydas 2017.
[3] Cf. Sousa e Silva 1987–1988; Hubbard 2007. The multifarious connections between Old Comedy and public oratory are also explored in the Introduction and in several contributions in this volume: see the chapters by Donelan, Apostolakis, Serafim, Kazantzidis and Hubbard.
[4] On the definition of invective and its function in ancient comedy see the introduction to this volume and cf. Serafim 2020, 23–42.

rums. Hence, they provide useful indications about the main practices and *topoi* of political oratory in contemporary Athens. By appropriately decoding the comic poets' satirical constructs, one may acquire a good glimpse into the rhetorical clashes and argument exchanges of the Athenian Assembly and courts.

In the present paper this close interaction between comic invective and Athenian political oratory will be investigated through a particular case study: the side-splitting episode of the dogs' trial in Aristophanes' *Wasps* (826–1008), which parodies the confrontation of two ideologically opposed statesmen in the final years of the Archidamian War.

2 The Trial of the Dogs and Its Historical Background

The elderly hero of the *Wasps*, Philocleon, suffers from an inveterate obsession with trials and passionately serves as a judge in the popular courts.[5] His sober son, the upper-class young Bdelycleon, tries to keep his incorrigible father away from the public trials. For this purpose, Bdelycleon inaugurates a domestic court of law, which operates at the threshold of their family house. The addicted old dicast will sit there, like a one-man jury, and judge any private disputes which may arise between the slaves or other members of his household, following all the formalities of Attic law. Philocleon is satisfied with this outrageous idea. Soon father and son set up an improvised courtroom outside their house door, making use of easily available household utensils. When everything is ready, Bdelycleon introduces the first case. A dog of the house, named Labes ("Snatcher"), has stolen from the pantry and eaten up a loaf of Sicilian cheese. Another dog, Kyon of Cydathenaeum, presents the accusation. This masterful parody of Attic court procedure is one of the most famous scenes of the comedy.

From the very names and attributes of the litigants the audience would quickly realise that the two dogs represent figures of Athenian public life. The defendant Labes symbolises, with a small phonetic change, the aristocratic general Laches, who was distinguished especially as a career military commander. Laches had served as *stratēgos* in an Athenian expedition to Sicily from 427 to 425 BC. As it seems, he had been accused for embezzlement or misuse of funds during his tenure of office; hence the charge of stealing a 'Sicilian' cheese from the larder. Kyon, who takes up the prosecutor's part, stands for the dema-

---

5 On Philocleon's obsession, which verges on insanity: Kazantzidis' chapter in this volume.

gogue Cleon, who was actually from the deme of Cydathenaeum and must have been the main instigator of the accusations against Laches.

It is impossible to fully reconstruct the historical circumstances of the affair, because the information provided by ancient sources is insufficient.[6] Laches should have been obliged to appear before the appointed functionaries and render account of his tenure of office (*euthynai*) as soon as his term of service was completed, in 425 BC. Eventual accusations concerning misappropriation of funds or other financial offences during the Sicilian campaign should normally have been brought and investigated during the procedure of Laches' regular *euthynai*. However, this procedure must have been carried out two or three years before the performance of the *Wasps* (422 BC).[7] It seems unlikely that Aristophanes would devote an extensive episode of his play to satirise a case of the past, which would have passed out of topicality by the time of the performance.[8] Like all topical satirical scenes of this kind in the Aristophanic *oeuvre*, the dogs' trial doubtless concerns a public affair of immediate relevance and seasonality, which must have occurred at most a few months before the presentation of the comedy and would have been still fresh in the audience's memory.

It is not necessary to assume that Cleon actually took Laches to court; there is no historical evidence for a judicial indictment, outside the comic scene of the *Wasps*. The trial, just like the household court and the personified animals, may be a product of Aristophanes' fertile imagination, a grotesque inflation of a more moderate and prosaic reality. Most probably Cleon denounced Laches in public speeches, maintaining that the general had made illegal profits or harmed the financial interests of Athens while exercising his office in Sicily.[9] Of course, the ruthless demagogue may have also threatened to bring formal court charges against Laches for those alleged offences, even though in point of fact there was no legal possibility of doing so in 423/422, over two years after the completion of the general's *euthynai*.

Significantly, in the spring of 423, some months before the performance of the *Wasps*, Laches took an active initiative for the conclusion of a yearly truce with Sparta: he moved the decree by which the Athenian Assembly accepted the

---

6 On the historical background of the conflict see Mastromarco 1974, 35–64; Moneti 1993; Braund 1999; Saldutti 2014, 155–164.
7 See Mastromarco 1974, 57–62; Moneti 1993, 450–452; Giangiulio 1997, 881; Biles and Olson 2015, lii, 165–166.
8 Cf. Mastromarco 1974, 59–63, 97–101; Storey 1995, 17; Olson 1996, 138; Reinders 2001, 229.
9 See Jacoby 1954, 500–501; Gomme 1956, 430–431; Westlake 1969, 122; MacDowell 1971, 164–165; Moneti 1993; MacDowell 1995, 167–168; Giangiulio 1997, 867–868, 880–882; Reinders 2001, 229–230; Biles and Olson 2015, 165–166.

suspension of hostilities, and thus opened the way for negotiations towards a definitive peace treaty (Thucydides 4.118). This effort was soon frustrated. Nevertheless, Laches' prominent role in these events brought him to the fore of Athenian foreign policy and promoted him as a rising champion of the pro-peace faction, and hence as a dangerous potential opponent of the belligerent demagogues.[10] Cleon would have been likely to target this ascending enemy and try to smear him with slander and suspicions. Laches' most recent major command in the Sicilian expedition would have come in handy as a hook on which to attach various accusations of misconduct.

Taking occasion from Cleon's demagogic proclamations and threats, Aristophanes dreams up a judicial process against Laches, filtered of course through comic phantasmagoria. A clash of the political arena is transplanted on the theatrical stage and metamorphosed into an imaginary lawsuit. The trial of the dogs is a piece of staged comic invective, in which both of the opponents are mocked for their public careers, even though Cleon is the main target of lampoon, as standardly in Aristophanes' early plays. The satirical depiction of the two litigants reflects a number of rhetorical devices (artful figures of speech, clever metaphors, exemplary narratives) which seem to have been drawn from the public discourses of Cleon and Laches or other members of their factions. In addition, the Aristophanic ēthopoiia of the two rivals reproduces ideological tenets and political statements which may have nourished the speeches delivered in the context of their conflict. Thus, the dramatised invective of comedy may be appropriately decoded to reveal significant details of the content and style of the orations held by the two opposed politicians.

In the following sections three elements of the dogs' trial will be explored in this respect. Firstly, the presentation of the two statesmen in the form of dogs is a grotesque scenic materialisation of a rhetorical metaphor which Cleon used in his speeches. Secondly, the plentiful motifs of animal imagery and fable, which permeate the episode of the trial, may have been inspired by the use of Aesopic fables as persuasive examples in the two opponents' discourses. Finally, the humorous character portraits of the two dogs reverberate with ideological principles and stereotypes that are familiar from the political struggle between radicals and moderates in Athenian public life and may have been used in rhetorical debates.

---

10 See Kagan 1974, 305–308; Mastromarco 1974, 34–53, 63–64; Carter 1986, 117; Giangiulio 1997, 868; Saldutti 2014, 158–159.

3 The Watchdog of the People

A core ingredient of the dogs' trial is the symbolic representation of the two political rivals, the arch-demagogue Cleon and general Laches, in the form of household dogs. This grotesque scenic metamorphosis provides the metaphorical framework which sustains the comic imagery of the entire scene. The image of the dogs may be directly inspired from Cleon's own rhetorical idiolect. Aristophanes and other comic poets often compare this particular demagogue with a hound, sometimes more specifically with Cerberus, the mythical watchdog of Hades.

In the *Knights*, produced two years before the *Wasps* (424 BC), Paphlagon, the arch-slave in the house of old Demos, is a transparent scenic representation of Cleon, the leader of the Athenian *dēmos*. In one scene (1014–1024) Paphlagon expressly compares himself to a jag-toothed dog which faithfully guards his master Demos and barks to protect him. The Sausage-Seller, Paphlagon's antagonist, cleverly reverses this metaphor and likens Paphlagon to a fawning, guileful and thievish dog, which steals his master's food, while Demos is inadvertently looking away (1025–1034). In the *Peace*, produced shortly after the *Wasps* (421 BC), Cleon, who was killed in battle in the meantime, is metonymically presented as Cerberus, the terrible guardian dog of the underworld (313); apparently, he is supposed to pursue his canine habits and behaviour even after death. Plato Comicus also called Cleon "Cerberus" in an unknown play (fr. 236 Kassel-Austin).

Furthermore, in the parabasis of the *Wasps* Cleon is pictured as a horrible conglomerate monster, composed of the parts of various animal and human creatures, according to the model of many mixed monsters of myth and popular fantasy (1031–1036). The first characteristic of this beast consists in his jagged, saw-like teeth (καρχαρόδοντι, 1031), which allude to the image of the jag-toothed hound familiar from the *Knights* (ἱερὸν κύνα καρχαρόδοντα, 1017).[11] Additionally, the creature's eyes are said to flash like those of Cynna (Κύννης, 1032), a well-known hetaira of the time, whose name also puns on the word κύων and fits with the overall canine imagery of the passage.[12] This piece of grotesque comic invective was apparently so successful that Aristophanes repeated it the following year in the parabasis of the *Peace* (754–759).

---

[11] Καρχαρόδους is a typical epithet of dogs in Archaic poetry, applied especially to the terrible Cerberus. See Desfray 1999, 45; Imperio 2004, 284; Corbel-Morana 2012, 131.
[12] Cf. Taillardat 1965, 405; Imperio 2004, 285–286; Corbel-Morana 2012, 131–132.

The frequency of this image in comic texts is remarkable.[13] It is a common scholarly assumption that the simile of the dog is drawn from public discourses of the time. Presumably Cleon pictured himself, in his own harangues, as the watchdog that guards the *polis* or the *dēmos*. His ideological comrades and collaborators, in their public utterances, may also have attached the nickname κύων to Cleon, with a view to praising him as a loyal guardian and protector of Athens.[14] Cleon's political opponents might have seized hold of the same figure of speech and inverted it, as Aristophanes does, so as to taunt the demagogue for his unpleasant, loud and "barking" voice or for his tail-wagging flattery of the people.[15]

An indirect confirmation of this hypothesis is found later in the corpus of extant fourth-century oratory. The first speech *Against Aristogeiton*, attributed to Demosthenes (Dem. 25),[16] was composed for a court case in which the Athenian politician Aristogeiton was prosecuted for debts to the state and disenfranchisement. In this oration the metaphor of the watchdog is used with the same political symbolism as was found in the texts of Old Comedy. The speaker condemns the defendant's supporters, who call Aristogeiton "the hound of the *demos*" (κύων [...] τοῦ δήμου, 25.40), that is, the watchdog that guards the democracy. The speaker holds on to the image of the dog but reverses its value

---

13 On this metaphorical image of Cleon see Taillardat 1965, 403–406; Lilja 1976, 70–74; Edmunds 1987, 55–56; Lind 1990, 223–228; Storey 1995, 16–20; Desfray 1999, 44–47, 54–56; Imperio 2004, 284–286; Lauriola 2004, 86–87, 93–94; Corbel-Morana 2012, 118–136; Fileni 2012, 96–97; Brock 2013, 118–119, 136–137. Eupolis was inspired from the same metaphor and produced a variation adapted to another figure of Athenian politics. In his comedy *Poleis* the politician Syrakosios, as he is pacing around on the speaker's stand, is likened to a dog's puppy which barks from atop the courtyard walls (fr. 220 Kassel-Austin). This mocking image may target the disorderliness of Syrakosios' public behaviour, the shrillness of his voice, the aggressiveness but also the ineffectiveness of his rhetoric. See Storey 2003, 225, 343–344; Fileni 2012, 101; Olson 2016, 238–241.
14 This suggestion is often made, from Dover 1972, 96–97 to Spatharas 2013, 88. See the bibliography cited above, n. 13.
15 Cf. Franco 2014, 93–94. For the "liminal" image of the dog, which can be presented both as a useful and as a harmful creature, cf. Serafim 2020, 38–40.
16 There is an ongoing debate about the authenticity of this speech. Convincing vindications of Demosthenes' authorship have been forwarded by Hansen 1976, 144–152; Carmignato 1999; MacDowell 2009, 298–313; Martin 2009, 182–202; Faraguna 2011, 75–77; Apostolakis 2014, 203–208. It seems in any case extreme to date the text to the Hellenistic period and brand it a mere rhetorical exercise: thus Sealey 1967; Sealey 1993, 237–239; Harris 2018, 193–197. Even if the oration is not a genuine work by Demosthenes, it may have been composed by another fourth-century orator and may thus testify to the familiarity of the dog metaphor in classical Athenian political discourse; thus Treves 1936, 252–258; Martin 2009, 182.

and political implications, as Aristophanes did for Cleon in the *Knights*. Aristogeiton, according to the speaker, is a useless and harmful dog because he does not bite the wolves but instead eats the sheep he is supposed to protect. In terms of political symbolism, this means that the accused statesman does not defend the Athenian citizens from their enemies but actually causes harm to the people.[17]

In Plutarch's *Life of Demosthenes* (23.4–6) the great orator applies the same metaphor to himself. When Alexander the Great demanded, after the destruction of Thebes in 335 BC, that the Athenians deliver to him the most prominent anti-Macedonian politicians, Demosthenes recited to the people the famous Aesopic fable of the wolves and the sheep (158 Hausrath/153 Perry). As the story goes, the wolves wanted to devour a flock of sheep but could not overpower the watchdogs and therefore used guile. They sent a deceitful embassy to the sheep and asked them to hand over the dogs, because the latter were the only causes of enmity between the sheep and the wolves and the only obstacles to a communal peace. The silly sheep did not understand the treachery and submitted to the wolves' demand. Thus, the wolves put the protective dogs out of the way and then ate up the defenceless flock.

The mention of sheep and wolves together with the watchdogs, both in *Against Aristogeiton I* and in the biographical anecdote about Demosthenes, highlights the political symbolism of the animal imagery. The sheep stand for the common people of Athens; the wolves represent the people's enemies, whether political evil-doers within the Athenian state (*Against Aristogeiton*) or menacing foreign powers (Plutarch's *Demosthenes*). The watchdogs correspond to the patriotic statesmen who protect the *polis* and foster its interests. All these motifs are already present in the Aesopic fable, which is indeed accompanied in the manuscripts by a suitable *epimythium* of political *allegorisation*: "In the same way, those cities which easily betray the leaders of their people, are themselves quickly subdued by the enemies, before they know it" (οὕτω καὶ τῶν πόλεων αἱ τοὺς δημαγωγοὺς ῥᾳδίως προδιδοῦσαι λανθάνουσι καὶ αὐταὶ ταχέως πολεμίοις χειρούμεναι). This traditional animal fable is therefore the model of reference for both Demosthenic rhetorical examples cited above.[18]

---

17 On Aristogeiton's image as a dog cf. Worman 2008, 230–232; Spatharas 2013, 88–91; Apostolakis 2014, 216–222; Serafim 2020, 38–40.

18 Cf. Jedrkiewicz 1989, 237; van Dijk 1997, 293–296; Kurke 2011, 148–149; Corbel-Morana 2012, 133–134; Spatharas 2013, 79, 88–91. The image survives in the early Hellenistic *Characters* of Theophrastus (29.5), applied again to a corrupt politician who speaks in the Assembly and is tried for public offences at court. His supporter calls him κύνα [...] τοῦ δήμου, because "he

Probably Cleon or his supporters also had in mind the same popular Aesopic story, when they used the symbol of the watchdog for the demagogue's political role. Like most of the classic Aesopic tales, the fable of the wolves, the sheep and the dogs must have been familiar and widespread among the Athenian public from an early age.[19] The very text of the *Wasps* supplements Cleon's canine metaphor by adducing the other, complementary parts of the animal allegory, as set out in the fable. In the prologue of the play the slave Sosias sees in his dream the common citizens of Athens transformed into sheep, which gather at the Pnyx and sit down for a session of the Assembly (31–36), a clear representation of the Athenian people's gregariousness and gullibility. Later, during the burlesque trial, Bdelycleon defends Labes/Laches and praises him as an excellent dog which is capable of chasing away the wolves (952) and overseeing many sheep (955). The sheep and the wolves may be taken again as respective symbols of the Athenian people and its enemies.[20]

Transforming Cleon and Laches into dogs, Aristophanes comically materialises the metaphor used by Cleon and/or his supporters in their political orations. The demagogue likened himself to a faithful watchdog of the *dēmos*, in the sense of a guardian of the state. Aristophanes takes this rhetorical figure literally and turns it into a visible and side-splitting spectacle on stage.[21] This kind of scenic materialisation of linguistic metaphors is a peculiar technique of Aristophanic comedy and one of its most impressive theatrical effects.[22] Thus, the comic writer's staged invective grows out of a rhetorical *topos* of contemporary political discourse.

---

barks at offenders". Cf. Kish's chapter in this volume for a Roman variant of the simile, recorded by Cicero.

19 Cf. Meuli 1954, 88; Jedrkiewicz 1989, 237, 377; van Dijk 1997, 293; Irwin 2005, 252–256; Corbel-Morana 2012, 111–112, 128.
20 On the sheep as ludicrous symbols of the docile Athenian *dēmos* cf. Ar. *Eq.* 264, *Nub.* 1203; Taillardat 1965, 255–256; Wright 2007, 422–423; Corbel-Morana 2012, 109–114. On the theme of the stupidity and naïveté of the Athenian people cf. also Apostolakis' chapter in this volume.
21 Cf. Taillardat 1965, 404–406, 505; Lind 1990, 225; Corbel-Morana 2012, 124–130; Lenz 2014, 33–34.
22 See Newiger 1957, 122–133; Taillardat 1965, 65–67, 337–338, 430–431, 504–506; Thiercy 1986, 103–119; Konstantakos 2021b.

4 Aesopic Fables and Political Oratory

The theriomorphic incarnation of the two political rivals is not the only element of Aesopic provenance in the Aristophanic episode. The trial of the dogs, in its entirety, is largely pieced together of motifs drawn from the repertoire of Aesopic animal stories. Philocleon's home trial may be read as an original mega-fable, which Aristophanes has created by ingeniously picking out and intertwining various characteristic elements of the Aesopic tradition, so as to forge a new synthesis of his own. This monumental satirical fable is cast in dramatic form and enlivened on stage.[23]

Firstly, the trial and court of animals is a widespread theme in folk narrative tradition. In the stories of many peoples, from the animal legends of medieval Europe to Russian fairy tales, from Indian and Iranian moral parables to African lore, wild beasts and domestic animals appear as judges or litigants, judge and sentence their fellow-creatures or are brought to trial before human arbiters.[24] In the ancient world this story-pattern mostly occurs in didactic animal fables. In a versified fable of Babrius (102, fable 334 Perry) the lion institutes a court to judge all the animals. In another fable (452 Perry), preserved in a collection of *Progymnasmata* from late antiquity,[25] the wolf tries the ass for his offences and condemns him to be eaten. The narrative includes much forensic vocabulary and details of a judicial procedure. The animals' court was also common in the fable traditions of the Near East, which provided a broader context to the Graeco-Roman Aesopic corpus and often constituted the ultimate source of its materials.[26]

The contrast between the two rival dogs in the Aristophanic scene is also based on fable motifs. In his oration in Labes' defence Bdelycleon compares the two dogs in some detail, so as to illuminate the peculiar nature of each one. The

---

[23] Cf. Giner Soria 1978; Jedrkiewicz 2006, 77; Pertsinidis 2009, 209; Schirru 2009, 59–64; Hutchinson 2011, 65; Corbel-Morana 2012, 129–130.
[24] See e.g. Thompson 1955–1958, motifs A2255.2, B270–275, J1172.3.1–2, K815.7, Z49.6; Uther 2004, tale types 53, 122K*, 207C, 220A, 926D.
[25] Walz 1832, 597–599.
[26] See e.g. the trial of the fox and the wolf in the Mesopotamian *Myth of the Fox* (mid-second millennium BC): Lambert 1960, 186–212; Kienast 2003; Jiménez 2017, 39–54, 377–395. Ancient Egyptian animal stories, illustrated on ostraca and papyri from the 12th century BC, portray the mouse and other animals as judges in official uniform, supervising the judicial execution of penalties: see Brunner-Traut 1968, 4–5, 14, 19–20; Omlin 1973, 29–30, 39; Houlihan 2001, 70–76. In the ancient Indian *Pañcatantra* a cunning old cat arbitrates a civil case between the partridge and the hare: Edgerton 1924, 369–371; Olivelle 1997, 118–120.

defendant Labes is pictured as a loyal and useful animal: he valiantly guards the door, watches over the sheep, chases wolves away and gives battle on his master's behalf; he is indefatigable, constantly moves around and endures hardship, to the point of feeding on scraps and bare bones (*Wasps* 950–969). By contrast, Kyon of Cydathenaeum remains at home and lives in laziness; yet he demands a share of every delicacy that is brought inside the house, and if he does not get it, he starts biting (970–972). Here the hard-working and tough hound, which assists his boss, is opposed to the spoiled and vociferous lazybones dog of the household.

Such contrasts between different types of dog are common in the Aesopic tradition. In a fable of the classic Greek collections (94 Hausrath/92 Perry) the bloodhound, which toils all day in the hunt, protests against the household dog, which remains at home and yet receives a share from the quarry. The domestic dog, however, blames the master, who assigned these roles to the two animals. This story displays the same antithesis between the indefatigable labour outdoors and the comforts of a well-fed housebound life, as applied to the pair of rival dogs in the *Wasps*.[27] In a tale of Babrius (153 Crusius, fable 329 Perry) the well-nurtured domestic dog, bred to fight against wild beasts in the arena, escapes and comes face to face with the stray dogs in the streets. The latter are lean and poorly fed, but do not need to risk their lives in fights. Analogous bipolar patterns are found in the age-old repertoire of Sumerian proverb-fables, from the early second millennium BC: the household dog, which tolerates the chain and collar, is opposed to the bloodhound or the shepherd's hound, which is accustomed to greater freedom.[28] The two dogs' portraits in the Aristophanic episode draw on this thematic repository.

It is not fortuitous that Aristophanes uses materials from the fable tradition to construct his scenic fantasy of the animal trial. The cantankerous Philocleon favours Aesopic fables and related didactic narratives; he uses them at various moments of the action, either as a means of amusement or as auxiliary rhetorical arguments when he confronts opposed parties.[29] Indeed, Philocleon expressly acknowledges his love for this genre, simultaneously revealing a fertile source from which he may have drawn a large part of his own repertoire of fables. When he enumerates the pleasures of his service at the Heliaia (548–630),

---

[27] See Giner Soria 1978; Schirru 2009, 59–60; Corbel-Morana 2012, 129.
[28] See Gordon 1958, 57; Alster 1997, 136.
[29] See Jedrkiewicz 1989, 347–348, 360–362; Rothwell 1995, 233, 239–254; van Dijk 1997, 38–39, 188–197; Pertsinidis 2009, 211–223; Schirru 2009, 20–21, 26–39, 56–70, 88–99, 150–165; Hall 2013, 289–293.

the old obsessive dicast includes among them the various ways by which the litigants try to amuse the judges and gain their favour. Some of the pleading men narrate myths; others recite jokes or funny stories of Aesop (Αἰσώπου τι γέλοιον, 566–567). Philocleon especially enjoys listening to Aesopic fables and other such stories at court. This is one of the greatest delights that he finds in his public office as a judge.[30]

This fact explains the subject-matter and the form that Bdelycleon selects for the domestic trial, which he offers to his father as a substitute of his beloved public processes. The young man's aim is to keep his father content at home, away from the popular courts. It is for this purpose that Bdelycleon sets up the household court in the first place, so that the old man may satisfy his obsessive passion without budging from the house. Most appropriately, Bdelycleon chooses a quarrel between two personified dogs as object of the trial: all the ingredients of this case (humanised animals, framework and motifs of the plot) recall the world of Aesopic animal fables. Philocleon had confessed, shortly before, that what he most enjoys in trials are the Aesopic stories which he hears from the contestants' lips. Fittingly, the son now enlivens before his father's eyes a mega-fable of the Aesopic type, in the form of a forensic lawsuit, so that the old man may take delight precisely in the kind of material he loves the most.

Bdelycleon's plan is not devoid of irony. Instead of assessing the content and importance of every judicial case, Philocleon admits that he expects to be entertained with Aesopic stories. Thus, the entire trial evolving in front of him becomes a large-scale Aesopic fable animated on stage. In Philocleon's eyes, this would look as though his best dream had come true: the tedious details of judicial procedure and litigating argumentation are put aside, and the whole process is occupied by the most enjoyable element of all. From the spectators' point of view, of course, the sarcastic parody of the Athenian legal system is evident. The low intellectual and moral level of the lot-appointed jurors, their gullibility and proneness to extra-judicial criteria and unrestrained favouritism, the cheap rhetorical artifices of the litigants and counsellors, all this is painfully discernible under the burlesque scenic metamorphosis of court practice.[31]

As indicated by Philocleon's comment on the litigants' means of *captatio benevolentiae*, the narration of Aesopic fables must have been a known practice

---

30 Cf. Jedrkiewicz 1989, 360; Pertsinidis 2009, 219–220; Hall 2013, 289–290. On this passage of the *Wasps* see also the comments of Donelan in this volume.
31 Cf. Sousa e Silva 1987–1988, 62–68.

in Athenian oratory,³² at least in court contexts. Aristotle confirms this in his *Rhetoric*, as he includes Aesopic stories (λόγοι [...] Αἰσώπειοι) among the common proofs employed in rhetorical speeches. Like other kinds of narrative (e.g. historical anecdotes), the Aesopic fables may be adduced as examples (παραδείγματα) to illustrate a point in a graphic manner or to support the speaker's argument (*Rh.* 1393a28–1394a18). Aristotle mentions two particular cases of this rhetorical application of fables; both occur, significantly, in speeches of a political character. Firstly, the wise poet Stesichorus told the fable of the horse and the stag to his fellow-citizens at Himera, in order to warn them against awarding excessive power to the ambitious dictator Phalaris. Secondly, the story of the fox and the dog-fleas was narrated by Aesop at Samos in defence of a demagogue, who was being tried on a capital charge related to public funds. Neither of these cases is taken from Attic oratory and both are anecdotal or legendary. Nevertheless, they testify to the incorporation of fables in political orations.³³

It is noteworthy, in this respect, that the bulk of Philocleon's experience as a dicast relates to trials of public offences, often with a clear political dimension: the old man and his comrades are called to judge Athenian politicians (157, 240–245), important officials who have stolen public money (552–558, 575, 626–627, 758–759), men accused of public misdeeds (590–600, 691–695) and cases related to the allies of Athens (281–285, 673–679). In combination, the references of Aristotle and of the *Wasps* suggest that the recital of fables was a recurrent auxiliary means of persuasion in speeches of political content— perhaps not only in public trials but also in the Assembly.³⁴

---

32 Cf. Bonner 1922; Meuli 1954, 87–88; Jedrkiewicz 1989, 360, 400–404; Rothwell 1995, 245–247; Hall 2006, 387–388; Kurke 2011, 156–158.
33 Cf. Jedrkiewicz 1987, 58–59; Rothwell 1995, 245–247; van Dijk 1997, 40–42; Kurke 2011, 150, 156.
34 There are also anecdotes in which the Athenian orators Demosthenes and Demades recite Aesopic fables while making political speeches before the *dēmos*: see Jedrkiewicz 1989, 401–403; van Dijk 1997, 296–305. However, no actual specimen of such stories is preserved in the extant corpus of Attic oratory from the fifth and fourth century. If the narration of fables was a known practice in Athenian public orations, why has it left no trace in the surviving published versions? This is a much-discussed question and various answers are proposed. The narration of fables may have been a rhetorical usage of the fifth century which starkly declined in the fourth, when the bulk of the extant Attic orations were composed; Meuli 1954, 87–88. According to other scholars, fables were employed in the oral delivery of the speeches; but since these stories were generally considered as popular and low-brow material, they were edited out by the prestigious fourth-century orators, when they revised their texts for definitive publication; see Bonner 1922, 103; Jedrkiewicz 1989, 401–403; Rothwell 1995, 246–247; Adrados 1999, 379–380; Hall 2006, 387; Kurke 2011, 156–158.

Thus, the ample presence of animal imagery and fable material in the Aristophanic trial of the dogs may also reflect rhetorical techniques used in the historical model of this scene. Cleon and Laches—or their supporters who were involved in the clash and the concomitant debates—may have included Aesopic animal tales in their speeches, in their effort to accuse the opponent or vindicate their own stance and services to the city.[35] These beast fables, told in the context of the rhetorical confrontations between Cleon and Laches, would have inspired Aristophanes to incorporate animal characters and various other fabulistic motifs in his fantastic scenic recast of the two politicians' conflict.

5 The Ideological Tenets of the Conflict

On the surface, the *Wasps* is a satire of the popular courts of the Heliaia and the judicial system of the Athenian democracy. In essence, the main targets of the comic attack are the populist demagogues, notably Cleon and his clique, as in all of Aristophanes' early plays.[36] The central issue in the first part of the comedy is the way in which Cleon manipulates the Athenian court system in order to annihilate his political enemies, blackmail his rivals or the allied states and collect large bribes. In the great *epirrhematic agōn*, which forms the ideological core of the play, Bdelycleon explains to his father in detail how the demagogues deceive the people and exploit the poor judges, in return for minimal remuneration, so as to forward their own political agenda, terrify their opponents and amass riches and offices (650–735).[37] As in earlier Aristophanic comedies, Cleon emerges as the greatest political villain, the veritable *katharma* of the state and the main source of corruption in the public life of Athens.[38]

---

35 On the use of animal imagery in Athenian public oratory, especially in rhetorical invective, see Apostolakis' chapter in this volume.
36 On Aristophanes' attacks against the demagogues cf. the chapters of Donelan, Apostolakis and Buis in this volume.
37 On Bdelycleon's arguments in the *agōn* cf. MacDowell 1995, 160–165; Olson 1996, 134–138; Rosenbloom 2002, 323–324; Edwards 2010, 331–335; Bertelli 2013, 115–116; Major 2013, 101–104; Saldutti 2014, 93–94; Biles and Olson 2015, xlix–lii. In spite of his overall dry image, Bdelycleon functions as Aristophanes' mouthpiece in this respect: see Thiercy 1986, 268; Reckford 1987, 254–255, 273–274; Hubbard 1991, 132–133, 136–137, 222–223; Olson 1996, 143–145; Telò 2010, 282–286; Biles 2011, 163–165; Biles and Olson 2015, lviii–lix.
38 On the satire against Cleon in the *Wasps* see Edmunds 1987, 51–57; Hubbard 1991, 126–133; MacDowell 1995, 162–170, 175–179; Storey 1995; Olson 1996, 145–149; Reinders 2001, 207–232, 240–242; Hutchinson 2011, 63–67; Saldutti 2014, 93–94, 155–159; Biles and Olson 2015, xliv–

The trial of the dogs forms part of the same strain of political critique. By use of comic invective and the figurative techniques of Aesopic narrative, this scene carries forward the anti-demagogic arguments set forth by Bdelycleon in the *agōn*.[39] The trial episode is a burlesque scenic representation of Cleon's effort to disgrace one of his major ideological opponents at that time. As noted above, Laches was on the rise as a representative of the moderate faction of Athenian politics, the one that wished to negotiate a peace treaty with the Spartans. Cleon's campaign to besmirch Laches' generalship in Sicily was aimed at discrediting one of the champions of this "pro-peace" party; by extension, Cleon's ultimate purpose must have been to combat the opponents of his and the other demagogues' belligerent policy. In many of his early plays Aristophanes blames indeed the demagogues for instigating and sustaining the Peloponnesian War because it serves their personal ambitions and benefits. Cleon and his corrupt clique are repeatedly shown to exploit the turbulent war situation in order to occupy state posts and consolidate their own power in the *polis*.[40] The mock trial of Laches/Labes is thus connected with Aristophanes' persistent criticism against the warmongering politicians and their pursuit of the disastrous war.[41]

In this context, it is interesting to examine again the two litigants' contrasting portrayals, as they emerge from the speeches for the prosecution and the defence (907–975).[42] In his discourse of accusation Kyon of Cydathenaeum admits that the basic motive of his complaint is not the theft of the Sicilian cheese *per se*; he is mostly annoyed because Labes ate the cheese alone and gave no share to Kyon (907–930). It is thus insinuated that Cleon does not care about the welfare of the *polis* but only about his personal profit. He is a rotten blackmailer, constantly in pursuit of bribes and illegal gains; and if someone dares push him aside and fails to buy off his complicity, Cleon sets up trials and manipulates the juries in order to destroy him. Similarly, in Bdelycleon's de-

---

lxii. On the Aristophanic vituperation of Cleon see also the chapters of Donelan and Buis in this volume. Donelan discusses, in particular, the presentation of the demagogue as an obnoxious villain (a *miaros* or *katharma*) in comic and oratorical invective.
39 Cf. Lenz 1980, 24–28; Olson 1996, 138–139; Hutchinson 2011, 65; Biles and Olson 2015, xliii, lii.
40 See e.g. Ar. *Ach.* 56–152, 595–619, *Eq.* 802–809, 1388–1395, *Vesp.* 672–695, *Pax* 632–648. Cf. Henderson 1990, 282–284; Olson 1991; MacDowell 1995, 46–79, 108, 191–192.
41 On the ideological background and political dimension of the dogs' trial see mainly Olson 1996, 138–142; Rosenbloom 2002, 294–300; Biles and Olson 2015, lii–lvi.
42 On the rhetorical structure and devices of these speeches cf. Murphy 1938, 86–87, 91–99, 106; Sousa e Silva 1987–1988, 64–68; Hubbard 2007, 500–502; Major 2013, 105–108.

fence of Labes Kyon is depicted as a self-interested loafer and coward, who remains securely at home and performs no labour, but always demands a share of the booty (970–972). Cleon is denounced as a ruthless opportunist who contributes nothing to the military effort but only takes advantage of the war to promote his own interests.

By contrast, Bdelycleon gives a much more favourable portrait of Labes/Laches. From the beginning of the episode the slave announces with certainty that the dog Labes has stolen the cheese, as though the animal has been caught red-handed in the larder (836–838). Throughout the procedure, Philocleon is convinced of the defendant's guilt (893–961); indeed, Labes' responsibility for the theft is never doubted. However, Bdelycleon adduces the testimony of the cheese-grater, one of the personified household utensils which are called as witnesses for the defence; according to this deposition, Labes did not himself devour the stolen cheese but had it grated and distributed to his soldiers (962–966). Bdelycleon also praises the other virtues of this faithful dog, who strenuously guards the house door and the flocks and indefatigably runs everywhere for his master's sake (950–969).

The symbolism is transparent. Laches is commended as a good soldier, who toils in expeditions all around the Greek world for the glory and benefit of Athens. Also, even though he is not impeccable in handling finances, Laches presents a significant difference from Cleon: he does not selfishly keep for himself the booty that he gains from military operations, but distributes it to the soldiers, the brave lads of the Athenian *dēmos*. The competent, zealous and dependable military commander is deemed far preferable to the manipulative demagogic leader. The good general looks after the city and its army; he keeps Athens safe.

These contrasting descriptions of the two opponents may reflect propagandistic stereotypes that were shared by factions in Athenian political life and were rhetorically recycled in the public strife between Cleon and Laches. General Laches or his supporters might have denigrated Cleon exactly as a war-mongering but non-combatant stay-at-home, who seeks to make profit from a war he does not actively wage. Laches, on the other hand, would have been extolled (or self-introduced) as a staunch defender of the security of the *polis* and a protector of the interests of troops and civilians alike. The argumentative Aristophanic portraits of the two litigant dogs are a grotesque scenic enlivenment of ideological tenets taken from the rhetorical confrontations between radicals and moderates in contemporary Athenian politics.⁴³

6 Conclusion

In the present essay, due to the limitations of space, the tracking of elements from Athenian political oratory has been restricted to a single Aristophanic scene. Many other plays of Aristophanes can be subjected to the same kind of analysis. The peace plays of the Archidamian War (*Acharnians*, *Peace*) reflect aspects of the discourse of the moderate, pro-peace faction of Athens, which tried to downplay the causes and the strategic importance of the war and to promote the idea of negotiations with Sparta.⁴⁴ The *Knights* may be ploughed in order to reconstruct Cleon's populist rhetoric and the reactions to it in the speeches of his upper-class opponents.⁴⁵ All this is material for a further, more extensive study.

We will never read the authentic orations of the statesmen of fifth-century Athens. Nevertheless, Attic Old Comedy, by means of its topical invective against political men of its time, may help us imagine their speeches and even hear the echo of some of their sensational phrases and key rhetorical techniques. Through the centuries-long relay of the textual tradition, our ears catch the sound of the words pronounced by the protagonists of a glorious and terrible age.

Bibliography

Adrados, F.R. (1999), *History of the Graeco-Latin Fable*, transl. L.A. Ray, ed. F.R. Adrados and G.-J. van Dijk, vol. I, Leiden/Boston.
Alster, B. (1997), *Proverbs of Ancient Sumer. The World's Earliest Proverb Collections*, Bethesda.
Apostolakis, K. (2014), 'Ιδιωτικά σκάνδαλα και δημόσια εικόνα: Ο Αριστογείτων στο στόχαστρο της δικανικής ρητορείας ([Δημ.] 25 και 26)', in: L. Athanassaki, T. Nikolaidis and D. Spath-

---

43 Cf. Mastromarco 1974, 60–61; Carter 1986, 117–119; Edmunds 1987, 55; MacDowell 1995, 166–170; Braund 1999; Reinders 2001, 230–231; Rosenbloom 2002, 296–299; Biles and Olson 2015, lii–lv. Cf. also Major's chapter in this volume for the conflict between democratic and oligarchic groups in classical Athens, as reflected and exploited in a law-court speech.
44 See Konstantakos 2021a.
45 Cf. Connor 1971, 96–108; Edmunds 1987; Fileni 2012.

aras (eds.), *Ιδιωτικός βίος και δημόσιος λόγος στην ελληνική αρχαιότητα και στον διαφωτισμό. Μελέτες αφιερωμένες στην Ιωάννα Γιατρομανωλάκη*, Herakleion, 201–230.

Bertelli, L. (2013), 'Democracy and Dissent: The Case of Comedy', in: J.P. Arnason, K.A. Raaflaub and P. Wagner (eds.), *The Greek Polis and the Invention of Democracy. A Politico-Cultural Transformation and Its Interpretations*, Malden, MA, 99–125.

Biles, Z.P. (2011), *Aristophanes and the Poetics of Competition*, Cambridge.

Biles, Z.P. and Olson, S.D. (2015), *Aristophanes: Wasps*, Oxford.

Bonner, R.J. (1922), 'Wit and Humor in Athenian Courts', in: *Classical Philology* 17, 97–103.

Braund, D. (1999), 'Laches at Acanthus: Aristophanes, *Wasps* 968–9', in: *Classical Quarterly* 49, 321–325.

Brock, R. (2013), *Greek Political Imagery from Homer to Aristotle*, London.

Brunner-Traut, E. (1968), *Altägyptische Tiergeschichte und Fabel. Gestalt und Strahlkraft*, Darmstadt.

Carmignato, A. (1999), 'A proposito dell'autenticità della XXV orazione del Corpus demostenico (*Contro Aristogitone I*)', in: *Aevum Antiquum* 12, 91–112.

Carter, L.B. (1986), *The Quiet Athenian*, Oxford.

Connor, W.R. (1971), *The New Politicians of Fifth-Century Athens*, Princeton.

Corbel-Morana, C. (2012), *Le bestiaire d'Aristophane*, Paris.

Desfray, S. (1999), 'Oracles et animaux dans les *Cavaliers* d'Aristophane', in: *L'Antiquité Classique* 68, 35–56.

Dover, K.J. (1972), *Aristophanic Comedy*, Berkeley/Los Angeles.

Edmunds, L. (1987), *Cleon, Knights, and Aristophanes' Politics*, Lanham.

Edgerton, F. (1924), *The Panchatantra Reconstructed. An Attempt to Establish the Lost Original Sanskrit Text of the Most Famous of Indian Story-Collections on the Basis of the Principal Extant Versions*, vol. II, New Haven.

Edwards, A.T. (2010), 'Tyrants and Flatterers: *Kolakeia* in Aristophanes' *Knights* and *Wasps*', in: P. Mitsis and C. Tsagalis (eds.), *Allusion, Authority, and Truth. Critical Perspectives on Greek Poetic and Rhetorical Praxis*, Berlin/New York, 303–337.

Faraguna, M. (2011), 'Lykourgan Athens?', in: V. Azoulay and P. Ismard (eds.), *Clisthène et Lycurgue d'Athènes. Autour du politique dans la cité classique*, Paris, 67–86.

Fileni, M.G. (2012), 'Commedia e oratoria politica: Cleone nel teatro di Aristofane', in: F. Perusino and M. Colantonio (eds.), *La commedia greca e la storia*, Pisa, 79–128.

Franco, C. (2014), *Shameless. The Canine and the Feminine in Ancient Greece*, transl. M. Fox, Oakland.

Giangiulio, M. (1997), 'Atene e la Sicilia occidentale dal 424 al 415', in: *Seconde giornate internazionali di studi sull'area Elima. Atti*, vol. II, Pisa, 865–887.

Giner Soria, M.C. (1978), 'El juicio del perro, *Vespae* 891–1008', in: *Actas del V Congreso Español de Estudios Clásicos*, Madrid, 269–275.

Gomme, A.W. (1956), *A Historical Commentary on Thucydides*, vol. II: *Books II-III*, Oxford.

Gordon, E.I. (1958), 'Sumerian Animal Proverbs and Fables: "Collection Five"', in: *Journal of Cuneiform Studies* 12, 43–75.

Hall, E. (2006), *The Theatrical Cast of Athens. Interactions between Ancient Greek Drama and Society*, Oxford.

Hall, E. (2013), 'The Aesopic in Aristophanes', in: E. Bakola, L. Prauscello and M. Telò (eds.), *Greek Comedy and the Discourse of Genres*, Cambridge, 277–297.

Hansen, M.H. (1976), *Apagoge, Endeixis and Ephegesis against Kakourgoi, Atimoi and Pheugontes. A Study in the Athenian Administration of Justice in the Fourth Century B.C.*, Odense.

Harris, E.M. (2013), 'How to Address the Athenian Assembly: Rhetoric and Political Tactics in the Debate about Mytilene (Thuc. 3.37–50)', in: *Classical Quarterly* 63, 94–109.
Harris, E.M. (2018), *Demosthenes: Speeches 23–26*, Austin.
Henderson, J. (1990), 'The *Dēmos* and the Comic Competition', in: J.J. Winkler and F.I. Zeitlin (eds.), *Nothing to Do with Dionysos? Athenian Drama in Its Social Context*, Princeton, 271–313.
Hornblower, S. (1987), *Thucydides*, London.
Houlihan, P.F. (2001), *Wit and Humour in Ancient Egypt*, London.
Hubbard, T.K. (1991), *The Mask of Comedy. Aristophanes and the Intertextual Parabasis*, Ithaca/London.
Hubbard, T.K. (2007), 'Attic Comedy and the Development of Theoretical Rhetoric', in: I. Worthington (ed.), *A Companion to Greek Rhetoric*, Malden, MA, 490–508.
Hutchinson, G.O. (2011), 'House Politics and City Politics in Aristophanes', in: *Classical Quarterly* 61, 48–70.
Imperio, O. (2004), *Parabasi di Aristofane: Acarnesi, Cavalieri, Vespe, Uccelli*, Bari.
Irwin, E. (2005), *Solon and Early Greek Poetry. The Politics of Exhortation*, Cambridge.
Jacoby, F. (1954), *Die Fragmente der griechischen Historiker*, vol. IIIb (Supplement): *A Commentary on the Ancient Historians of Athens*, Leiden.
Jedrkiewicz, S. (1987), 'La favola esopica nel processo di argomentazione orale fino al IV sec. a.C.', in: *Quaderni Urbinati di Cultura Classica* 27, 35–63.
Jedrkiewicz, S. (1989), *Sapere e paradosso nell'antichità: Esopo e la favola*, Roma.
Jedrkiewicz, S. (2006), 'Bestie, gesti e *logos*. Una lettura delle *Vespe* di Aristofane', in: *Quaderni Urbinati di Cultura Classica* 82, 61–91.
Jiménez, E. (2017), *The Babylonian Disputation Poems. With Editions of the Series of the Poplar, Palm and Vine, the Series of the Spider, and the Story of the Poor, Forlorn Wren*, Leiden.
Kagan, D. (1974), *The Archidamian War*, Ithaca/London.
Kienast, B. (2003), *Iškar šēlebi: Die Serie vom Fuchs*, Stuttgart.
Konstantakos, I.M. (2021a), 'Divided Audiences and How to Win Them Over: The Case of Aristophanes' *Acharnians*', in: A. Michalopoulos, A. Serafim, A. Vatri and F. Beneventano della Corte (eds.), *The Rhetoric of Unity and Division in Ancient Literature*, Berlin/Boston, 191–211.
Konstantakos, I.M. (2021b), 'Staged Suspense: Scenic Spectacle, Anxious Expectation, and Dramatic Enthralment in Aristophanic Theatre', in: I.M. Konstantakos and V. Liotsakis (eds.), *Suspense in Ancient Greek Literature*, Berlin/Boston, 191–226.
Kremmydas, C. (2017), '*Ēthos* and Logical Argument in Thucydides' Assembly Debates', in: S. Papaioannou, A. Serafim and B. de Vela (eds.), *The Theatre of Justice. Aspects of Performance in Greco-Roman Oratory and Rhetoric*, Leiden, 93–113.
Kurke, L. (2011), *Aesopic Conversations. Popular Tradition, Cultural Dialogue, and the Invention of Greek Prose*, Princeton.
Lambert, W.G. (1960), *Babylonian Wisdom Literature*, Oxford.
Lauriola, R. (2004), 'Aristofane, Eracle e Cleone: sulla duplicità di un'immagine aristofanea', in: *Eikasmos* 15, 85–99.
Lenz, L. (1980), 'Komik und Kritik in Aristophanes' "Wespen"', in: *Hermes* 108, 15–44.
Lenz, L. (2014), *Aristophanes: Wespen*, Berlin.
Lilja, S. (1976), *Dogs in Ancient Greek Poetry*, Helsinki.
Lind, H. (1990), *Der Gerber Kleon in den "Rittern" des Aristophanes. Studien zur Demagogenkomödie*, Frankfurt a. M.

MacDowell, D.M. (1971), *Aristophanes: Wasps*, Oxford.
MacDowell, D.M. (1995), *Aristophanes and Athens. An Introduction to the Plays*, Oxford.
MacDowell, D.M. (2009), *Demosthenes the Orator*, Oxford.
Major, W.E. (2013), *The Court of Comedy. Aristophanes, Rhetoric, and Democracy in Fifth-Century Athens*, Columbus, OH.
Martin, G. (2009), *Divine Talk. Religious Argumentation in Demosthenes*, Oxford.
Mastromarco, G. (1974), *Storia di una commedia di Atene*, Firenze.
Meuli, K. (1954), 'Herkunft und Wesen der Fabel', in: *Schweizerisches Archiv für Volkskunde* 50, 65–88.
Moneti, I. (1993), 'Il presunto processo contro Lachete', in: *Civiltà Classica e Cristiana* 14, 245–254.
Murphy, C.T. (1938), 'Aristophanes and the Art of Rhetoric', in: *Harvard Studies in Classical Philology* 49, 69–113.
Newiger, H.-J. (1957), *Metapher und Allegorie. Studien zu Aristophanes*, Munich.
Olivelle, P. (1997), *Pañcatantra. The Book of India's Folk Wisdom*, Oxford.
Olson, S.D. (1991), 'Dicaeopolis' Motivations in Aristophanes' *Acharnians*', in: *Journal of Hellenic Studies* 111, 200–203.
Olson, S.D. (1996), 'Politics and Poetry in Aristophanes' *Wasps*', in: *Transactions of the American Philological Association* 126, 129–150.
Olson, S.D. (2016), *Eupolis: Heilotes – Chrysoun Genos. Translation and Commentary, Fragmenta Comica* 8.2, Heidelberg.
Omlin, J.A. (1973), *Der Papyrus 55001 und seine satirisch-erotischen Zeichnungen und Inschriften*, Torino.
Pertsinidis, S. (2009), 'The Fabulist Aristophanes', in: *Fabula* 50, 208–226.
Reckford, K.J. (1987), *Aristophanes' Old-and-New Comedy. Six Essays in Perspective*, Chapel Hill.
Reinders, P. (2001), *Demos Pyknites. Untersuchungen zur Darstellung des Demos in der Alten Komödie*, Stuttgart/Weimar.
Rosenbloom, D. (2002), 'From *Ponēros* to *Pharmakos*: Theater, Social Drama, and Revolution in Athens, 428–404 BCE', in: *Classical Antiquity* 21, 283–346.
Rothwell, K.S. (1995), 'Aristophanes' *Wasps* and the Sociopolitics of Aesop's Fables', in: *Classical Journal* 90, 233–254.
Saldutti, V. (2014), *Cleone. Un politico ateniese*, Bari.
Schirru, S. (2009), *La favola in Aristofane*, Berlin.
Sealey, R. (1967), 'Pseudo-Demosthenes XIII and XXV', in: *Revue des Études Grecques* 80, 250–255.
Sealey, R. (1993), *Demosthenes and His Time. A Study in Defeat*, Oxford.
Serafim, A. (2020), 'Comic Invective in the Public Forensic Speeches of Attic Oratory', in: *Hellenica* 68, 23–42.
Slater, N.W. (2002), *Spectator Politics. Metatheatre and Performance in Aristophanes*, Philadelphia.
Sommerstein, A.H. (2004), 'Harassing the Satirist: The Alleged Attempts to Prosecute Aristophanes', in: I. Sluiter and R.M. Rosen (eds.), *Free Speech in Classical Antiquity*, Leiden/Boston, 145–174.
Sousa e Silva, M. de F. (1987–1988), 'Crítica à retórica na comédia de Aristófanes', in: *Humanitas* 39–40, 43–104.

Spatharas, D. (2013), 'The Sycophant's Farm: Animals and Rhetoric in *Against Aristogeiton I*', in: *Ariadne* 19, 77–95.
Storey, I.C. (1995), '*Wasps* 1284–91 and the Portrait of Kleon in the *Wasps*', in: *Scholia* 4, 3–23.
Storey, I.C. (2003), *Eupolis. Poet of Old Comedy*, Oxford.
Taillardat, J. (1965), *Les images d'Aristophane. Études de langue et de style*, Paris.
Telò, M. (2010), 'Embodying the Tragic Father(s): Autobiography and Intertextuality in Aristophanes', in: *Classical Antiquity* 29, 278–326.
Thiercy, P. (1986), *Aristophane: fiction et dramaturgie*, Paris.
Thompson, S. (1955–1958), *Motif-Index of Folk-Literature*, vol. I-VI, Bloomington.
Treves, P. (1936), 'Apocrifi demostenici', in: *Athenaeum* 14, 233–258.
Uther, H.-J. (2004), *The Types of International Folktales. A Classification and Bibliography Based on the System of Antti Aarne and Stith Thompson*, vol. I, Helsinki.
van Dijk, G.-J. (1997), Αἶνοι, Λόγοι, Μῦθοι. *Fables in Archaic, Classical, and Hellenistic Greek Literature. With a Study of the Theory and Terminology of the Genre*, Leiden.
Walz, C. (1832), *Rhetores Graeci*, vol. I, Stuttgart.
Westlake, H.D. (1969), *Essays on the Greek Historians and Greek History*, Manchester.
Worman, N. (2008), *Abusive Mouths in Classical Athens*, Cambridge.
Wright, M. (2007), 'Comedy and the Trojan War', in: *Classical Quarterly* 57, 412–431.

Wilfred E. Major
Democracy, Poverty, Comic Heroism and Oratorical Strategy in Lysias 24

> Some folks are born, silver spoon in hand.
> Lord, don't they help themselves...
> but when the taxman comes to the door,
> Lord, the house looks like a rummage sale, yes.
> It ain't me, it ain't me, I ain't no millionaire's son, no...
>
> John Fogerty, "Fortunate Son"

Abstract: The disabled speaker of Lysias 24 argues for the retention of his public disability pension, but with little discussion of either his physical disability or his financial resources. Rather he primarily attacks his elite prosecutor as jealous, delusional and morally compromised. Unaddressed in scholarship is the question of why these techniques constitute effective oratorical strategy. Here two dynamics of stage comedy are relevant: (1) the success of a protagonist braggart and (2) how this model of success maps onto democratic ideology in Athens. Within the political landscape of democratic Athens, poverty was a major ideological flashpoint that elites struggled to navigate with the mass democratic working class. In the corpus of Classical Greek oratory, Lysias 24 is unique in its rhetorical stance in this ongoing discourse, in that it boldly asserts the moral superiority of the poor and resulting moral weakness of the wealthy. Taking this stance re-enacts the pattern of engagement from stage comedy and signals allegiance to the priorities of the democratic poor in Athens. This speech thus preserves a valuable and underrepresented dynamic in the dialogue in democratic Athens between the poor and the wealthy, and the role of comic abuse in that conversation.

The brief speech in Lysias' oratorical corpus wherein a disabled man defends the continuation of a public stipend for himself has prompted confusion among modern scholars and more than its fair share of derision. As Usher summarises, "The lack of firm evidence of any kind in this speech has baffled some commentators and exasperated others, and has led yet more to suppose that it was never delivered in an actual trial".[1] Usher himself supposes that that Lysias published

---
1 Usher 1985, 263.

the speech to display his ability to be successful with a difficult case. This, at least, provides a motive that results in the extant text of the speech, but he does not address what technique the speech demonstrates. Carey fills in this omission with what he sees as the cynical deployment of "diversionary digression" and summarises the speech's effectiveness as "based on a cool assessment of the remarkable weakness of the case and the need to discourage close scrutiny by the Boule, but not of course in the sense that it is meant to present a statement of the case which appeals to logic. The logographer's technique in this speech may reasonably be described as verbal guerrilla tactics, a regular sequence of attacks on his subject followed by retreats into entertaining or emotive irrelevance".[2] Harding is still harsher, finding the defendant "an *alazōn*, if there ever was one, and one who, through the perverse incongruity of his arguments, personified the comic representation of rhetoric", and the entire speech a parody.[3] As to how and why Lysias would ever have taken this case, Todd speculates that Lysias might have reduced his usual fee because of a personal connection to the defendant and suspects that Lysias had the goal of "encouraging [the Boule] to laugh the case out of court".[4]

The intensity of these comments suggests that these scholars find the speech effective enough to demand explanation (Harding even acknowledges that it is a "superb speech", 204), yet disturbing enough to require deflating it. Somehow this speech strikes a nerve, and I suggest that this nerve vibrates deep in the scholars' elitist preferences for the context and purpose of Athenian oratory. Ironically, the angst and derision among scholars arise from much the type of elitism that the defendant in this ancient speech criticises and mocks. Specifically Lysias has the defendant weaponise a democratically comic invective against the prosecutor. Whereas, as this volume as a whole demonstrates, comedy permeates invective performance in oratory, the particular invective in Lysias 24 is unique in extant Athenian oratory, though it likely represents a perspective and technique that was more common than this chance survival indicates.[5] Where most personal invective in Greek oratory offers variations on the ways elites undercut the status of other elites, in this speech the defendant comically undercuts an elite prosecutor, not so much for the prosecutor's indi-

---

[2] Carey 1990, 49.
[3] Harding 1994, 202–206.
[4] Tod 2000, 253–254; cf. Dillon 1995, 37–39 on the tradition of further marginalising the speech by impugning its authenticity.
[5] See especially Donelan, Apostolakis and Serafim in this volume for surveys and analysis of the use of comic invective in Attic oratory.

vidual failings, but simply on the basis of his wealth and, as Lysias 24 presents it, the inevitable hubris that attends such wealth.

My argument requires peeling back several layers of the contextual and cultural assumptions that previous scholars consider axiomatic when analyzing Lysias 24 and, indeed, the Greek oratorical corpus in general. I identify these expectations as: (1) that the legal case is fundamentally about the defendant's financial assets, lack of them, and his consequent merit in receiving a public pension, so demonstrating the level of these assets should resolve the case; (2) the personality and social life of the defendant should not play a role in deciding the case, but the speech implies that this could be a factor in both the prosecution and the defence; (3) Lysias is selecting and deploying techniques from a warehouse of canonical rhetorical techniques to win a case that is legally and morally compromised.

These assumptions range from wrong to implausible to problematic. To begin with the last assumption, while Lysias 24 cannot be dated to a specific year, the legal case and this case must have been during the first third of the fourth century, because the defendant lived as an adult during the reign of the Thirty in 403 BC (24.25). As such, the formal discipline of rhetorical training was much less focalised than these scholars assume. It would take another generation or more before speakers in court and the logographers supplying them had a canon of techniques and rhetorical structures that they would, by default, follow or depart from.[6] Thus, for example, Carey assumes that certain topics are "digressions" based on criteria about what was supposed to be "central" to Greek oratory, but this was not yet the case during the time of Lysias' career. Lysias could well choose to make the techniques and topics that Carey identifies central to this speech and not consider them digressions.

As for the first assumption, it is unlikely, even unreasonable, to expect that a basic financial audit of the defendant's assets would resolve this case. If it had been so straightforward, there is little to no reason to expect that this speech would exist. Legal cases that resulted in extant oratory were complex and fraught. As Scafuro has documented and analysed, there were layers of strategy, motions and arbitration to resolve an issue rather than have it reach a full trial.[7] If this case involved straightforward documenting of the defendant's fraudulent recording of his assets, the case would not have developed into one complex enough that our speech would serve as but one component. Something

---

6 Schiappa 1999.
7 Scafuro 1997.

larger was at stake and something more difficult to resolve than adding up the *minae* of the defendant's assets.

This folds into the second assumption, for, at some level, previous scholars have recognised this tension, that there must be some reason that this case continued to the point that this speech presumes. At best, the speculation is that there was something charismatic about the defendant that obviated the straightforward auditing and settling of the charge. What scholars have refused to consider or give credence to, however, is that the defendant and the speech were plausible because of the characterisation of the prosecutor as an elite bully who was persecuting a member of the *penētes* in Athens. Scholars are ready to believe that the "poor" defendant is a fraud, but they never consider it credible that the wealthy prosecutor is an envious bully. Moreover, although Lysias builds this particular defence speech around the idea that the prosecutor is a psychologically unbalanced abuser, scholars never address why such a characterisation might resonate with members of the Boule, either in this particular case or more broadly.[8] Quite the contrary, at best they think that the members of the Boule would find the tactic so comic that they would let the defendant continue his fraud as a sort of reward for being entertaining. In this line of reasoning, scholars, especially Harding, can see some of the techniques of Greek stage comedy at play in the speech, but miss entirely why these motifs are especially relevant and effective.

I propose to turn the dismissals by Harding and others on their heads by analyzing the speech from the perspective that the ideas and characterisations in it are legitimate, that they resonated for logical reasons within the sociopolitical context of early fourth-century democratic Athens. I mean specifically that the case represented, even typified, an instance of an elite litigant obsessively manoeuvring the levers of state authority against a vulnerable member of the working class in Athens.[9] The use of techniques and traditions from stage comedy is especially appropriate, then, as these techniques dramatised and gave voice to characters whose economic options were constricted because of their dependence on pay for labour and a level of financial assets that were thus attainable in this economic bracket. Consequently, the speech is not a remote

---

8 See the analysis of 24.3 and 24.14 for the speech's references to the prosecutor's irrationality, and cf. Kazantzidis in this volume for context of this type of invective in comedy and oratory.
9 I use the term "working class" for those grouped together under the rubric *penia*, because of the embedded associations of *penia* with individuals depending on pay for labour as sustenance for their daily needs, as contrasted with the *ptochoi*, which maps better onto the modern term "poverty", as designating individuals whose income is insufficient to acquire basic needs consistently. See Taylor 2017, 34–38.

curiosity, but a valuable document about the power and urgency of class abuse in fourth-century Athens, along with the techniques in the theatre and the courtroom where so much dialogue and negotiation about these tensions took place.

As the assumptions, methodology and conceptual frameworks previous commentators have used to dismiss this speech are ill-matched to the speech itself as I plan to analyse it, I will also use different frames to chart the workings of the speech. First, this speech snaps to the grid of socio-political negotiations between mass and elite factions of the citizen population of Athens, negotiations, as charted by Josiah Ober, that took place in political gatherings and via public debate and oratory, continually, with ideological consistency, from the restoration of the democracy in 403 BC until the disenfranchisement of citizens in the wake of the Macedonian conquest in 322 BC.[10] Ober's influential analysis pursues multiple axes by which elite litigants are distinguished from the non-elite judges, but for this speech I wish to focus on two of these axes, since Lysias and the defendant, as do many voices from fourth-century democratic Athens, weave these two together: (1) the financial axis with wealthy elites, especially the liturgical class, toward one pole, and the *penētes*, those working in "poverty" toward the opposite pole and (2) the axis of moral behaviour, labelled as *agathos, kalos* and so on toward one pole, and *ponēros, kakos, aischros* and so on toward the other pole.

Recent scholarship on *penia* in democratic Athens is relevant and informative for one of these axes more than the other.[11] This work seeks to map *penia* in the Athenian democracy onto modern sociological analyses of the poor and poverty-stricken. For noble reasons, modern categories try to uncouple the moral hierarchy that that has so long demonised the poor. Doing so is valuable and revealing in many ways, but of limited application to the current project, because it blunts the criticism that Lysias and his defendant level at the elite litigant. In the case of Lysias 24, there is nothing controversial about saying that the defendant projects himself as one of the citizen *penētes* of Athens, in opposition to his elite prosecutor. For present purposes, the contours of these identifications matter much more than how this depiction of *penia* matches onto modern analyses of poverty. Here I put a priority on unpacking how the speech explicitly and implicitly subverts the hierarchal rungs in the ideology of the elites in Athens, an ideology that maintained that financial assets rise in tandem with moral behaviour and political rectitude. Lysias, with the expectation

---

10 Ober 1989, cf. Sinclair 1988, esp. 77–105.
11 Notably Cecchet 2015 and Taylor 2017.

that the Boule will sympathise with subverting this ideology, promotes the dynamic that a financially elite citizen, especially one who prefers some citizens of the democracy to be poor, is morally deficient and politically at odds with the democracy.

As for rhetorical technique, rather than citing parallels from eras when catalogues of such techniques suffused pedagogical curricula and became a wellspring of references for modern scholars, I want to begin with a more basic technique, the building of rapport with the audience, as characterised and analysed by Serafim, who focuses on "sincerity", which he explains, "if used skilfully, enables the speaker to forge a rapport with the audience and reinforces his or her ability to communicate a message to the recipient and move hearers and viewers into a state of receptivity".[12] Serafim brings rhetorical sincerity into union and contrast with theatrical sincerity, where a performer, an actor, a *hypocritēs*, generates sincerity and rapport with spectators. There is, accordingly, a certain tension involved in a performer creating such a rapport and urging action based on it, whether via oratory or theatrical performance, because the rapport based on sincerity can run into conflict with the creative and staged creation of the "sincere" character. Lysias in fact finds a way to incorporate the traditions of stage comedy in a way that bolsters his defendant's appeal rather than threatening to undermine it, as we will see. Overall, though, the hazards and fraught tensions of stage performance are not so much my focus as articulating how Lysias and his defendant developed a strategy, based on prejudices, ill-founded or not, or even personal experiences, that they believed would be effective in this component of their defence before the sitting members of the Boule in the early fourth century.

Scholars to date have all but unanimously reckoned that this effectiveness resulted from Lysias' subversion of logical and noble reasoning, but I suggest the effectiveness, whatever its extent, would have come from the sitting members of the Boule having direct and indirect experience of financially elite Athenian citizens imposing their will on the working-class citizens of Athens, individually or collectively. The resulting speech portrays the elite prosecutor as an individual of character and morality quite inconsistent with the ideological hierarchy dictating that financial resources, birthright and moral rectitude proceed upward and downward in tandem with each other.

The defendant of Lysias 24 bluntly challenges this idea and, conversely, puts himself forward as a democratic individual simultaneously of deformed physical ability, limited financial assets, yet of the highest order of civic right-

---

[12] Serafim 2019, 347.

eousness. Lysias and the defendant expect that the particulars of the defendant's financial assets are less important than targeting the realities of economic inequality in Athens. Whether they were right in their calculus on this particular occasion, we do not, and almost certainly will never, know, but it is crucial to recognise that the moral failings of the character of the financial elite in Athens at the time were such that it seemed pragmatic to make the perception of these failures the centrepiece of this defence. As such, the text of this speech is extraordinarily valuable, for it, unusually among all surviving texts from democratic Athens, articulates a voice that is exceptionally frank in deriding the hypocrisy of the wealthy. It is unsettlingly revealing that scholars have felt motivated to short-circuit such a depiction before, or rather, instead of, giving any consideration to the possibility that such a depiction could reflect the reality of life in democratic Athens at the time.[13]

In response to, even contradicting, previous scholarly judgments, then, I offer a reading of Lysias 24 predicated on the supposition that enough members of the Boule would recognise and sympathise with the idea that the wealthy would obsessively persecute and prosecute members of the working class of Athens. The result would be that, if such a working class individual represented even a symbolic contrast to the elite's insistence that those in *penia* were in need of moral resurrection, while those in *penia* themselves rejected this ideological notion, and for a few generations in democratic Athens, the *demos* had the political leverage to render judgment accordingly, so this could be a formula for legal success.

In Lysias 24, the defendant declares immediately that his defence will address equally the quality of the life that he leads and expose the poor character of his prosecutor, specifically that he is a jealous liar (ψευδόμενον... φθόνου... φθόνον, 24.1). Commentators have focused mostly on denying the success of the defendant's portrayal of his own situation but little explored the portrait of the prosecutor. It will be, however, the prosecutor's behaviour and character that the defendant develops more and where he raises the stakes about what the legal case entails, so the defendant immediately extends his characterisation. The prosecutor is a liar to allege that personal enmity (ἐχθρόν, 24.2) drives the case. The defendant would not even associate with the prosecutor because of

---

13 See Akrigg 2019, who argues that the economic and demographic patterns of Athens in the fifth century precipitated the conflict over inequality in the fourth century.

the prosecutor's immorality (πονηρίας).[14] These two related counter-charges, that the prosecutor is immoral and is barely capable, if capable at all, of speaking the truth, become the key components of the defence on which the speech expands and increasingly links to the prosecutor's status as an obtuse member of the financial elite. Commentators take this shift as deceitful and inappropriate, for they take it for granted that the charge brought by the elite prosecutor has merit and that the defendant should respond according to the terms brought by the prosecutor. Instead, however, Lysias advances the idea that the prosecution is simply invalid because of the prosecutor's inferiority of character, a deficiency evident because of the prosecutor's wealth. Lysias next declares the moral hierarchy between the defendant in specific terms: the defendant is the better citizen (βελτίων εἰμὶ πολίτης). It is the health of his soul (τοῖς τῆς ψυχῆς ἐπιτηδεύμασιν ἰᾶσθαι) that trumps his physical disability (τὰ τοῦ σώματος δυστυχήματα). Otherwise his mental health (τὴν διάνοιαν) would be afflicted as his body is and, by that measure, the same as that of the prosecutor (τί τούτου διοίσω; 24.3), i.e., the prosecutor is as crippled in his mental capacities as the defendant is in his body.

The defendant now declares that his exposition about his right to the pension will be as brief as possible (διὰ βραχυτάτων ἐρῶ, referring to 24.4). The exposition itself has drawn the greatest ire from scholars. Adams imagines that the prosecutor is a well-intentioned "reformer" and so calls the speech's summary of the charges "an absurd travesty", for example, although there is no external evidence about the charges.[15] The defendant summarises his income, family situation and physical ability (24.4–6). The point, the speech promptly emphasises, is not the exact level of the defendant's net worth or income. The key issues are the conduct of the Boule and the ramifications for other citizens in similar straits in Athens. The Boule must not, insists the speaker, abandon its reputation for being exceptionally merciful (ἐλεημονέστατοι) even toward those who had not experienced wrong (περὶ τοὺς οὐδὲν ἔχοντας κακόν), because it would dishearten others in Athens who are similarly disabled (μηδ' ἐμὲ τολμήσαντες ἀδικῆσαι καὶ τοὺς ἄλλους τοὺς ὁμοίως ἐμοὶ διακειμένους ἀθυμῆσαι ποιήσητε, 24.7–8).[16]

---

14 My thanks to one of the reviewers of this volume who points out helpfully that the label *ponēria* here is consistent with mass democratic invective, while elites on the other side use it to characterise the *penētes*.
15 Adams 1905, 233, 236, 240. Contrast the moderate assessment of Dillon 1995.
16 See Serafim 2017, 54–60 on this technique in the context of oratory and performance. Cf. Loraux 1986 on the trope of Athens as exceptionally merciful.

The deeper issue is the chasm between the rich and poor among Athenian citizens. The speaker has declared how good a citizen he is, but to this wealthy prosecutor, he is not poor enough. The defendant calls out the prosecutor's hypocrisy on this point: δοκεῖ δέ μοι τῆς πενίας τῆς ἐμῆς τὸ μέγεθος ὁ κατήγορος ἂν ἐπιδεῖξαι σαφέστατα μόνος ἀνθρώπων, "I think the extent of my *penia* is such that he alone could identify it quite clearly" (24.9), but, of course, only if the context were one where the property of the wealthy were at stake. The defendant explains, εἰ γὰρ ἐγὼ κατασταθεὶς χορηγὸς τραγῳδοῖς προκαλεσαίμην αὐτὸν εἰς ἀντίδοσιν, δεκάκις ἂν ἕλοιτο χορηγῆσαι μᾶλλον ἢ ἀντιδοῦναι ἅπαξ, "if I were appointed the liturgy of producing a tragedy and brought the legal challenge of a property exchange in court, he would sponsor a tragedy ten times before he would exchange his property for mine just once". These are the different scales of poverty and wealth, depending on whose wealth is at stake. The wealthy prosecutor, because he is a bald liar driven by envy (24.1), is obsessed with the defendant not quite being poor enough for public welfare. If this were a court case where the prosecutor had to sponsor the production of a tragic performance, a public expense imposed on wealthy individuals, who could, if they pursued the measure, use the *antidosis* procedure to exchange property with a wealthier individual to avoid the burden,[17] well, then, to this prosecutor, this defendant would seem frighteningly poor and the wealthy litigant would rather take on the burden of this liturgy ten times than live the "poor" life of the defendant. Such is the hypocrisy of the wealthy in this example.

How would this idea appear to members of the Boule? There is no reason to suppose that any individual on the Boule at any time would react identically to any other, of course, but we can consider a range of options.[18] Shuckburgh, for example, finds "grim humour in such a man talking of an 'exchange of properties'" (326), which suits not only the horror of a number of scholars about this speech but plausibly also how those of the liturgical class in Athens would likely react.[19] For supporters of the prevailing democracy, however, the defendant's point could well have been a stinging warning more than ghoulish nightmare. As Dillon (1995) has argued, the state-subsidised allowance for this type of defendant was not, at least not exclusively or predominantly, a grant driven by humanitarian concerns. Rather, like other public pay, and like the ever-increasing strictures put on jury activity, it was a bulwark against the financial elite in Athens using their wealth to wield undue, and undemocratic, influence

---

17 See Christ 1998 for analysis of elite litigants the *antidosis* procedure.
18 On "interpretive communities" in the audience of Attic oratory, see Serafim 2017, 5–6.
19 Christ 1998.

by using their financial leverage on poorer citizens. It is one thing for there to be rich and poor in Athens, but another for the rich to subvert democratic egalitarianism by using wealth to influence political decision-making.[20] The defendant of Lysias 24 raises the spectre of a wealthy litigant who wants to make sure that a certain citizen is poor. Why? So that the citizen can be bribed into the sphere of influence of an influential wealthy citizen. It will not be the last statement in this speech to raise this spectre. From the perspective of the elite, this is perhaps a discursive digression, as Carey would characterise it, but from a democratic perspective, this is putting a case directly in the cross-currents of a powerful issue in the ongoing governance of the Athenian democracy.

Lysias next wants to firm up the speaker's credibility in terms of *penia*, by demonstrating that he understands what disability and financial constraints really mean. Personal travel, for example, means riding on borrowed horses. The prosecutor thinks that riding a horse derives from hubris and wealth. It really derives from the limited opportunities facing those in *penia*, that the defendant must borrow horses to travel, for if someone like him had adequate financial means, he would choose to ride a mule with a saddle (24.12), a sort of choice that the wealthy prosecutor would not understand, but one Lysias expects that members of the Boule will find sympathetic. As Lysias characterises it in this speech, it is yet another mark of the prosecutor's moral failing, his absolute shamelessness (ἀναισχυντία, 24.13), that from this example the prosecutor seeks to prove that the speaker is not even disabled.

Lysias now again brings an example of the hypocrisy of the rich. Imagine, suggests the defendant, that he is not disabled, so now, in the eyes of the prosecutor, he is not disabled and not poor. But, continues Lysias, let him enter the lottery for the position of one of the nine archons, a prominent office that would be confer prestige upon its holder, traditionally an aristocrat. No doubt in this scenario the prosecutor would consider the defendant disabled, poor and unqualified for office (24.14). Hypocrisy now becomes outright absurdity, he continues and concludes: οὔτε ὑμεῖς τούτῳ τὴν αὐτὴν ἔχετε γνώμην "you do not think this", and even the prosecutor does not believe it, when he is thinking clearly (εὖ φρονῶν).[21] The rich aristocrat is thinking of this case as if it were one about inheritance with an heiress (ὥσπερ ἐπικλήρου), that is, a type of case that wealthy litigants get involved in (yet still involving a citizen who cannot or

---

[20] On the history of this dynamic, see Lenfant 2013.
[21] Carey's OCT retains the MS' ποιῶν here, but I prefer Markland's emendation, also followed by Usher, as unobtrusive and making better sense here. Hude's φρονεῖ makes much the same sense for my purposes.

should not control wealth), not the sort of case relevant for those who are poor, disabled and democratic.

These assertions are not digressions, for Lysias continues and expands on this theme. The prosecutor has alleged that the defendant is hubristic, violent and out of control (ὑβριστής εἰμι καὶ βίαιος καὶ λίαν ἀσελγῶς, 24.14), extreme charges that the defendant says were used for shock value, because the truth would be pedestrian. "But in the interest of expressing clarity, members of the Boule", he now says, "I think that you have to distinguish those who have the manoeuvring room to act with hubris from those without the option, because those in *penia* and stuck without the means are unlikely to act with hubris, as opposed to those who have acquired much more than they need" (24.15–16). It was a truism of Greek morality already for centuries that hyperabundance fuelled hubris and uncivilised behaviour and, by contrast, that relative poverty kept people on a more sensible and moral path, but the truism has a more specific referent here. The prosecutor in this case is seen to embody this very moral principle in action by his obsessive persecution of a good, albeit poor, citizen of the Athenian democracy. After some examples of the general principle with reference to the young and old, disabled and those bodily strong, and the strong versus the weak, comes an even more blunt contrast between the rich and poor: "the wealthy buy their way out of trouble, but the *penētes*, because of lack of opportunity, are constrained to behave decently" (24.17).

It is now that Lysias invokes comedy. In view of the moral hierarchy just asserted, the speaker, as he did a little earlier, avers that the prosecutor has devolved into comic absurdity: "So I think the prosecutor, when he speaks of my hubris, is not being serious, but just telling a joke. He's not even trying to convince you that I'm like that. He wants to make fun of me, as if that's a decent thing to do" (24.18).

Lysias is shrewd in the way he incorporates comedy into his invective against the prosecutor. Harding would have it that the defendant's bravado invokes comic protagonists like some of those in Aristophanes' comedies, making manifest that the defendant is a fraud but an entertaining one, as the only way to garner sympathetic votes.[22] Harding is half right: Lysias does imbue the defendant with qualities of a comic protagonist, but not to acknowledge tacitly that he is a fraud. This is yet another technique for establishing the defendant's credentials as a democrat.

Harding calls the defendant an *alazōn*, which is comically true, but it is worth emphasising that there is a crucial difference in being an *alazōn* and be-

---

22 Harding 1994.

ing *hubristic*. Hubris involves a disdain, which in this speech is being aligned solely with the financial elite, who are capable and have the freedom to behave hubristically. The working class, that is, those restrained by *penia*, do not have such freedom. An *alazōn* in stage comedy, however, brags but in a way that is respectful of his audience and predicated on a rapport with them,[23] thus, as Serafim has it and paradoxical as it might seem, a bond of sincerity. The prosecutor, as the Lysias frames him, cannot use comedy effectively, for he does not understand it. The defendant can brag like an appealing comic *alazōn* and build rapport with the Boule, while the prosecutor tries to tell a joke and fails, because he is too disconnected from democratic life to understand how comedy works.

This is because traditions in theatre embraced both oligarchic and democratic bonds, but Lysias makes sure in this speech to link the oligarchic traditions with the prosecutor and the democratic traditions with the defendant. Scholars have become increasingly sensitive to the ways that performance in the theatre was enmeshed broadly in the political mechanisms of Athens. As an institution, theatre was linked to the democratic government in ways that was refracted differently for poor and elite citizens.[24] Lysias capitalises on this refraction, in particular when he brings up the liturgy for sponsoring a tragedy. This characterises the prosecutor as someone who would know tragic theatre, whatever its democratic associations, in a context exclusive to the liturgical class, i.e., to the wealthy elite. Lysias links the defendant, by contrast, with comedy, and, at that, comedy in performance engaging with the issues prioritised by the *demos*. Even during the Peloponnesian War, Greek stage comedy addressed rhetoric, oratory and other issues in terms that spoke to the democratic populace rather than to the elite.[25] Closer to the time of this case, comedy continued this trend even more radically than before. In the late 390's, Aristophanes' *Ecclesiazusae* dramatised a radical redistribution of wealth based on communal ownership of property, and a few years later (388 BC), *Wealth* dramatised another radical redistribution of financial assets, this one based on civic morality. It is the radical protagonists of such plays whom Lysias invokes in characterising his defendant. Thus Harding is right about the particulars of these comic heroes, but wrong about the resonance it would have, or was expected to have, on the members of the Boule. Such a characterisation testified that the defend-

---

[23] Major 2006.
[24] See Carter 2011, esp. 1–7, for an outline of how tragedy's roles embrace many opposing poles in Athenian cultural and political discourse.
[25] Major 2013.

ant knew and experienced the anxieties and hardships of working-class members of the *demos*, and, moreover, implied that this particular case was an instantiation of the struggles of the *demos* against oligarchic elites. Lysias expects, not without reason, that the Boule will vote to exonerate a citizen *penēs* against the aggression of anti-democratic aristocrat, not at all an irrational strategy.

The last few minutes of the speech hammer this point one way after another, every statement reinforcing the democratic credentials of the defendant and the suspicious allegiances of the elite prosecutor. "Because of this prosecutor, should I be deprived of what the City, thoughtful about people in [my] situation, provided?" (24.23). Has the defendant ever caused anyone to lose their property (24.24), he asks, again invoking the type of court case that a wealthy elite might initiate or become entangled in. Does he meddle boldly and love to quarrel, or, again, is he hubristic and violent (24.24–25)? As Lysias has already established, these are prerogatives of the rich, so no. Did the defendant grab power and use it against citizens of Athens under the Thirty Tyrants (24.25)? No, he was a loyal democrat who went into exile "with your crowd" (μετὰ τοῦ ὑμετέρου πλήθους, 24.25), to make explicit where the Boule is oriented politically related to those events and that the defendant is aligned the same way.[26] This is not a case about an audit of public funds or about a public office (24.26), again cases that a citizen of the defendant's standing would not be involved in. The entire speech ends on what has now become the linchpin of the defence: "This man will learn from now on not to plot against the weak but instead to challenge those equal to him" (24.27). Let the rich plunder each other and leave working class democrats alone.

Such repudiation of the rich is hard to find outside of this speech and stage comedy, although the angst about how wealth relates to good citizen behaviour does also surface in texts composed by the elite. Aristotle literally makes a virtue out of a wealthy man using his resources toward good moral ends.[27] Plato, in his mammoth dilation on how to make a *polis* behave and prosper, borrows from the Spartans the idea of a guiding elite who literally never handle money.[28] Xenophon, ever more pragmatic, tries to systematise the Athenian finances to resolve the tension, but he is more direct about the problem than most. Introducing *Revenue-Sources* (*Poroi*), he writes: "For my part I have always believed that the constitution of a state matches what sort of leaders it has. Still, some of

---

26 See Serafim 2017, 47–54 on this technique in the context of oratory and performance.
27 Taylor 2017, 49.
28 Taylor 2017, 57–58.

the leaders in Athens reckon that they understand justice no less than anyone else, but, because of the *penia* of the masses, they say, they are forced to be rather unjust..." (1.1). Xenophon acknowledges the cascading effects of financial inequality, but, typically of his elitist perspective, he sees the problem as the limits on the elite. The defendant of Lysias 24 articulates the limits that this same inequality imposes on the working class. This crucial perspective, developed in extant texts of the period elsewhere only in Aristophanes' last two surviving comedies, makes this speech not something to be denigrated as laughable and fraudulent, but preserving a voice and perspective that, for the 21st century, is particularly valuable and rewarding.

Bibliography

The text of Lysias 24 follows that of Carey's 2007 OCT, except where noted.

Adams, C.D. (1905), *Lysias: Selected Speeches*, New York.
Akrigg, B. (2019), *Population and Economy in Classical Athens*, Cambridge.
Carey, C. (1990), 'Structure and Strategy in Lysias 24', in: *Greece & Rome* 37, 44–51.
Carter, D.M. (ed.) (2011), *Why Athens?: A Reappraisal of Tragic Politics*, Oxford.
Cecchet, L. (2015), *Poverty in Athenian Discourse: From the Eve of the Peloponnesian War to the Rise of Macedonia*, Stuttgart.
Christ, M. (1998), *The Litigious Athenian*, Baltimore.
Dillon, M. (1995), 'Payments for the Disabled at Athens: Social Justice or Fear of Aristocratic Patronage?', in: *Ancient Society* 26, 27–57.
Harding, P. (1994), 'Comedy and Rhetoric', in: I. Worthington (ed.), *Persuasion: Greek Rhetoric in Action*, London, 196–221.
Lenfant, D. (2013), 'Intégrés ou dénoncés: La place faite aux pauvres dans les discours grecs sur la démocratie', in: *Ktèma* 38, 37–51.
Loraux, N. (1986), *The Invention of Athens: The Funeral Oration in the Classical City*, Cambridge, MA.
Major, W. (2006), 'Aristophanes and *Alazoneia*: Laughing at the Parabasis of the *Clouds*', in: *Classical World* 99, 131–144.
Major, W. (2013), *The Court of Comedy: Aristophanes, Rhetoric and Democracy in Fifth-Century Athens*, Columbus, OH.
Ober, J. (1989), *Mass and Elite in Democratic Athens: Rhetoric, Ideology, and the Power of the People*, Princeton.
Scafuro, A. (1997), *The Forensic Stage: Settling Disputes in Graeco-Roman New Comedy*, Cambridge.
Schiappa, E. (1999), *The Beginnings of Rhetorical Theory in Classical Greece*, New Haven.
Serafim, A. (2017), *Attic Oratory and Performance*, London.

Serafim, A. (2019), 'Thespians in the Law-Court: Sincerity, Community and Persuasion in Selected Speeches of Forensic Oratory', in: A. Markantonatos and E. Volonaki (eds.), *Poet and Orator: A Symbiotic Relationship in Democratic Athens*, Berlin, 347–364.
Sinclair, R.K. (1988), *Democracy and Participation in Athens*, Cambridge.
Taylor, C. (2017), *Poverty, Wealth, and Well-Being: Experiencing Penia in Democratic Athens*, Oxford.
Whitehead, D. (2019), *Xenophon: Poroi (Revenue-Sources)*, Oxford.

Notes on Editors and Contributors

Kostas Apostolakis is Associate Professor of Ancient Greek at the University of Crete.

Emiliano Buis is Professor of International Law, Associate Professor of Ancient Greek at the University of Buenos Aires and a permanent Researcher at the Argentinean National Scientific Research Council (CONICET).

Hanna Maria Degener is a Research Associate in Ancient History at the Interdisciplinary Collaborative Research Centre 1285 "Invectivity. Constellations and Dynamics of Disparagement", University of Dresden.

Jasper Donelan is Doctor of Philosophy at the University of Nottingham.

Jan Lukas Horneff is a Research Associate at the Interdisciplinary Collaborative Research Centre 1285 "Invectivity. Constellations and Dynamics of Disparagement", University of Dresden.

Thomas K. Hubbard is Professor of Classics and holder of the James R. Dougherty, Jr. Centennial Professorship of Classics at the University of Texas at Austin.

George Kazantzidis is Assistant Professor of Latin Literature at the University of Patras.

Nathan Kish is Visiting Assistant Professor of Classical Studies at Tulane University.

Ioannis Konstantakos is Professor of Ancient Greek Literature at the National and Kapodistrian University of Athens.

Wilfred E. Major is Associate Professor of Classics at Louisiana State University.

Sophia Papaioannou is Professor of Latin at the National and Kapodistrian University of Athens.

Dennis Pausch is Professor of Latin at Dresden University of Technology.

Andreas Serafim is a Research Fellow at the Research Centre for Greek and Latin Literature of the Academy of Athens.

General Index

Abuse 7, 15, 25–26, 28, 30–31, 33–38, 44–45, 48, 50, 52, 54, 61, 67, 83, 86, 94, 97, 107–109, 114, 122, 126, 150, 152, 158, 175, 179, 183, 212, 214–215, 227, 257, 261
Acharnians 16, 29–30, 47, 51–52, 57, 81, 83–84, 86–90, 92–94, 97–102, 180, 187, 251
Actor 8, 18, 38, 45–46, 50, 53, 56, 76, 128, 132, 139, 147–148, 150, 152, 156, 163–164, 171, 176, 187–188, 204, 262
Adulescens 17, 130, 132–133, 140
Agōn 4, 16, 81, 83, 99, 102–103, 187, 248–249
Agonistic 199
Aischrologia 10, 12
Alazōn 46, 48–49, 69, 75, 258, 267
Ambassador 46–47
Animal fable 242, 244, 246
Antiphrasis 50
Apology 4, 16, 81–102, 187

Barbarian 14, 28, 56–58
Blame 6, 12, 46, 59, 95, 136, 148, 245, 249
Body 1, 18, 28–29, 65, 68, 151, 163, 171–177, 179, 181–185, 187, 188, 201, 264
–Civic 119–120
Braggart 48–49, 69–70
Bribery 16, 43, 54, 61, 219
Buffoon 6, 16, 18, 191–192, 194, 202, 204

Captatio benevolentiae 17, 147, 246
Charlatan 46, 48–49
Cinaedus 18, 211, 213, 224–225, 228
Clothing 14–15, 224, 228
Comedy 1–5, 7–9, 12–13, 15–18, 149, 151, 153, 155, 163, 175–181, 187–188, 196, 198, 211, 220–222, 225, 228, 248, 257–258, 260, 262, 267–269
–Middle 4–5, 16, 18, 43, 45–46, 48, 53, 60–61
–New 48, 58, 60, 128, 157, 160, 164
–Old 180, 251

–Plautine 198
–Roman 7, 130, 132, 149, 151, 218, 222
Comicness 1–2, 14, 16, 65–66, 69, 74–75, 77
Comic invective 3, 5, 7, 9–19, 43–47, 49, 51, 53, 55–59, 61, 65–77, 81–91, 93–95, 97–103, 113, 122, 124, 127, 129, 131, 133, 135, 137, 139, 141, 143, 147, 152, 162, 191, 193. 195, 197, 199, 201, 203, 205, 207, 211, 213, 215, 217, 219, 221, 223, 225–227, 229, 235, 237, 239, 241, 243, 245, 247, 249, 251, 258
Community 2, 11–12, 14, 27, 34, 43–44, 83, 120–121, 154, 158, 196–197, 199
Costume 73, 84, 150–151, 161, 164
Court of animals 244
Cowardice 14–15

Deception 16, 26–27, 43, 46, 51–52, 54, 61
Decorum 18, 191–195, 197, 199–201, 203–205, 207–208, 211, 213, 215–217, 219, 221, 223, 225, 227, 229
Defence 1, 9, 16–17, 19, 65, 68–69, 74, 77, 81–83, 85, 87, 89, 92, 95–98, 101, 111, 125, 130, 137, 141, 143, 157, 173, 188, 192, 213–215, 219–221, 228, 247, 249–250, 262–264, 269
Demagogues 28, 51–52, 85, 92, 98, 236, 239, 248–249
Democracy 19, 26, 56, 73, 100, 163, 235, 241, 248, 257, 259, 261–263, 265–267, 269
Descent 17, 177
Diadikasia 16, 68, 75, 77
Disease 48, 113, 116, 120, 173
Disgust 175
Disparagement 8, 125, 127, 148–151, 162, 212
Division 1–2, 10–11, 73, 195, 205
Doctor 45, 75
–Quack 48–49, 69
Dogs 18–19, 235, 237–240, 242–246, 248–250

https://doi.org/10.1515/9783110735536-015

General Index

Education 17, 34, 213, 222–224
Effeminacy 18, 31, 179, 213, 219, 224, 227–228
Elitism 258
Emotions 11–12, 34, 75, 136, 148, 152, 195
Emotional community 12, 44
Envy 6, 118, 265
Ēthos 32, 39, 70, 74–75, 93, 158, 181
Ēthopoiia 43, 75, 115, 239
Euthynai 238
Evidence 33, 37–3972, 75, 85, 89, 107, 113, 118, 122, 141, 150, 171, 173, 175, 177–183, 185, 187, 211–212, 215, 221, 227, 238, 257, 264

Fable 19, 235, 242–248
Fabula Palliata 7, 140
Family 4, 16, 32, 43, 55, 59, 61, 84, 130, 139–140, 162, 213–214, 228, 237, 264

Gender 14, 34, 66, 113, 140, 211, 216, 219
Graeculus 18, 213, 222–224
Graffiti 31, 151

Hamartia 174
Heroism 19, 257, 259, 261, 263, 265, 267, 269
Homosexuality 181
Humour 3–4, 6, 8–11, 13, 18, 25, 38–39, 83, 86, 90–91, 127, 141, 148–150, 153, 163, 191–206, 208, 211, 228, 265
Hubris 163, 259, 266–269

Identity 8, 72, 113, 155, 163, 177, 222
Image/Imagery 2, 5, 19, 32, 43, 45, 51, 71, 76, 90–91, 94–95, 97, 134–135, 141, 147, 172, 179, 207, 223–224, 235, 239, 240–242, 248
Impostor 45, 49
Incongruity 5, 65, 68, 72, 76, 193, 223, 258
Insanity 17, 107, 109–122, 156, 237
Insults 4, 11, 13, 15, 25–39, 44, 85, 109, 131, 149–150, 156–157, 213–215, 224

Jokes 6–7, 11, 36, 38, 83, 99, 135, 153, 163, 192–198, 201, 204–205, 223, 225–226, 246
–Sexual 7

Kinaidos 31, 173

Language 191, 198–199, 204, 213–214, 216, 220
–Body 151, 163
–Comic 44, 128, 175
–Foul 10, 14, 32, 68
Laughter 1–6, 8–11, 13, 25, 86, 102, 137, 143, 149, 163–164, 188, 191–196, 200–201, 203, 208, 222, 228
Law-court 13, 15, 25–27, 29, 31, 33, 35–37, 39, 70, 76, 219
Loidoria 16, 27, 33, 35–39, 86
Ludi Scaenici 148–149, 153

Madness 15, 17, 107, 111, 113–122
Malice 6, 9, 95, 113
Mask 8, 84, 99, 139, 164, 179
Mental 3, 5, 264
Metaphor 19, 45, 113, 174, 185, 206, 235, 239–243
Military 37, 75–76, 179, 183, 218, 237, 250
Mime 18, 49, 133, 161, 164, 191, 194, 202, 204
Mimēsis 53

Natura 18, 156, 191, 194, 202, 205–207
Non-Athenian 45, 57–58
Non-elite occupation 7, 14–15

Onomasti kōmōidein 4, 44–45, 52, 93
Oratory 1, 3–5, 7, 9, 11–19, 25–27, 29–32, 35, 43–48, 51–52, 61, 99, 102, 107, 113–114, 117, 119, 121, 128, 156, 178, 181, 193, 198–199, 205, 207, 216, 219, 223, 225, 235–237, 241, 244, 247, 251, 258–262, 264–265, 268–269
–Athenian 198, 247, 258
–Attic 1, 5, 13, 16, 44, 47, 65–67, 71, 75, 77, 128, 247, 265

–Forensic 1, 13, 16, 65, 223
–Roman 1, 3–5, 7, 9, 11, 13–15, 17, 19, 38

Pantomime 152
Parabasis 97
Parasite 151, 157, 177–178, 187
Physical disability 19, 257, 264
Performance 34–35, 44, 53, 56, 76, 82, 84, 126, 130, 133–134, 138–139, 142–143, 147–149, 152–154, 157–164, 174, 176, 203, 206, 213, 216–219, 221–222, 225, 229, 238
–Invective 4, 258
Personificatio 138–139
Pimp 8, 15, 151
Politics 10, 13, 26–27, 47, 54, 59, 66, 83, 100, 108, 121, 181, 197, 200, 241, 249, 251
Poverty 19, 36, 74, 257, 259–261, 263, 265, 267, 269
Praeteritio 137, 208
Prosecution 1, 16, 33, 65, 70, 72, 74, 77, 171, 180–181, 183–184, 187, 219–220, 222, 249, 259, 264
Prostitution 18, 131, 133, 135, 171, 173, 180–187
Protagonist 30, 84, 87, 93, 108–109, 178, 187, 195–196, 213, 251, 257, 267–268

R. Descartes 9
Religious 28,
Ridicule 3–4, 6, 10, 35–36, 57, 60, 73, 76, 87, 96, 151, 153, 175, 177, 179, 185, 195–196, 201, 211, 226, 235–236

S. Freud 9
Satire 55
Scapegoat 4, 9, 13, 43–44, 47, 52, 55–56, 61, 224, 248
Sermocinatio 138
Servile heritage 14
Sexuality 1, 13, 15, 17–18, 149, 176, 186
Slander 9–10, 17, 26, 33–35, 37–38, 49, 56–57, 59, 90–93, 95, 107, 111, 113, 122, 126, 131, 136–137, 155, 214–215, 239

Slave 7, 48, 56–57, 60, 132, 140, 149, 151, 154, 161–162, 164, 185–186, 237, 240, 243, 250
Social status 16, 43, 60–61, 151, 161–163, 206
Speeches 13–16, 25–26, 29–31, 35–36, 38, 43, 45–46, 53–54, 58–59
–Deliberative 54, 61
–Epideictic 66, 77
–Forensic 1, 14, 16, 45, 54, 58–59, 61, 128, 155, 183, 225
–Logographic 1
–Non-logographic 1
–Private 65–71, 73–77
–Public 14, 16, 61, 65, 67–68, 75–76, 238
Sycophant 28–29, 51, 55, 94, 182–183

T. Hobbes 9
Theatre 3, 5, 18, 39, 44–45, 50, 85, 126, 133, 147–153, 162, 176, 179, 211, 213, 215–217, 219, 221, 223, 225, 227, 229, 236, 261, 268
Theory
–Disparagement 12, 102
–Social identity 3, 11, 72
–Superiority 9–10
Thievery 7, 14, 55
Tragedy 46, 65, 68, 99, 129, 265, 268
Tritagonist 176

Unity 1, 10
Urbanitas 126–127, 135, 149, 196, 207, 216, 220

Violence 2, 34, 73, 81, 86, 94, 96, 100–101, 125, 141, 143, 149–151, 199, 203
Vituperation 1, 6, 81, 83, 101, 149, 214, 249

Women 30, 60, 66, 74, 76, 82, 108–109, 113–114, 119–121, 134, 138, 143, 177

Index Locorum

Aesop
Fable 94 Hausrath/92 Perry 245
Fable 158 Hausrath/153 Perry 242

Aeschines
1	170–190
1.18–19	172
1.19–20	182
1.26	175
1.75	172
1.192	29
2.34	49 f.
3.156	47
3.172	56

Aristophanes
Acharnians
37–39	100
61–72	47
79	32
120–121	52
287–288	30
377–382	93 f.
378	85
407–479	84
440–444	99
497–503	91 f.
497	95
502	95
628–632	84 f.
629	89
630	90
631	99
633–635	99
641–645	99
650–651	89
655–658	92
659–664	92 f.
676–684	97
685–691	97
713–718	97
714	99

Clouds
218 ff.	82
844–846	117
909	32

Ecclesiazusae
241–253	108–114
1043	31

Frogs
465	30
466	31
560–575	35

Knights
304–305	30
1014–1034	224
1362–1363	28
1405	28

Lysistrata
137	31
554–559	120 f.
620–624	52
969	31
1082–1085	53

Peace
183	31
1318–1319	28

Wasps
826–1008	237
fr. 194 K.–A.	53

Aristotle
Nicomachean Ethics
1108a24–25	12
1128a34–1128b1	12

Poetics
1449a32–34	196 n. 15
1416b34–35	53

Rhetoric
1379a30–b32	34
1379a38–40	34
1393a28–1394a18	247
1393a28–31	35
1394a2–5	35
1379b23–27	34

Cicero

De oratore

1.1–4	200
1.24–27	199
2.182–184	201 n. 30
2.216–290	193, 194 f.
2.216	148 n. 4, 195, 205 f.
2.218	202
2.219–220	197 n. 18
2.220	195 n. 9, 197 n. 18, 203 n. 34
2.236	201
2.237	200
2.239	202
2.240–241	203
2.240	203
2.242	203
2.247	204 f.
2.255	5, 196 n. 12, 198
3.2–6	200
3.9–12	200
3.13–14	200

In Pisonem

1	224 n. 52
70	224 n. 52

Pro Caelio

1	136 n. 55
1–2	128 n. 13
3–4	128 n. 17
6	126
18	129 f., 136 n. 56
30–36	136–140
32	137 f.
33	139
36	139–141
37–38	132
61–67	132 n. 38
62	133 n. 43
64	132 f.
65	133
67	132

Pro Cluentio

57–59	218–222

Demosthenes

3.54	118
9.54	37, 44 n. 2
10.70–73	54
10.75	36
18.3	9, 44 n. 4, 102 n. 53
18.15	36
18.126	38
18.127	38
18.139	38
18.209	38
18.242	38
18.262	38
18.138	44 n. 2
18.242	51
18.243	48, 69, 75 f.
19.95	38
19.20	38
19.314	38
19.260	115 n. 19, 119 f.
21.2	29
21.98	29
21.103	29
21.114	29
21.117	29
21.135	29
21.151	29
21.185	29
201	29
21.79	32
25.8	28
25.16	28
25.31	28
25.52	28
25.58	28
25.77	28
25.95	28
96	28
25.99	28
21.185	38
25.40	241 f.
35.46	29
36.41	69
45.63–66	70 f.
48.52–56	111 f.
54.8–9	33
54.9	72
57	59 f.
57.18	59
57.33–34	60

57.44–45	60	17d	96
57.45	74 n. 32	17d–18a	93 n. 36
58.17	55 n. 43	18a	95 n. 40
58.40	36 n. 30, 53 n. 37	18d	97
60.26	37	19b–c	82
		20d	88, 102

Dinarchus

1.99	36 n. 30, 53 n. 37	20e	100
		21a	89, 100 n. 50
		24a	95 n. 41

Gellius
Noctes Atticae

		25a	90
		26e	96
6.12.5	15, 227	27b	100 n. 50
		28a	95

Lysias

		28d	88
24	257–271	30a	96
24.1–2	263	40c–d	97

Philebus

24.3	264	50a	102
24.7–8	264		

Symposium

24.9	265	193b	91
24.14	266 f.	193d	91
24.15–16	267		

Plato Comicus

24.18	36, 267	fr. 183 K.–A.	58
24.24–25	269		
fr. 195.10–12 Carey	32		

Plutarch

Lucian

		Cicero 5.6	193 n. 2, 197 n. 19
Hist. Conscr. 51	207 n. 46	*Comp. Dem. et Cic.* 1.4	191 f.
		Demosthenes 23.4–6	242

Macrobius

Quintilian
Inst. Or.

Sat. 2	54, 224–226, 162 f.		
2.1.1–13	226	4.1.39	128
2.2.6	226	4.2.19	207 n. 44, 220 n. 34
2.7.4	162	4.2.34	206 f. n. 44
		6.3.3	10, 193 n. 2, 220 n. 34

Menander
Aspis

		6.3.7–8	149
339–342	48	6.3.8	196 n. 15, 197 n. 20, 207 n. 46
374–375	48 f.		
		6.3.13	198 n. 24

Pliny

		6.3.81	197 n. 20
Epist. 2.19.2–6	117 f.	6.3.89	207 n. 46
		10.3.1	195 n. 9

Plato
Apology of Socrates

		10.5.2	195 n. 9
17a	94		
17b	95		
17c	96		

Terence
Adelphoe 1–25 158
Andria 1–27 154 f.
Eunuchus 1–45 156 f.
H(e)autontimorumenos 1–52 155 f.

Timocles
fr. 12 K.–A. 50

Xenophon
Poroi 1 269 f.

www.ingramcontent.com/pod-product-compliance
Lightning Source LLC
Chambersburg PA
CBHW020223170426
43201CB00007B/302